Foreign Relations of the PRC

*The Legacies and Constraints of
China's International Politics since 1949*

Second Edition

Robert G. Sutter

ROWMAN & LITTLEFIELD
Lanham • Boulder • New York • London

Executive Editor: Susan McEachern
Editorial Assistant: Katelyn Turner
Senior Marketing Manager: Kim Lyons

Credits and acknowledgments for material borrowed from other sources, and reproduced
with permission, appear on the appropriate page within the text.

Published by Rowman & Littlefield
An imprint of The Rowman & Littlefield Publishing Group, Inc.
4501 Forbes Boulevard, Suite 200, Lanham, Maryland 20706
https://rowman.com

Unit A, Whitacre Mews, 26-34 Stannary Street, London SE11 4AB,
United Kingdom

British Library Cataloguing in Publication Information Available

Library of Congress Cataloging-in-Publication Data
Names: Sutter, Robert G., author.
Title: Foreign relations of the PRC : the legacies and constraints of China's international
    politics since 1949 / Robert G. Sutter.
Description: Second edition. | Lanham : Rowman & Littlefield, 2019. | Includes biblio-
    graphical references and index.
Identifiers: LCCN 2018012998 (print) | LCCN 2018013710 (ebook) | ISBN
    9781538107485 (ebook) | ISBN 9781538107461 (hardback : alk. paper) | ISBN
    9781538107478 (pbk. : alk. paper)
Subjects: LCSH: China—Foreign relations—1949– | World politics—1945–1989. | World
    politics—1989–
Classification: LCC DS777.8 (ebook) | LCC DS777.8 .S879 2018 (print) | DDC 327.51—
    dc23
LC record available at https://lccn.loc.gov/2018012998

Printed in the United States of America

Contents

Map

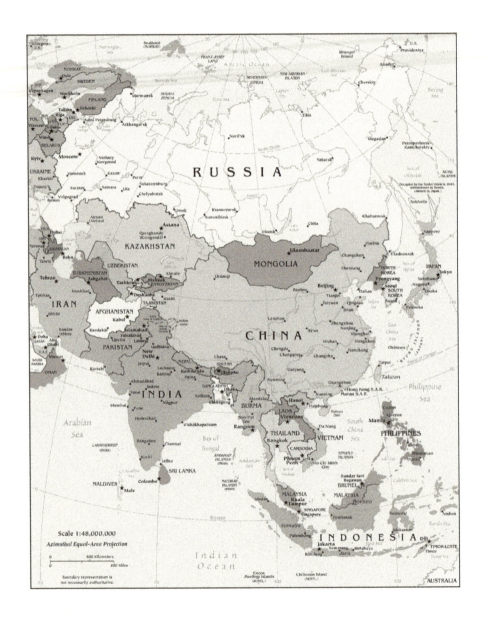

Scale 1:48,000,000
Azimuthal Equal-Area Projection

0   600 Kilometers
0   600 Miles

Boundary representation is
not necessarily authoritative.

Acknowledgments

The second edition of this volume was undertaken with great appreciation of the strong support of Susan McEachern, vice president and executive editor, Rowman & Littlefield. Rowman & Littlefield colleagues Rebeccah Shumaker, Katelyn Turner, and Janice Braunstein helped guide the manuscript through the production process. Special thanks go to three professors, who use the book in their classes, for offering anonymously important suggestions on how the second edition should be written.

In line with the reviewers' suggestions, a list of key terms, a list of study statements and questions related to the material discussed in each of the ten chapters of the book, and a detailed chronology of salient developments in the almost seven decades of PRC foreign relations are available to readers of this volume at https://rowman.com/ISBN/9781538107478.

In addition to information cited in source notes, the assessments in this volume benefited from close and frequent interchange with numerous colleagues in Washington, DC, and throughout the United States, Asia, and elsewhere who have a strong interest in Chinese foreign relations and share their perspectives during conferences, more informal meetings, and conversations in Internet groups. And special thanks go to the students who participate actively in the several classes I teach each year dealing with China and its role in world affairs.

Chapter One

Assessing China's Role
in World Affairs

China's ascendance as a world power represents the most important change in the still developing international dynamics of the twenty-first century. A wide range of expert commentaries and assessments judge that China in recent decades has established a clear strategy of developing wealth and power in world affairs. They see expanding Chinese economic, military, and political influence that entails a change in leadership in the Asia-Pacific region and a power shift in world affairs. The United States and its partners among developed countries are viewed in decline as China rises, and thus their choices are depicted in sometimes stark terms. They are advised by some to appease and accommodate China, and by others to resist.[1]

This study joins some other specialists and commentators in judging that the above assessments of China's rise and its consequences are premature and may be mistaken.[2] The following chapters focus first on a chronological examination of the actual impact, legacies, and constraints of the foreign relations of the People's Republic of China (PRC); later chapters assess Chinese relations with specific countries and regions for the same purpose. Overall, the review provides reasons for the conclusion that China's rise has not and may not in the future result in the regional and international power shift that some predict.

One reason has to do with conflicts evident in China's purported strategy for acquiring leadership in Asian and world affairs. The Chinese Communist Party and state apparatus has long fostered an image of China following correct principles in accord with international conditions that insure a consistently effective foreign strategy. The Chinese effort has reinforced the assessments of foreign specialists that China in recent decades has been pursuing a coherent strategy to develop wealth and power within the evolving interna-

tional system that many believe foreshadows Chinese international primacy
and leadership as the influence of developed countries declines.

Yet the record of China's actual behavior in world affairs shown in this
volume demonstrates repeated changes, shifts in emphasis, and adjustments
that belie a coherent foreign strategy. Mao Zedong (d. 1976) shifted China
between violent revolutionary behavior and more pragmatic accommodation
to the existing world order. Deng Xiaoping (d. 1997) curbed revolutionary
excesses but shifted China's foreign approach repeatedly; he notably sought
advantage in alternative overtures to the United States and the Soviet Union.
Both leaders left a legacy among concerned countries, especially around
China's periphery, that China was an unpredictable actor, prone to changes in
course and periodic violence. Later Chinese leaders tried to focus on domestic economic development and on sustaining a peaceful international environment conducive to such nation building. Nevertheless, time and again,
they have shifted toward assertive, coercive, disruptive, and sometimes violent behavior, especially in the pursuit of disputed Chinese sovereignty
claims and security interests around China's periphery.

This book argues that the repeated shifts and hard-to-predict instances of
assertiveness, intimidation, and violence have seriously encumbered China's
rising influence in regional and world affairs. They have put many of China's
neighbors and other concerned powers, including the United States, on
guard; and they have reinforced the tendencies of these powers to develop
contingency plans to deal with possible Chinese pressure and dominance in
the years ahead. Those plans pose a strong impediment to Chinese leadership
in areas around China's periphery, the part of the world that remains by far
China's top concern in international affairs.

The second reason for this study's judgment that China's rise remains
encumbered centers on the book's examination in some detail of the extent of
the actual influence China exerts among the countries along its rim and with
other large powers involved in those countries, notably the United States.
The study shows that the People's Republic of China has always exerted its
greatest influence in nearby Asia, and that this area has always received the
lion's share of Chinese foreign policy attention. The region is essential to
China's national security; it contains the disputed sovereignty issues that
remain of top importance to the Chinese leaders as well as to the strongly
patriotic Chinese popular and elite opinion. Nearby Asia is more important
than any other world area to China's economic development; it determines
the peaceful international environment seen by post-Mao Chinese leaders as
essential in China's pursuit of economic development, the primary source of
legitimacy for continued Communist Party rule in China.

The examination of China's actual influence in nearby Asia shows widespread shortcomings, especially in relations along China's eastern and southern frontiers, despite impressive recent advances in Chinese economic, diplo-

matic, and military engagement with the region. These shortcomings often are rooted in the legacies of past violence and unpredicted shifts toward neighboring countries, which support wariness as these states respond to China's rise in the current period. Episodes dating back more than a decade show unexpected Chinese assertiveness, coercion, and violence toward Japan, along with similar behavior in recent years toward Southeast Asian states, South Korea, India, and the United States over disputed territorial claims and other issues, underlining regional concerns and strengthening contingency planning and preparations to deal with possible increased pressure and coercion from China as it gains in wealth and power.

The study finds that the Chinese party-state apparatus, fostering a positive image of Chinese foreign relations with the countries of nearby Asia, strongly influences thinking among the Chinese people that is far from reality, making it very difficult for China to acknowledge the grievances and concerns of neighbors with past and recent Chinese assertiveness and coercion. The party-fostered worldview also is accompanied by a strong nationalistic resentment at the exploitation of Chinese weaknesses by foreign powers in the nineteenth and much of the twentieth centuries. This victim mentality is accompanied by other patterns of behavior, explained below, that prompt China to overreact to foreign actions in many areas of nearby Asia. Such overreaction in turn reinforces the concern and contingency planning of neighbors and the United States that limit China's actual influence in the region.

Regarding China's positive international contributions, the record shows continued preoccupation among Chinese leaders with ongoing and serious domestic problems and priorities that reinforce their unwillingness to undertake risks, costs, or commitments supporting regional or broader "common goods." The narrow China-centered mind-set that has characterized PRC foreign relations is seen in the ubiquitous "win-win" principle guiding Chinese foreign deal making in the post–Cold War period. At bottom, China is reluctant to undertake obligations that it wouldn't ordinarily do unless there is a clear "win" for a narrowly defined win-set of Chinese interests. In nearby Asia, China's actual contributions to regional common interests appear small and reflect China's hard-to-reverse reputation as a "cheap rider" that exploits the prevailing international order supported by others. China's willingness to contribute monetary resources that will not be paid back or to place its military in harm's way for the sake of regional or global common goods is notably small in comparison with the massive costs and great risks undertaken by the United States, which sustains such commitments in line with its unusual broad view of its interest in preserving regional and global stability. There is little change in strong American international defense commitments under the Donald Trump administration, while its targeting of perceived unfair trade and other economic practices represents a small adjustment in the overall openness of the US market that remains of central importance to international economic development.

Against this background, the inventory of China's relationships with countries of nearby Asia provided in chapter 8 shows that even though China is advancing in power and influence, it has a long way to go to overshadow America and become the leader of the Asia-Pacific region. Chapter 9 shows advances in Chinese interests in other world areas, with the major caveat that the range of Chinese interests in these areas is significantly narrower and the interests themselves substantially less important to Chinese decision makers. In these areas, China is focused heavily on commercial concerns that mesh fairly well with the leaders and business elites in a number of these countries. Nevertheless, economic realities—notably the stagnation of China's trade in 2015 and 2016—have diminished Chinese influence. Chapter 10 forecasts developments in the next five years by examining the foreign policy plans of the government of party leader and President Xi Jinping in his second five-year term following China's Nineteenth Communist Party Congress in late 2017. It contrasts the widely publicized grand visions of Xi Jinping's foreign ambitions with realities that continue to constrict China's regional and international ascent.

SOURCES OF POWER AND INFLUENCE

The manifestations of China's growing impact and salience in world affairs start with the remarkable growth of the Chinese economy, which is strongly integrated with international economic developments. Since the beginning of economic reforms following the death of Mao Zedong in 1976, China has been the world's fastest-growing major economy. From 1979 to 2011, the average annual growth rate of China's gross domestic product (GDP) was about 10 percent. By 2010, China became the world's second-largest economy, after the United States. It was the world's largest exporter and second-largest trader. In 2011, it became the largest manufacturer, surpassing the United States, and in 2012, the world's largest trader. China has become the second-largest destination of foreign investment, the largest holder of foreign exchange reserves, and the largest creditor nation. Per capita gross domestic product in China has surpassed $8,000 in nominal terms and was much higher using measurements of international financial institutions.[3]

Looking to the future, some Chinese government officials and specialists warned of significant Chinese economic weaknesses due to a wasteful economic model of diminishing returns requiring fundamental reform. Grossly inefficient use of energy and resources resulted in massive environmental problems, and China's strong dependence on the health of the global trading economy saw absolute trade levels decline in 2015 and 2016.[4] On the whole, however, a broad range of expert opinion in China and abroad projects continued growth. Several predictions say that China is on track to surpass the United States, the world's largest economy, within a decade.[5]

In foreign affairs, the growing importance of the Chinese economy is manifested most notably by the growth in economic interchange between China and foreign countries throughout the world. Most important in this regard has been the strong growth until recently of trade and foreign investment in China. Chinese investment abroad also is growing rapidly from a low base. Beginning about twenty years ago and getting a major boost with China's various Silk Road infrastructure initiatives in Eurasia and Africa beginning in 2013, notable increases in Chinese commercial and concessional financing have assisted some developing countries in Africa and Asia in particular. As discussed below, the Silk Road initiatives became consolidated into an overall Chinese plan called the Belt and Road Initiative (BRI). Its poorly defined scope was very wide, featuring Chinese investment, infrastructure construction, and trade throughout Eurasia and nearby parts of Africa. As the plan developed amid intensive Chinese publicity, Chinese leaders continued to broaden its scope. In 2018, Xi Jinping announced that Latin America and the Caribbean were within the scope of this amorphous Chinese foreign policy approach.[6]

The major share of Chinese trade and investment involves neighboring Asian countries, the European Union, and the United States. However, the demand for resources to support China's economic growth deepened and broadened Chinese economic interchange with developing countries. Chinese purchases of raw materials and sales of manufactured goods in these markets grew rapidly in the twenty-first century. China in recent years became the most important trading partner for Africa, Brazil, and many developing countries in Asia.[7] Chinese financing, economic assistance, and construction have transformed the way many developing countries trade, with a focus on the China market and Chinese goods and services. Such Chinese-fostered development in these developing economies often overshadows the support offered by developed countries and the international financial institutions they support.

Against this background, a number of foreign specialists and commentators in recent years have portrayed China as a clear leader in international economic affairs, surpassing Japan, India, and the European powers, as it closes the gap with the United States. Thus, they commonly assert the following key judgments:

- China already is an economic superpower.
- It is likely to continue rapid growth and gather greater economic and geopolitical strength.

- China's growth is the main engine changing the post–Cold War Asian and international order, where the United States was dominant, into a more multipolar order where US dominance is diminished by China's rising stature and importance.
- China's emergence is unique among major powers in that China has risen by being widely open to economic interaction with the rest of the world, building international dependence on China's economy.
- The speed, scope, and scale of China's economic expansion on the global stage create very strong adjustment pressures on the United States, other developed countries, and many developing nations as well.[8]

Chinese economic growth has supported concurrent advances in Chinese military power. Chinese military modernization programs have been under way for thirty years. They involve usually double-digit increases in annual defense budgets that pay for marked improvements in China's ability to project military power in nearby regions of Asia by modern air, naval, and missile forces. They also involve new capabilities to counter adversaries in space and cyber warfare. The modernization efforts have reached the point where they strongly suggest that the objective of the Chinese leadership is to build Asia's most powerful defense force to assure regional dominance in the face of US and other challenges. Overall, Chinese defense acquisition and advancement show broad ambitions for Chinese military power. While they appeared focused recently on dealing with US forces in the event of a Taiwan contingency, these forces can be used by Chinese leaders as deemed appropriate in a variety of circumstances. The Chinese advances mean that China's military power dominates continental Asia. With the possible exception of Japan, no Asian country will be capable of challenging China's naval power and airpower in maritime eastern Asia. Should Beijing choose to deploy naval and air forces to patrol the sea-lanes in the Indian Ocean, only India conceivably would be capable of countering China's power.[9]

The sinews of economic and military power underline China's greater prominence in international governance and leadership. China's growing involvement with and dependence on the world economy heads the list of reasons explaining China's ever-broadening and deepening involvement with foreign governments and various multilateral organizations. There have been remarkable changes and increased Chinese activism in Asian regional multilateral organizations, with China in recent years taking a leading role in creating such structures as the ASEAN-China Free Trade Agreement and a regional security body that includes Russia and four central Asian states known as the Shanghai Cooperation Organization (SCO). The Chinese approach in these endeavors strives to meet the interests of the other participants while ensuring that Chinese interests of security, development, and stability are well served. China also has participated actively in recent years in loosely structured global groups, notably the G-20, involving the world's twenty leading powers, and the BRICS, composed of Brazil, Russia, India, China, and South Africa. Beginning in 2013, President Xi Jinping's signature foreign policy initiative has involved a very broad-based effort to connect and integrate Eurasian and some African economies under the auspices of China's varied Silk Road infrastructure and development plans that involve sixty-eight countries with China at the center. [10]

China's approach to multilateralism and broader foreign relations has changed markedly since China became a participant in such endeavors on entry into the United Nations in 1971. There has been a trend since then toward closer Chinese government cooperation with the United Nations and an ever-widening range of multilateral organizations and the international norms supported by the UN. The record of Chinese adherence to multilateral guidelines and norms remains somewhat mixed, however. And Beijing registers strong disagreement with key aspects of US-led international institutions, especially regarding security matters.

Chinese engagement with international economic organizations has been the most active and positive. The reasons seem obvious: these organizations provide numerous material benefits for China's development, and China's active participation ensures that China will play an important role in decisions affecting the world economy on which Chinese development depends. There are some limits on Chinese cooperation with international economic institutions. For example, China does not cooperate closely with international organizations that seek to regulate scarcities in the global oil market.

China's recently more active and positive approach in Asian regional economic, security, and political organizations seems to reflect the strong recent priority of the Chinese government to portray China's rising power and influence as benign and not a danger to China's neighbors and the region's leading outside power, the United States. Chinese leaders see the recent period as a "strategic opportunity" to advance China's modernization; they do not want to prompt these states, out of concern that China's rise could hurt their interests, to obstruct or complicate China's development. China's attentive diplomacy and periodic deference to the interests of its neighbors have helped to reassure many of them about Chinese intentions, giving rise to significant improvement in Chinese relations throughout its periphery. On the other hand, as noted above, many regional governments remain on guard, especially given the greater Chinese assertiveness over sovereignty and security issues with Asian neighbors and the United States in recent years. For example, many regional governments and many in the United States have judged that the recent rise of Chinese military power, along with China's economic power and positive multilateral diplomacy, is inconsistent with China's avowed peaceful intentions toward its neighbors and poses a serious threat to their security and regional stability. [11]

In the case of international regulation of environmental practices, China remains reluctant to commit to international norms if they infringe on Chinese efforts to expand economic growth. In recent years, Beijing's growing concern with massive pollution and the related very wasteful Chinese use of energy has brought China closer to environmentally sensitive world leaders seeking reductions in pollution and greenhouse gases leading to climate change. The Chinese government's approach to international human rights regimes has long focused on engaging in protracted dialogues and cooperating where possible or needed in order to avoid international sanction. China nonetheless consistently avoids significant commitments that would impede its ability to coerce those in China who are seen as challenging the Communist authorities. Such coercion remains a common feature of Chinese governance. China's cooperation with international arms control measures has grown steadily in the past two decades, although the Chinese government continues to avoid commitments that would impede Chinese independence in certain areas important to Chinese interests.[12]

The impressive and continuing advance of Chinese economic, military, and political power and influence contrasts with prevailing and widely publicized difficulties facing developed nations, notably Japan, the European Union, and the United States. As noted at the start of this chapter, a range of specialists and forecasters aver that a power shift is under way in world affairs. They believe that the prevailing order in the Asia-Pacific region, the most economically important world region in the twenty-first century, is witnessing a decline in the power and influence of the United States, as well as Japan, while China has emerged on a steady course as the region's new dominant power. Many experts judge that the power shift will soon involve other areas of the world as well. China's massive size, rapid economic growth, strengthening military power, and growing political influence will increasingly determine world affairs as the United States and other developed nations deal with protracted problems.[13]

International relations scholars are well aware that power shifts are dangerous phenomena in world affairs; they often are accompanied by military conflict and major wars that determine leadership in the emerging new order. These and other concerns have prompted closer examination of forecasts of China's rise to Asian and world leadership. Some specialists, including this writer, find the forecasts lacking in several respects. In particular, they do a poor job of accurately assessing various Chinese domestic limitations with important foreign policy implications involving leadership legitimacy, corruption, widening income gaps, widespread social turmoil, highly resource-intensive economic development, environmental damage, and slowing reform of an economic model seen as unsustainable. In addition, they have a hard time showing how China actually exerts influence in world affairs, notably by getting other countries to do things they wouldn't ordinarily do.[14]

Because of pervasive secrecy surrounding Chinese leadership decision making and the absence of accurate data on salient domestic developments in China, there is wide-ranging debate about how the various domestic limitations noted in the previous paragraph actually influence Chinese foreign behavior. On one side are those who see these difficulties as severe and bringing China to the brink of protracted decline or even collapse. On the other side are those who see them as comparatively small given the success of China's modernization and international prominence.[15]

The impact of these domestic determinants in contemporary Chinese foreign relations can be assessed indirectly through careful study of actual Chinese behavior in international affairs. The latter approach also has the added benefit of providing more clear and concrete evidence regarding what Chinese representatives in fact are doing in various international arenas and how successful their efforts have been in meeting Chinese goals. Once such an assessment has been made, it can provide a comparatively sound basis for discerning how influential China is in contemporary world affairs and the prospects for a power shift in China's direction.

This book endeavors to provide such an assessment. It pays close attention to the context of contemporary Chinese foreign relations. To do otherwise would ignore legacies and patterns of past behavior that influence Chinese contemporary behavior in ways that enhance or detract from Chinese pursuit of international influence and particular foreign policy goals. And assessing in some detail contemporary Chinese foreign relations in light of the recent past provides good indications as to how much progress China actually is making in pursuit of its objectives and in regard to regional and global leadership.

After this first chapter, which introduces the purpose and scope and provides key findings of the book, chapters 2, 3, and 4 review the remarkable course of the foreign relations of the People's Republic of China (PRC) during its almost seven decades of international involvement. While Chinese leaders have tended to emphasize the consistency of China's approach in foreign affairs, the record of change seems overwhelming.

Chapters 5 and 6 address, respectively, patterns of decision making of the Chinese elite and their world outlook along with that of broader Chinese constituencies, and China's changing importance in world affairs since the founding of the PRC in 1949. There follow three chapters dealing with international relationships considered in order of importance for China: the United States (chapter 7); countries located around China's rim (chapter 8); and other developing and developed countries (chapter 9). The conclusion in chapter 10 forecasts the next five years by contrasting the stated vision of Xi Jinping's foreign ambitions with realities that continue to constrict China's rise.

CHINA'S IMAGE IN FOREIGN AFFAIRS

The record of Chinese foreign relations since 1949 shows gaps between the image of China in foreign affairs fostered by the Chinese government and the actual practice seen in the events of Chinese foreign relations. One of the first issues a student or other observer encounters in dealing with Chinese foreign relations involves how much weight to give to China's image building in foreign affairs and what are its actual implications for Chinese foreign behavior.

Examining the record of Chinese foreign behavior shows long-standing efforts by Chinese officials to support the positive in China's pursuit of its objectives abroad. In recent years, China's salience as an international economic, military, and political power has been reinforced by attentive efforts by the Chinese Foreign Ministry; various other government, party, and military organizations that deal with foreign affairs; various ostensibly non-government organizations with close ties to the Chinese government; party and military offices; and the massive publicity/propaganda apparatus of the Chinese government. The opinions of these officials, nongovernment representatives, and media accounts provide sources used by international journalists, scholars, and officials in assessing Chinese foreign relations. On the whole, they boost China's international stature while they condition people in China to think positively about Chinese foreign relations. Such efforts have been common in past periods of Chinese foreign relations. Points of emphasis in these efforts include the following:

- China's foreign policy is consistent.
- It follows principles in dealing with foreign issues, which assures a moral position in Chinese foreign relations.
- The Chinese government deals effectively with international events and adopts policies and takes actions in accord with Chinese principles and moral leadership.
- Abiding by principles and seeking moral positions provide the basis for effective Chinese strategies in world affairs.
- Such strategies ensure that China does not make mistakes in foreign affairs, an exceptional position reinforced by the fact that the People's Republic of China is seen to have avoided publicly acknowledging foreign policy mistakes or apologizing for its actions in world affairs. [16]

Many in China and some foreign observers base their analyses of Chinese foreign relations on the information provided by the above-noted Chinese outlets. Their analyses show how China's image-building efforts, which enjoy support from the Chinese people and various constituencies in China, support a leading role for China in Asian and world affairs. They conclude optimistically that China will follow a contemporary policy emphasizing recent themes stressed by the Chinese government. The themes include promoting peace and development abroad, eschewing dominance or hegemonic policies in dealing with issues with neighbors or others even as China's power grows, and following the purported record of historical Chinese dynasties in not seeking expansionism as China's power increases. [17]

Some specialists in China and many others abroad, including this writer, duly consider Chinese-provided information but also examine closely the actual behavior of China in its foreign affairs, behavior that can be measured from both the perspective of China and the perspective of foreign governments and others concerned. This book also shows that Chinese image building may help China's pursuit of goals in foreign affairs in some ways, but it also represents a serious liability in China's pursuit of effective policies, especially toward its Asian neighbors and the United States.

Principles versus Interest-Based Foreign Policy

While China's foreign policy actions are usually said to be based on adherence to righteous and moral principles, there are notable weaknesses in China's long-avowed adherence to such morally correct principles. Chinese foreign policy expert Samuel Kim over twenty years ago labeled China's "peculiar" operational code of conduct "firmness in principle and flexibility in application." The result for Kim and other foreign observers is a gap between principle and practice, with China repeatedly attempting to show through often convoluted discussion of a sometimes dizzying array of various and often newly created sets of principles governing Chinese foreign relations that China is an exception to the interest-based policies and practices of great powers. Chinese discourse does not address the net effect of all the different sets of Chinese principles, which, as seen by Kim and others, allows China to be all things to all nations on all salient international issues, and thereby provides little in the way of concrete guidance on how and why China behaves in a particular set of circumstances. [18]

The course of Chinese foreign relations is littered with examples where principles were reinterpreted or put aside in favor of other sets of principles as Chinese interests in a foreign relationship changed. Jawaharlal Nehru seemed truly surprised when his efforts to nurture a cooperative relationship with Zhou Enlai under the rubric of the Five Principles of Peaceful Coexistence seemed to count for little as China pursued border interests at odds with India's interests. Noncommunist Southeast Asian leaders could be forgiven for skepticism as they observed China's flawed observance of its principle of noninterference in another state's internal affairs at various times in their checkered relationships with China. For example, Deng Xiaoping reached out to improve relations with noncommunist Southeast Asian neighbors in

the mid-1970s as China was constructing a broad front of nations to oppose
Soviet-backed Vietnam's pending attack against the Chinese-backed Khmer
Rouge government in Cambodia. Deng did so on the understanding that these
governments would accept reconciliation with China while Beijing at the
same time continued support for the tens of thousands of insurgents China
had trained, supplied, and supported in their armed struggles against the very
Southeast Asian leaders with whom Deng was seeking to improve relations.[19]

Albania's Enver Hoxha was more vocal than other more important Com-
munist leaders in Hanoi and Pyongyang as well as less prominent Communist leaders aligned with Beijing whose interests were adversely impacted by
China's surprising opening to the United States in the early 1970s despite
long-standing Chinese commitments to them in the struggle against
American imperialism. Meanwhile, Pakistan, the only country with which
China has been able to sustain a close relationship since the early 1960s, saw
China's commitment to an "all-weather" relationship diminish for many
years as China in the post–Cold War period backed away from previous
support for Pakistan's position in the Kashmir dispute in order to open the
way for improved Chinese relations with India. More recently, China has
increased support for Pakistan, alienating India.[20]

China's Exceptional Exceptionalism

It is common for states to redefine their foreign policies as their interests
change in light of changing circumstances at home or abroad. And when
states follow those changed interests and shift stated policies and commitments deemed principled and moral in new directions to the detriment of
others, they rarely apologize; they tend to only grudgingly acknowledge
negative consequences and mistakes.

Leaders of my own country, the United States, are widely seen as prone to
an arrogant sort of exceptionalism in foreign affairs. They are loath to apologize for policy changes or international actions that sometimes grossly hurt
others or are at odds with American principles. Nonetheless, the American
political process, open media, active interest groups, and regularly scheduled
elections allow for recognition of foreign policy failings and proposed reme-
dies. In contrast, Chinese exceptionalism in foreign affairs is much more
exceptional than that of the United States. One reason is the continuing need
for the Chinese Communist Party–led system to sustain its legitimacy partly
through an image of correct behavior in foreign affairs consistent with Chinese-supported principles. Another reason is that while there have been some
recent debates on foreign policy issues in Chinese media, they fail to deal
well with many Chinese legacies of egregious malfeasance in the past. And
no corrective is provided by elections or a legitimate political opposition.

The unwillingness and seeming inability of the Chinese government to address forthrightly some of the major negative features of the PRC history is well represented. Samuel Kim acknowledged that Chinese Communist leaders have addressed and corrected some of their large domestic policy failures, while sustaining an image of correctness in foreign affairs.[21] Reflecting a tendency to avoid attention to the negatives of the PRC's record, the Great Leap Forward and the Cultural Revolution merit only tiny displays in the otherwise detailed recounting of the history of the modern Chinese revolution in the large National Museum in Beijing.

This writer's frequent lectures to university audiences and otherwise well-informed citizen groups in China show very weak understanding of such sensitive issues as Chinese support for the Khmer Rouge as well as other Communist insurgencies in Southeast Asia during the latter years of Mao Zedong's leadership (1949–76) and most of the period of Deng Xiaoping's leadership (1977–97). Many Chinese elites and broad popular opinion truly believe that the People's Republic of China has always followed morally correct foreign policies based on principles in support of progressive world forces. Against this background, it was not surprising that a senior Chinese foreign policy researcher associated with the Chinese Foreign Ministry presented a written keynote address to a trilateral international meeting in the United States of Vietnamese, Chinese, and American specialists in 2011 that was attended by the author and emphasized that "the People's Republic of China has always been a stabilizing force in Asia." The speaker seemed oblivious to the reaction of the Vietnamese delegates as they squirmed in their seats. He showed little awareness that the Vietnamese are among China's neighbors with the strongest reasons to disagree.

Explaining China's Interest-Based Behavior in Foreign Affairs— Change and Uncertainty

Whatever importance one gives to the wide array of principles and moral norms that are said by the Chinese government to govern Chinese foreign relations, the fact is that the private calculus of Chinese leaders in making key foreign and domestic policy decisions remains shrouded in secrecy. It is a crime subject to serious punishment to disclose such matters. Thus, the explanation of Chinese foreign policy decisions provided in this volume joins other studies in basing analysis mainly on patterns of Chinese behavior that can be observed and supported by evidence from Chinese and international sources.[22]

A defining feature of the foreign policy behavior of the People's Republic of China is change. As noted above, it seems impossible to explain these changes realistically on the basis of the muddled array of principles used in Chinese foreign relations over the past sixty years. The discussion in this

book finds greater accuracy in explaining Chinese decisions as heavily interest based. As seen from the list below and as explained in later chapters, the
Chinese foreign policies changed markedly and frequently, apparently driven
by changing calculations of Chinese interests that were in turn driven by
changing circumstances at home or abroad. Perceiving the reasons for the
changes in the course of Chinese policy is easier in retrospect. At the time,
the changes often came as a surprise, adding to China's reputation as a power
prone to unpredictable change, often leading to coercion and violence.

Because of the secrecy that has continued to surround Chinese leaders'
decision making, it is hard to know with precision why Chinese leaders
shifted course in foreign policy at different times over the years. During
Mao's rule (1949–76), the interests seen driving Chinese foreign policy were
often perceived as focused on fostering and promoting domestic and international revolution, though Mao also valued domestic development and made
several policy initiatives, including the opening to the United States in the
late 1960s, in pragmatic moves to buy time and gain leverage in order to
protect China's national security. Deng Xiaoping's leadership (1977–97) and
following leaders had a clearer focus on the top priorities of sustaining Communist Party rule through effective economic development. Foreign policy
was to serve these primary goals.

Nevertheless, the leaders wrestled periodically with conflicts in interests.
Thus, for example, questions over how far to go in accommodating the
United States in the interest of fostering a strong united front against Soviet
expansion were superseded after the Cold War and collapse of the USSR
(1991) with questions about how to balance Chinese goals to lead the international struggle against US superpower "hegemonism" and seek a multipolar world order versus a more pragmatic pursuit of peace and development
beneficial to China and others it interacted with. As the issue of Taiwan
independence rose to prominence with the Taiwan president's visit to the
United States in 1995, Chinese leaders struggled to balance imperatives to
protect China's claim to Taiwan and prevent Taiwan independence with the
need to sustain and deepen their advantageous economic and other ties with
Taiwan's main protector, the United States. Most recently, since 2009, advocates of a more assertive Chinese posture on sensitive territorial and other
issues involving the United States and many of China's neighbors have seriously complicated China's ongoing effort to reassure those and other concerned governments that China's rise would be peaceful and not adverse to
their interests.

Key periods with intervening changes in Chinese foreign relations can be
broken down as follows:

1949–53—Amid domestic consolidation, China showed strong support
for revolution at home and abroad in opposition to the United States.

Against this background, miscalculations resulted in war with the United States in Korea.

1954–57—Chinese-backed Viet Minh forces defeated French forces in Indochina. China echoed Soviet-backed peaceful coexistence and improved relations with India and other neighbors.

1958–65—Mass domestic mobilization in the ultimately disastrous Great Leap Forward was accompanied in 1958 by Chinese artillery attacks on islands held by Chiang Kai-shek's forces in the Taiwan Strait. The United States reacted with threats of nuclear war and the Soviet Union chafed over China's provocative international behavior and irrational economic policies involving large amounts of Soviet assistance. Moscow ended aid in 1960 and Sino-Soviet polemics spread from the international communist movement to competition among newly independent developing countries and insurgents resisting colonial rule. Radical Chinese policies in support of various foreign groups and nations generally failed to make many lasting gains; growing Chinese influence in Indonesia collapsed with a bloody purge in 1965 of Communists and pogroms against ethnic Chinese, killing half a million.

1966–68—Excesses during a violent radical phase of "Red Guard diplomacy" in the early years of the Cultural Revolution saw the collapse of the senior levels of the foreign ministry. China's relations with all but a handful of states suffered serious setbacks. Chinese mobs assaulted Soviet diplomats and set fire to the British mission with foreign officers forced to flee the flames into the mob.

1969–78—Soviet military pressure and the threat of nuclear attack forced China's opening to other states helpful in China's search for security. The United States for its own reasons was seeking reconciliation. Cooperation against Moscow would bind the United States and China together amid an intense leadership struggle in China that did not subside until the death of Mao and arrest of the Gang of Four in 1976 and the ascendance of Deng Xiaoping to leading power in 1978.

1979–89—China repeatedly maneuvered for advantage between the United States and the Soviet Union. Most of the time, it found improvements with the Soviet Union less beneficial than the advantages of cooperative relations with the United States.

1989–2001—China used generally pragmatic means to climb back to international importance following the imposition of Western isolation of China after the Tiananmen crackdown in 1989, the decline of China's strategic importance to the West as a result of the end of the Cold War, and Taiwan's international prominence as a new democracy. In the mid-1990s, China's strong actions in defense of claims to Taiwan and territories in the South China Sea alarmed and alienated many neighbors. It then adopted a new set of principles in a "new security concept" (NSC) that recalled the Five Principles of Peaceful Coexistence in pledging a policy of reassurance to China's neighbors. Nevertheless, China's moderation was not directed to the United States. China persisted with steady attacks against perceived US hegemonism and took careful aim at US alliances in the Asia-Pacific.

2001–9—Faced with an initially tough American stance against China under the George W. Bush administration, China broadened its reassurance efforts to now include the United States. Its objections to US alliances subsided; China did not want to be seen pressing Asian neighbors to have to make a choice they didn't want to make between aligning with the United States and aligning with China. US-China relations remained smooth until the first year of the Obama administration.

2009–18—Beginning in starts and stops in 2009 and becoming a more general trend under the rule of party leader and President Xi Jinping (2012–), there was an upsurge of Chinese opposition to US security and other policies in the Asia-Pacific, more assertive Chinese positions and commentary directed at China's neighbors, and for a time stepped-up Chinese support for North Korea during a period of leadership succession that also featured egregious North Korean attacks on South Korea. The Chinese behavior and assertiveness raised serious concerns throughout its eastern and southern flanks. The behavior saw major advances in Chinese control in contested islands in the South China Sea to which the usually restrained government of President Barack Obama eventually reacted with strong criticism and some concrete measures against Chinese behavior in this matter and in other sensitive trade and human rights issues in Sino-American relations.

FEATURES OF CHINA'S CHANGING FOREIGN POLICY PRIORITIES AND BEHAVIOR

In addition to recurring change and related uncertainty over the course of Chinese foreign relations during the almost seventy-year history of the People's Republic of China, other aspects of Chinese foreign relations need to be considered when assessing the impact and effectiveness of China's varied approaches to the world.

Chinese-Centered Calculus

A common feature in the changing Chinese priorities and behavior in foreign affairs is that the changes seem to be China-centered—grounded in a fairly clear and narrow set of Chinese interests. Mao Zedong talked often about world revolution, but he generally focused on China-centered interests. For example, available scholarship shows how Mao was prepared to confront the American military–backed containment system designed to halt China's advance in Asia in the 1950s, in part in order to better mobilize support for domestic change and revolution in China.[23] Domestic Chinese interests also were involved in governing Chinese foreign policy at the end of the Maoist period. Recent disclosures show how Mao ensured that considerations of Chinese domestic politics were reflected in defining the principles used by Deng Xiaoping in his inaugural speech at the United Nations in 1974 setting forth China's renowned "Three Worlds" theory in foreign affairs.[24]

Deng Xiaoping's first decade as China's most important leader beginning in 1978 focused foreign policy on protecting China in the face of Soviet pressure and coercion. Against this background, Deng turned out to be as supportive of the reviled Khmer Rouge as were Mao and the revolutionary leaders in China during the previous decade known as the Gang of Four. Deng's interest in backing this unsavory and radical Cambodian group seemed carefully calculated to support China's security interests, as the Khmer Rouge fielded the best fighting force available to counter Soviet-backed Vietnam's expansion along China's southeastern flank.[25]

Post-Deng leaders have created a new principle, the "win-win principle," which underlines their China-centered concerns. The formula is useful for reassuring neighboring countries and other nations China interacts with that China is interested in their development and concerns along with China's interest in its own development and concerns. China's partners like the approach as it generally does not require them to do anything they wouldn't ordinarily do. For its part, China also does not do anything it wouldn't ordinarily do, thereby avoiding initiatives that don't have a payoff for a narrowly defined Chinese win-set.[26]

Concern with the United States and Nearby Asia-Pacific Countries

The long record of the policy and behavior of the People's Republic of China in the Asia-Pacific region shows repeated maneuvering to keep China's periphery as free as possible from hostile or potentially hostile great-power pressure. Asia, especially the countries around China's periphery, has been the main arena of Chinese foreign relations. At bottom, this area has contained sovereignty issues and security issues that have been at the very top of the list of Chinese foreign policy priorities in most years. They involve such sovereignty issues as China's long-standing goal of reunifying Taiwan and the Chinese mainland, and such security issues as opposition to US containment in the 1950s and 1960, followed by opposition to perceived Soviet use of military force and alignments with Vietnam, India, and others to "encircle" and constrain China during the 1970s and 1980s, followed in turn by renewed public opposition to US alliances and military deployments in the 1990s and into the twenty-first century.

Chinese efforts to keep this periphery free of potentially hostile great-power presence and pressure have represented a long-lasting trend that shows persistent wariness and sometimes overt hostility toward such large outside powers, notably the United States. China has used sometimes offensive and sometimes defensive measures to thwart the perceived great-power ambitions in the region, which is seen as central to Chinese security. This trend has continued, along with growing Chinese economic integration, increasing political and security cooperation, and active engagement with various multilateral organizations in the region, since the 1990s. Thus, as Chinese officials in recent years declare greater confidence and China rises in influence in Asia, they work assiduously in trying to ensure that the United States and its allies and associates do not establish influence along China's periphery that is adverse to Chinese interests.[27]

Victim Mentality

China's enduring concern with the United States (or in the past, the Soviet Union) working with countries near China to establish a strong presence around China's periphery has been reinforced by a strong sense among Chinese elites and public opinion that China has been the victim of foreign imperialism and dominance for much of the past two centuries and should work assiduously to prevent such dominance in the future. Chinese and foreign specialists acknowledge that citizens and leaders of the People's Republic of China have long been conditioned through the education system, government-sponsored media coverage, and various other means to think of China as having been victimized by international powers beginning in the early nineteenth century. Emphasis on this historical conditioning was strengthened after the Chinese Communist Party (CCP) crisis at the time of the Tiananmen demonstrations and bloody crackdown in 1989 and continues up to the present. Sensing that communism no longer provided adequate ideological support for continued CCP rule, the authorities instituted a patriotic education campaign and other measures that encouraged regime-supporting patriotism in China by recalling the more than one hundred years of foreign affronts to Chinese national dignity. On one hand, the victim mentality has been created and used by the Chinese authorities to foster unity and support for the regime in the face of foreign challenges. On the other hand, it has become so widespread and deeply rooted in Chinese elite and public opinion that it requires Chinese officials to deal with the United States and other powers, notably Japan, with an often prickly sense of nationalism that impedes collaboration, even in some areas of mutual interest.[28]

United Front Tactics, Seeking Leverage against the "Main Enemy"

In its maneuvers against the United States and the Soviet Union focused on the Asia-Pacific region, China resorted repeatedly to tactics used during the wars against Japan (1937–45) and Chiang Kai-shek's Nationalist government (1945–49). Mao Zedong and post-Mao leaders focused on the main enemy and sought leverage and influence against it through mobilization of support within China and cooperation with other states or international forces. Sometimes the search for support brought China into close contact with international radicals, like the Khmer Rouge, or abusive authoritarians including Zaire's Sese Mobutu, Chile's Augusto Pinochet, the Shah of Iran, and Serbia's Slobodan Milosevic. China's depiction of its adversary as a threat often was exaggerated, presumably in order to foster greater domestic Chinese vigilance and international resolve. Thus, even though the end of the Cold War saw the People's Republic of China for the first time face no imminent threat of superpower military attack, the Chinese debate following the US bombing of the Chinese embassy in Belgrade during the US-led air war against the regime of Slobodan Milosevic in 1999 featured authoritative Chinese media arguing for a strong international united front against President Bill Clinton, whose actions in the war were equated with the atrocities and expansionist threat of Adolf Hitler.[29] Meanwhile, China on its part repeatedly employed building leverage and using united front tactics against lesser powers—notably Taiwan and Japan, but also including Vietnam, Burma, Thailand, and others—that were important targets for Chinese use of sometimes attractive and sometimes coercive levers of influence to bend these countries more to China's will.

THE UNITED STATES AT THE CENTER OF CHINESE FOREIGN CALCULATIONS

The subsequent chapters show that the United States was often the "main enemy" in Chinese foreign policy calculations. When China shifted focus to the Soviet Union as the main enemy as the United States seemed to be in significant decline beginning in the late 1960s, Chinese leaders remained focused on the importance of relations with the United States as it represented the chief bulwark against feared Soviet expansion. Although foreign and Chinese specialists advise in the post–Cold War period that China is increasingly less focused on the United States, as American primacy is seen to be in decline and for other reasons, available evidence shows strong Chinese awareness of China's increasing dependence on international commons and key world regions controlled or heavily influenced by America, notably many of the oil-producing countries of the Persian Gulf. Meanwhile, the Obama administration's reengagement efforts around China's rim in the

Asia-Pacific became notable with its so-called rebalance policy or "pivot" to Asia in 2011 and were viewed with carefully measured Chinese concern as they impacted areas of direct salience to Chinese security and sovereignty.[30]

China Often Reactive, Not in Control of Developments

In contrast with the image fostered by Chinese officials that Chinese foreign policy has been effective and moral under the guidance of far-seeing officials, more often than not the twists and turns in Chinese foreign policies and practices listed above resulted from unforeseen developments that required Chinese policy makers to make adjustments and shift course. China obviously was surprised by the US reaction to China-supported North Korea's attack on South Korea in 1950, and it may not have anticipated Soviet threats to invade China and destroy its nuclear facilities following a series of clashes on the Sino-Soviet border in 1969. Also, internal Chinese turbulence or other developments sometimes have spilled over into foreign affairs, causing Chinese policy officials to respond. Examples include reactions to the excesses of so-called Red Guard diplomacy at the start of the Cultural Revolution. Chinese assertiveness over sovereignty and security concerns over the past decade is commonly seen to have arisen in part from domestic pressure for a bolder and tougher foreign policy on nationalistic issues, compelling Chinese diplomats and senior officials who had been emphasizing China's "unwavering" interest in peace and development to respond accordingly.[31]

Competing Goals = Muddled Strategy

As explained earlier in this chapter, the zigzag pattern of adjustments and major changes in Chinese foreign relations suggests that China has had a hard time coming up with a coherent foreign policy strategy. A closer look at developments in the following chapters underlines this finding. Even with the more consistent policy priorities of Deng Xiaoping and later leaders, Chinese decision makers repeatedly wrestle with competing priorities that remain hard to reconcile in a national strategy worthy of the name.

LEGACIES AND VOLATILITY ADD TO COMPLICATIONS IN THE ASIA-PACIFIC

To repeat a key finding of the assessment of Chinese foreign relations in this book noted earlier, the Asia-Pacific region and its main outside power, the United States, represent the focus of Chinese foreign policy efforts. Unfortunately for contemporary Chinese influence in the region, the zigzag pattern of often intense and violent Chinese behavior toward the United States and neighboring Asia has not been forgotten. Available scholarship and other evidence have reinforced the findings of this writer's interviews with 260 officials in ten Asia-Pacific countries since 2004 to underscore the importance of this powerful and largely negative Chinese legacy to China's neighbors. US awareness of this negative legacy comes notably because the United States has a very large intelligence and security apparatus as well as a variety of scholars and specialists who delve into the past as well as the future in discerning dangers to American interests. All Asia-Pacific governments were relieved and pleased as China after the Cold War embarked with some twists and turns on an approach emphasizing reassurance of its neighbors. There is no interest among regional officials for digging up major negative episodes from the past. Nevertheless, the past is not forgotten, and China has an awful lot to live down given the record of its changing and often violent behavior. [32]

For example, the People's Republic of China arguably was the most disruptive element in the Asia-Pacific for forty of its sixty-plus years. Most bordering countries have experienced intrusion or invasion by PRC security forces. They and others somewhat further away have experienced armed insurgencies for decades whose strength depended on training, financial support, and arms from China.

The twists and turns of changing Chinese foreign policies in the region have baffled senior foreign leaders. Nehru was surprised and shamed by the Chinese border incursions and later armed attack on India. Nikita Khrushchev led the Soviet Union from 1954 to 1964. In 1958, he was appalled by Mao's reckless behavior confronting the United States in the Taiwan Strait crisis that year and by what the Soviet leader called Mao's "harebrained schemes" involving misuse and waste of Soviet aid during the disastrous Great Leap Forward. Ho Chi Minh in the 1960s sought a united Sino-Soviet front in his war against America, which China rebuffed. His successor, Le Duan, in the 1970s may not have expected China to invade Vietnam and create a Vietnamese government in exile in reaction to the Vietnamese war against the provocative Khmer Rouge regime in Cambodia. Chinese willingness to follow up well into the 1980s with years of periodic massive artillery attacks into Vietnamese border regions and other aggression underlined Chinese resolve to pursue its interests with determined use of military force and coercion. [33]

The United States was surprised with the Chinese-backed invasion by North Korea of South Korea in June 1950 and the subsequent massive Chinese intervention into the Korean conflict with the United States at the end of that year. After that negative experience, Americans tended to be careful to avoid direct war with China in following years, but they were surprised again by China's militant reaction to the Taiwan president's visit to the United States in 1995. They worried about further abrupt Chinese behavior and violence directed at the United States after the US bombing of China's embassy in Belgrade in 1999, and after the crash of a Chinese fighter jet and an

American surveillance plane in 2001. The harassment of a US surveillance ship by several Chinese government vessels in 2009 and Chinese public warnings against any further deployments of US aircraft carriers into the Yellow Sea in 2010 served as public warnings that China could react to perceived affronts from the United States or its allies and associates in disruptive and perhaps violent ways. [34]

Japan has reason to be very perplexed with China's changing priorities. China's pragmatic turn to Japan in the 1960s for economic support after the Chinese break with the Soviet Union and disastrous collapse of the Great Leap Forward was broadly welcomed in Japan, which maneuvered for exceptions regarding the US-led economic embargo of China. Japan was surprised by the US-China announcement in 1971 of Nixon's visit in 1972. The Japanese government changed leaders and quickly established diplomatic relations with China. China's strident opposition to Soviet expansion muted past worries about Japanese militarism, and Deng Xiaoping and his colleagues in the 1970s encouraged Japan to more strongly adhere to a Chinese-supported international front against the USSR. Japan was not seeking confrontation with Moscow and reluctantly signed a peace treaty with China in 1978 that contained a clause seen as targeting Moscow. The strong Ronald Reagan–Yasuhiro Nakasone relationship fended off Soviet expansion in Asia in the 1980s to China's general satisfaction.

Disputes with Japan over history books and past Japanese atrocities in China during the first half of the twentieth century were put aside as China welcomed Japan's efforts in 1990–91 to renew normal economic relations, including substantial foreign assistance, with China after the Tiananmen crackdown and subsequent allied isolation of China. The Japanese emperor—the living symbol of imperial Japan—was warmly welcomed by a grateful China in 1992. But relations soon declined as Chinese leaders reflected the stronger Chinese emphasis during the 1990s on patriotism and resolve to avoid any repetition of foreign, especially Japanese, infringement on China. Historical issues as well as territorial disputes and competition for Asian and international leadership saw relations decline, and they further deteriorated with Japanese prime minister Junichiro Koizumi (2001–6) and his repeated visits to a controversial Japanese war memorial. How sour the overall relation had become was seen in mass and sometimes violent demonstrations in some Chinese cities that broke out without Chinese government support in 2005, resulting in extensive property damage. Japan was a major target of the Chinese assertiveness over territorial and related issues that began in 2009 and became increasingly important in subsequent years. Chinese government–backed mass demonstrations in 120 Chinese cities, considerable property damage, and Chinese threats against Japan marked the dispute over Japanese policy toward the disputed Diaoyu/Senkaku Islands in 2012. They marked the largest public outpouring against a foreign target in the history of China.[35]

For their part, the South Koreans had worked hard in the post–Cold War period to win Chinese favor regarding issues on the Korean peninsula while building ever-closer economic relations. Relations were very close and growing in 2004, a time of major decline in South Korea's relations with the United States. Persisting differences over some historical issues and divergence over how to deal with North Korea checked further forward movement in China–South Korean relations, but the South Korean leadership and public were not prepared for China's strong support for North Korea during 2010, despite two North Korean military attacks on South Korea resulting in dozens of military personnel killed and some civilian casualties. Later, in the face of blatant and provocative North Korean actions and threats to use newly developed nuclear missiles, South Korea's outgoing conservative government and incoming progressive government in 2016–17 accepted advanced US missile defense systems that China opposed. In a crude demonstration of power to force Seoul to reverse its position, China used harsh criticism accompanied by strong diplomatic and widespread economic sanctions that surprised and seriously alienated South Korean leaders and public opinion.[36]

India too found that agreements during seemingly warm meetings with Chinese leaders in the past decade did not translate into significant progress on pending issues. The border dispute flared repeatedly with officials on both sides making strong accusations and military forces preparing for action.

Other countries moving from close convergence to wariness in dealing with China during the past decade include Australia and New Zealand. Vietnam, the Philippines, and others in the Association of Southeast Asian Nations (ASEAN) became deeply concerned with China's perceived assertiveness in recent years in the South China Sea and how that blocked their ambitions to use the sea's resources. The Philippines changed leaders and radically changed China policy in 2016, seeking accommodation with China.

As will be discussed in chapters 7 and 8, the legacies of negative behavior and volatile change add to the many differences between China and its neighbors and the United States over issues fundamentally important to China's security, stability, development, and national ambition. China's exceptionalism and image building make dealing with these issues realistically and effectively very difficult. The result is prevailing suspicion and wariness in the United States and among many of China's important neighbors as they deal with China's increasing power.

As explained in chapter 8, China's relations with central Asia are notably smoother than elsewhere around China's periphery.

PROGRESS IN AREAS FARTHER FROM CHINA

The discussion in chapter 9 will show various and sometimes serious complications and obstacles to expanding Chinese influence among countries beyond China's periphery. However, in these countries, legacies and volatility count for less, as China is often seen as a newcomer, without the negative historical baggage of other outside powers that have been interacting with them for many decades. Also, Chinese objectives in these areas appear more limited than Chinese objectives around China's rim. Security and sovereignty are not directly involved. China's main objectives focus on advantageous economic interchange; this focus appears broadly in line with the indigenous countries' interests in promoting mutual development. Nevertheless, relations in these regions sometimes stall with stagnant trade, economic disputes, and other differences.

CONCLUDING JUDGMENT

The mixed outlook for China's rise in line with Xi Jinping's often dramatic vision of China in the emerging world portrayed in chapter 10 endeavors to answer the question of whether or not a power shift is under way in Asian and world affairs. It shows that China remains seriously constrained where it matters most to China—in the Asia-Pacific region. Chinese behavior and interactions with the states of this region and with the United States in the region do not show the confidence that one would assume would accompany a power shift in China's favor. China's unwillingness to move beyond the restricted win-sets of the prevalent win-win formula governing Chinese foreign relations means that it remains reluctant to undertake significant risks or costs for the sake of regional or broader common goods. Part of the reason for this continued reluctance to lead in substantive as opposed to rhetorical ways appears related to the various internal problems noted earlier requiring that resources be used at home, not abroad. Meanwhile, the chapter demonstrates that the expanded footprint in regions farther from China remains more narrowly based than Chinese relations in nearby Asia, and under the win-win rubric it does not show much influence toward actually getting countries to do what they wouldn't ordinarily do.

NOTES

1. Aaron L. Friedberg, *Contest for Supremacy: China, America and the Struggle for Mastery in Asia* (New York: Norton, 2011); Hugh White, *The China Choice* (Collingwood, Australia: Black, 2012).

2. Stephen Brooks and William Wohlforth, "The Once and Future Superpower: Why China Won't Overtake the United States," *Foreign Affairs* (April 2016): pp. 91–104, https://

digitalcommons.dartmouth.edu/cgi/viewcontent.cgi?article=1133&context=facoa; Paul Dibb and John Lee, "Why China Will Not Become the Dominant Power in Asia," *Security Challenges* 10, no. 3 (2014): pp. 1–21, https://www.regionalsecurity.org.au/Resources/Files/SC10-3%20Dibb_Lee.pdf; Michael Beckley, "China's Century? Why America's Edge Will Endure," *International Security* 36, no. 3 (Winter 2011/2012): pp. 41–78.

3. Wayne Morrison, *China's Economic Conditions*, Report RL 33534 (Washington, DC: Library of Congress, Congressional Research Service, June 26, 2012), pp. 2–10; Cui Liru, "A Multipolar World in the Globalization Era," *Contemporary International Relations* (Beijing) 20, Special Issue (September 2010): pp. 1–11; World Bank, "China Per Capita GDP 2016," https://www.google.com/search?q=china+per+capita+gdp&rlz=1C1CHBF_enUS733US733&oq=china+per&aqs=chrome.5.69i57j0j69i60l3j0.13144j0j7&sourceid=chrome&ie=UTF-8 (accessed August 29, 2017).

4. Yu Yongding, "A Different Road Forward," *China Daily*, December 23, 2010, p. 9; "China's Reforms: The Second Long March," *Economist*, December 11, 2008, http://www.economist.com; "China Posts Worst Exports Fall since 2009," Reuters, January 13, 2015, http://www.reuters.com/article/us-china-economy-trade-idUSKBN14X0FD (accessed August 29, 2017); Zhong Nan, "Trade Volume Up Sharply, Ending a Two-Year Dip," *China Daily*, January 13, 2018, p. 1.

5. Arvind Subramanian, "The Inevitable Superpower: Why China's Rise Is a Sure Thing," *Foreign Affairs* 90, no. 5 (September/October 2011): pp. 66–78; Arthur Kroeber, *China's Economy: What Everyone Needs to Know* (New York: Oxford University Press, 2016), pp. 234–37).

6. Fabian Cambero and Dave Sherwood, "China Invites Latin America to Take Part in One Belt, One Road," Reuters, January 22, 2018, https://www.reuters.com/article/us-chile-china/china-invites-latin-america-to-take-part-in-one-belt-one-road-idUSKBN1FB2CN.

7. Trade figures used in this section are from the UN COMTRADE database at http://comtrade.un.org/db.

8. Carl Dahlman, *The World under Pressure: How China and India Are Influencing the Global Economy and Environment* (Stanford, CA: Stanford University Press, 2011).

9. US Department of Defense, *Annual Report to Congress: Military and Security Developments Involving the People's Republic of China 2017* (Washington, DC: US Department of Defense, May 2017); Ian Rinehart, *The Chinese Military: Overview and Issues for Congress*, CRS Report 44196 (Washington, DC: Congressional Research Service of the Library of Congress, March 24, 2016).

10. Jing-Dong Yuan, "China's Role in Establishing and Building the Shanghai Cooperation Organization (SCO)," *Journal of Contemporary China* 19, no. 67 (November 2010): pp. 855–70; Wu Xinbo, "Chinese Perspectives on Building an East Asian Community in the Twenty-First Century," in *Asia's New Multilateralism*, ed. Michael Green and Bates Gill (New York: Columbia University Press, 2009), pp. 55–77; Nadege Rolland, *China's Eurasian Century? Political and Strategic Implications of the Belt and Road Initiative* (Seattle, WA: National Bureau of Asian Research, 2017).

11. Michael Yahuda, *The International Politics of the Asia-Pacific* (London: Routledge, 2011), pp. 195–202; Linda Jacobson, "Australia-China Ties: In Search of Political Trust," *Policy Brief*, Lowy Institute, June 2012; Robert Blackwill and Ashley Tellis, *Council Special Report: Revising U.S. Grand Strategy toward China* (Washington, DC: Council on Foreign Relations, April 2015); Orville Schell and Susan Shirk, Chairs, *U.S. Policy toward China: Recommendations for a New Administration*, Task Force Report (New York: Asia Society, 2017).

12. Evan Medeiros, *Reluctant Restraint: The Evolution of China's Nonproliferation Policies and Practices, 1980–2004* (Stanford, CA: Stanford University Press, 2007); US Department of State, *2016 Country Reports on Human Rights Practices*, March 3, 2017, https://www.state.gov/j/drl/rls/hrrpt/2016/ (accessed July 1, 2017); Joanna Lewis, "US-China Climate Cooperation More Crucial Than Ever," *Chinafile*, July 10, 2014, http://www.chinafile.com/reporting-opinion/environment/us-china-climate-cooperation-more-crucial-ever (accessed January 17, 2018); Elizabeth Economy, "Why China Is No Climate Change Leader," *Politico*, June 12,

2017, https://www.politico.com/magazine/story/2017/06/12/why-china-is-no-climate-leader-215249 (accessed January 17, 2018).

13. Gideon Rachman, *Easternization: Asia's Rise and America's Decline* (New York: Penguin Random House, 2017); Wu Xinbo, "Understanding the Geopolitical Implications of the Global Financial Crisis," *Washington Quarterly* 33, no. 4 (October 2010): pp. 155–63.

14. Beckley, "China's Century?"

15. Minxin Pei, *China's Trapped Transition* (Cambridge, MA: Harvard University Press, 2007); David Shambaugh, "The Coming Chinese Crack-Up," *Wall Street Journal*, March 6, 2015, http://www.wsj.com (accessed July 1, 2017); Michael Forsythe, "Q and A: Roderick MacFarquhar on Xi Jinping's High-Risk Campaign to Save the Communist Party," *New York Times*, January 30, 2015, http://sinosphere.blogs.nytimes.com (accessed July 1, 2017); David Michael Lampton, *The Three Faces of Chinese Power* (Berkeley: University of California Press, 2008); Bruce Dickson, "Updating the China Model," *Washington Quarterly* 34, no. 4 (Fall 2011): pp. 39–58.

16. Denny Roy, *China's Foreign Relations* (Lanham, MD: Rowman & Littlefield, 1998), pp. 36–39; Samuel Kim, "China's International Organizational Behavior," in *Chinese Foreign Policy: Theory and Practice*, ed. Thomas Robinson and David Shambaugh (New York: Oxford University Press, 1994), pp. 401–5; Harry Harding, "China's Changing Role in the Contemporary World," in *China's Foreign Relations in the 1980s*, ed. Harry Harding (New Haven, CT: Yale University Press, 1985), pp. 177–79.

17. Dai Bingguo, "Adhere to the Path of Peace and Development," Xinhua, December 6, 2011, http://china.usc.edu/ShowArticle.aspx?articleID=2325 (accessed July 3, 2012).

18. Kim, "China's International Organizational Behavior," p. 402.

19. Ezra Vogel, *Deng Xioaping and the Transformation of China* (Cambridge, MA: Harvard University Press, 2011), pp. 266–92.

20. Robert Sutter, *Historical Dictionary of Chinese Foreign Policy* (Lanham, MD: Scarecrow, 2011), pp. 117–18, 194; Andrew Small, "First Movement: China and the Belt and Road Initiative," *Asia Policy* 24 (July 2017): pp. 80–87.

21. Roy, *Chinese Foreign Relations*, p. 38.

22. In addition to works already cited, see among others, A. Doak Barnett, *China and the Major Powers in East Asia* (Washington, DC: Brookings Institution Press, 1977); Michael Yahuda, *China's Role in World Affairs* (New York: St. Martin's, 1978); Allen Whiting, *The Chinese Calculus of Deterrence: India and Indochina* (Ann Arbor: University of Michigan Press, 1975); Robert Ross and Jiang Changbin, eds., *Reexamining the Cold War* (Cambridge, MA: Harvard University Press, 2001); Michael Hunt, *The Genesis of Chinese Communist Foreign Policy* (New York: Columbia University Press, 1996); Harold Hinton, *China's Turbulent Quest* (New York: Macmillan, 1972); Peter Van Ness, *Revolution and Chinese Foreign Policy* (Berkeley: University of California Press, 1970); Melvin Gurtov and Byong-Moo Hwang, *China under Threat* (Baltimore: Johns Hopkins University Press, 1981); John Garver, *Foreign Relations of the People's Republic of China* (Englewood Cliffs, NJ: Prentice Hall, 1993); Lowell Dittmer, *Sino-Soviet Normalization and Its International Implications, 1945–1990* (Seattle: University of Washington Press, 1992); Yong Deng, *China's Struggle for Status: The Realignment of International Relations* (New York: Cambridge University Press, 2008); M. Taylor Fravel, *Strong Borders, Secure Nation: Cooperation and Conflict in China's Territorial Disputes* (Princeton, NJ: Princeton University Press, 2008); Bobo Lo, *Axis of Convenience: Moscow, Beijing, and the New Geopolitics* (Washington, DC: Brookings Institution Press, 2008); Lorenz M. Luthi, *The Sino-Soviet Split: Cold War in the Communist World* (Princeton, NJ: Princeton University Press, 2008); Andrew Nathan and Andrew Scobell, *China's Search for Security* (New York: Columbia University Press, 2012); James Reilly, *China's Economic Statecraft: Turning Wealth into Power* (Sydney: Lowy Institute, November 2012); David Shambaugh, *China Goes Global: Partial Power* (New York: Oxford University Press, 2013); David Shinn and Joshua Eisenman, *China and Africa* (Philadelphia: University of Pennsylvania Press, 2012); Thomas Christensen, *The China Challenge: Shaping the Choices of a Rising Power* (New York: Norton, 2015); Rosemary Foot and Andrew Walter, *China, the United States and the Global Order* (New York: Cambridge University Press, 2011); David Michael Lampton, *Following the Leader: Ruling China from Deng Xiaoping to Xi Jinping*

(Berkeley: University of California Press, 2014); Evelyn Goh, *The Struggle for Order: Hegemony, Hierarchy and Transition in Post–Cold War East Asia* (Oxford: Oxford University Press, 2013); John Garver, *China's Quest: The History of the Foreign Relations of the People's Republic of China* (New York: Oxford University Press, 2016); Hu Sheng, *Imperialism and Chinese Politics* (Beijing: Foreign Language Press, 1985); Jiang Changbin and Robert S. Ross, eds., *Cong Duizhi Zouxiang Huanhe: Lengzhan Shiqi Zhong Mei Guanxi zai Tantao* [From confrontation toward détente: A reexamination of US-China relations during the Cold War] (Beijing: Shijie Zhishi Chubanshe, 2000); Pei Jianzhang, *Yanjiu Zhou Enlai: Waijiao sixiang yu shijian* [Researching Zhou Enlai: Diplomatic thought and practice] (Beijing: Shijie Zhishi Chubanshe, 1989); Wang Taiping et al., *Zhonghua renmin gongheguo waijiao shi, 1957–1969* [A diplomatic history of the People's Republic of China, 1957–1969] (Beijing: Shijie Zhishi, 1998); Gong Li, *Kuayue: 1969–1979 nian Zhong Mei guanxi de yanbian* [Across the chasm: The evolution of China-US Relations, 1969–1979] (Henan: Henan People's Press, 1992); Lin Qing, *Zhou Enlai zaixiang shengya* [The career of Prime Minister Zhou Enlai] (Hong Kong: Changcheng Wenhua Chubanshe, 1991); Wang Shuzhong, ed., *Mei-Su zhengba zhanlue wenti* [The question of contention for hegemony between the United States and the Soviet Union] (Beijing: Guofang daxue chubanshe, 1988); Wang Yu-san, ed., *Foreign Policy of the Republic of China* (New York: Praeger, 1990); Xie Yixian, *Zhongguo Waijiao Shi: 1949–1979* [China's diplomatic history: 1949–1979] (Henan: Henan Renmin Chubanshe, 1988); Men Honghua, *China's Grand Strategy: A Framework Analysis* (Beijing: Beijing Daxue Chubanshe, 2005); Yan Xuetong, *Zhongguo guojia liyi fenxi* [The analysis of China's national interest] (Tianjin: Tianjin Renmin Chubanshe, 1996).

23. Chen Jian, *Mao's China and the Cold War* (Chapel Hill: University of North Carolina Press, 2001); Thomas Christensen, *Useful Adversaries: Grand Strategy, Domestic Mobilization, and Sino-American Conflicts, 1949–1958* (Princeton, NJ: Princeton University Press, 1996).

24. Vogel, *Deng Xiaoping*, pp. 83–87.

25. Vogel, *Deng Xiaoping*, pp. 266–92.

26. Michael Chambers, "China and Southeast Asia: Creating a 'Win-Win' Neighborhood," in *China's "Good Neighbor" Diplomacy: A Wolf in Sheep's Clothing?* Special Report 126, ed. Gang Lin (Washington, DC: Woodrow Wilson Center for Scholars Asia Program, January 2005); "Wen Rolls Out 'Win-Win' Strategy in Africa," IPS News, June 21, 2006, http://ipsnews.net/news.asp?idnews=33702 (accessed July 16, 2010).

27. Yan Xuetong, "The Instability of China-US Relations," *Chinese Journal of International Politics* 3, no. 3 (2010): pp. 1–30; Zhang Liping, "A Rising China and a Lonely Superpower America," in *Making New Partnership: A Rising China and Its Neighbors*, ed. Zhang Yunlin (Beijing: Social Sciences Academic Press, 2008), pp. 324–55; Wu Xinbo, "The End of the Silver Lining: A Chinese View of the U.S.-Japanese Alliance," *Washington Quarterly* 29, no. 1 (Winter 2006): pp. 119–30; Tuan Phan, "Why the US 'Rebalance to Asia' Is More Important Than Ever," *Diplomat*, June 28, 2016, https://thediplomat.com/2016/06/why-the-us-rebalance-to-asia-is-more-important-than-ever/ (accessed January 17, 2018).

28. Suisheng Zhao, *A Nation-State by Construction: Dynamics of Modern Chinese Nationalism* (Stanford, CA: Stanford University Press, 2004); Peter Gries, *China's New Nationalism* (Berkeley: University of California Press, 2004); Anne-Marie Brady, *Marketing Dictatorship: Propaganda and Thought Work in Contemporary China* (Lanham, MD: Rowman & Littlefield, 2008), pp. 151–74; John Garver, *Foreign Relations of the People's Republic of China* (Englewood Cliffs, NJ: Prentice Hall, 1993), pp. 1–28.

29. David M. Lampton, *Same Bed, Different Dreams* (Berkeley: University of California Press, 2001), p. 60.

30. Martin Indyk, Kenneth Lieberthal, and Michael O'Hanlon, *Bending History: Barack Obama's Foreign Policy* (Washington, DC: Brookings Institution Press, 2012), pp. 61–62.

31. Thomas Christensen, "The Advantages of an Assertive China," Brookings Institution Press, March 25, 2011, https://www.brookings.edu/articles/the-advantages-of-an-assertive-china-responding-to-beijings-abrasive-diplomacy (accessed January 17, 2018).

32. Evelyn Goh, "Southeast Asia: Strategic Diversification in the 'Asian Century,'" in *Strategic Asia 2008–2009*, ed. Ashley Tellis, Mercy Kuo, and Andrew Marble (Seattle: National Bureau of Asian Research, 2008), pp. 261–96.

33. Vogel, *Deng Xiaoping*, pp. 266–92.

34. Robert Sutter, *U.S.-Chinese Relations: Perilous Past, Pragmatic Present*, 2nd ed. (Lanham, MD: Rowman & Littlefield, 2013), p. 163.

35. Ming Wan, *Sino-Japanese Relations: Interaction, Logic and Transformation* (Stanford, CA: Stanford University Press, 2006); Richard Bush, *The Perils of Proximity* (Washington, DC: Brookings Institution Press, 2010); Michael Yahuda, *Sino-Japanese Relations after the Cold War* (London: Routledge, 2014); June Teufel Dreyer, *Middle Kingdom and Empire of the Rising Sun* (New York: Oxford University Press, 2016); Richard McGregor, *Asia's Reckoning* (New York: Penguin Random House, 2017); Robert Sutter, *Chinese Foreign Relations: Power and Policy after the Cold War*, 4th ed. (Lanham, MD: Rowman & Littlefield, 2016), p. 12.

36. Scott Snyder, *South Korea at the Crossroads* (New York: Columbia University Press, 2018), epilogue.

Chapter Two

Mao's Changing Course in Foreign Affairs, 1949–69

The foreign relations of the People's Republic of China (PRC) have experienced dramatic changes since 1949. Mao Zedong's rise in the 1930s and 1940s as the undisputed leader of the Chinese Communist Party (CCP) heralded the strong-man rule and Mao's dominance of Chinese foreign policy decision making for three decades, until his death in 1976. Under Mao's rule, the period of 1949–76 witnessed dramatic swings in alignment, repeated and strong commitments to revolutionary goals and ideals along with more pragmatic emphasis on fostering China's national interests, and spasms of destructive mass campaigns within China that spilled over to impact Chinese foreign relations.

Chinese relations with the Soviet Union went from close alignment to the brink of war from 1950 to 1969. Under the pressure of Soviet military–backed coercion and intimidation, Mao in the early 1970s shifted course and aligned pragmatically with the United States, heretofore his main international adversary and the target of animus in a pervasive worldview fostered throughout China by Mao and the Communist government.

Coming after the disastrous results of the radical Great Leap Forward (1958–61), fostered and perpetuated by Mao and which resulted in the deaths of thirty million Chinese, Mao initiated in 1966 the Cultural Revolution that brought a massive purge of Chinese government and party officials and destroyed the lives of hundreds of thousands of Chinese elites and their families—an estimated one-half million to two million died as a result. The movement ended conventional Chinese relations with most of the world for several years. The resulting searing experiences for the leaders and people of China occurred in an international atmosphere of repeated episodes of tense Cold War confrontation and competition between two superpowers, the United States and the Soviet Union, which alternatively viewed China as a major adversary or as an asset in their ongoing contests with one another.

China reached the nadir of its international relationships and influence during the early years of the Cultural Revolution (1966–76) when conventional diplomacy and experienced diplomats were put aside and dismissed in favor of strident ideological fervor bordering on xenophobia. China became alienated from all but a handful of remaining international friends. The road back to more conventional diplomacy and international interchange was slow and difficult amid stark differences over domestic and foreign policy issues among Chinese leaders engaged in what turned out to be life-or-death struggles for power. The process toward more conventional diplomacy and international interchange was expedited because Sino-Soviet frictions reached a point in 1969 where the Soviet Union, backed by its large military buildup along the Chinese border, warned it would invade China and destroy China's nuclear facilities. The Soviet threat forced China to put aside the rigidities of the recent past and seek common ground with international forces helpful in countering the Soviet threat, leading to China's opening to many countries, especially the United States. [1]

CONFLICT AND CONTAINMENT

Mao Zedong and his Communist Party–led fighters faced daunting challenges as they endeavored to consolidate their rule after defeating Chiang Kai-shek's Nationalist Party (Kuomintang—KMT) forces in the Chinese Civil War and established the People's Republic of China on the Chinese mainland in 1949. Chiang and his remaining forces retreated to Taiwan. The Communist armies prepared to attack Taiwan and finish the civil war. Prospects for Communist success in the assault improved as US president Harry Truman decided that the United States should end support for Chiang's Nationalists.

China had been war ravaged for decades and arguably had been without effective governance for over a century. The collapse of the decaying Chinese empire in 1911 was followed by decades of warlord violence throughout the country. The interlude of Chinese Nationalist rule in the late 1920s and early 1930s ended with Japan's war against China. With one million Japanese troops and the support of Chinese collaborators, Japan controlled the most productive eastern half of China. Chinese deaths in the war with Japan (1937–45) were about twenty million.

The Chinese Communists were a rural-based movement with over two decades of experience in guerrilla war and supporting administrative efforts in the Chinese countryside, but with little experience in managing the complicated affairs of China's cities, its urban economy, or its national administration. Seeking needed technical and economic backing as well as guarantees and support for China's national security, the Maoist leadership endeavored to consolidate relations with the Soviet Union in an international environment heavily influenced by the United States, the main international supporter of its Chinese Nationalist adversary, and America-associated states influential in Asian and world politics. Mao made his first trip abroad and traveled to Moscow. He waited for weeks before Soviet leader Joseph Stalin, calculating Communist advances in Europe and Asia and uncertain of Mao's reliability, was ready to conclude an agreement on February 14, 1950, establishing the Sino-Soviet alliance.

These circumstances and determinants led to a strong current in analyses of Chinese relations, which emphasized Chinese imperatives of consolidation and development domestically and reactions internationally to perceived threats and occasional opportunities posed by circumstances involving notably the United States and the Soviet Union. In particular, as the Cold War spread from Europe and came to dominate international dynamics in Asia for several decades beginning in the late 1940s, Chinese foreign relations were seen as dominated in the 1950s and 1960s by Chinese efforts to deal with what emerged as a massive US-led military, economic, and political containment of China. Chinese interactions with the United States and Chinese foreign relations more broadly in this period often were assessed in terms of Chinese reactions to perceived threats posed by the power and actions of the United States and associated countries.[2]

Heading the list of strengths that the Maoist leaders brought to bear as they began national leadership in China were the Chinese Communist Party's broad experience in political organization and related social and economic mobilization, and a strong revolutionary ideology.[3] Mao Zedong and supporting leaders were committed to seeking revolutionary changes in China and in international affairs affecting China, and they had the determination and ability to move Chinese people along these paths. This set of determinants and circumstances led to another strong current in analyses of Chinese relations, which emphasized the importance of the Chinese leadership's resolve to challenge and confront the United States and its allies and associates in Asia as the Communist Chinese leadership sought to promote revolutionary change in Asian and world affairs. The analyses also showed a related tendency of the Chinese leadership to exploit episodes of confrontation with America as means to mobilize greater support within China for the often revolutionary changes sought there by the Maoist leadership.[4]

Assessments of the record of the Maoist period show a complicated mix of revolutionary imperatives and more conventional imperatives of security and nation building driving Chinese decision making. Adding to the mix was the emergence of the dominant role of Mao Zedong and how his strong-man rule came to determine Chinese decision making regarding Chinese foreign relations in particular, notably relations with the United States and the Soviet Union. One consequence was the ability and the actual tendency of the PRC to shift direction dramatically in foreign affairs. China's strong alignment with the Soviet Union in 1950 and break with Moscow ten years later exemplify the kinds of major shifts in China's foreign policy during this period.[5]

EARLY EXPERIENCES IN FOREIGN AFFAIRS

The roots of Chinese Communist calculus and shifts in foreign affairs lay heavily with the protracted experience of Mao Zedong and his associates as leaders of a guerrilla revolutionary movement struggling for success against great odds in the two decades prior to the establishment of the People's Republic of China in 1949. Chiefly concerned with the survival of their movement against Chiang Kai-shek's Nationalist Party–led government, the Communist leaders devoted only secondary attention to events outside China.

Chiang's armies forced Mao and his cohort to retreat from base areas in southern China, embarking on the so-called Long March, which ended after great hardship with the remnants of the group arriving in northwestern China in 1936, where they developed new base areas. A mutiny among troops ostensibly under his command forced Chiang in late 1936 to agree to a united front with the Communists against Japan and its expansionist moves in China. Japan's launch of full-scale war against China in 1937 focused mainly against Chiang's forces, which were compelled after strong resistance to retreat from coastal China into the interior. The Nationalist-Communist united front eroded. The Japanese assault on Chiang's armies provided opportunity for Mao and the Communists to consolidate their bases in northwestern China, in particular.

Reflecting their isolation and apparent lack of information about foreign affairs, the CCP leaders showed little evidence of a sophisticated view of world events. In particular, they relied heavily on guidelines set by the Soviet Union–dominated international communist movement (the Communist International, or Comintern) in assessing the policies of capitalist states such as the United States. Thus, when the USSR opposed the foreign policies of the United States and other Western powers in the early 1930s, Chinese party representatives carefully followed suit. A few years later, the CCP promptly echoed the Comintern's "united front" line, which drew a distinction between the "principal" enemy—that is, the fascist states—as opposed to the capitalist democracies, calling for alliance with the latter against the former. This line conformed to the CCP interests inside China, allowing the Communists to exploit an anti-Japanese approach in order to broaden their appeal within the country.[6]

The CCP also followed the Comintern line in foreign affairs even when it proved damaging to the Communists' position in China, as during the period of erratic shifts in Soviet foreign policy in 1939–41. Mao Zedong personally supported the Comintern position on the most notorious example of expedient Soviet policy—the German-Soviet pact of August 1939—even though it seriously tarnished the CCP image in China. The Soviet move notably disappointed a prevailing Chinese hope that the USSR would unite with the capitalist democracies against the Axis powers, which came to include imperial Japan along with Adolf Hitler's Germany and Benito Mussolini's Italy, and accordingly would assist China, which was bearing the brunt of Japanese military might.[7]

The significance of the Chinese Communists' subservience to Moscow's line in foreign affairs remains unclear. It may be, as some have argued, that the CCP was in fact demonstrating an intense desire to win favor with Moscow as well as a genuine, ideologically based determination to follow the Soviet lead.[8] On the other hand, the CCP leaders may have been demonstrating little more than pro forma backing for the Comintern line, in a relatively unimportant sphere of foreign affairs, in order to keep on good terms with the Soviet-led international communist movement—the source of foreign support that the Chinese Communists had at this time.

At the same time, the Chinese Communists judged the United States and associated Western powers negatively on the basis of their ideological training in Marxism-Leninism and their particular belief in Vladimir Lenin's theory of imperialism. Prior to World War II, the Communists generally assessed the policies of the "imperialist" powers in China, including the United States, as motivated chiefly by economic gain; the desire for financial return was seen to cause the powers to intervene actively in China's internal affairs, militarily dominate the Chinese treaty ports, patrol rivers and coastal waterways, and supply warlords and other perceived nonprogressive power holders in China with arms and loans to suppress the CCP-supported, anti-imperialist movement.[9]

The twists and turns of the CCP's shifting emphasis in foreign affairs were reflected in on-again off-again initiatives toward the United States in the 1930s and 1940s. The termination of the Nationalist blockade and military campaigns against the Communists following the start of the CCP-KMT united front in late 1936 prompted the Communist leaders to try to break out of their isolated position. Overlooking past disputes and negative feelings toward the United States, they endeavored to win favor with American news reporters and other Westerners who visited their base in northwestern China. This opening to the West, highlighted by Mao's meetings with journalist Edgar Snow, was short lived. Nationalist forces reimposed a tight blockade around the Communist base while American interest was diverted to Japan's expansion in East Asia.[10]

Following the Japanese attack on Pearl Harbor and American entrance into the Pacific war, the Chinese Communist leadership initiated a more serious effort to win US support. In China's wartime capital, Chongqing, CCP representatives led by Zhou Enlai made concerted efforts in private conversations with American officials to explain the Communists' positions that were at odds with those of the ruling Nationalist government. They also encouraged the Americans to send official representatives to the Communist-held areas in northern China for liaison work with the CCP officials in the war against Japan. The Communists' accommodating approach toward the United States came in spite of their past ill feeling toward Washington and their ideologically based antagonism toward the capitalist American government. It no doubt was in part prompted by the general line of the Communist International at this time, which emphasized the need for world Communists to unite with the capitalist democracies in order to defeat the fascist powers. However, the intensity of Communists' efforts to woo American favor also appeared to be closely tied to the situation in China and to the CCP's competition for power with the Kuomintang. [11]

America emerged during World War II as the predominant foreign power in East Asia, and in China it brought its power, influence, and aid to bear solely on the side of Chiang Kai-shek's Nationalists. Facing this adverse trend, the Communists sought closer association with the United States. Their efforts resulted in the establishment of military and political connections, notably through a US liaison office in the Communist headquarters at Yenan. US mediation between the Communists and Nationalists beginning in 1944 failed to bridge the gap between the two and failed to end one-sided American support for Chiang Kai-shek's Nationalists. In the Chinese civil war following Japan's defeat the Americans sided strongly with the Nationalists, reinforcing the CCP's leaders' view of the United States as an enemy of the newly founded People's Republic of China. [12]

CONTAINMENT AND CHINA'S RESPONSE

The foreign policy plans of the newly established People's Republic of China (PRC) were confronted at the outset by miscalculations over Korea, which resulted in Sino-American war and the establishment of a massive US military–led effort to surround and check Chinese Communism. The American deployments, alliances, and related economic embargo under the rubric of the policy of containment came to dominate the foreign policy calculations of the PRC for two decades. How China chose to deal with the American threat and other salient concerns in foreign affairs varied greatly, reinforcing a pattern of swings in Chinese foreign policy behavior that were hard to foresee. [13]

Neither the government of Mao Zedong nor the administration of President Harry S. Truman in the United States sought or foresaw a US-China war in early 1950. The Americans were surprised when North Korean forces, with the support of Soviet and Chinese leaders, launched an all-out military attack against South Korean forces in June 1950. The Chinese Communist leaders and their Korean and Soviet Communist allies apparently calculated that the better-organized and better-armed North Koreans would attain victory quickly without provoking a major or effective US military response. Thus, it was their turn to be surprised when the United States promptly intervened militarily in the Korean War and also sent the US Seventh Fleet to prevent a Chinese Communist attack on Taiwan, where Chiang Kai-shek and his remaining forces had retreated after their defeat on the Chinese mainland. US forces and their South Korean allies halted the North Korean advance and carried out an amphibious landing at Inchon in September 1950 that effectively cut off the North Korean armies in the South, leading to their destruction.[14]

The string of miscalculations continued. With the support of the United Nations, US and South Korean forces proceeded into North Korea. The Chinese warned and prepared to resist them, but US leaders thought the warnings were a bluff. By November hundreds of thousands of Chinese Communist forces were driving the US and South Korean forces south in full retreat. Eventually, the Americans and their allies were able to sustain a line of combat roughly in the middle of the peninsula, as the two armies faced off for over two more years of combat, casualties, and destruction.[15]

Chinese Communist leaders also launched domestic mass campaigns to root out pro-American and other Western influence and seize control of US and Western cultural, religious, and business organizations that remained in China. The United States began wide-ranging strategic efforts to contain the expansion of Chinese power and Chinese-backed Communist expansion in Asia. A strict US economic and political embargo against China, large US force deployments, eventually numbering between one half and one million troops, massive foreign aid allocations to US Asian allies and supporters, and a ring of US defense alliances around China were used to block Chinese expansion and to drive a wedge between the PRC and its Soviet ally.[16]

President Dwight D. Eisenhower's administration used threats and negotiations in reaching an armistice agreement that stopped the fighting in Korea in 1953. But American efforts to strengthen military alliances and deployments to contain Chinese Communist–backed expansion continued unabated. The US-led efforts faced off against enhanced Chinese efforts in the wake of the Korean armistice to strengthen support for Communist insurgents working against American-backed forces in French Indochina and direct Chinese military probes and challenges against the United States and their Chinese Nationalist allies in the Taiwan Strait.

Mao Zedong and his Communist Party–led government continued their consolidation of control inside China, notably through mass campaigns led by Communist activists targeting landlords, leading urban political and economic elites, and others deemed abusive or uncooperative with Communist goals. They prepared for major nation-building efforts with the support of their Soviet and Soviet bloc supporters to establish an administrative structure, often along the lines of that of the Soviet Union, to govern Chinese civil administration, economic planning, military modernization, intelligence collection, and other endeavors. They pursued efforts to tap into the surplus wealth being created in China's rural sector for investment in their planned expansion of China's industrial economy. After a brief period where peasants held land as a result of the mass campaign for land reform in rural China in the early 1950s, Chinese leaders saw the need to emulate the Soviet model and began to collectivize the land under government administration so as to better control the surplus rural wealth and to maximize its utility to the state's interests in promoting industrial development. The Soviet Union was providing over one hundred major projects to assist Chinese industrialization and modernization, but they had to be paid for. The Chinese saw collectivization in the rural areas and concurrent establishment of greater state control of the urban economy along Soviet lines as the appropriate way forward.

These dramatic and massive shifts in domestic policy and direction occurred frequently in conjunction with crises and confrontations with the United States and its allies and associates around China's periphery in Asia. At one level, the Chinese determination to work against and confront the US-backed French forces in Indochina and the US-supported forces of Chiang Kai-shek in the Taiwan Strait reflected a deeply held determination to confound and wear down the American-fostered containment system. The Chinese Communist leadership held a strong revolutionary commitment to change the international order dominated by the United States and its allies and to support Communist-led forces struggling against what they saw as foreign imperialism.[17]

The US effort also directly threatened China's national security and sovereignty, often in graphic and severe ways. The Eisenhower administration threatened China with nuclear attack in order to push it toward an armistice in Korea, and the US government used the threat of nuclear attack at other times in the face of perceived Chinese provocations in the 1950s. Mao Zedong's China had no viable defense against US nuclear weapons and put top priority on developing Chinese nuclear weapons to deal with such repeated US efforts at intimidation. At the same time, the Chinese Communist leaders also were seen to continue to use the crisis atmosphere caused by confrontations with outside threats posed by the United States and its allies as a means to strengthen their domestic control and their mobilization of resources for advancement of nation building and administrative competence.[18]

Defeat of US-backed French forces in Indochina led to the 1954 Geneva Conference and accords that formalized French withdrawal. China backed the Communist-led Viet Minh victors with supplies and advisors, while the United States provided supplies to forces of France that ultimately were defeated at their Indochina stronghold, Dien Bien Phu, on May 7, 1954. France sought peace at the Geneva Conference in 1954, while the United States deepened involvement in Vietnam and elsewhere in Southeast Asia to check Chinese-backed Communist advances in Southeast Asia. After the conference, US policy worked to support a non-Communist regime in South Vietnam, backing the regime when it resisted steps toward reunification set forth in the Geneva Accords. The United States also deepened and broadened defense and other links with powers in Southeast Asia in order to check Chinese-backed Communist gains in the region.

President Eisenhower and Secretary of State John Foster Dulles were wary of Chiang Kai-shek's maneuvers that might drag the United States into a war with the Chinese Communists over Taiwan. Using the fortuitous turn of events caused by the Korean War, Chiang Kai-shek's Nationalists consolidated their rule in Taiwan and with American support rapidly built up Taiwan's military forces with the objective of eventually taking the battle to mainland China. The political atmosphere inside the United States was supportive of Chiang and his harsh anti-Communist stance. The so-called China Lobby supporting Chiang and his Nationalist administration included liberals as well as conservatives in a variety of respected organizations. Thus, US military and economic assistance to Chiang Kai-shek and the Nationalist forces on Taiwan expanded dramatically.[19]

Though Dulles and other leaders of the US government were privately unsure of the wisdom of such close and formal US ties to Chiang's Nationalists, Washington eventually brought Taiwan into the web of formal military alliances that provided the foundation of the US containment system against Chinese-backed Communist expansion in Asia. The United States and Nationalist China signed a bilateral defense treaty on December 2, 1954.

The PRC reacted with harsh rhetoric and military assaults against Nationalist Chinese–controlled islands off the coast of the Chinese mainland. Great Britain and other US allies, as well as some US congressional leaders and other elites, did not welcome this new and potentially very dangerous military crisis between the United States and China so soon after the bloody conflict in Korea. But the US administration firmly backed the Chinese Nationalists and their Republic of China (ROC). US forces helped Nationalist forces on some exposed islands to withdraw as the Taiwan Strait crisis of 1955 continued, raising fears of a renewed US-China war.

PEACEFUL COEXISTENCE

Against this background, the Chinese Communist government's stance against the United States moderated. The reasoning appeared related to a shift in Soviet policy toward the West following Stalin's death in 1953. The incoming Soviet leaders were more interested than Stalin had been in arranging an advantageous modus vivendi with Western powers in Europe. While they continued to give some public support to their Chinese ally in its dispute with the Chinese Nationalists and the United States, they also signaled Soviet wariness about getting involved in Asian conflicts. They played down the applicability to Asia of the Sino-Soviet alliance; Soviet official commentary implied that China was to bear the major responsibility for dealing with the United States and its allies and associates in Asia. The Chinese government also began at this time to endeavor to broaden productive economic and diplomatic ties with countries in Asia, Africa, and Europe, and Chinese leaders found that their hard line and confrontational behavior in the Taiwan Strait were counterproductive for this effort. Washington, for its part, had not sought to escalate military tensions with China, as this would complicate US efforts to work with European and Asian allies to explore Soviet moderation and to build lasting alliance relationships to contain Asian Communist expansion.[20]

Thus, Beijing by early 1955 was faced with an increasingly counterproductive campaign over Taiwan, a potentially dangerous military confrontation with Washington, lukewarm support from its primary international ally, and increased alienation from world powers. In this context, Chinese leaders understandably chose to move to a more moderate stance when presented with the American offer in mid-January 1955 of a cease-fire in the armed conflict in the Taiwan Strait. Beijing responded to the US proposal with criticism but indirectly signaled interest in the offer by gradually reducing Chinese demands concerning Taiwan.

Chinese Premier Zhou Enlai used the venue of the Afro-Asian Conference in Bandung, Indonesia, in April 1955 to ease tensions and call for talks with the United States. How serious the Chinese were in pursuing their avowed interest in such engagement with the United States was never shown, as the Chinese overtures met with a nuanced but firm rebuff from Washington. Secretary of State Dulles was wary that direct talks with the PRC would undermine Chiang Kai-shek's Nationalist government on Taiwan. Dulles's private strategy of vigorously pursuing a containment policy against China favored a tougher US policy toward China than toward the Soviet Union. He endeavored thereby to force Beijing to rely on Moscow for economic and other needs, which the Soviet Union could not meet. In this and other ways, he hoped to drive a wedge between China and the USSR. On the other hand, Dulles faced congressional and allied pressures to meet with the Chinese, so he agreed to low-level ambassadorial talks that began in Geneva in 1955. The talks met frequently for a time but little progress was made, as the United States repeatedly rejected Chinese initiatives and accused China of perfidy regarding the agreements that were reached.[21]

Zhou's overtures at Bandung also included Chinese efforts to improve relations with growing numbers of newly independent governments in the developing world by reassuring them with Chinese pledges to follow moderate foreign policies consistent with what became known as the Five Principles of Peaceful Coexistence. China established relations and improved ties with various governments and notably advanced Chinese relations with governments of such key large developing countries as Egypt, India, and Indonesia. Over time, those advances flagged as China pursued more radical and confrontational policies directed against the United States and eventually the Soviet Union in the late 1950s and 1960s. Nonetheless, Beijing's diplomatic relations broadened with a number of developing and some developed countries during this period.

In 1958, China moved into a more radical phase of foreign as well as domestic policy, and its resolve against the United States remained firm and deepened over the next decade. Beijing's public break with the Soviet Union by 1960 brought on stronger Chinese competition with the Soviet Union in the international communist movement and especially among developing nations. China's strident antagonism regarding both superpowers exacerbated differences with the wide range of countries and world leaders who maintained or sought amicable ties with either Washington or Moscow.

China sustained strong interest in ties with Egypt following the coming to power of Gamal Abdel Nasser in the 1950s. Nasser gave a strongly anti-Western cast to the prevailing ideas in the Afro-Asian and nonaligned movements. He also was a proponent of pan-Arabism and sought to reduce Western influence in Egypt, notably by nationalizing the Suez Canal. Egypt's confrontation with Great Britain and France over this move led it to establish diplomatic relations with China in 1956. It became the first country in Africa or the Middle East to do so. Egypt's militant anticolonialist stance and its role as the largest and most influential Arab state reinforced Chinese interest in maintaining close relations. The two governments differed, however, notably over China's strident opposition to the Soviet Union, which caused a major split with Egypt and others in the Afro-Asian People's Solidarity Organization in the 1960s. After the Egyptians' defeat to US-backed Israel in 1967, China's advice to Nasser was to engage in protracted guerrilla war with Israel; this advice was deemed unhelpful and naïve among the Arab leaders.[22]

Other features of Chinese diplomacy in the 1950s included efforts to reach out to Japan, which was interested in trade and other conventional relations despite the American-led international embargo against China. Several European countries improved relations with China, as did some South and Southeast Asian nations interested in taking advantage of China's emphasis on peaceful coexistence.

Greater Chinese international activism in the mid-1950s also saw the PRC take a leading position on two major crises in the international communist movement, perhaps the most important arena of Chinese foreign policy activity in the 1950s. China reacted differently to anti-Soviet trends in Poland and Hungary. As dedicated Marxist-Leninists, Chinese leaders supported the intervention of Soviet troops in Hungary in November 1956, as the existing Communist regime was seen as unable to contain a burgeoning mass movement that was increasingly taking outright anti-Communist forms. By contrast, Chinese officials that same year supported the leadership of Poland where the Communist Party resisted Soviet pressure to curb what was deemed by Moscow as excessive nationalism and defiance of Soviet instructions.[23] The lesson of these concurrent episodes was that China supported Communist regimes and forceful Soviet actions in support of Communist regimes against anti-Communist challenge but favored resistance to the Soviet Union's efforts to intimidate and coerce neighboring Communist regimes for the sake of Moscow's stature as leader of the international communist movement. In both cases, China's actions showed willingness to undertake a greater role regarding international communist matters following the death of Stalin and in emerging Chinese disagreements with Stalin's successors.

REVIVED RADICALISM

With the shift back to a more radical posture in foreign affairs in 1958, Mao Zedong's Communist forces used artillery barrages in an effort to challenge and halt resupply of the Nationalist Chinese forces holding the fortress island Quemoy and other Nationalist-controlled islands located only a few miles off the coast of the Chinese mainland. The military attacks predictably created another major crisis and war scare, with the United States firmly supporting Chiang Kai-shek's forces and threatening nuclear attack. Chiang Kai-shek refused to consider withdrawal from the Quemoy fortress, where a large portion of his best troops were deployed as part of his broader military preparations to attack mainland China and reverse Communist rule.

The absence of landing craft and other preparations for an invasion suggested that Mao was testing Nationalist and US resolve regarding the offshore island and did not intend to invade Taiwan itself. The crisis atmosphere played into Mao's efforts at the time to mobilize national resources for a massive "Great Leap Forward" in Chinese development. Later, foreign analysts argued persuasively that the domestic mobilization was a major Chinese objective in launching the military aggression on the offshore islands held by the Chinese Nationalists.[24]

Another line of analysis argued that the Chinese leader also used the confrontation with the United States to test Soviet resolve in supporting China in what was seen in China as a weakening Sino-Soviet alliance. The Chinese-Soviet alliance indeed began to unravel by the late 1950s. Ideological debates emblematic of the Sino-Soviet split came into public view by 1960, and Soviet leader Nikita Khrushchev ended assistance to China that year. The dispute broadened to include intense Sino-Soviet competition for influence in the international communist movement and among developing countries in world affairs. The Sino-Soviet border became an issue of public dispute in 1964. By that time, Leonid Brezhnev and Alexei Kosygin had replaced the deposed Khrushchev; they undertook a major buildup of Soviet forces along the Sino-Soviet border and in Mongolia. Escalating border clashes in 1969 foreshadowed a full-scale Soviet military attack.[25]

The Soviet withdrawal of assistance to China in 1960 came at a time of acute economic crisis in China caused by the collapse and abject failure of the Great Leap Forward campaign. The staggering damage to China from the three-year effort included the premature deaths of thirty million people from starvation and nutrition deficits. During this period of weakness China became more concerned about border security in the face of Chiang Kai-shek's avowed plans to attack and India's perceived encroachments along its border with China. China prepared to use force against Chiang's armies, and in 1962 it launched a major assault destroying India's border defenses.[26]

As the first prime minister of independent India until his death in 1964, Jawaharlal Nehru presided over, and in many cases directed, the tortuous turns of Sino-Indian relations during this formative period of relations. Nehru charted a course for India independent of the United States and the Soviet Union. He pioneered a policy on nonalignment and became a leader of the Non-Aligned Movement composed mainly of newly emerging and developing countries. He quickly established diplomatic relations with China, argued in favor of China's entry into the United Nations, and refused to condemn China as the aggressor in the Korean War. In the mid-1950s, Nehru built a relationship with Chinese premier Zhou Enlai, who was then emphasizing Chinese moderation consistent with the Five Principles of Peaceful Coexistence. He seemed surprised by revelations in 1958 of Chinese road building across Indian-claimed territory along the border with China known as the Aksai Chin. In 1959, he allowed the Dalai Lama and many thousands of his followers, escaping a Chinese crackdown in Tibet, to reside in India. Chinese-Indian border tensions worsened, though Nehru again seemed surprised by the Chinese military action overrunning Indian defenses along the eastern boundary in 1962, the nadir of Sino-Indian relations in the modern period.[27]

Elsewhere, China used diplomacy, established relations, and employed other conventional means to stabilize sensitive issues. In neighboring Laos, China fully supported the armed struggle against the rule by France in Indochina that resulted in the 1954 Geneva Accords and the creation of an independent Laos. The unstable Laotian government was subjected to pressures from rightist forces and forces associated with a Communist insurgency, which China supported. China established diplomatic relations with Laos in 1961. In 1961–62 a second Geneva Conference, attended by US and Chinese officials, eventually reached an understanding on the Communist versus non-Communist armed struggle in Laos. The understanding temporarily defused this flash point of US-Chinese conflicting interests, although the United States and China subsequently deepened military involvement in the country, as did the Chinese-backed forces from North Vietnam. The escalation of fighting in the Vietnam War involving Vietnamese Communist forces and forces of the United States in the 1960s dominated developments in the country. China fully backed the Vietnamese Communists and their Communist-led allies in Laos.[28]

China also advanced relations with Nepal. The Himalayan mountain state had deepened economic and security ties with India in the aftermath of China's military occupation of Tibet in 1950, and a Nepal-India Peace and Friendship Treaty was signed that year. Nepal improved relations with China in the mid-1950s in tandem with improvement in India's relations with China; subsequently, relations with Nepal continued to improve while Indian-Chinese relations declined. Nepal and China established diplomatic relations in 1955; Nepal recognized Tibet as part of China; and the two countries exchanged resident ambassadors by 1960. That year, Nepal and China signed a boundary settlement agreement and a treaty of peace and friendship. Nepal also began supporting China's entry into the United Nations. In 1961, Nepal and China agreed to build an all-weather road connecting the Nepalese capital, Kathmandu, with Tibet. During the Sino-Indian War of 1962, Nepal maintained neutrality.[29]

China's early involvement with Africa featured sometimes visionary efforts to help African countries throw off the influence of colonial or other foreign powers and to foster rapid development and social progress. China supported Gamal Abdel Nasser's leading Egypt against Western powers in the 1950s. In the 1960s, it supported newly emerging nations and armed resistance groups targeting colonial and white-ruled African regimes. It favored nations and groups that opposed or remained independent of the Soviet Union, the United States, and colonial powers of Europe. Major assistance projects included the TanZam Railway linking Zambia and Tanzania, representing a high point in Chinese assistance to Africa, and support for the pro-China leaders of the countries, Zambia's Kenneth Kaunda and Tanzania's Julius Nyerere.[30]

Among developed countries, China reached out to Japan in the 1960s for trade, technology, and other economic support following the end of Soviet assistance to China. The Japanese government and businesses found ways around the US-led international embargo against China in order to reach understandings with Beijing that made Japan China's most important international economic partner in the 1960s. France, under the leadership of independent-minded President Charles de Gaulle, also broke with American-led efforts to isolate China and established diplomatic relations with the PRC in 1964.

TURMOIL IN THE CULTURAL REVOLUTION

During the 1960s, a disastrous result of the twists and turns in Chinese domestic and foreign policy following the widespread starvation and other calamities caused by the collapse of the Great Leap Forward were years of violence and life-or-death political struggle. Elites and other groups, mainly in Chinese cities, maneuvered and fought during the Cultural Revolution that began in 1966 and did not end until Mao's death in 1976.[31] At first, the sharply deteriorating domestic situation in the early 1960s caused Mao to retreat from regular involvement in administrative matters. His subordinates pursued more moderate and pragmatic policies designed to revive agricultural and industrial production on a sustainable basis without reliance on the highly disruptive and wasteful mass campaigns and excessive collectivization of recent years. The economy began to revive, but the progress was marred in Mao's eyes by a reliance on the kinds of incentives prevalent in the "revisionist" practices of the Soviet Union and its allied states and the controlling bureaucratic elites in those states, who were seen as restoring the kind of unequal and exploitative practices typical of capitalism.

Mao found that two of the three main pillars of power and control in China, the Communist Party and the Chinese government, continued to move in the wrong direction. The third pillar of power and control, the Chinese military, was under the leadership of Lin Biao following the purge of Defense Minister Peng Dehuai, who dared to resist Mao's Great Leap policies during a leadership meeting in 1959. Defense Minister Lin positioned his leadership in support of Maoist ideals of revolution, equality, and service to the people. Indoctrination and involvement in civil society and popular affairs often took precedence over professional military training. The distillation of Mao's wisdom from volumes of selected works was distributed throughout the Chinese military, the broader masses of China, and abroad in the form of a plastic covered "little red book," *Quotations from Chairman Mao Tsetung*, published with a preface by Lin Biao.

Mao was not prepared to break with his party and government colleagues until 1966. By that time he had become sufficiently opposed to prevailing administrative practices and tendencies. Also he had built up enough support outside normal administrative structures in order to challenge and reverse what was later portrayed as a drift toward revisionism and the restoration of capitalism. Relying on his personal charisma, organizational support from military leaders like Lin Biao, security forces controlled by radical leaders like Kang Sheng, and various political radicals and opportunists, Mao launched his unorthodox efforts, including the creation of legions of millions of young Red Guards leading the attack against established authority in urban China. The result was confusion, some resistance from political and government leaders often unaware of Mao's commitment to the radical Red Guards and their allies, and ultimately mass purges and persecution of senior and lesser authorities amid widespread violence and destruction carried out by Red Guard groups and others. By 1968, numerous neighborhoods in cities in China had burned during clashes between rival Red Guard groups, and the party and government structure had collapsed. The military was called into the cities to restore order. With Mao's support, they proceeded to transport the millions of Red Guards from the cities and to disperse them into various areas in the Chinese countryside where they were compelled to stay and work for the indefinite future. It was during this crackdown that over half of the estimated half million to two million deaths attributed to the Cultural Revolution took place.[32]

The disaster and disruption in domestic affairs was duplicated in the shift toward radicalism in Chinese foreign relations. The Chinese split with the Soviet Union deepened and broadened in the 1960s. Beijing not only opposed the Soviet Union on ideological grounds but strongly attacked Moscow's willingness to cooperate with the United States in international affairs. Chinese leaders saw the newly independent Asian and African states as providing an important arena for struggle with Moscow as well as with the United States. Though weak economically and having little to spare following the deprivations of the Great Leap Forward, China provided economic and military aid to left-leaning governments, and it provided training, military assistance, and financial support to armed insurgents struggling against colonial powers or right-leaning third world governments.

Chinese premier Zhou Enlai visited Africa in 1964 and said it was "ripe for revolution." China endeavored to compete with the Soviet Union in support of various anticolonial insurgencies and to supply significant aid to African governments prepared to align closer to the PRC than to the Soviet Union or the West. In Asia, China strongly supported the Vietnamese Communist forces directed by the North Vietnamese government in Hanoi in the face of increased American military involvement in South Vietnam and other parts of Indochina. The Chinese government also organized and/or strengthened support for Communist-led insurgencies targeted against governments in Southeast Asia seen by China as pro-American or insufficiently accommodating to Chinese influence and interests.[33]

Although one of the first governments to recognize the People's Republic of China and despite its neutral stance during the Cold War, the government of Burma came under sometimes violent pressure from China. China was long involved with Communist insurgencies and dissident ethnic groups along the porous Sino-Burmese border. The border was finally settled in 1960. Relations deteriorated seriously in 1967 when clashes inspired by Cultural Revolution zealots led to full-scale anti-Chinese riots, leaving over one hundred Chinese dead. China subsequently organized, armed, and trained a large (twenty thousand fighters) insurgency against the Burmese government under the rubric of the Burmese Communist Party, which posed a major security threat to the Burmese government for the next twenty years.[34]

China followed two tracks in developing relations with Indonesia in the early 1960s. One track involved supporting President Sukarno in his radical nationalist policies of confrontation with Malaysia, which was backed by Great Britain, over whether Malaysia or Indonesia should control the disputed regions of Sarawak and Sabah. The other involved closer cooperation with the Indonesian Communist Party (PKI), the world's largest nonruling Communist party, which was growing rapidly in influence under Sukarno's regime. In 1965 the only organized opposition to the PKI was the army. In September, radical officers attempted a coup against the top-level, anti-Communist leadership of the army. Several army leaders were assassinated, but others escaped to organize a counterstrike. With much of the army's top leadership either dead or missing, General Suharto took control of the army and put down the abortive coup. The army quickly blamed the coup attempt on the PKI and instigated an Indonesia-wide anti-Communist propaganda campaign. An anti-Communist reign of terror developed; it was fed by popular Islamic and anti-Chinese prejudices. Hundreds of thousands of Communists, ethnic Chinese, and others were killed; the PKI was crushed. General Suharto outmaneuvered Sukarno politically and was appointed president in 1968, consolidating his influence over the military and government. The new order in Indonesia was led by military leaders among the most suspicious of China in the world. Relations between China and Indonesia were suspended in 1967.[35]

Following the poor record of Chinese advances among developing countries as it pursued a strong agenda against the United States and the Soviet Union in the 1960s, Maoist China during the early years of the Cultural Revolution that began in 1966 came to sacrifice conventional diplomacy in pursuing revolutionary fervor. The foreign minister and much of the senior foreign policy elite were purged. Ambassadors were recalled and forced to undergo extensive ideological retraining. Lower-level embassy officials often endeavored to show their loyalty to Mao and his revolutionary teaching by unauthorized demonstrations and proselytizing with often unreceptive and hostile foreign audiences. They and the staff of foreign policy organs in Beijing followed a radical line that alienated China from most foreign governments.[36]

The low point of Chinese diplomacy seemed evident in several developments in 1967. Huge Red Guard demonstrations were mobilized against the Soviet embassy in Beijing, which was kept under siege in January and February. Later in 1967, Red Guards invaded the Soviet embassy's consular section and burned its files. When Moscow withdrew its diplomats' dependents in February 1967, some were beaten or forced to crawl under pictures of Mao Zedong on their way to planes to take them home. When Red Guard demonstrators in Hong Kong were arrested by British authorities for public disruption and disorder, a major crisis in Chinese-British relations ensued. A mob of thousands of Chinese surrounded British diplomatic offices in Beijing and set fires in the building. Escaping British diplomats ran into the hands of the Chinese mob.[37]

NOTES

1. Past major overviews of modern Chinese foreign relations include A. Doak Barnett, *China and the Major Powers in East Asia* (Washington, DC: Brookings Institution Press, 1977); Michael Yahuda, *China's Role in World Affairs* (New York: St. Martin's, 1978); Harold Hinton, *China's Turbulent Quest* (New York: Macmillan, 1972); John Garver, *Foreign Relations of the People's Republic of China* (Englewood Cliffs, NJ: Prentice Hall, 1993); Andrew Nathan and Andrew Scobell, *China's Search for Security* (New York: Columbia University Press, 2012); David Shambaugh, *China Goes Global: Partial Power* (New York: Oxford University Press, 2013). The most complete assessment is John Garver, *China's Quest: The History of the Foreign Relations of the People's Republic of China* (New York: Oxford University Press, 2016).

2. A. Doak Barnett, *Communist China and Asia: Challenge to American Policy* (New York: Harper and Brothers, 1960); Barnett, *China and the Major Powers in East Asia*; Allen Whiting, *The Chinese Calculus of Deterrence: India and Indochina* (Ann Arbor: University of Michigan Press, 1975).

3. Franz Schurman, *Ideology and Organization in Communist China* (Berkeley: University of California Press, 1966).

4. Chen Jian, *Mao's China and the Cold War* (Chapel Hill: University of North Carolina Press, 2001).

5. Odd Arne Westad, *Brothers in Arms: The Rise and Fall of the Sino-Soviet Alliance, 1945–1963* (Stanford, CA: Stanford University Press, 1998).

6. Warren Cohen, "The Development of Chinese Communist Policy toward the United States, 1922–1933," *Orbis* 11 (1967): pp. 219–37; James Reardon-Anderson, *Yenan and the Great Powers* (New York: Columbia University Press, 1980); Michael Hunt, *The Genesis of Chinese Communist Foreign Policy* (New York: Columbia University Press, 1996); Robert Sutter, *China-Watch* (Baltimore: Johns Hopkins University Press, 1978), pp. 10–18.

7. Sutter, *China-Watch*, p. 11.

8. Tang Tsou, *America's Failure in China* (Chicago: University of Chicago Press, 1963), pp. 208–19.

9. Cohen, "The Development of Chinese Communist Policy toward the United States, 1922–1933"; Sutter, *China-Watch*, p. 11.

10. Kenneth Shewmaker, *Americans and Chinese Communists, 1927–1945: A Persuading Encounter* (Ithaca, NY: Cornell University Press, 1971).

11. Reardon-Anderson, *Yenan and the Great Powers*; Sutter, *China-Watch*, pp. 14–15.

12. Tsou, *America's Failure in China*; Barbara Tuchman, *Stilwell and the American Experience in China* (New York: Macmillan, 1971).

13. Harold Hinton, *Communist China in World Politics* (Boston: Houghton Mifflin, 1966).

14. William Stueck, *The Korean War: An International History* (Princeton, NJ: Princeton University Press, 1997); Bruce Cumings, *The Origins of the Korean War* (Princeton, NJ: Princeton University Press, 1990); Chen Jian, *China's Road to the Korean War* (New York: Columbia University Press, 1994).

15. Allen Whiting, *China Crosses the Yalu* (New York: Macmillan, 1960).

16. Robert Ross and Jiang Changbin, eds., *Reexamining the Cold War* (Cambridge, MA: Harvard University Press, 2001).

17. Hinton, *Communist China in World Politics*.

18. Barnett, *China and the Major Powers in East Asia*; Chen Jian, *Mao's China and the Cold War* (Chapel Hill: University of North Carolina Press, 2001); Thomas Christensen, *Useful Adversaries: Grand Strategy, Domestic Mobilization, and Sino-American Conflicts, 1949–1958* (Princeton, NJ: Princeton University Press, 1996).

19. Nancy Bernkopf Tucker, *Strait Talk: United States–Taiwan Relations and the Crisis with China* (Cambridge, MA: Harvard University Press, 2009).

20. Sutter, *China-Watch*, pp. 31–46.

21. Steven Goldstein, "Dialogue of the Deaf? Sino-American Ambassadorial-Level Talks, 1955–1970," in *Re-examining the Cold War: U.S.-China Diplomacy, 1954–1973*, ed. Robert Ross and Jiang Changbin (Cambridge, MA: Harvard University Press, 2001), pp. 200–237.

22. Robert Sutter, *Historical Dictionary of Chinese Foreign Policy* (Lanham, MD: Scarecrow, 2011), pp. 175–76.

23. John Garver, *Foreign Relations of the People's Republic of China* (Englewood Cliffs, NJ: Prentice Hall, 1993), pp. 125–27.

24. Chen, *Mao's China and the Cold War*, pp. 163–204; Christensen, *Useful Adversaries*.

25. Alice Lyman Miller and Richard Wich, *Becoming Asia* (Stanford, CA: Stanford University Press, 2011), pp. 116–36, 182–93.

26. Allen Whiting, *The Chinese Calculus of Deterrence: India and Indochina* (Ann Arbor: University of Michigan Press, 1975).

27. Sutter, *Historical Dictionary of Chinese Foreign Policy*, p. 178.

28. Arthur Lall, *How Communist China Negotiates* (New York: Columbia University Press, 1968); Hinton, *Communist China in World Politics*, pp. 348–55.

29. Sutter, *Historical Dictionary of Chinese Foreign Policy*, pp. 178–79.

30. Philip Snow, "China and Africa," in *Chinese Foreign Relations: Theory and Practice*, ed. Thomas Robinson and David Shambaugh (New York: Oxford University Press, 1994), pp. 283–89.

31. Roderick MacFarquhar and Michael Schoenhals, *Mao's Last Revolution* (Cambridge, MA: Harvard University Press, 2006); Joseph W. Esherick, Paul G. Pickowicz, and Andrew G. Walder, eds., *The Chinese Cultural Revolution as History* (Stanford, CA: Stanford University Press, 2006).

32. "The Cultural Revolution: All You Need to Know about China's Political Convulsion," *Guardian*, May 10, 2016, https://www.theguardian.com/world/2016/may/11/the-cultural-revolution-50-years-on-all-you-need-to-know-about-chinas-political-convulsion (accessed January 17, 2018).

33. Peter Van Ness, *Revolution and Chinese Foreign Policy* (Berkeley: University of California Press, 1970).

34. Sutter, *Historical Dictionary of Chinese Foreign Policy*, p. 55.

35. Sutter, *Historical Dictionary of Chinese Foreign Policy*, p. 125.

36. David Mozingo, *China's Foreign Policy and the Cultural Revolution* (Ithaca, NY: Cornell University Press, 1970); Barbara Barnouin and Yu Changgen, *Chinese Foreign Policy during the Cultural Revolution* (New York: Columbia University Press, 1997).

37. Raymond Whitaker, "Peking Embassy Siege Veterans Recall the Red Guards' Summer of Hate," *Independent*, August 16, 1997, http://www.independent.co.uk/news/world/peking-embassy-siege-veterans-recall-the-red-guards-summer-of-hate-1245933.html (accessed January 18, 2018).

Chapter Three

Maneuvering between the United States and USSR, 1969–89

The middle decades of the foreign relations of the People's Republic of China (1969–89) featured extraordinary changes. At the start of these two decades, the growing power of the Soviet Union supported Soviet Communist Party General Secretary Leonid Brezhnev's determination to use military and international pressure to compel China to come to terms favored by the USSR over border disputes, leadership in Asia, and a range of international and security differences. The danger of war with the Soviet Union rose in 1969 and compelled Mao and his often divided associates to curb the revolutionary excesses of the Cultural Revolution in developing an international approach that would protect China from Soviet coercion and the threat of war. The Chinese leaders found the United States weakened notably by the protracted and unsuccessful war in Vietnam and willing to end its containment of China and cooperate with Beijing, especially on common interests in dealing with the dangers both saw in Moscow's rising power.[1]

The development of China's approach in the US-USSR-China triangular relationship, the so-called Great Power Triangle, was anything but smooth. During the period from 1970 until the end of the Cold War in 1989, with the collapse of the Soviet Bloc and the dismantling of the Berlin Wall, changes in US and Soviet policies and practices prompted shifts in the Chinese approaches. China also shifted course for its own reasons. Until his death in 1976, Mao worked carefully to sustain his influence and to preserve a positive legacy amid subordinates divided by political ambitions and glaring differences on how to deal with China's international and other priorities. Mao's frequent interventions included, at first, policy moves to support an opening to the United States as a check against the USSR, and, later, policy moves reflecting disappointment with the results of the opening and criticism

49

of senior leaders Zhou Enlai and Deng Xiaoping, who were charged at the time with managing the Chinese approaches toward the United States and the Soviet Union.[2]

After being purged for a second time under Mao's direction in 1976, Deng Xiaoping returned to a leading position in 1977 and established primacy among Chinese leaders by late 1978. He inherited the Maoist mantle of strong-man rule in Chinese foreign policy, and for much of the next fifteen years, Deng guided policies and practices that supported his top priority of fostering more efficient and effective economic development and nation building in China that would sustain the legitimacy of Communist Party rule. He reached out to Japan, other Western-aligned countries, and international financial institutions for economic and other support. As most developed countries and related international financial and economic institutions at this time were poised to cooperate more closely with China, the main challenges Deng faced in fostering greater international economic exchange came from inside China. After so many years of Maoist emphasis on self-reliance, ideological rigidity, and deeply rooted institutions and attitudes favoring state-directed economic development, Deng had to promote reforms that would allow for such pragmatic interchanges with other nations.

In this context, the focus in foreign affairs was on creating and sustaining a favorable international environment for the economic development and related economic and political reforms sought by Deng and his associates. The United States and other developed countries had the military power to balance and offset Soviet expansion, and they also supplied economic assistance, technology, and markets sought by China. Thus, these countries tended to receive high priority in China's foreign policy at this time. Nevertheless, volatile international circumstances and changing policies and practices of the Soviet Union and the United States prompted repeated recalibration and adjustments in China's approach toward the two superpowers and their allies and associates, as well as in other foreign affairs. China endeavored to maximize its advantage in an increasingly pragmatic pursuit of its interests in an international setting controlled more by others, notably the USSR and the United States, than by China.[3]

As will be discussed further in chapters 8 and 9, China's opening to conventional international exchange beginning in the late 1960s also dramatically broadened its foreign relations. Over the next few years, scores of countries established diplomatic relations with China, and China gained entry into the United Nations in 1971. Post-Mao leaders sought international assistance, and in the 1980s China advanced relations with the World Bank, the International Monetary Fund, the Asian Development Bank (ADB), and other assistance organizations. As a result, China became the leading or one of the leading recipients of foreign assistance by the late 1980s and early 1990s.

NORMALIZATION AND OPENING

The dramatic turnabout leading to China's opening to the United States and Western-aligned powers, and China's entry into the United Nations in the early 1970s, began in what were very adverse circumstances. Maoist China had descended through phases of ideologically driven excess in foreign and domestic affairs, reaching a point of unprecedented international isolation. The United States had over five hundred thousand troops in Vietnam fighting a Communist-led adversary supported by China with supplies, financing, and the provision of many thousands of Chinese support troops. US leaders were particularly fearful of an escalation of the prolonged and increasingly unpopular conflict that would somehow bring China more directly into a war that the American leaders were unsure how to win under existing conditions. The US containment effort along China's periphery continued, as did the political isolation and economic embargo the United States brought to bear against the Beijing regime. Nascent US efforts to consider greater flexibility in relations with the PRC ran up against Maoist hostility, disinterest, and contempt, and were overshadowed by the broad implications of the Vietnam quagmire. [4]

The turn toward normalization and opening in Chinese foreign relations at this time has been subject to different scholarly interpretations. One view sees a flagging of Mao's revolutionary drive and vigor, opening the way for the Chinese leader to consider and ultimately pursue pragmatic understanding with the United States and its allies and associates. [5] Another sees a reconfiguring in the US calculus of China's position in world politics and its implications for the United States. This view highlights the importance of an apparent trend whereby US leaders privately came to see China in the late 1960s as less threatening than in the past; eventually they came to view the Maoist regime as a potential asset in American strategy, which was focused increasingly on dealing with a rising and threatening Soviet Union. [6]

Despite these and other divergent views, assessments of this period and the opening in Sino-American relations and other aspects of Chinese foreign relations find it hard not to give priority to interpretations focused on the acute strategic necessities of both the United States and China amid circumstances of a regional and international order featuring a rising and powerful Soviet Union challenging their critical national interests. Only the threat of nuclear war with a domineering Soviet Union at a time of acute internal disruption and weakness in China appears sufficient to explain the remarkable turnabout in Beijing's foreign policy calculus and the approach to the United States and other foreign actors at this time. Given China's size and the preoccupation Chinese rulers have long evidenced with the tasks of managing the complicated internal affairs of this vast country, China historians and specialists of contemporary affairs often have given pride of place to Chinese domestic determinants in Chinese foreign policy. There was no better example during Maoist rule of how domestic Chinese policies and practices determined Chinese foreign policy than during the violent and disruptive early years of China's Cultural Revolution. Moving Chinese leaders out of their self-initiated isolation probably would have taken many years under more normal circumstances. But circumstances in the late 1960s were far from normal, giving rise to the real danger of the Soviet Union militarily invading China, destroying its nuclear and other strategic installations, and forcing China to conform to Soviet interests.[7]

Mao succeeded in removing political rivals in the early years of the Cultural Revolution, but at tremendous cost. Many burned urban areas testified to widespread violence and arson among competing groups. The party and government administration were severely disrupted. Experienced administrators were often purged, persecuted, or pushed aside by proponents of radical Maoist ideals or political opportunists. Expertise in economics, development, and other fields essential to nation building came to be seen as a liability in the politically charged atmosphere of repeated mass campaigns. Political indoctrination and adherence to Mao Zedong overshadowed education and training in practical tasks.[8]

Military forces called in to Chinese cities in order to restore order duly removed millions of disruptive Red Guards and began to lead the process of reconstituting a party and government infrastructure on the basis of military-led rule. As noted in the previous chapter, the process was deadly, with more people killed than in any other phase of the ten-year Cultural Revolution.[9] Not surprisingly in this context, Defense Minister Lin Biao and his People's Liberation Army (PLA) associates rose to new prominence in the Chinese hierarchy. Military representation in various party and government bodies was high. Not all military leaders were as supportive of the radical policies and practices of the Cultural Revolution as Lin Biao and his associates in the high command. Some experienced civilian and military cadres survived in office. But they appeared in the minority in a leadership featuring factional chieftains like the Gang of Four, involving Mao's wife and three other extremist party Politburo members; such luminaries as Mao's speechwriter and sometime confidant, Chen Boda; and security forces and intelligence operative Kang Sheng.[10]

Under these circumstances, the PRC was not prepared for a national security shock. Chinese troops were engaged in domestic peacekeeping and governance. They also for many years had followed Maoist dictates under the leadership of Defense Minister Lin Biao and eschewed professional military training in favor of ideological training and promoting popular welfare in China. Chinese military programs for developing nuclear weapons and ballistic missiles generally were excluded from the violence and disruption of the Cultural Revolution, but the PLA on the whole was poorly prepared to deal with conventional military challenges.[11]

In August 1968, the Soviet Union invaded Czechoslovakia and removed its leadership, putting in power a regime more compliant to Soviet interests. The Soviet Union also made clear that it reserved the right to take similar actions in other deviant Communist states, a view that came to be known as the Brezhnev doctrine, named after the Soviet party leader Leonid Brezhnev, who remained in control from the mid-1960s until the early 1980s. Of course, Chinese leaders well knew that, from the Soviet perspective, there was no Communist state more deviant than China. Moreover, since Brezhnev's takeover in 1964, the Soviet Union had backed political opposition to China with increasing military muscle, deploying ever-larger numbers of forces along the Manchurian border and, as a result of a new Soviet defense treaty with Mongolia, along the Sino-Mongolian border. The Soviet forces, mainly mechanized divisions designed to move rapidly in offensive operations, were configured in a pattern used by Soviet forces when they quickly overran Japanese forces in Manchuria and northern China in the last days of World War II.[12]

The Sino-Soviet dispute had emerged in the late 1950s as an ideological dispute with wide implications. The dispute broadened to include stark differences on international issues and how to deal with the United States. Chinese accusations of Soviet weakness in the face of the firm US stance against Soviet missiles during the Cuban missile crisis of 1962 were answered by the Soviets accusing China of accommodating colonial "outhouses" held by Great Britain and Portugal in Hong Kong and Macao, respectively. Mao responded by reminding the world that imperialist Russia took by far the greatest tracts of Chinese territory by virtue of the so-called unequal treaties imposed on China by imperialist powers in the nineteenth and twentieth centuries.[13] The Sino-Soviet debate now focused on competing claims to disputed border territories, against the background of new uncertainty over the legitimacy of the boundaries established by the unequal treaties. Sino-Soviet negotiations soon after Brezhnev took power following the ouster of Nikita Khrushchev in 1964 failed to resolve border uncertainties, prompting the new Soviet leader to make the force deployments and arrangements noted above in order to deal with the Chinese disputes from a position of strength. With the declared Soviet ambitions under the terms of the Brezhnev doctrine and Moscow's military preparations, the stage was set for the border dispute to evolve into the most serious national security threat ever faced by the People's Republic of China.[14]

The combination of perceived greater threat and internal weakness caused a crisis and debate in the Chinese leadership that lasted into the early 1970s. Chinese leadership decision making in the Cultural Revolution was not at all transparent. Mao seemed to remain in overall command, but official Chinese media reflected competing views on how to deal with the new and apparently dangerous situation in relations with the Soviet Union.[15]

Some commentary presumably encouraged by some Chinese leaders favored reaching out to the United States as a means to offset the Soviet threat. In November 1968, the Chinese Foreign Ministry under Premier Zhou Enlai's direction called for renewed ambassadorial talks with the newly elected administration of Richard Nixon in a statement that was notable for the absence of the then usual Chinese invective critical of the United States. The argument used in media commentary proposing a reaching out to the United States was that the United States was in the process of being defeated in Indochina and was no longer the primary threat to China. It too faced a challenge from the expanding USSR, and China could take advantage of the differences between the competing superpowers in order to secure its position in the face of the newly emerging Soviet danger.[16]

Other commentary presumably backed by other Chinese leaders strongly opposed an opening to the United States. These commentaries were associated with Lin Biao and his lieutenants, along with the radically Maoist leadership faction, the Gang of Four. They argued in favor of continued strong Chinese opposition to both Washington and Moscow. Though weakened by the defeat in Vietnam, the United States could not be trusted in dealings with China. In particular, any sign of Chinese weakness toward either superpower likely would prompt them both to work together in seeking to pressure China and gain at its expense.[17]

The latter leaders held the upper hand in Chinese leadership councils during much of 1969. Chinese media rebuked and ridiculed the new US president as he took office. At the last moment Chinese leaders canceled the slated ambassadorial talks in February. The Chinese authorities took the offensive in the face of Soviet military pressure along the border, ambushing a Soviet patrol on a disputed island in early March and publicizing the incident to the world. Far from being intimidated, Brezhnev's Soviet forces responded later in the month by annihilating a Chinese border guard unit, setting the stage for escalating rhetoric and military clashes throughout the spring and summer of 1969. The clashes were capped by an all-day battle along the western sector of the border in August that saw the Soviets inflict many casualties on the Chinese. Soviet officials followed with warnings to Americans, and other foreigners sure to relay the warnings to the Chinese, that the Soviet Union was in the process of consulting with foreign powers to assure they would stand aside as the Soviet Union prepared an all-out attack on China, including the possible use of nuclear weapons.[18]

In the face of such threat and pressure, Chinese leaders were compelled to shift strategy. Zhou Enlai was brought forward to negotiate with Soviet leaders. It was clear that while negotiating with the USSR would temporarily ease tensions and the danger of war, China would not accept Soviet demands. Beijing now viewed the USSR as China's number one strategic threat. Seeking international leverage and support, it took measures to improve strained relations with neighboring countries and with more distant powers. It was nonetheless evident that while helpful, these improvements would not fundamentally alter China's strategic disadvantage in the face of Soviet intimidation and threat. Only one power, the United States, had that ability. Zhou and like-minded officials in the Chinese leadership were encouraged that the United States was weakened by the Vietnam War, and that it was also beginning to withdraw sizable numbers of troops from Asia and dismantle the US military containment against China. On this basis, Beijing could pursue relations with Washington as a means to deal with the Soviet threat. However, Lin Biao and others continued to argue that both superpowers were enemies of China and in the end they would cooperate together to isolate and control China.[19]

The debate seemed to get caught up with the broader struggle for power in this period of the Cultural Revolution. Mao Zedong came to side with the view associated with Zhou Enlai. Repeated initiatives by the Nixon administration to China ultimately succeeded in Sino-US ambassadorial talks being resumed in Warsaw in early 1970. China used the image of restored contacts with the United States to offset and undermine Soviet efforts to intimidate China. Chinese officials arranged for the meeting to be held in the secure area of their embassy in Warsaw. The usual venue, a palace provided by the Poles, was long suspected of being riddled with secret listening devices that would give the USSR and Warsaw Pact allies the full transcript of the US-Chinese discussions. The Chinese diplomats also made a point of being unusually positive to Western reporters during the photo opportunity as American officials were welcomed to the Chinese embassy at the start of the official talks. As Chinese officials presumably hoped, Soviet commentary on the secret talks and improved atmosphere in US-China relations viewed the developments as complicating Soviet border negotiations with China and nuclear armament limitation talks with the United States. Soviet commentators even charged that Beijing, fearful of Soviet intentions, was seeking to come to terms with the United States in order to play one nuclear power off against the other.[20]

The Nixon administration's expansion of the Vietnam War by invading Cambodia in spring 1970 caused China to cancel the talks and slowed forward movement. Mao highlighted a mass demonstration in Beijing on May 20, 1970, where he welcomed the Cambodian leader, Norodom Sihanouk, who had been deposed by the US-backed military leaders in Cambodia. The Chinese chairman in his last major public statement denouncing the United States called on the people of the world to rise up against US imperialism and their running dogs. Outwardly, it appeared that Mao was siding with the Chinese advocates of a harder line against the United States. However, clandestine US-China communication continued, as did the withdrawal of US forces from Vietnam and other parts of Asia, so that by October 1970 Mao was prepared to tell visiting US journalist Edgar Snow that Nixon could visit China.[21]

The shift in Mao's stance was accompanied by other moves that appeared to undermine the leadership standing of Lin Biao and his radical allies in the Chinese leadership. A key radical leader, Chen Boda, dropped from public view in late 1970 in what later was shown to be intensified factional maneuvering leading up to the alleged coup plans by Lin and his allies.[22]

What role the differences over the opening to the United States played in the struggle in the Chinese leadership remains hidden by pervasive secrecy in Chinese leadership decision making. Emblematic of the significance of the opening to the United States in Chinese politics at the time was the unusual greeting of US National Security Advisor Henry Kissinger on arrival in Beijing on his secret mission in July 1971 to open US-China relations. The first Chinese official to greet Kissinger on arrival was not a protocol officer from the foreign ministry or some other appropriate official. It was Marshall Ye Jianying. Ye was one of the most senior Chinese military leaders. He had survived the Cultural Revolution, advised Mao to use connections with the United States in the face of the Soviet threat, later played a key role in the arrest of the Gang of Four following Mao's death in 1976, and became president of China. His approach was close to Zhou Enlai and at odds with Lin Biao.[23]

The announcement of Kissinger's successful secret trip appeared to represent a serious defeat for Lin Biao and his allies in their debate with opponents on how to deal with the Soviet Union and the United States. The setback came amid rising pressures and adverse developments affecting the military leader. The stakes apparently were very high. Two months later, Lin, his wife, son, and close aides were dead as a result of an airplane crash in Mongolia, as they were allegedly trying to escape China following a failed coup attempt against Mao and his opponents. The military high command in the PLA, who had risen to power under Lin's tenure as defense minister, were arrested, removed from power, and not seen again until they eventually were brought out for public trial along with the discredited radical leaders of the Gang of Four in the years after Mao's death.[24]

MANEUVERING BETWEEN THE SUPERPOWERS IN THE 1970s

The PRC's emerging openness to international interchange prompted many Western countries to establish relations with China. With the strong support of developing countries, China in 1971 gained entry into the United Nations, and Taiwan withdrew. China and the United States made progress in normalizing relations and established liaison offices directed by high-ranking officials in Washington and Beijing in 1973. Against this background and in the course of a few years, dozens of countries, many closely aligned with the United States, established diplomatic relations with China. China also seemed satisfied with the 1973 Paris Peace Agreement that ended major US combat operations in Vietnam as US forces continued to withdraw from Vietnam and from around the periphery of China. [25]

President Nixon's resignation over the Watergate scandal in 1974 precluded progress toward normalization with China. Mao signaled Chinese dissatisfaction with the slow progress in US withdrawal from Taiwan and with perceived US use of ties with China as a means to advance US détente with the Soviet Union in ways seen as disadvantageous for China. He backed criticism of Zhou Enlai for being too accommodating in dealing with the Americans. He supported Deng Xiaoping's debut as China's foreign policy spokesman in a speech to the United Nations in 1974 propounding the Three Worlds theory critical of the United States as well as the Soviet Union that was said to guide China's foreign policy in the new international situation. [26]

As Maoist China in the latter stages of the Cultural Revolution moved away from ideologically driven support for radical insurgent movements targeting established governments and sought to develop conventional relations with existing administrations beneficial to China, it employed the Three Worlds theory featured in the speech by Deng Xiaoping at the United Nations in 1974. The theory divided the world into three categories of governments: the first were the two superpowers, the United States and the Soviet Union, whose domineering policies and practices were seen as the main cause of international problems; the second were the other developed countries of Europe, North America, and the Asia-Pacific; the third were the vast majority of countries that made up the developing world, or the so-called third world. China saw the third world as the main source of resistance to the "hegemonism" of the superpowers, and it sought to align with them and, where possible, countries of the second world in order to resist the superpowers and create a more equitable and just international order. [27]

At a very general level, the framework of the Three Worlds theory helped to guide China's foreign approach, though in practice Chinese leaders repeatedly adjusted and changed course within the broad framework. Thus, the timing of the 1974 speech signaled a shift reflecting Mao's dissatisfaction with the results of the opening to the United States and US détente with the USSR. In practice, however, China's approach in world affairs for the most part reflected strong preoccupation with the danger posed by growing Soviet power targeted against China and its interests, especially in Asia. China relied heavily on the United States and its allies and associates to deal with this danger. The third world played a very secondary role in helping China to secure the favorable environment it sought in order to carry out reforms fostering efficient and effective nation building in China. [28]

Chinese leaders came to be preoccupied with Mao's declining health and the most important leadership succession struggle in the history of the People's Republic of China. Zhou Enlai died in January 1976, followed by Mao in September of that year. Zhou's purported successor, recently rehabilitated veteran leader Deng Xiaoping, gave the eulogy at the memorial service for Zhou and then disappeared from public view, purged from the leadership for a second time. The radical Gang of Four seemed to exert more influence for a time, but demonstrations of support for Zhou and his relatively moderate policies by thousands of people placing flowers and wreaths in his memory at the monument for revolutionary martyrs in the capital in April appeared to underline that the days of radicalism were numbered. The death of senior military leader Zhu De in July preceded Mao's by two months, setting the stage for the struggle for succession. [29]

That China had far to go in creating a foreign policy that dealt with the United States and other countries in conventional and normal ways was underlined by the tragedy of an earthquake in July that demolished the industrial city of Tangshan, 105 miles southeast of Beijing, and did severe damage in nearby areas including the capital and the major port and industrial city of Tianjin. It later was disclosed that hundreds of thousands of Chinese died in the quake and that the needs for relief were enormous. Nevertheless, in a remarkable and extremely damaging demonstration of Maoist "self-reliance," the radical leadership in Beijing at the time refused to acknowledge these needs or to allow foreign countries and groups to assist in efforts to save lives and reduce misery. [30]

Deng Xiaoping, who was purged at the start of the Cultural Revolution and purged again in 1976, was brought back to power. By 1978, Deng was able to consolidate a leading position among party, military, and government officials and to launch the economic and policy reforms that provided the foundation for China's recent approach to international affairs. Deng and his supporters were compelled to maneuver amid competing interests and preferences within the Chinese leadership and the broader polity in order to come up with changes that they felt would advance China's wealth and shore up the legitimacy of the Chinese Communist Party, which had been severely damaged by the excesses and poor performance of the past. [31]

While Chinese leaders were preoccupied internally, their priorities internationally focused on dealing with Soviet intimidation and threat. The United States was weakened by Nixon's resignation and the Gerald Ford government was hobbled by the president's pardon of Nixon. Ford was in a poor position to continue strong support for the struggling South Vietnamese government and the neighboring Cambodian government aligned with the United States. Strong Soviet assistance to Vietnamese Communist forces bolstered their efforts to take control of the South. The Cambodian regime collapsed and Chinese-backed Khmer Rouge insurgents entered Phnom Penh in April 1975. The new regime immediately began carrying out radical and brutal policies that would see the evacuation of the capital and the massive repression and deaths of over one million Cambodians. North Vietnamese forces launched an all-out assault in South Vietnam. The Saigon regime disintegrated; the Americans and what Vietnamese associates they could bring with them fled in ignominious defeat; and the Communist forces barged through the gates of the presidential palace and occupied Saigon in late April.[32]

Chinese officials showed considerable alarm at the turn of events around China's periphery. Stronger efforts by the Soviet Union to use military power and relations with allies around China like Vietnam and India to contain and pressure China, mimicked the US-led containment effort against China earlier in the Cold War. Under these circumstances, Chinese leaders focused on shoring up US resolve and the resolve of other governments and forces seen as important in what China depicted as a united front against expanding Soviet power and influence in Asian and world affairs.

Over the next few years, Chinese officials reached out to conservative world leaders seen as useful in the struggle against the USSR, including the Shah of Iran and Sese Mobutu in Zaire. They were less generous in foreign assistance to developing countries, seeking instead to focus Chinese resources on China's own modernization. They also endeavored to cut back support for insurgents they had long supported in the past directed against neighboring governments and governments in places like Africa and the Middle East. And they encouraged resistance to what they called Soviet "hegemonism" on the part of Japan, leading European powers, and countries in Southeast Asia, among others.[33]

With the support of President Jimmy Carter, National Security Advisor Zbigniew Brzezinski was in the lead in seeking rapid progress in normalizing US-China relations in 1978, and in subsequent steps to advance US-China relations as a means to counter Soviet power and expansion. Soviet and Soviet-backed forces had made gains and were making inroads that seemed at odds with common US and Chinese interests in different parts of Africa, the Middle East, Central America, and Southwest and Southeast Asia. Chinese officials were prominent among international advocates in warning the United States to avoid the dangers of "appeasement" and to stand firm and work with China against the expanding Soviet power.[34]

US and, especially, Chinese leaders used the signs of improved US-China relations in a communiqué establishing relations on January 1, 1979, and during Chinese leader Deng Xiaoping's widely publicized visit to the United States in January 1979 to underline Sino-US cooperation against "hegemony," notably a Soviet-backed Vietnamese military assault against Cambodia beginning in late December 1978. Returning from the United States, Deng launched a large-scale Chinese military offensive into Vietnam's northern region. Chinese forces withdrew after a few weeks, though they maintained strong artillery attacks and other military pressure against Vietnamese border positions until the Vietnamese eventually agreed to withdraw from Cambodia ten years later.[35]

President Carter and his aides were less successful than President Nixon in winning US domestic support for their initiatives toward China. Many in Congress were satisfied with the stasis that had developed in US relations with the PRC and with the Republic of China on Taiwan in the mid-1970s. They were unconvinced that the United States had any strategic or other need to formalize already existing relations with the PRC that was worth the price of breaking a defense treaty and other official ties with Taiwan. Bipartisan majorities in Congress resisted the president's initiatives and passed laws, notably the Taiwan Relations Act (TRA), that tried to tie the hands of the administration on Taiwan and other issues.

Nevertheless, the backlash from Congress and a variety of American interest groups failed to halt the forward movement in US relations with China. Notably, the United States met Chinese conditions for normalization, broke all official relations with Taiwan, and ended the defense treaty with Taiwan. The TRA and other congressional initiatives, however, made clear the continuing strong opposition among important elements in the United States to the rapid development of relations with China that appeared to them to come at the expense of American values and interests.[36]

MANEUVERING BETWEEN THE SUPERPOWERS IN THE 1980s

Throughout much of the 1970s, China was more vocal than the United States in warning of the dangers of the Soviet Union's expansion, which was seen as the greatest threat to China's security and integrity. Chinese officials saw the US approach to Moscow as vacillating between a tough line and accommodation. In late 1979 the Soviet Union sent forces to invade and occupy Afghanistan in support of a pro-Soviet government there, resulting in an intense backlash by the United States and allied powers. The overall situation prompted the Chinese leaders to again begin to recalculate their respective approaches to the Soviet Union and the United States. The previous perceived danger, that the United States would appease the Soviet Union and thereby allow Moscow to direct its pressure against China, now appeared remote. Carter's last year in office and President Ronald Reagan's initial stance toward the USSR saw a large increase in US defense spending and military preparations. Closely allied with the United States, European powers and Japan also were building forces and taking tough positions against the USSR. Meanwhile, the Soviet Union was experiencing increasing complications and weaknesses, including problems of leadership succession, economic sustainability, and tensions in Poland and elsewhere in the Warsaw Pact. Faced with such adverse circumstances, prior to his death in 1982, Brezhnev reached out with positive initiatives toward China, attempting to improve relations.[37]

Despite the continued political and rhetorical interest in ties with developing countries under the overall rubric of the Three Worlds theory, China's pragmatic leadership under Deng Xiaoping cut back sharply China's previously generous assistance to developing countries. China now became a major competitor with these countries in seeking international financial and other support from the World Bank, UN assistance agencies, and developed countries. China had few illusions that the developing countries could provide a suitable foundation for its efforts to secure an advantageous international position. Instead, it deepened domestic reforms designed in considerable measure to open opportunities for economic, technical, and other interchange with developed countries.[38]

Against this background, particularly the perceived Soviet decline and recently strong strategic resolve by the United States and its allies and associates, Chinese officials saw an opportunity to exert a freer hand in foreign affairs and to position China in a stance less aligned with the United States. The priority to stay close to the United States in order to encourage resolute US positions against Soviet expansion was no longer as important as in the recent past. Also, there were salient Chinese differences with the Reagan administration over Taiwan and new opportunities to negotiate with Soviet leaders calling for talks. Thus, by 1981 China's new "independent foreign policy" featured a modest revival of Chinese interest in relations with the developing third world and in the international communist movement on a basis sometimes critical of the United States, which had been broadly neglected in favor of emphasis on the anti-Soviet front in the 1970s despite the stated framework of China's Three Worlds theory.[39]

China between the United States and the Soviet Union

A key turning point in China's "independent foreign policy" and maneuvering in favor of closer ties with the USSR and away from one-sided alignment with the United States came with the resignation in 1982 of US Secretary of State Alexander Haig. Haig was widely known to favor a strong US effort to meet Chinese demands on Taiwan and other issues in order to preserve a close Sino-American relationship directed against the Soviet Union. Amid continued strong Chinese pressure tactics on a wide range of US-China disputes, American policy shifted with Haig's resignation in 1982 and the appointment of George Shultz as secretary of state. Reagan administration officers who were at odds with Haig's emphasis on the need for a solicitous US approach to China came to the fore. They were led by Paul Wolfowitz, who was chosen by Shultz as assistant secretary of state for East Asian affairs; Richard Armitage, the senior Defense Department officer managing relations with China and East Asia; and the senior National Security Council staff aide on Asian affairs and later assistant secretary of state for East Asian affairs, Gaston Sigur. Officers who had backed Haig's pro-China slant were transferred from authority over China policy, and the new US leadership contingent with responsibility for East Asian affairs moved US policy toward a less solicitous and accommodating stance toward China, giving much higher priority to US relations with Japan, as well as other US allies and friends in East Asia. There was less emphasis on China's strategic importance to American competition with the Soviet Union, and there was less concern among US policy makers about China possibly downgrading relations over Taiwan and other disputes.[40]

The significance of this perceived change in US policy and behavior toward China can be better understood against the background of developments since the Nixon administration. As noted earlier, the scholarship on the US opening to China beginning in the Nixon administration focuses on powerful strategic and domestic imperatives that drove the United States and China to cooperate together in a pragmatic search for advantage for their respective national and leadership interests. The scholarship also underlines the primacy of China in American foreign policy in Asia while relations with Japan and other East Asian allies and friends remained secondary and were sometimes viewed as declining assets or liabilities.[41]

Some scholars discern an important adjustment in US strategy toward China and in East Asia more broadly beginning in 1982.[42] The reevaluation of US policy toward China under Secretary of State George Shultz is seen to have brought to power officials who opposed China's high priority in US strategy toward East Asia and the world and who gave much greater importance to US relations with Japan and other US allies in securing American interests amid prevailing conditions. The reevaluation on the whole is depicted as working to the advantage of the United States. Notably it is seen to have worked with the changing balance of forces affecting Chinese security and other interests in Asian and world affairs that prompted heretofore demanding Chinese leaders to reduce pressures on the United States for concessions on Taiwan and other disputed issues. The changes in Chinese policy helped to open the way for several years of comparatively smooth US-China relations after a period of considerable discord in the late 1970s and early 1980s.

Other scholars explain the improvement in US-China relations with a focus on the dynamics of the relations themselves.[43] They discern American compromises and accommodations that assuaged Chinese demands and met Chinese interests over Taiwan and other issues. They tend to shun analysis of how any shift in emphasis in US policy away from China toward Japan and the East Asian region might have altered Chinese calculations and the overall dynamic in US interaction with China.

The analysis in this volume supports the former view. It shows that the Chinese leaders, despite their emphasis on a new independent foreign policy, grudgingly adjusted to the new US stance, viewing their interests being best served by less pressure and more positive initiatives directed to the Reagan administration, as evidenced by their warm welcome for the American president on his visit to China in 1984. Cooperative Chinese relations with the United States were critically important to the Chinese leadership in maintaining Chinese security in the face of continuing pressure from the Soviet Union and in sustaining the flow of aid, investment, and trade essential to the economic development and modernization under way in China—the linchpin of the Communist leadership's plans for sustaining their rule in China. Meanwhile, the Reagan leadership learned not to provoke the Chinese over issues like military and other support for Taiwan with overt and heavy-handed action. Thus, the accommodations that characterized US-China relations in Reagan's second term in office were mutual, but they involved significant Chinese adjustments and changes influenced by the firmer posture toward China undertaken by Secretary of State Shultz and his colleagues. US firmness in the face of Chinese demands had the seemingly counterintuitive effect of improving US-Chinese relations. US firmness also was much more acceptable to congressional members, others in American politics, and the media, who had been alienated by the secrecy and perceived excessive US deference to China in the previous decade. It made executive-congressional relations over China policy much smoother than in the previous six years.[44] Meanwhile, the actions of the Chinese and US governments during the tenure of Secretary Shultz also reflected the primacy of relations with the United States in Chinese foreign policy calculations, despite China's rhetorical emphasis on developing countries, assertions of independence, and active maneuvering within the US-Soviet-Chinese triangular relationship.[45]

China's Changing Strategic Calculus and the Importance of the United States

Chinese foreign policy throughout the period 1969–89 was strongly influenced by Chinese assessments of the relative power and influence of the Soviet Union and the United States. Throughout much of the 1970s, China viewed expansion by the Soviet Union as the greatest threat to its security and integrity: the Soviet Union was aggressively seeking to contain China in Asia through its military buildup and advanced nuclear ballistic missile deployments along the Sino-Soviet border, its deployments of mobile mechanized divisions in Mongolia, its stepped-up naval activity in the western Pacific along the China coast, its military presence in Vietnam including active use of formerly American naval and air base facilities, its ever-closer military relationship with India, and its growing involvement with and eventual invasion of Afghanistan. These Soviet actions were seen as part of a wider expansion of Soviet power and influence that China wanted countered by a united international front including China and led by the United States.[46]

Chinese disappointment with perceived US ambivalence toward the Soviet Union showed in criticism of senior officials in the Ford and Carter administrations for being too soft toward Moscow.[47] The strong Western reaction to the Soviet invasion of Afghanistan in late 1979 caused Chinese leaders to recalculate. The previous perceived danger that the United States would "appease" the Soviet Union and thereby allow Moscow to direct its pressure against China now appeared remote.[48] And Brezhnev also was seen in a weaker position as he tried to improve ties with China.[49]

However, the shift in Chinese policy away from the United States and somewhat closer to the Soviet Union did not work very well. By 1983, Chinese leaders showed increasing concern about the stability of the nation's surroundings in Asia at a time of unrelenting buildup of Soviet military and political pressure along China's periphery, and of a serious and possibly prolonged decline in relations with the United States, caused in part by strong Chinese demands on various issues. Against this backdrop, they decided that the foreign policy tactics of the previous two years, designed to distance China from the policies of the United States and to moderate and improve Chinese relations with the Soviet Union, were less likely to safeguard the important Chinese security and development concerns affected by the stability of the Asian environment.[50]

Thus, in 1983, Beijing began to retreat from some of the tactical changes made the previous two years under the rubric of an independent approach to foreign affairs. The result was a substantial reduction in Chinese pressure on the United States over Taiwan and other issues; increased Chinese interest and flexibility in dealing with the Reagan administration and other Western countries across a broad range of economic, political, and security issues; and heightened Sino-Soviet antipathy. Beijing still attempted to nurture whenever possible the increased influence it had garnered by means of its independent posture in the developing third world and the international communist movement, but it increasingly sided with the West against the USSR in order to secure basic strategic and economic interests.[51]

Among Chinese calculations leading to the new independent foreign policy begun in 1981 were:

- The United States had reasserted a balance in East-West relations likely to lead to a continued major check on possible Soviet expansion. Chinese worries about US "appeasement" of the USSR seemed a thing of the past.

- The Soviet ability to pressure China appeared to be at least temporarily blocked by US power, the determination of various US allies to thwart Soviet expansion, and Soviet domestic and international problems. China added to Soviet difficulties by cooperating with the United States in clandestine operations, supporting fighters resisting the Soviet occupation of Afghanistan, and cooperating in allowing the US to use sites in China to monitor Soviet missile launches, following the US loss of such facilities in Iran.
- At least some important American leaders, notably Secretary of State Alexander Haig and his subordinates in the East Asia Bureau of the State Department, continued to consider preserving and developing good US relations with China as a critically important element in US efforts to confront and contain Soviet expansion.[52]

By mid-1983, China saw these calculations upset. In particular, the United States under Secretary of State George Shultz adopted a new posture that publicly downgraded China's strategic importance—a marked contrast from Haig and his subordinates. The posture was reflected in speeches by Shultz and Wolfowitz later in the year.[53] US planners now appeared to judge that efforts to improve relations with China were less important than in the recent past because:

- China seemed less likely to cooperate further with the United States (through military sales or security consultations, for instance) against the Soviet Union at a time when the PRC had publicly distanced itself from the United States and had reopened talks on normalization with the USSR.
- At the same time, China's continued preoccupation with pragmatic economic modernization and internal development made it appear unlikely that the PRC would revert to a highly disruptive position in East Asia that would adversely affect US interests in the stability of the region.
- China's demands on Taiwan and a wide variety of other bilateral disputes, and the accompanying threats to downgrade US-Chinese relations if its demands were not met, seemed open-ended and excessive.
- The US ability to deal militarily and politically with the USSR from a position of greater strength had improved, particularly as a result of the Reagan administration's large-scale military budget increases and perceived serious internal and international difficulties of the USSR.
- US allies, for the first time in years, were working more closely with Washington in dealing with the Soviet military threat. This was notably true in Asia, where Prime Minister Yasuhiro Nakasone took positions and initiatives underlining common Japanese-US concerns against the Soviet danger, setting the foundation for the close "Ron-Yasu" relationship between the US and Japanese leaders.

- Japan and US allies and friends in Southeast Asia—unlike China—appeared to be more important to the United States in protecting against what was seen as the primary US strategic concern in the region—safeguarding air and sea access to East Asia, the Indian Ocean, and the Persian Gulf from Soviet attack. China appeared less important in dealing with this perceived Soviet danger. [54]

The ability of China to compel the United States to meet its demands on Taiwan and other questions was less than in the recent past. As Beijing threatened retaliation, the Reagan administration remained firm. [55] Eventually, Chinese commentary and discussions with Chinese officials suggested that Beijing perceived its leverage in the United States to have diminished. Chinese media duly noted the strong revival in the US economy in 1983 and the positive political implications this had for President Reagan's reelection campaign. China also had to be aware, through contacts with leading Democrats, notably House of Representatives Speaker Tip O'Neill who visited China at this time, that Beijing could expect little change in US policy toward Taiwan under a Democratic administration. Indeed, a new worry for China was support of self-determination for Taiwan—anathema to Beijing—in legislation backed by leading Democrats, notably Senator Claiborne Pell on the Foreign Relations Committee. [56]

Meanwhile, although Sino-Soviet trade and cultural and technical contacts were increasing, Beijing saw few signs of Soviet willingness to compromise on basic political and security issues during vice-ministerial talks on normalizing Sino-Soviet relations that began in October 1982. And the Soviet military buildup in Asia—including the deployment of highly accurate SS-20 intermediate-range ballistic missiles—continued. [57]

In short, if Beijing continued its demands and harder line of the previous two years against the United States, pressed the United States on various issues, and risked downgrading relations, it faced the prospect of a period of prolonged decline in Sino-American relations—possibly lasting until the end of Reagan's second presidential term. This decline brought the risk of cutting off China's implicit but vitally important strategic security understanding with the United States with regard to the threat of the USSR.

The Chinese also recognized that a substantial decline in Chinese relations with the United States would undercut their already limited leverage with Moscow; it probably would reduce Soviet interest in accommodating China in order to preclude closer US-Chinese security ties or collaboration against the USSR. It also would possibly upset China's ability to gain greater access not only to American markets and financial and technical expertise, but also to those of other important capitalist countries. Now that the Chinese economy was successfully emerging from some retrenchments and adjustments undertaken in 1981–82, the Western economic connection seemed more important to PRC planners. Yet many US allies and friends, notably Japan, were more reluctant to undertake heavy economic involvement in China at a time of uncertain US-China political relations. The United States also exerted strong influence in international financial institutions that were expected to be the source of several billion dollars of much needed aid for China in the 1980s.

China also had to calculate that a serious decline in US-Chinese relations would likely result in a concurrent increase in US-Taiwanese relations. As a result, Beijing's chances of using Taiwan's isolation from the United States to prompt Taipei to move toward reunification in accord with PRC interests would be set back seriously.

Moderation toward the United States

Appearing anxious to moderate past demands and improve relations with the United States, the Chinese responded positively to the latest in a series of Reagan administration efforts to ease technology transfer restrictions—announced by Commerce Secretary Malcolm Baldrige during a trip to China in May 1983. The Chinese followed up by agreeing to schedule the long-delayed visit by Secretary of Defense Caspar Weinberger in September and to exchange visits by Premier Zhao Ziyang and President Reagan at the turn of the year. In order to not appear too anxious to improve relations with China, Reagan administration officials were successful in getting Premier Zhao to visit Washington for a summit in January 1984, before the US president would agree to go to China later that year. Beijing media attempted to portray these moves as Chinese responses to US concessions and consistent with China's avowed "independent" approach in foreign affairs and its firm stance on US-Chinese differences. But as time went on, it became clear just how much Beijing was prepared to moderate past public demands and threats of retaliation over Taiwan and other issues for the sake of consolidating Sino-American political, economic, and security ties.[58]

- In 1981, Beijing had publicly disavowed any interest in military purchases from the United States until the United States satisfied China's position on the sale of arms to Taiwan. Beijing continued to note that China was dissatisfied with US arms transfers to Taiwan after the August 1982 communiqué, which continued at a pace of over $700 million a year; but it now was willing to negotiate with the United States over Chinese purchases of US military equipment. Defense Minister Zhang Aiping disclosed that negotiations on arms sales were revived during Secretary Weinberger's visit to China in September 1983.

- Chinese officials and official media moderated past demands, threats, and accusations that the United States was not fulfilling the 1979 and 1982 Sino-American communiqués.
- Beijing backed away from previous demands that the United States repeal or amend the Taiwan Relations Act or face a decline in relations.
- Beijing muffled previous demands that the United States alter its position regarding Taiwan's continued membership in the Asian Development Bank.
- China reduced criticism of official and unofficial US contacts with counterparts in Taiwan. Beijing was even willing to turn a blind eye to the almost thirty members of Congress who traveled to Taiwan in various delegations in January 1984—coincident with Zhao Ziyang's trip to Washington. It even welcomed some of the members who traveled on to the mainland after visiting Taiwan.
- Beijing allowed Northwest Airlines to open service to China in 1984, even though the airline still served Taiwan. This was in marked contrast with the authoritative and negative Chinese position adopted in 1983 in response to Pan American Airline's decision to reenter the Taiwan market while also serving the mainland.
- China reduced complaints about the slowness of US transfers of technology to China and about the continued inability of the administration to successfully push through legislative changes that would have allowed the Chinese to receive American assistance. [59]

China's greatest compromise was to give a warm welcome to President Reagan, despite his continued determination to maintain close US ties with "old friends" on Taiwan.

When the US-Chinese nuclear cooperation agreement, which had been initialed during the president's visit, became stalled because of opposition from nonproliferation advocates in the United States who were concerned about China's support for Pakistan's nuclear weapons program, China only managed a minor complaint and went along with the Reagan administration's explanations of their inability to overcome the opposition. [60] On the question of Taiwan, Beijing gave lower priority to Chinese complaints about President Reagan's interpretations of the communiqué at odds with China's position and gave lower priority to Chinese complaints over the US president's continued strong determination to support US interests in helping the defense of Taiwan. The Chinese downplayed previous routine criticism of methods used by the United States to calculate the value of arms sales to Taiwan at high levels, thereby allowing over $500 million of US sales to the island's armed forces for years to come. And most notably China chose not to contest vigorously the ultimately successful maneuvers used by Taiwan and US defense manufacturers that allowed the United States to support, through

commercial transfers of equipment, technology, and expertise, the development of a new group of over one hundred jet fighters, the so-called indigenous fighter aircraft, for Taiwan's air force.[61]

Continued Sino-Soviet Differences

China's incentive to accommodate the United States was reinforced by Beijing's more somber view of Sino-Soviet relations. China appeared disappointed with its inability to elicit substantial Soviet concessions—or even a
slowing in the pace of Soviet military expansion in Asia—during the brief
administration of Yuri Andropov (d. 1984). Beijing saw the succeeding
government of Konstantin Chernenko (d. 1985) as even more rigid and uncompromising. In response, China hardened its line and highlighted public
complaints against Soviet pressure and intimidation—an approach that had
the added benefit of broadening common ground between China and the
West, especially the strongly anti-Soviet Reagan administration.[62]

The Sino-Soviet vice-ministerial talks on normalizing relations were revived in October 1982 following their cancellation as a result of the Soviet
invasion of Afghanistan in late 1979. These talks were unable to bridge a
major gap between the positions of the two sides on basic security and
political issues. Beijing stuck to its preconditions for improved Sino-Soviet
relations involving withdrawal of Soviet forces from along the Sino-Soviet
border and from Mongolia (later China added a specific reference to Soviet
SS-20 ballistic missiles targeted against China), an end to Soviet support for
Vietnam's military occupation of Cambodia, and withdrawal of Soviet forces
from Afghanistan.[63]

In part to get around this roadblock, a second forum of vice-foreign-
ministerial discussions began in September 1983. The discussions covered
each side's views of recent developments in the Middle East, Central America, the Indian Ocean, Afghanistan, and Indochina; concerns over arms control, including the deployment of SS-20 missiles in Asia; and other questions.
No agreement was noted.

Progress in both sets of talks came only in secondary areas of trade,
technology transfers, and educational and cultural exchanges. Both sides
attempted to give added impetus to progress in these areas coincident with
the exchange of high-level Sino-American visits in early 1984. In particular,
Moscow proposed and Beijing accepted a visit to China by First Deputy
Prime Minister Ivan Arkhipov, the highest-level Soviet official to visit China
since Premier Alexei Kosygin stopped in Beijing airport to talk with Zhou
Enlai amid preparations for a Sino-Soviet war in September 1969.[64] The visit
was timed to occur just after President Reagan's departure from China in
early May 1984. It was postponed until December 1984 on account of rising
Sino-Soviet frictions.

Chernenko's leadership went out of its way to publicize strong support for Mongolia and Vietnam against China, and underlined Soviet unwillingness to make compromises with China at the expense of third countries. Beijing also saw Moscow as resorting to stronger military means in both Europe and Asia in order to assert Soviet power and determination against China and others. In February and March, the Soviet Union deployed two of its three aircraft carriers to the western Pacific; one passed near China in late February, on its way to Vladivostok. And in March, the USSR used an aircraft carrier task force to support its first joint amphibious exercise with Vietnam, which was conducted fairly close to China and near the Vietnamese port city of Haiphong. This followed the reported stationing of several Soviet medium-range bombers at Cam Ranh Bay, Vietnam, in late 1983—the first time Soviet forces were reported to be stationed outside areas contiguous with the USSR.

Meanwhile, the Chinese escalated their artillery barrages and other military pressure against the Vietnamese—taking their strongest action precisely at the time of President Reagan's visit to China in late April and early May 1984. Beijing at the same time escalated charges regarding the Soviet threat to Chinese security, especially via Vietnam, and attempted to establish publicly an identity of interests with both Japanese prime minister Nakasone, during a visit to China in March, and President Reagan in April–May, on the basis of opposition to Soviet expansion in Asia. The overall result of these and other developments was the most serious downturn in Sino-Soviet relations since the Soviet invasion of Afghanistan in late 1979.

In sum, the record of developments in China's approach toward and relations with the United States and the Soviet Union in the 1980s showed that the approach adopted by Secretary of State George Shultz and the senior officials responsible for Asian affairs during this period of the Reagan administration worked effectively in support of American interests in policy toward China in several important ways. The approach was firmer than in the past on various US-China differences. The new US stance notably played into an array of concerns and uncertainties in Chinese foreign policy calculations and interests, causing the Chinese leaders to move to a more accommodating posture toward the United States that played down issues that in the recent past Chinese officials had said threatened to force China to take steps to downgrade the US-China relationship. US officials made sure that their Chinese counterparts understood that the United States was no longer as anxious as evident in the first decade of Sino-American rapprochement and normalization to seek China's favor as a source of influence against Moscow. The United States was increasingly confident in its strategic position vis-à-vis the Soviet Union, and had begun a process to roll back the gains the Soviets had made in the previous decade in various parts of the developing world. It was China that appeared to face greater difficulties posed by Soviet military buildup and expansion. China needed the US relationship as a counterweight to this Soviet posture, and it increasingly needed a good relationship with the United States to allow for smooth economic interchange with the developed countries of the West and Japan and the international financial institutions they controlled.[65]

In the mid-1980s, with the rise to power of Mikhail Gorbachev and his reform-minded colleagues in the Soviet Union, China and the Soviet Union slowly moderated past differences and appeared determined to improve political, economic, and other bilateral concerns. Chinese and Soviet leaders focused on internal economic and political reforms, and expressed interest in fostering a stable, peaceful international environment conducive to such domestic change. Ideological, territorial, and leadership differences between Beijing and Moscow were deemed less important. However, the two sides remained divided largely over competing security interests in Asia. Gorbachev gradually began to accommodate China's interests in this area by starting to pull back Soviet forces from Afghanistan, Mongolia, and other places around China's periphery. Concurrently, Chinese military planners began to revise substantially China's strategic plans. They downgraded the danger of Soviet attack and allowed for a major demobilization of Chinese ground forces.[66]

The Soviet initiatives also reduced Chinese interest in cooperating closely with the United States and its allies and associates in Asia in order to check possible Soviet expansion. But China's growing need for close economic and technical ties with these countries compensated to some degree for its decreased interest in closer security ties with them. Chinese officials also wished to improve relations with the Soviets in order to keep pace with the rapid improvement in Gorbachev's relations with the United States and Western Europe. Otherwise, Chinese leaders ran the risk of not being consulted when world powers debated international issues important to China. The agreement marking the Soviet withdrawal from Afghanistan was reached without China playing an active role in the negotiations, for example.

During this period, the United States and its allies found the Soviet Union more accommodating than China on matters of interest to the West. At the same time, the changes in US-Soviet relations and in China's policy to the Soviet Union reduced the perceived American need to sustain and develop close strategic cooperation with China against the Soviet Union. Meanwhile, some specialists judged that the United States did not consider economic interchange with China important enough to compensate for the reduced anti-Soviet strategic cooperation, even though China remained important for Asian security and international arms control. Reflecting this slow change in US-China relations, long-standing bilateral and other irritants in China-US relations over human rights, treatment of intellectuals, and Tibet appeared to take on more prominence in Sino-American relations.[67]

RELATIONS APART FROM THE "GREAT POWER TRIANGLE"

As noted at the outset of this chapter and discussed in chapters 8 and 9, China changed during this two-decade period from an inward-looking and myopic international approach characterized by Maoist ideological rigidity and self-reliance to an approach that increasingly integrated China with neighboring countries, international economic organizations, and countries farther from China. In addition to the security concerns related to dealing with the danger posed by the Soviet Union and the opportunities and disputes associated with the United States, discussed in detail above, Chinese motivation for burgeoning international relationships focused on how they assisted China's economic development and how they added to the prestige and standing of China in world affairs.

As highlighted earlier in the chapter, Chinese leaders gave a much higher profile to being a recipient of foreign assistance, technology, and trade than they did to China's unique role under Mao as an impoverished country spreading influence through generous provision of foreign assistance to a range of states and movements seen as deserving of support. China now actively competed with developing states for the foreign assistance provided by developed countries and international economic institutions, and it competed with developing countries for access to advanced foreign technology and markets for Chinese manufactured and other products.

Chinese officials endeavored to get along with countries and groups that they had in the past shunned or opposed for ideological, strategic, or other reasons. Efforts continued to improve China's relations with non-Communist governments along China's periphery, including notably Japan and the governments that were members of the Association of Southeast Asian Nations (ASEAN). Economic ties grew with the advancing South Korean economy, though political ties were to wait until after the end of the Cold War. By the end of the period, China was reciprocating efforts by countries that were aligned with the now rapidly declining Soviet Union, notably India and Vietnam, to begin the process of normalizing their heretofore very strained relations with China.

Chinese friendships and mutually advantageous relationships with developing countries in Africa, the Middle East, and to a degree Latin America remained active, though China generally avoided costly assistance projects of the past. China's willingness to provide nuclear weapons technology and ballistic missiles to Pakistan headed the list of egregious Chinese weapons proliferation practices that served to solidify Chinese relations with key countries like Pakistan and Saudi Arabia; and China rose to prominence as a leading provider of conventional arms to both Iran and Iraq in their protracted war during the 1980s. China further distanced itself from the terrorist practices of the Palestine Liberation Organization (PLO) and other such groups, while it moved pragmatically to develop closer relations with Israel involving intelligence exchanges; arms sales; and in the early 1990s, official diplomatic relations.

Chinese interest in developed countries like Japan and West European countries centered on their role in working with the United States in dealing with the expansion of the Soviet Union and in their economic prowess, the source of assistance, technology, and markets important to Chinese development. In international organizations and governance, China tended to avoid controversy, endeavoring to remain on good terms with most states and eschewing costs or commitments that might hamper the nascent growth of China's economy as it integrated more closely with the world economy. China was glad to keep its UN dues and payments to UN peacekeeping very low. For the most part, it avoided using its Security Council veto, preferring to abstain on issues it did not approve of.

NOTES

1. Alice Lyman Miller and Richard Wich, *Becoming Asia* (Stanford, CA: Stanford University Press, 2011), pp. 161–93.

2. Ezra Vogel, *Deng Xiaoping and the Transformation of China* (Cambridge, MA: Harvard University Press, 2011), pp. 91–183.

3. John Garver, *Foreign Relations of the People's Republic of China* (Englewood Cliffs, NJ: Prentice Hall, 1993), pp. 70–112.

4. A. Doak Barnett, *A New U.S. Policy toward China* (Washington, DC: Brookings Institution Press, 1971); Rosemary Foot, *The Practice of Power: U.S. Relations with China since 1949* (New York: Oxford University Press, 1997); Evelyn Goh, *Constructing the U.S. Rapprochement with China, 1961–1974* (New York: Cambridge University Press, 2005); Gong Li, *Kuayue: 1969–1979 nian Zhong-Mei guanxi de yanbian* [Across the chasm: The evolution of relations between China and the United States, 1969–1979] (Zhengzhou: Henan Renmin Chubanshe, 1992); Pei Jianzhang, ed., *Zhonghua renmin gongheguo waijiao shi* [Diplomatic history of the People's Republic of China] (Beijing: Shijie zhishi chubanshe, 1994); Xie Yixian, *Zhongguo Waijiao Shi: 1949–1979* [China's diplomatic history: 1949–1979] (Henan: Henan Renmin Chubanshe, 1988); Wang Taiping et al., *Zhonghua renmin gongheguo waijiao shi, 1957–1969* [A diplomatic history of the People's Republic of China, 1957–1969] (Beijing: Shijie Zhishi, 1998); Xie Xide and Ni Shixiong, *Quzhe de licheng: Zhong Mei jianji ershi nian* [From normalization to renormalization: Twenty years of Sino-US relations] (Shanghai: Fudan Daxue Chubanshe, 1999).

5. Chen Jian, *Mao's China and the Cold War* (Chapel Hill: University of North Carolina Press, 2001).

6. Foot, *The Practice of Power*; Goh, *Constructing the U.S. Rapprochement with China*.

7. A. Doak Barnett, *China and the Major Powers in East Asia* (Washington, DC: Brookings Institution Press, 1977); Robert Ross, *Negotiating Cooperation: The United States and China, 1969–1989* (Stanford, CA: Stanford University Press, 1995); Robert Sutter, *China-Watch: Toward Sino-American Reconciliation* (Baltimore: Johns Hopkins University Press, 1978), pp. 83–102; Thomas Gottlieb, *Chinese Foreign Policy Factionalism and the Origins of*

the Strategic Triangle (Santa Monica, CA: RAND, 1977); John Garver, *China's Decision for Rapprochement with the United States, 1968–1971* (Boulder, CO: Westview, 1982); Wang Zhongchun, "The Soviet Factor in Sino-American Normalization, 1969–1979," in *Normalization of U.S.-China Relations*, ed. William Kirby, Robert Ross, and Gong Li (Cambridge, MA: Harvard University Press, 2005).

8. Li Jie, "China's Domestic Politics and the Normalization of Sino-U.S. Relations, 1969–1979," in Kirby, Ross, and Li, eds., *Normalization of U.S.-China Relations*, pp. 56–89; Philip Bridgham, "Mao's Cultural Revolution: The Struggle to Seize Power," *China Quarterly* 41 (1970): pp. 1–25.

9. "The Cultural Revolution: All You Need to Know about China's Political Convulsion," *Guardian*, May 10, 2016, https://www.theguardian.com/world/2016/may/11/the-cultural-revolution-50-years-on-all-you-need-to-know-about-chinas-political-convulsion (accessed January 17, 2018).

10. Gottlieb, *Chinese Foreign Policy Factionalism and the Origins of the Strategic Triangle*; Roderick MacFarquhar and Michael Schoenhals, *Mao's Last Revolution* (Cambridge, MA: Harvard University Press, 2006).

11. Harlan Jencks, *From Muskets to Missiles: Politics and Professionalism in the Chinese Army, 1945–1981* (Boulder, CO: Westview, 1982).

12. Miller and Wich, *Becoming Asia*, pp. 161–93; Allen Whiting, "The Sino-American Détente: Genesis and Prospects," in *China and the World Community*, ed. Ian Wilson (Sydney: Australian Institute of International Affairs, 1973), pp. 70–89; Thomas Robinson, "The Sino-Soviet Border Dispute: Background, Development and the March 1969 Clashes," *American Political Science Review* 66, no. 4 (December 1972): pp. 1175–78; Harold Hinton, *Bear at the Gate: Chinese Policymaking under Soviet Pressure* (Stanford, CA: Hoover Institute, 1971).

13. Garver, *Foreign Relations of the People's Republic of China*, p. 64. For Mao's statements, see Ministry of Foreign Affairs of the People's Republic of China and Document Research Office of the CCP Central Committee, *Mao Zedong Waijiao Wenxuan* [Selected works of Mao Zedong on diplomacy] (Beijing: Zhongyang Wenxian Chubanshe and Shijie Chubanshe, 1994).

14. Garver, *Foreign Relations of the People's Republic of China*, pp. 304–20.

15. David Bachman, "Mobilizing for War: China's Limited Ability to Cope with the Soviet Threat," *Issues and Studies* 43, no. 4 (December 2007): pp. 1–38; Gottlieb, *Chinese Foreign Policy Factionalism*; Roger Brown, "Chinese Politics and American Policy: A New Look at the Triangle," *Foreign Policy* 23 (Summer 1976): pp. 3–23.

16. Sutter, *China-Watch*, pp. 72–75.

17. Sutter, *China-Watch*, pp. 75–78; for background, see among others Wang Shuzhong, ed., *Mei-Su zhengba zhanlue wenti* [The question of contention for hegemony between the United States and the Soviet Union] (Beijing: Guofang daxue chubanshe, 1988).

18. Miller and Wich, *Becoming Asia*, pp. 166–70; Garver, *Foreign Relations of the People's Republic of China*, pp. 306–10.

19. Sutter, *China-Watch*, pp. 78–102.

20. Michael Schaller, *The United States and China: Into the Twenty-First Century* (New York: Oxford University Press, 2002), p. 170; Garver, *Foreign Relations of the People's Republic of China*, pp. 74–83; Ross, *Negotiating Cooperation*, pp. 33–34.

21. Ross, *Negotiating Cooperation*, pp. 28, 34–35.

22. Garver, *Foreign Relations of the People's Republic of China*, pp. 74–83; Ross, *Negotiating Cooperation*, p. 34; Immanuel C. Y. Hsu, *The Rise of Modern China* (New York: Oxford University Press, 2000), pp. 711–14, 822.

23. Robert Sutter, *Historical Dictionary of United States–China Relations* (Lanham, MD: Scarecrow, 2006), pp. 190–91.

24. Hsu, *The Rise of Modern China*, pp. 710–14, 820–23.

25. Sutter, *China-Watch*, pp. 109–12.

26. Vogel, *Deng Xiaoping and the Transformation of China*, pp. 76–119.

27. Sutter, *Historical Dictionary of Chinese Foreign Policy*, pp. 240–41.

28. Vogel, *Deng Xiaoping and the Transformation of China*, pp. 76–88.

29. Hsu, *The Rise of Modern China*, pp. 763–73; for background, see among others Wang Taiping, ed., *Zhonghua renmin gongheguo waijiao shi* [History of the diplomacy of the People's Republic of China], vol.3 (*1970–1978*) (Beijing: Shijie Zhishi Chubanshe, 1999).

30. Wang Wenlan, "Tangshan Earthquake: Unforgotten History," *China Daily*, July 26, 2006, http://www.chinadaily.com (accessed September 14, 2009); John K. Fairbank and Merle Goldman, *China: A New History* (Cambridge, MA: Harvard University Press, 1999), pp. 404–5.

31. Vogel, *Deng Xiaoping and the Transformation of China*, pp. 217–48.

32. Nayan Chanda, *Brother Enemy: The War after the War* (New York: Harcourt Brace Jovanovich, 1986).

33. Garver, *Foreign Relations of the People's Republic of China*, pp. 166–77, 310–11.

34. Robert Sutter, *U.S.-Chinese Relations* (Lanham, MD: Rowman & Littlefield, 2010), pp. 76–80.

35. Ross, *Negotiating Cooperation*, pp. 125–26; James Mann, *About Face* (New York: Knopf, 1999), pp. 98–100.

36. House Committee on Foreign Affairs, *Executive-Legislative Consultations over China Policy, 1978–1979* (Washington, DC: US Government Printing Office, 1980).

37. Robert Sutter, *Chinese Foreign Relations: Developments after Mao* (New York: Praeger, 1986), pp. 18–96; Garver, *Foreign Relations of the People's Republic of China*, pp. 98–103, 317–19.

38. Sutter, *Chinese Foreign Relations*, pp. 104–7.

39. Ross, *Negotiating Cooperation*, pp. 164–74.

40. Nancy Bernkopf Tucker, *Strait Talk: United States–Taiwan Relations and the Crisis with China* (Cambridge, MA: Harvard University Press, 2009), pp. 153–60.

41. Harry Harding, *A Fragile Relationship* (Washington, DC: Brookings Institution Press, 1992); Ross, *Negotiating Cooperation*; Mann, *About Face*; David M. Lampton, *Same Bed, Different Dreams* (Berkeley: University of California Press, 2001); Robert Suettinger, *Beyond Tiananmen* (Washington, DC: Brookings Institution Press, 2003); Jean Garrison, *Making China Policy: From Nixon to G. W. Bush* (Boulder, CO: Lynne Rienner, 2005). Garrison's analysis (pp. 80–85) identifies two competing groups of US decision makers regarding China policy in the early 1980s as the "China-first" group and the "pan-Asian" group. The analysis in this chapter builds on the Garrison analysis.

42. Ross, *Negotiating Cooperation*, pp. 170–245; Mann, *About Face*, pp. 119–36; Garrison, *Making China Policy*, pp. 79–106; Tucker, *Strait Talk*, pp. 153–60.

43. Harding, *Fragile Relationship*, pp. 131–45; David Shambaugh, "Patterns of Interaction in Sino-American Relations," in *Chinese Foreign Policy: Theory and Practice*, ed. Thomas Robinson and David Shambaugh (New York: Oxford University Press, 1994), pp. 203–5.

44. Sutter, *U.S.-Chinese Relations*, pp. 82–84.

45. The scholarship that portrays the improvement in US-China relations at this time as largely based on the dynamics of those relations seems too narrowly focused. The United States is seen to make compromises that accommodate Chinese interests and thus allow for smoother US-Chinese relations. By limiting the focus to the dynamics of US-China ties, this scholarship seems to miss the importance of the shift in American emphasis during the tenure of George Shultz. Yet overall, that shift significantly enhanced US influence over China in negotiations over Taiwan and other disputes, and it compelled China to make concessions of its own in order to insure a positive relationship with the United States. This changed the dynamic, with the United States in a more commanding position vis-à-vis China.

46. Garver, *Foreign Relations of the People's Republic of China*, pp. 310–19.

47. Sutter, *Chinese Foreign Relations*, pp. 18–96.

48. Garver, *Foreign Relations of the People's Republic of China*, pp. 98–103, 317–19.

49. Ross, *Negotiating Cooperation*, pp. 164–74.

50. Sutter, *Chinese Foreign Relations*, p. 182.

51. Sutter, *Chinese Foreign Relations*, p. 178.

52. Garver, *Foreign Relations of the People's Republic of China*, pp. 98–103; Ross, *Negotiating Cooperation*, pp. 170–200.

53. Tucker, *Strait Talk*, pp. 153–60; Mann, *About Face*, pp. 128–33.

54. Sutter, *Chinese Foreign Relations*, p. 178.

55. Richard Nations, "A Tilt Towards Tokyo," *Far Eastern Economic Review*, April 21, 1983, p. 36; Ross, *Negotiating Cooperation*, pp. 228–33.

56. Sutter, *Chinese Foreign Relations*, pp. 178–79.

57. Sutter, *Chinese Foreign Relations*, pp. 178–79.

58. Ross, *Negotiating Cooperation*, pp. 233–45; Tucker, *Strait Talk*, pp. 160–61.

59. Sutter, *Chinese Foreign Relations*, pp. 180–81.

60. Ross, *Negotiating Cooperation*, pp. 233–44; Sutter, *Chinese Foreign Relations*, pp. 181–82.

61. Tucker, *Strait Talk*, pp. 155–60.

62. Gerald Segal, *Sino-Soviet Relations after Mao*, Adelphi Papers, no. 202 (London: International Institute for Strategic Studies, 1985).

63. The review of Sino-Soviet relations in the remainder of this section is adapted from Sutter, *Chinese Foreign Relations*, 182–86. See also Segal, *Sino-Soviet Relations after Mao*.

64. Ann Scott, "First Vice Premier Ivan Arkhipov, the Highest Ranking Soviet Official to Visit China in More Than 15 Years," UPI, December 20, 1984, https://www.upi.com/Archives/1984/12/20/First-Vice-Premier-Ivan-Arkhipov-the-highest-ranking-Soviet-official/3889472366800/ (accessed January 17, 2018).

65. Sutter, *U.S.-Chinese Relations*, pp. 93–94.

66. Miller and Wich, *Becoming Asia*, pp. 194–202.

67. Harding, *Fragile Relationship*, pp. 173–214.

Chapter Four

Chinese Foreign Relations after the Cold War

This chapter deals with the evolution of Chinese foreign relations in the post–Cold War period in two ways. First, important developments in Chinese foreign relations and relevant domestic Chinese events in the 1990s are discussed in chronological order. Second, there follows a more detailed assessment of the internal and external factors, providing an overall context of developments in Chinese foreign relations in the twenty-first century that are featured in more detail in later chapters of this book. The assessment of the policies and priorities of the Chinese government relevant to China's approach to foreign affairs concludes with discernment of goals motivating Chinese policy and practice in contemporary international affairs. As noted earlier and discussed in later chapters, the goals often conflict with one another, resulting in unexpected changes and precluding a clear and predictable strategy in foreign affairs.[1]

DEVELOPMENTS IN THE 1990s

The weakening and collapse of the Soviet threat to China improved China's overall security situation. For the first time, the People's Republic of China was not facing an immediate foreign threat to its national security. However, the sharp international reaction to China's harsh crackdown on dissent after the June 1989 Tiananmen incident caught Chinese leaders by surprise. They reportedly had expected industrialized nations to restore stable relations with China after a few months. They had not counted on the rapid collapse of Communism in Eastern Europe, the subsequent march toward self-determination and democratization throughout the Soviet republics, and ultimately the end of the Soviet Union in 1991. These unexpected events for several years diverted industrialized nations' return to China with advantageous investment, assistance, and economic exchanges, called into question China's strategic importance as a counterweight to the Soviet Union, and posed the most serious challenge to the legitimacy of the Chinese Communist regime since the Cultural Revolution. Taiwan's concurrent moves toward greater democracy and self-determination received greater positive attention in the United States and the West, adding to China's concerns about broad international trends and what to do about them.[2]

The United States was seen as both the greatest threat and most important partner in Chinese foreign policy. In response to US-led sanctions and criticisms in the late 1980s and early 1990s, the Chinese government endeavored to use foreign affairs to demonstrate the legitimacy and prestige of its Communist leaders. High-level visits to Asian capitals and elsewhere in the non-Western world were used along with trade and security arrangements in order to strengthen China's image before skeptical audiences at home and abroad. To reestablish internal political stability, Chinese leaders also gave high priority to the resource needs of the military and public security forces. Thus began a long series of often double-digit annual increases in China's defense budget that has persisted up to now and has made China a more formidable military competitor of the United States and Asia's leading military power.[3]

Recognizing that communist ideology was not popular enough to support their continued monopoly of power, leaders in Beijing played up more traditional themes of Chinese patriotism and nationalism to support their rule. US and other foreign criticisms of the communist system in China were portrayed not as attacks against unjust arbitrary rule but as assaults on the national integrity of China. These attacks were equated with earlier "imperialist" pressures on China in the nineteenth century and the first half of the twentieth century.[4]

Meanwhile, statements and initiatives by Deng Xiaoping spurring economic reform and opening during a tour of southern China in 1992 pushed other Chinese senior leaders away from their hesitant approach to economic modernization and reform after the Tiananmen crackdown. Deng called for faster growth and increased economic interchange with the outside world, especially the developed economies of Asia and the West. This call coincided with the start of an economic boom on the mainland that continued for several years of double-digit growth and then declined a bit to the still rapid pace of 7–8 percent annual growth. The consequences of such rapid growth initially included serious inflation as well as broader economic dislocation and many social problems, but the growth also caught the attention of foreign business and government leaders. Many of China's well-to-do neighbors such as Hong Kong and Taiwan already had become well positioned to take advantage of the mainland's rapid growth. They were followed rapidly by

West European, Japanese, Southeast Asian, and Korean entrepreneurs. American business interest in the China market grew markedly from 1992, and was credited with playing an important role in convincing the William Clinton administration in 1994 to stop linking US most-favored-nation trade treatment to improvements in China's still poor human rights conditions.[5]

Deng Xiaoping and the new third generation of leaders headed by president and party leader Jiang Zemin continued the post-Mao policies, emphasizing fostering a better economic life for the people of China in order to justify their continued monopoly of political power. As the prestige of Mao and Communism had faded rapidly, Chinese leaders found themselves depending heavily on foreign trade, and related foreign investment and assistance, for China's needed economic development. China depended particularly on its Asian neighbors for aid, investment, and trade benefits, and on the United States and other major consumer markets to absorb its exports, which were growing at double the rate of the fast-developing Chinese economy. To insure their political survival, China's leaders continued to emphasize the maintenance of a peaceful international environment, especially in nearby Asia, which would facilitate the continued trade, investment, and assistance flows so important to Chinese economic well-being.[6]

The leadership followed earlier steps to put aside self-reliance and to broaden international contacts by increasing efforts to meet the requirements of the United States and others regarding market access, intellectual property rights, and other economic issues, and to become a member of the World Trade Organization (WTO). Chinese leaders accepted more commitments and responsibilities stemming from their participation in such international economic organizations as the World Bank, the Asian Development Bank, and the Asia-Pacific Economic Cooperation (APEC) forum.[7]

Chinese leaders remained sensitive on matters of national sovereignty and international security issues close to home. But they adjusted to world pressure when resistance appeared detrimental to broader Chinese concerns. Examples of this adjustment included Chinese cooperation with the international peace settlement in Cambodia in 1991, willingness to join the 1968 Treaty on Non-Proliferation of Nuclear Weapons and to halt nuclear tests by the end of 1996 under an international agreement, willingness to abide by terms of the Missile Technology Control Regime (MTCR), and efforts to help the United States reach an agreement with North Korea in October 1994 over the latter's nuclear weapons development program. Beijing also endeavored to meet international expectations on other transnational issues, such as policing drug traffic, curbing international terrorism, and working to avoid further degradation of the global environment.[8]

China's consistent hard line against outside criticism of its political authoritarianism and poor human rights record continued to illustrate limits of China's accommodation to international norms. China continued to transfer sensitive military technology or dual-use equipment to Pakistan, Iran, North Korea, and other potential flash points, despite criticism from Western countries. Furthermore, Chinese political and military leaders were not reluctant to use rhetorical threats or demonstrations of military force to intimidate those they believed were challenging China's traditional territorial or nationalistic claims in sensitive areas such as Taiwan, the South China Sea, and Hong Kong.[9]

As a general rule, Chinese leaders tended to approach each foreign policy issue on a case-by-case basis, each time calculating the costs and benefits of adherence to international norms. This kind of approach applied especially to security and political issues, while Chinese leaders came to view economic norms differently, seeing China generally well served by embracing economic globalization and at least some of the norms associated with it. By 1991, Chinese officials saw that maintaining past support for the Khmer Rouge in Cambodia would counter broader Chinese interests in achieving a favorable peace settlement in Cambodia and solidifying closer Chinese relations with Association of Southeast Asian Nations (ASEAN) members, Japan, and the West—all of whom saw continued Chinese aid to the Khmer Rouge as a serious obstacle to peace. Similarly, in 1994, China had to announce its decision to stop nuclear testing by the end of 1996 and to join the comprehensive nuclear test ban, or it would have risked major friction in its relations with the United States, Japan, Western Europe, and Russia.[10]

Influencing the case-by-case approach was a rising sense of nationalism among Chinese leaders and the Chinese people more broadly. Tending to view the world as a highly competitive, state-centered system, Chinese leaders were slow to embrace multilateralism and interdependence, though they came to accept these trends regarding economic issues. In security and political affairs, however, they were inclined to see the world in fairly traditional balance-of-power terms. They stressed that the world was becoming more multipolar (that is, having a number of competing nation states), though in the face of undiminished US dominance, they came to play down multipolarity for the time being in favor of multilateralism. The latter required the United States to sacrifice some freedom of maneuver for the sake of an interdependent international order, thereby constraining US power that could be used against Chinese interests.[11]

Chinese suspicions of the prevailing Asian and international order centered on the dominant role of the United States and its allies and associates. These nations were seen as setting the agenda of many international regimes in order to serve their own particular national interests, in the process giving short shrift to the interests and concerns of newly emerging powers like China. For example, many leaders in China during the 1990s saw foreign efforts to encourage or pressure China to conform to standards on international security, human rights, and economic policies and practices as moti-

leadership and global power. As part of this effort, Chinese leaders have become more active in bilateral and multilateral diplomacy. In international forums (the United Nations, the WTO, arms control discussions, and other arenas), China increasingly has tried to ensure that it is one of the rule makers for the global environment of the twenty-first century.[63] Beijing has also perceived that it needs to continue to build its military capabilities to be able eventually to back up its diplomacy, especially over the status of Taiwan, other territorial claims, and a widening range of important interests regarding energy security and the security of sea lines of communications, space, and other global commons. In particular, China has shown that it is willing to use military-backed actions by an array of Chinese security forces, trade sanctions, violent and destructive demonstrations in China, and other means in pursuit of its goals regarding sensitive security, sovereignty, and other contested issues involving the United States and governments along China's rim in nearby Asia.[64]

NOTES

1. Notable reviews include Ashley J. Tellis and Travis Tanner, eds., *Strategic Asia 2012–13: China's Military Challenge* (Seattle: National Bureau of Asian Research, 2012); Andrew Nathan and Andrew Scobell, *China's Search for Security* (New York: Columbia University Press, 2012); Ye Zicheng, *Inside China's Grand Strategy: The Perspective from the People's Republic* (Lanham, MD: Lexington, 2011); David Shambaugh, *China Goes Global: Partial Power* (New York: Oxford University Press, 2013); Jessica Chen Weiss, *Nationalist Protests in China's Foreign Relations* (New York: Oxford University Press, 2014); John Garver, *China's Quest: The History of the Foreign Relations of the People's Republic of China* (New York: Oxford University Press, 2016); Howard French, *Everything under the Heavens* (New York: Knopf, 2016); Fei-Ling Wang, *The China Order: Centralia, World Empire, and the Nature of Chinese Power* (Albany: State University of New York Press, 2017); Yan Xuetong et al., *Ancient Chinese Thought, Modern Chinese Power* (Princeton, NJ: Princeton University Press, 2011); Rosemary Foot and Andrew Walter, *China, the United States and the Global Order* (New York: Cambridge University Press, 2011); Zhu Liqun, *China's Foreign Policy Debates* (Brussels: Chaillot Papers, September 2010); Zhang Yunling, *Rising China and World Order* (Tokyo: World Scientific, 2010); David Michael Lampton, ed., *The Making of Chinese Foreign and Security Policy* (Stanford, CA: Stanford University Press, 2001); Robert S. Ross and Zhu Feng, eds., *China's Ascent: Power, Security, and the Future of International Politics* (Ithaca, NY: Cornell University Press, 2008); Yong Deng and Fei-Ling Wang, *China Rising: Power and Motivation in Chinese Foreign Policy* (Lanham, MD: Rowman & Littlefield, 2005); Allen Carlson and Ren Xiao, *New Frontiers in China's Foreign Relations* (Lanham, MD: Lexington, 2011); Bates Gill, *Rising Star* (Brookings Institution Press, 2007); Susan Shirk, *China: Fragile Superpower* (New York: Oxford, 2007); David Michael Lampton, *Three Faces of Chinese Power* (Berkeley: University of California Press, 2008); T. Robinson and D. Shambaugh, eds., *Chinese Foreign Policy* (New York: Oxford, 1994); Andrew Nathan and Robert Ross, *The Great Wall and Empty Fortress* (New York: Norton, 1997); Elizabeth Economy and Michel Oksenberg, *China Joins the World* (New York: Council on Foreign Relations, 1999); Alastair Iain Johnston and Robert Ross, *New Directions in the Study of China's Foreign Policy* (Stanford, CA: Stanford University Press, 2006); Alastair Iain Johnston, *Social States: China in International Institutions, 1980–2000* (Princeton, NJ: Princeton University Press, 2008); Yong Deng, *China's Struggle for Status: The Realignment of International Relations* (New York: Oxford University Press, 2008); Ann Kent, *Beyond Compliance: China, International Organ-*

izations, and Global Security (Stanford, CA: Stanford University Press, 2007); Allen Carlson, *Unifying China, Integrating with the World: Securing Chinese Sovereignty in the Reform Era* (Stanford, CA: Stanford University Press, 2005); Peter Hays Gries, *China's New Nationalism* (Berkeley: University of California Press, 2004); Suisheng Zhao, *A Nation-State by Construction* (Stanford, CA: Stanford University Press, 2004); Christopher Hughes, *Chinese Nationalism in a Global Era* (London: Routledge, 2006); Yufan Hao and Lin Su, eds., *Chinese Foreign Policy Making: Societal Force and Chinese American Policy* (Burlington, VT: Ashgate, 2005).

2. Robert Sutter, *Shaping China's Future in World Affairs* (Boulder, CO: Westview, 1996), pp. 32–33.

3. Harry Harding, *A Fragile Relationship* (Washington, DC: Brookings Institution Press, 1992), pp. 235–39; Tellis and Tanner, *Strategic Asia, 2012–13.*

4. Joseph Fewsmith, *China since Tiananmen* (New York: Cambridge University Press, 2001), pp. 21–43, 75–158.

5. Robert Suettinger, *Beyond Tiananmen: The Politics of U.S.-China Relations, 1989–2000* (Washington, DC: Brookings Institution Press, 2003), pp. 194–99.

6. Sutter, *Shaping China's Future in World Affairs*, pp. 33–34.

7. Nathan and Ross, *The Great Wall*, pp. 158–77.

8. Sutter, *Shaping China's Future in World Affairs*, pp. 33–34.

9. Shirley Kan, *China as a Security Concern in Asia*, Report 95-465 (Washington, DC: Library of Congress, Congressional Research Service, December 22, 1994).

10. Lampton, *The Making of Chinese Foreign and Security Policy*, pp. 34–36.

11. Evan Medeiros and Taylor Fravel, "China's New Diplomacy," *Foreign Affairs* 82, no. 6 (November–December 2003): pp. 22–35; Zhang Yunling and Tang Shiping, "More Self-Confident China Will Be a Responsible Power," *Straits Times*, October 2, 2002, http://www.Taiwansecurity.org (accessed October 4, 2002); Denny Roy, "Rising China and U.S. Interests: Inevitable vs. Contingent Hazards," *Orbis* 47, no. 1 (2003).

12. Sutter, *Shaping China's Future in World Affairs*, p. 35.

13. Chinese Academy of Social Sciences, *Trends of Future Sino-US Relations and Policy Proposals* (Beijing: Institute for International Studies of the Academy of Social Sciences, September 1994).

14. David M. Lampton, *Same Bed, Different Dreams* (Berkeley: University of California Press, 2001), pp. 59–60.

15. Fewsmith, *China since Tiananmen*, pp. 159–89.

16. H. Lyman Miller and Liu Xiaohong, "The Foreign Policy Outlook of China's 'Third Generation' Elite," in *The Making of Chinese Foreign and Security Policy*, ed. David M. Lampton (Stanford, CA: Stanford University Press, 2001), pp. 143–50.

17. Robert Sutter, *Chinese Policy Priorities and Their Implications for the United States* (Lanham, MD: Rowman & Littlefield, 2000), p. 18.

18. Barry Naughton, "China's Economy: Buffeted from Within and Without," *Current History*, September 1998, pp. 273–78.

19. Joseph Fewsmith, "China in 1998," *Asian Survey* 39, no. 1 (January–February 1999): pp. 99–113.

20. Cheng Li, "Fourth Generation Leadership in the PRC," in *China's Future: Implications for U.S. Interests*, Conference Report CR99-02 (Washington, DC: US National Intelligence Council, September 1999), pp. 13–36.

21. Jean-Pierre Cabestan, "The Tenth National People's Congress and After," *China Perspectives* 47 (May–June 2003): pp. 4–20.

22. Thomas Christensen, "China," in *Strategic Asia: Power and Purpose, 2001–2002*, ed. Richard Ellings and Aaron Friedberg (Seattle, WA: National Bureau of Asian Research, 2001), pp. 27–70; Thomas Christensen, "China," in *Strategic Asia: Power and Purpose, 2002–2003*, ed. Richard Ellings and Aaron Friedberg (Seattle, WA: National Bureau of Asian Research, 2002), pp. 51–94.

23. C. Fred Bergsten, Charles Freeman, Nicholas Lardy, and Derek Mitchell, *China's Rise: Challenges and Opportunities* (Washington, DC: Peterson Institute for International Economics and Center for Strategic and International Studies, 2008); *2010 Report to Congress of US-China Economic and Security Review Commission*, http://www.uscc.gov (accessed February

19, 2011); Harry Harding, "Has U.S. China Policy Failed?" *Washington Quarterly* 38, no. 3 (2015): 95–122; Robert Blackwill and Ashley Tellis, *Council Special Report: Revising U.S. Grand Strategy toward China* (Washington, DC: Council on Foreign Relations, April 2015); Orville Schell and Susan Shirk, Chairs, *US Policy toward China: Recommendations for a New Administration* (New York: Asia Society, 2017).

24. Li, *China's Emerging Middle Class.*

25. Kerry Brown, "The Path to the 19th Party Congress," *Diplomat*, May 15, 2017, http://thediplomat.com/2017/05/on-the-chinese-campaign-trail-the-path-to-the-19th-party-congress(accessed November 1, 2017).

26. For discussion of these various Chinese actions, see Schell and Shirk, *US Policy toward China: Recommendations for a New Administration.*

27. Cheng Li, *China's Leaders: The New Generation* (Lanham, MD: Rowman & Littlefield, 2001); Cheng Li, "Power Shift in China—Part I," YaleGlobal Online, April 16, 2012, http://yaleglobal.yale.edu.

28. Alice L. Miller, "Institutionalization and the Changing Dynamics of Chinese Leadership Politics," in *China's Changing Political Landscape: Prospects for Democracy*, ed. Cheng Li, pp. 61–79 (Washington, DC: Brookings Institution Press, 2008).

29. Jing Huang, "Institutionalization of Political Succession in China," in Li, *China's Changing Political Landscape*, pp. 80–98.

30. Dennis Blasko, *The Chinese Army Today* (London: Routledge, 2012).

31. David Shambaugh, "China's 17th Party Congress: Maintaining Delicate Balances," *Brookings Northeast Asia Commentary*, November 11, 2007; Bergsten et al., *China's Rise*, pp. 92–94; Li, "Power Shift in China—Part I"; "China Premier's Lavish Praise Shows Xi's Power," *Bloomberg*, March 5, 2017, https://www.bloomberg.com/news/articles/2017-03-05/chinese-premier-s-lavish-praise-shows-xi-power-before-reshuffle.

32. Bergsten et al., *China's Rise*, pp. 105–30; Wayne Morrison, *China's Economic Rise*, Report RL33534 (Washington, DC: Library of Congress, Congressional Research Service, 2017).

33. Morrison, *China's Economic Rise.*

34. Tony Saich, *Governance and Politics of China* (London: Palgrave, 2004), pp. 135, 233–67; Bruce Dickson, "Updating the China Model," *Washington Quarterly* 34, no. 4 (Fall 2011).

35. Bergsten et al., *China's Rise*, pp. 75–90.

36. Morrison, *China's Economic Conditions*, Report RL33534 (Washington, DC: Library of Congress, Congressional Research Service, 2012), pp. 17–18.

37. Minxin Pei, *China's Trapped Transition* (Cambridge, MA: Harvard University Press, 2006), pp. 83–84, 189, 200–204; Thomas Lum, *Human Rights in China and U.S. Policy*, Report RL 34729 (Washington, DC: Library of Congress, Congressional Research Service, July 18, 2011), pp. 28–29; "Strikes and Protests by China's Workers Soar to Record Heights in 2015," *China Labor Bulletin*, July 1, 2016, http://www.clb.org.hk/en/content/strikes-and-protests-china%E2%80%99s-workers-soar-record-heights-2015 (accessed January 20, 2018).

38. Lum, *Human Rights in China and U.S. Policy*, p. 6; Martin King Whyte, "Chinese Social Trends: Stability or Chaos," in Li, *China's Future: Implications for U.S. Interests*, pp. 67–84; Bergsten et al., *China's Rise*, pp. 96–97, 103; Martin King Whyte, "China's Dormant and Active Volcanoes," *China Journal* (January 2016): pp. 9–37.

39. US Department of Defense, *Annual Report to Congress: Military and Security Developments Involving the People's Republic of China 2012* (Washington, DC: US Department of Defense, May 2012).

40. "Friend or Foe? A Special Report on China's Place in the World," *Economist*, December 4, 2010, pp. 6–8.

41. David M. Lampton, *Three Faces of Chinese Power* (Berkeley: University of California Press, 2008), pp. 40–42; Mark Manyin, coord., *Pivot to the Pacific? The Obama Administration's "Rebalancing" toward Asia*, Report R42448 (Washington, DC: Library of Congress, Congressional Research Service, March 28, 2012).

42. Shirley Kan and Wayne Morrison, *U.S.-Taiwan Relationship: Overview of Policy Issues*, Report R41952 (Washington, DC: Library of Congress, Congressional Research Service,

June 15, 2012), pp. 1–10; Bonnie Glaser, *Prospects for Cross-Strait Relations as Tsai Ing-wen Assumes the Presidency in Taiwan* (Washington, DC: CSIS, April 2016).

43. David Shambaugh, *China's Communist Party: Atrophy and Adaptation* (Washington, DC: Woodrow Wilson Center, 2008), pp. 161–82; Bruce Dickson, *The Dictator's Dilemma: The Chinese Communist Party's Strategy for Survival* (New York: Oxford University Press, 2016).

44. Lampton, *The Three Faces of Chinese Power*, p. 208; Stapleton Roy, "Power Shift in China—Part II," YaleGlobal Online, April 18, 2012, http://yaleglobal.yale.edu.

45. Morrison, *China's Economic Conditions* (2012); Susan Lawrence and Thomas Lum, *U.S.-China Relations: Policy Issues*, Report R41108 (Washington, DC: Library of Congress, Congressional Research Service, March 11, 2011); Elizabeth Perry, "Growing Pains: Challenges for a Rising China," *Daedalus* 143, no. 2 (Spring 2014): pp. 5–13.

46. Yongnian Zheng, "China in 2011," *Asian Survey* 52, no. 1 (January–February 2012): pp. 28–41; Whyte, "China's Dormant and Active Volcanoes."

47. Richard Baum, "Political Implications of China's Information Revolution: The Media, the Minders, and Their Message," in Li, *China's Changing Political Landscape*, pp. 161–84; Peter Mattis, "Executive Summary for 'China in 2012,'" *China Brief* 12, no. 2 (January 20, 2012): pp. 1–3; Ching Kwan Lee, "State and Social Protest," *Daedalus* 143, no. 2 (Spring 2014): pp. 124–34.

48. Mattis, "Executive Summary"; Li, "Power Shift in China—Part I"; Dickson, *The Dictator's Dilemma.*

49. Susan Lawrence and Michael Martin, *Understanding China's Political System*, Report R41007 (Washington, DC: Library of Congress, Congressional Research Service, May 12, 2013).

50. "Friend or Foe?" pp. 6–8; Phillip Saunders and Andrew Scobell, eds., *PLA Influence on China's National Security Policymaking* (Stanford, CA: Stanford University Press, 2015).

51. Lawrence and Martin, *Understanding China's Political System*, pp. 10–16.

52. Zheng, "China in 2011"; Li, "Power Shift in China—Part I"; Linda Jacobson and Dean Knox, *New Foreign Policy Actors in China*, SIPRI Policy Paper 26 (September 2010); David Shambaugh, "Coping with a Conflicted China," *Washington Quarterly* 34, no. 1 (Winter 2011): pp. 7–27; Robert Sutter, *Chinese Foreign Relations: Power and Policy since the Cold War* (Lanham, MD: Rowman & Littlefield, 2016), p. 44.

53. Michael Swaine, "China's Regional Security Posture," in *Power Shift: China and Asia's New Dynamics*, ed. David Shambaugh (Berkeley: University of California Press, 2005), pp. 266–88. Manyin, "Pivot to the Pacific?" pp. 8–9, 15–16, 18–19, 23–24.

54. Suisheng Zhao, "China's Pragmatic Nationalism: Is It Manageable?" *Washington Quarterly* 29, no. 1 (2005): 131–44; Lum, *Human Rights in China and U.S. Policy*, p. 1.

55. Peter Gries refers to this kind of sensibility as "face nationalism." See Peter Hayes Gries, "A China Threat? Power and Passion in Chinese 'Face Nationalism,'" *World Affairs* 162, no. 2 (Fall 1999): p. 67.

56. On Chinese leaders' goals, especially as they relate to world affairs, see the discussion in subsequent chapters and in the selected bibliography in this book.

57. Avery Goldstein, *Rising to the Challenge: China's Grand Strategy and International Security* (Stanford, CA: Stanford University Press, 2005); Yong Deng, "Hegemon on the Offensive: Chinese Perspectives on U.S. Global Strategy," *Political Science Quarterly* 116, no. 3 (Fall 2001): pp. 343–65; Qian Qichen, "The International Situation and Sino-U.S. Relations since the 11 September Incident," *Waijiao Xueyuan Xuebao* (Beijing) 3 (September 25, 2002): pp. 1–6.

58. Jacobson and Knox, *New Foreign Policy Actors in China*; Shambaugh, "Coping with a Conflicted China."

59. David Shambaugh, "China's Military Views the World," *International Security* 24, no. 3 (Winter 1999–2000): pp. 52–79.

60. Robert Sutter, *The United States and Asia: Regional Dynamics and Twenty-First-Century Developments* (Lanham, MD: Rowman & Littlefield, 2015), pp. 69–108.

61. "Friend or Foe?" 8–15; Dai Bingguo, "Stick to the Path of Peaceful Development," *Beijing Review* 51, December 23, 2010, http://www.bjreview.com.cn; Shambaugh, "Coping with a Conflicted China."

62. Robert Sutter, *Chinese Policy Priorities and Their Implications for the United States* (Lanham, MD: Rowman & Littlefield, 2000), pp. 46–53; Shambaugh, "Coping with a Conflicted China."

63. Evan Medeiros, *China's International Behavior* (Santa Monica, CA: RAND Corporation, 2009); Michael Swaine, *The 19th Party Congress and Chinese Foreign Policy*, Carnegie Endowment for International Peace, October 16, 2017, http://carnegieendowment.org/2017/10/16/19th-party-congress-and-chinese-foreign-policy-pub-73432 (accessed January 21, 2018).

64. Lampton, *The Three Faces of Chinese Power*, pp. 25–36; Stephanie Kleine-Ahlbrandt, "Dangerous Waters," *Foreign Policy*, September 17, 2012, http://www.foreignpolicy.com/articles/2012/09/17/dangerous_waters (accessed October 7, 2012): Sutter, *Chinese Foreign Relations*, pp. 26–28.

Chapter Five

Patterns in Decision Making and International Outlook

The foreign policy and behavior of the People's Republic of China (PRC) is determined by leaders who make the decisions on the basis of what they think about the issues being decided. The patterns of decision making and the international outlook of Chinese leaders have changed in the post–Cold War period:[1]

- China's greater opening to the outside world since the death of Mao and China's remarkable integration with international economic, security, political, and other multilateral organizations have accompanied greater transparency and openness in Chinese foreign policy decision making.
- The number of people in and outside the Chinese government with an interest and influence in Chinese foreign policy decision making has grown enormously from the Maoist period. At that time, the Chinese Communist Party (CCP) chairman made most of the key decisions, often changing policy in radical directions, with the assistance of a few advisors.
- The Chinese decision makers today also represent a much broader set of Chinese interests in international affairs, notably in international economics and overall global stability and welfare. This trend contrasts with the predominantly security-oriented interests that dominated Chinese leadership concerns over foreign affairs during much of the Cold War. These security-oriented interests were focused on narrower concerns about preserving national sovereignty and security against superpower opposition.
- The outlook of Chinese decision makers on international affairs at times appears more cosmopolitan and compatible with prevailing international trends and norms, with less emphasis than in the past on the need for China to be on guard and prepared to take assertive and forceful action

against dangerous and predatory powers seeking to exploit, oppress, and constrain China. At other times, guarded suspicion seems more salient.

This chapter reviews highlights of what is known of the evolving structure and processes in the Chinese government's decision making on foreign policy and important features of the international outlook of Chinese decision makers. The assessment shows that in the Chinese government, the CCP, and the People's Liberation Army (PLA), the three key administrative groups governing China, the structure and processes in Chinese decision making on foreign policy have become more regularized and institutionalized than in the past. Also in contrast to past practice, Chinese leaders often are more accommodating to international trends and more in conformity with prevailing international norms.

However, the assessment also shows significant areas of secrecy; long-standing suspicion of other world powers, especially in nearby Asia; nationalistic and military ambitions; and other trends that seem at odds with or contradict cosmopolitan and accommodating Chinese foreign policy and behavior. The net result reinforces a finding in this book that while much of the recent orientation of China's foreign policy should be encouraged and welcomed by the international community, world leaders should not assume that these Chinese policy trends will uniformly prevail or that Chinese policy and behavior will invariably continue in directions of peace and development. Leaders in China long have held conflicting views over how far to go in accommodating other countries and in conforming to international norms.

Foreign policy decision making at the top levels of the Chinese leadership, notably in the past and at times in the present, can lead to arbitrary and abrupt decisions that can prompt the Chinese leadership to shift course under certain circumstances in directions that could be adverse to other international interests in peace, stability, and prosperity. Several examples from recent Chinese foreign relations illustrate why uncertainty and caution seem to be appropriate in predicting implementation of avowed Chinese foreign policy that does not threaten others and is in the broad international interest.

For instance, Chinese foreign policy in recent years repeatedly has shown abrupt shifts toward confrontation during international crises involving China. The accidental US bombing of the Chinese embassy in Belgrade in May 1999 prompted an abrupt shift toward the negative in China's approach toward the United States.[2] The danger of abrupt reversal in Chinese policy toward the United States surfaced again in 2001 as a result of the April 1 clash between a Chinese jet fighter and a US reconnaissance aircraft in international airspace near China's southern coast.[3] In contrast with China's accommodating approach toward neighboring countries, labeled China's "good-neighbor" policy, mass demonstrations against Japanese diplomatic and business installations in China in 2005 resulted in damage and destruction. Contrary to international norms, Chinese government officials allowed demonstrators to carry out violent actions for several days before using coercive measures to stop the destruction.[4] Repeated assertive actions beginning in 2008 and continuing into following years by the PLA Navy, maritime surveillance forces, and Chinese foreign policy organizations employed intimidation, coercion, harassment, and other forceful actions along with often extraordinary rhetorical attacks against fishing, energy prospecting, maritime surveillance, and military and diplomatic actions by foreigners involving Chinese-claimed territorial and other rights in waters along China's rim. Efforts by Japan, South Korea, and several Southeast Asian nations to support their claimed rights and interests, along with complaints from the United States, met with truculent Chinese charges featuring authoritative accusations of foreign "attacks" against and "containment" of China.

The Chinese assertiveness appeared to subside as President Hu Jintao reaffirmed China's focus on moderation and negotiation during a summit with President Obama in January 2011 and during later meetings with Asian leaders, but observers inside and outside of China were unsure whether or not the trend toward moderation would hold. Their uncertainty was justified, as 2012 featured extraordinary demonstrations of Chinese use of a wide-ranging means of power and force short of direct military action to coerce, intimidate, and compel neighbors with claims to territory in the South China Sea and the East China Sea to give way to China's demands. The means involved repeated shows of force by Chinese civilian-controlled maritime security forces, diplomatic threats, economic sanctions at odds with established international norms, and in the case of Japanese claims in the East China Sea, mass demonstrations in over one hundred Chinese cities for a weeklong period in September 2012 that resulted in widespread violence including burning and looting of Japanese properties and beatings of Japanese citizens in China.[5]

As discussed in chapters 7 and 8, sharp criticism by the heretofore reticent US president Barack Obama and other concerned leaders of such Chinese "bullying" to have its way at others' expense in disputed maritime territories failed to halt China's assertiveness and expansionism. It gradually became clear that Chinese leaders had decided to put aside Deng Xiaoping's advice to keep a low profile in foreign affairs. Now favored in the "new era" under the leadership of Xi Jinping (2012–) were Chinese disruptive, assertive, and bold approaches in pursuit of an ever-stronger and reunified China with regional leadership and global prominence specified in the overall goal of the "China Dream."

Adding to the uncertainty among Chinese and foreign observers regarding how and why Chinese foreign policy decisions are made is the prevailing secrecy that continues to surround Chinese policy on key foreign policy questions. To this day, Chinese and foreign specialists remain in the dark about how senior Chinese leaders deliberated in the weeks following the crises with the United States in May 1999 and April 2001.[6] Similar uncertainty pervades reviews of what is known of Chinese decision making during the April 2005 demonstrations against Japan and in the repeated episodes of coercion, intimidation, and extralegal actions including trade sanctions and periodic violence beginning in 2008 that impacted China's neighbors and the United States.[7] Even key Chinese decisions in international economics, such as the considerations that top leaders focused on in making the final decision for China to accept significant compromises in 1999 to reach agreement in order to join the World Trade Organization (WTO), are not clearly known.[8] One of the most important international security issues that has faced Chinese decision makers involved the international crisis brought about by North Korea's development of nuclear weapons and North Korea's concurrent leadership transition. Yet Chinese officials and specialists were frank in acknowledging that they remained in the dark and uncertain about the emphasis top Chinese decision makers gave to these and other concerns in the secret deliberations they carried out with reclusive North Korean leader Kim Jong Il during his several visits to China in the period before his death in 2011.[9] Taking over from his father, Kim Jong Un kept China at arm's length as he pursued rapid development of nuclear armed ballistic missiles capable of threatening Asian neighbors and the United States. Harsh Chinese media criticism of Kim's provocations and China's endorsement of UN sanctions against them failed to explain the calculations of senior Chinese leaders as they avoided pressures that would risk regime collapse and instability on the Korean peninsula.

KEY DECISION MAKERS IN CHINESE FOREIGN POLICY

There is general agreement among Chinese and foreign specialists regarding the continued decisive role of the "paramount" leader at the top of the hierarchy of central administration actors influencing Chinese foreign policy decision making. Mao Zedong, Deng Xiaoping, Jiang Zemin, and Hu Jintao played that role in past years. Xi Jinping became Communist Party general secretary, government president, and chairman of the Central Military Commission in late 2012 and early 2013; he is in this key final decision-maker role. It is generally held that Mao and Deng were strong and decisive in guiding Chinese foreign policy, where Jiang and Hu were much more consultative and cautious in their foreign policy roles. Party leader and President Xi consolidated his leadership power and emerged as a foreign policy ruler comparable with Mao and Deng. The Nineteenth Chinese Communist Party Congress in October 2017, which marked the end of Xi's first term as party general secretary, saw Xi dominate the proceedings. His "thought" was written by name into the party constitution along with that of Mao and Deng.

Among other notable accolades of Xi Jinping's foreign policy leadership, the senior Chinese foreign policy official, State Councilor Yang Jiechi, eased his selection to membership in the CCP Politburo with a laudatory exposition on the merits of Xi Jinping's foreign policy thought in a lengthy article highlighted by official Chinese media in the lead-up to the party congress. [10]

Xi maintained command of the leadership positions on the various foreign policy–related Communist Party groups dealing with different aspects of foreign affairs, including military and security, diplomacy, economic, and other issues. [11] In contrast, under Hu Jintao's leadership (2002–12), others in the CCP Politburo Standing Committee played leading roles in foreign policy. Prime Minister Wen Jiabao, who was more active than President Hu in dealing with foreign affairs, was most prominent. During the leadership of Jiang Zemin, who left his last official leadership post in 2004, specialists assessed that the broader CCP Politburo and the CCP secretariat under the Politburo played supporting roles as the paramount leader made decisions. And in the Leading Small Group for Foreign Affairs during Jiang's tenure as party leader and president, this decision-making and deliberative body on foreign affairs was at first chaired by Premier Li Peng (until sometime in the 1990s) and then by Jiang himself. Also a member was Vice Premier Qian Qichen, a former foreign minister, who played a key decision-making and advisory role on foreign affairs throughout Jiang Zemin's rule. Then as now, also represented were the top-level officials of the Foreign Affairs, Defense, and State Security ministries. [12]

The Financial and Economic Affairs Leading Small Group was the most important organ in economic decision making. Premier Zhu Rongji was the leader of this group during his five-year tenure (1998–2003), and Premier Wen Jiabao chaired the group beginning in 2003. As the Chinese authorities increasingly integrated the Chinese economy into the world economy, this body made decisions on these matters. Xi Jinping chairs this group along with a new group that manages Chinese economic reforms.

National security matters influencing foreign policy have been dealt with routinely by the party's Central Military Commission, which was headed by the party leader, now Xi Jinping. The commission is made up of key representatives from PLA departments and services. Meanwhile, policy toward Taiwan has been dealt with by the Leading Group on Taiwan Affairs, which Jiang and then Hu headed and now Xi directs. [13]

Xi also created a National Security Commission, which he directs. That commission remained poorly understood, though its focus seemed to be more on domestic Chinese security than on national defense and foreign policy. [14] One purpose of these leading groups is to allow key government, party, and military components to have input into important foreign policy decisions. A second purpose is to allow the paramount leader and his close advisors to benefit from these contributions as they seek to formulate effective policies that reflect the expertise and interests of relevant parts of the Chinese govern-ment, party, and military. Among administrative actors consulted in such decision making are the Ministry of Foreign Affairs, the Commerce Ministry, the Ministry of State Security, the Xinhua news agency, the International Liaison Department, the United Front Work Department of the CCP, and components of the PLA dealing with intelligence, military exchanges, and arms transfers.

The importance of leading small groups and other organizational struc-tures in the making of Chinese foreign policy has depended heavily on the leadership and decision-making approach of the paramount leader. What is known about usually secret foreign policy decision making under Mao Ze-dong indicates that Mao at times consulted with other senior leaders about key decisions and used the expertise of China's foreign policy and national security bureaucracies. Senior leaders concerned with particular issues also would deliberate prior to offering policy recommendations. In the end, Mao would decide on the path China would take, with varying and sometimes little consideration of the views of foreign policy professionals and other leaders with a stake in the decision. [15]

Such strong-man rule was reinforced by Chinese leaders' deference to Mao's wishes in most policy areas, especially national security and foreign affairs. The danger of challenging Mao's authority was enormous, as shown in Mao's harsh reaction to criticism of Defense Minister Peng Dehuai and other senior leaders in 1959 regarding Mao's push for development in the disastrous Great Leap Forward. Though the collapse of the Chinese economy eventually allowed more pragmatic Chinese leaders to nudge Mao to the sidelines and move domestic policies to less radical development policies in the early 1960s, Mao remained predominant in foreign affairs. The Cultural Revolution disrupted and destroyed much of China's foreign policy appara-tus, resulting in Mao making decisions with the advice of senior leaders like Zhou Enlai and a small circle of other advisors. [16]

The abrupt changes in Chinese foreign policy in the Maoist period cannot be explained without reference to Mao's dominant leadership role. He was in a position to steer China toward closer ties with the Soviet Union and then change course after a few years toward ever-greater hostility to Moscow. It appears that only such a paramount leader as Mao could support China's position in the early 1960s of opposition to both nuclear weapons–wielding superpowers at a time when China seemed very weak and vulnerable because of internal economic collapse. Mao subsequently led China from decades of violent opposition to the United States to the surprising opening to the Nixon administration and other developed countries.

Even as his health declined, Mao's leadership in foreign affairs remained supreme. Available scholarship shows successful efforts by Mao after the opening to the United States to check the rising stature of Premier Zhou Enlai in foreign affairs and to push Chinese policy toward the United States in directions more assertive than the moderate approaches favored by Zhou. Deng Xiaoping is seen to have been well aware of Mao's dominance, as he made his debut as Zhou's replacement as China's top foreign policy representative with a speech at the United Nations in 1974 propounding China's Three Worlds theory. As noted in chapter 3, the speech underlined Maoist resolve to remain tough toward the United States while seeking support from Washington in China's ongoing search for security and support against the Soviet Union.[17]

Upon Deng Xiaoping's ascendance as China's top leader following his return to top levels of power in 1978, the Chinese reformer began to exert a dominant influence in Chinese foreign relations that lasted until the end of the Cold War and the decline in his health in the 1990s. Unlike Mao, whose drive toward visionary goals led China to repeated domestic disasters and wide swings in China's foreign approach, Deng was more focused and consistent in domestic and international affairs. In general, he saw foreign relations as secondary to promoting economic development in China, which provided the basis for the continued legitimacy of Communist Party rule in the country. Effective nation building on the one hand required a stable international environment that at the time was challenged by perceived dangers to China from the expanding power of the Soviet Union. On the other hand, also required was China's opening to increased interchange with developed countries, led by the United States, which had the capital, technology, and markets needed for advancing Chinese economic development.

Deng favored patterns of leadership decision making more regularized and predictable than the often idiosyncratic means used by Mao. Nevertheless, he kept decision making on foreign and national security matters firmly in his own hands. Thus, he relied on the expertise of professionals and leaders dealing with foreign and national security matters, but he made and took responsibility for final decisions.[18]

The consequences of these decisions were often dramatic and far reaching. Thus, Deng was at the center of the Chinese decisions in late 1978 and early 1979 to invade Vietnam over its invasion of Cambodia and toppling of the Chinese-backed Khmer Rouge regime. Vietnam had recently aligned formally with the Soviet Union, which backed the Vietnamese invasion of Cambodia and had many divisions poised in offensive configurations along the northern border of China. Despite the clear danger of Soviet military action against China if China attacked Moscow's new ally in Vietnam, Deng decided to invade Vietnam in February 1979. At the time he also endeavored to use his leading role as the final arbiter of China's normalization agreement with the United States in December 1978 and China's peace agreement with Japan earlier in the year with his trips to the United States and Japan in 1979 in order to align China closely with these powers in directions that opposed Soviet expansion and dominance.[19]

Subsequently, Deng was in charge of charting China's course in dealing with the Soviet invasion of Afghanistan in late 1979, cooperating clandestinely with the United States in supporting Afghan resistance and allowing US monitoring stations in China to assess advances in Soviet missile developments. He led efforts to deal with Ronald Reagan's backsliding on US agreements with China over Taiwan and to move China toward a more "independent" and evenhanded public posture in dealing with the two superpowers, eventually seeing the wisdom of consolidation of China's relations with the United States in the face of uncompromising Soviet positions. Deng faced off with Britain's Margaret Thatcher, compelling the "iron lady" to back down and meet China's requirements in an agreement returning Hong Kong to China.

Deng's vision of how China should deal with the international isolation it faced following the Tiananmen crackdown of 1989 and the end of the Cold War remained the foundation of Chinese foreign policy calculus until the ascendance of Xi Jinping.[20] Pronouncements at the CCP Congress in October 2017 made clear that Xi's rule marked a "new era" for communist rule that entailed a much more prominent Chinese role in world affairs involving the "rejuvenated" China seen in Xi's vision of the China Dream.[21]

THE FOREIGN POLICY CONCERNS AND WORLDVIEWS OF CHINESE LEADERS

Assessments of Chinese foreign policy thinking at the start of this century made the case that Chinese foreign policy and behavior were changing markedly in directions more in line with international norms, especially regarding economic and cultural matters and constructive participation in multilateral organizations. These changes in Chinese policy were seen as influenced by a more pluralistic range of Chinese decision makers, whose diverse interests were reflected in foreign policy and behavior. These decision makers represented a variety of government, party, and military bureaucracies, government-affiliated and nongovernment think tanks, and provincial and local governments, as well as broad segments of Chinese people, reflecting aroused public opinion, especially on nationalistic issues. According to the assessments, the broad range of those influencing Chinese foreign policy meant that the Chinese foreign policy process needed to be more consultative and attentive to wide-ranging inputs. As a result, the decision-making process often was slower and more cumbersome than in the past, when the top leader could decide changes in policy on his own authority.[22]

As Chinese policy and practice became increasingly engaged in international relations, better-educated and younger officials and nongovernment specialists played a more important role in informing and guiding the decision-making process. They contributed on such complicated issues as economic regulations, intellectual property rights, environmental compliance, arms control regulations, human rights, and international law. Another feature of the recent foreign policy–making process in China was that foreign governments, businesses, and other nongovernment groups had more entry points that allowed them to influence some or all of the diverse range of Chinese actors that have influence in determining Chinese foreign policy and behavior. These outside influences tended to push China toward behavior more in line with international norms.

The assessments acknowledged the still secretive and hierarchic structure of Chinese foreign policy decision making, with the top-level party, government, and military leaders exerting dominant influence on final decisions, especially on national security questions.[23] They also highlighted a prevailing worldview among this elite that emphasized seeing international affairs in terms of competing states, with China required to maintain its guard against exploitation and oppression as it seeks to develop national wealth and power and greater influence in Asian and world affairs. Nonetheless, the assessments pointed out that these leaders needed the expertise and broad inputs that came from consulting the wide range of bureaucratic and nongovernment specialists and interests noted previously. To do otherwise risked ineffective or mistaken policies that could have a direct impact on top Chinese leaders, whose legitimacy rested heavily on demonstrating an ability to advance Chinese power and influence without major international complications or confrontation. In sum, there was some optimism that the recent trend of increasing Chinese foreign policy conformity with and adherence to international norms, along with continued emphasis on promoting general trends toward world peace and development, were likely to continue.[24]

On assuming the leading CCP position in 2002, Hu Jintao appeared to follow the pattern of generally cautious moves toward moderation in Chinese foreign affairs seen in the latter years of Jiang Zemin. Hu's leadership featured emphasis on "peaceful development" and supporting a "harmonious" world.[25] However, beginning in 2008, repeated episodes of Chinese assertiveness and truculence over sensitive issues with the United States, Japan, South Korea, India, several Southeast Asian states, and other countries seemed at odds with Hu's stated policy goals. They raised questions regarding whether the Chinese leader had the will and the ability to control China's interagency foreign policy coordination process and its various stakeholders, as well as influential elements outside the formal process, including public opinion fanned by sometimes sensational media coverage of sensitive foreign policy issues. As noted above, Hu strongly reaffirmed a moderate line in foreign affairs during 2011, but impressive demonstrations of coercive and truculent Chinese behavior toward neighboring states in 2012 assured that questions about the durability of Chinese moderation and other longer-term trends would remain unresolved. An authoritative study of Chinese foreign policy actors in 2010 concluded that foreign policy decision making had become more "fractured"; the Chinese military and other conservative forces had become more prominent, a development that was strengthened by widespread Chinese opinion that China should be "less submissive" and defend more strongly its interests in disputes with other countries. Subsequently, a leading American specialist on China, David Shambaugh, warned of the implications of the "current consensus among the more conservative and nationalist elements to toughen its policies and selectively throw China's weight around."[26] Subsequent foreign policy developments under newly assertive Xi Jinping corroborate this forecast.

A review of the various worldviews propounded by leaders of the People's Republic of China since 1949 indicates how difficult it remains for China to fully accept existing international norms and an accommodating posture to the Western countries and other leaders and large stakeholders in the prevailing international mechanisms. As specialists in China have repeatedly emphasized in recent years, China's rising international prominence has brought to the fore nationalistic and zero-sum realist foreign policy calculations on the part of a variety of influential foreign policy actors in China that have put those Chinese leaders arguing for progressive accommodation to existing international norms in a more defensive and increasingly less influential position. These nationalistic and realist calculations come in spite of Chinese publicists claiming that China does not engage in such zero-sum competitive calculations; they tap into deeply rooted Chinese views of world affairs.

There is little disagreement among Chinese and foreign specialists that Chinese officials and the rest of the Chinese people have long been conditioned through the education system and government-sponsored media coverage to think of China as having been victimized by international powers since the early nineteenth century. Emphasis on this historical conditioning was strengthened after the CCP crisis at the time of the Tiananmen demonstrations and bloody crackdown in 1989 and continues up to the present. Sensing that communism no longer provided adequate ideological support for continued CCP rule, the authorities instituted a patriotic education campaign with related media coverage. The campaign was designed to encourage regime-supporting patriotism in China by recalling the more than one hundred years of foreign affronts to Chinese national dignity. With this focus, foreign complaints about human rights and other abuses in China after the Tiananmen crackdown were depicted as the latest in a long series of foreign efforts to abuse and victimize China. As such, they were likely to elicit negative responses from Chinese people directed at foreign governments rather than result in Chinese people agreeing with the foreign criticism of the abuses of Chinese Communist rule.[27]

The historical record since the first Opium War (1839–42), featured in Chinese indoctrination, education, and media efforts, provides a rich legacy for those seeking to view China as an aggrieved party in international affairs.[28] For example, foreign powers, mainly Great Britain but including the United States, used the opium trade as a way to balance their purchases of tea and other commodities from China in the early nineteenth century. Backed by superior military power, British, and later joint British-French, military expeditions defeated Chinese forces and compelled the opening of several so-called treaty ports along Chinese rivers and coastal areas, where foreigners lived under their own jurisdiction, not Chinese law, and foreign missionaries were free to spread religious beliefs seen as heterodox by Chinese officials. Foreign military power coerced the Chinese government to give large swaths of territory to foreign rule. After Japan unexpectedly defeated China in a war over dominance in Korea and took Taiwan from China in 1895, the foreign powers seemed poised to divide up China into their respective colonies or spheres of influence.[29]

China probably would have been divided by the foreign imperialists had not the tensions leading to World War I caused the European powers to withdraw forces from China in order to prepare for war in Europe. The field was then open for Japan to dominate China, which it did. Other foreign powers did little other than object to Japan's expansion and eventual takeover of Manchuria.

In 1937, as full-scale war broke out between China and much stronger and technologically superior Japanese forces, China stood basically alone. Through brutal and rapacious attacks, one million Japanese soldiers occupied the most productive parts of China. With Japan's defeat in 1945, the United States sided with Chiang Kai-shek against the Chinese Communists in three years of Chinese civil war, ending with the Communist victory on the Chinese mainland in 1949 and Chiang Kai-shek's retreat to Taiwan.

The Chinese Communists then confronted the United States following the June 1950 US intervention in the Korean War as well as the US intervention in the Taiwan Strait that prevented the Communists from reunifying Taiwan with the mainland. In the Chinese view, twenty years of hostility, confrontation, and abuse of China at the hands of American leaders were followed by twenty years of similar treatment of China by the Soviet Union, which emerged as China's main security threat in the late 1960s. Finally, at the end of the Cold War, the PRC experienced an international situation where for the first time it did not face immediate danger of war with one or two nuclear-armed superpowers.

The lessons of this sordid experience, which continues to be strongly emphasized by Chinese education, media, and propaganda organs, heavily influence the world outlook of Chinese leaders and people:[30]

- The world is viewed darkly. It is full of highly competitive, unscrupulous, and duplicitous governments that are seeking their selfish interests at the expense of China and others.
- To survive and develop, China needs power—military power backed by economic power and political unity. If there is disunity at home, foreign powers will use Chinese differences to exploit China, just as they did in the past.
- China is an aggrieved party. It has suffered greatly at foreign hands for almost two centuries. It needs to build its power and influence to protect what it has and to get back what is rightfully China's. This means restoration of Taiwan to Chinese sovereignty and securing other Chinese territorial claims.
- China does not dominate the world order; other powers do—during the Cold War, the United States and Soviet Union; after the Cold War, the United States. China needs to work toward an international balance that helps Chinese interests and avoids outside dominance. In this vein, Chinese leaders in recent years have emphasized the benefits of a multipolar world order where China would have greater freedom of maneuver and security than in an international order dominated by the United States.

Complementing this historical discourse showing China as the victim of predatory outsiders are other features influencing China's worldview to various degrees:

- The ideological and revolutionary drive of Mao Zedong and his colleagues to foster revolution in China and abroad has largely ended, though as noted in the previous chapter, China's leaders remain determined to preserve Communist Party rule in the face of perceived political challenges and values supported by the West.
- Chinese self-reliance, so important in the latter Maoist period discussed in chapters 2 and 3, has been put aside with China's ever-growing interdependence with the world, especially in economics and trade. Nevertheless, with the exception of North Korea, China scrupulously avoids alliances with or formal dependence on other states as it seeks ties with other countries based on the "win-win" formula that determines Chinese foreign relations recently. Chinese cooperation with others is contingent on a "win" for China that is within the scope of a win-set defined narrowly in terms of tangible benefit for the Chinese state.

- Chinese officials recently have fostered an idealized depiction of benevolent Chinese imperial interaction with China's neighbors. The hierarchic order of international relations with China at the center seen during much of the Ming and Qing dynasties from the fourteenth to the nineteenth centuries is depicted showing Chinese naval expeditions and other foreign interchange that reflects China's unwillingness to be expansionist.[31]
- As discussed in chapter 1, Chinese official discourse and related scholarship tend to play down foreign depictions of Chinese leaders changing foreign policies and even overall alignments as Chinese interests shift with changing circumstances at home and abroad. Rather, they portray Chinese policies and practices as consistent, based on appropriate principles in line with broad moral goals, and aligning China's approach with the "progressive" forces in international affairs.
- China's "peculiar" operational code of conduct—"firmness in principle and flexibility in application," as Samuel Kim labels it—is another aspect foreign observers find troubling. For Kim and others there is a gap between principle and practice, with China repeatedly attempting to show through sometimes adroit and sometimes awkward use of a wide range of old and new sets of principles that interest-based changes in Chinese foreign relations remain consistent with righteous principles.
- And, as discussed in chapter 1, one result of such Chinese reasoning is an acute sense of Chinese exceptionalism. Many Chinese truly believe that the People's Republic of China has always followed morally correct foreign policies in the interest of progressive world forces. They believe China has done nothing wrong in world affairs; if difficulties arise with other states over foreign policy concerns, the fault naturally lies with the other party.

The overall implications of China's acute sense of grievance against past international victimization of China on the one hand and the strong sense of righteousness in the foreign policy and practice of the PRC on the other hand support a Chinese popular and elite worldview of poor self-awareness of Chinese international shortcomings and sharp sensitivity to international pressure.

Meanwhile, although some foreign and Chinese specialists look on the bright side and see China conforming more to international norms, more sober views see China adjusting to circumstances. They see that adjustments could shift in ways at odds with international stability if the circumstances were to change, say, for example, with a rise in Chinese power and decline of the power of the United States.

Indeed, the rise of Chinese power and the perceived decline of the power of the United States prompted Chinese leaders under Xi Jinping to shift foreign policy in ways that disrupted the regional status quo in Asia and challenged the interests of the United States. Xi's and other authoritative statements in the lead-up to and during the Nineteenth CCP Congress in October 2017 made clear that China no longer looked to conform to patterns and norms of behavior favored by the United States and its allies and partners. In their place Xi emphasized that Chinese foreign and domestic policies would adhere to "Chinese characteristics," which were emphasized in virtually all areas of public policy. These characteristics stressed stronger authoritarian CCP control at home, and Communist-ruled China's burgeoning dominance in Asia and other practices abroad that challenged and undercut the prevailing international order backed by the United States.[32]

As discussed in the following chapters, putting aside the past "low profile" in foreign affairs favored by Deng Xiaoping, the Chinese authoritarian and state-directed political, economic, and social system now publicly eschewed examples from the West and asserted that it was China and not the West that represented a model of development for other developing countries. Various concurrent Chinese government actions reinforcing this new thrust in foreign policy included new China-created or China-supported multilateral international finance, development, security, and political organizations engaged in Asian and broader world leadership. They ranged from the China-created Asian Infrastructure Investment Bank and the New Development Bank carried out by the five BRICS countries (Brazil, Russia, India, China, and South Africa), with China the most important, to such regional groupings fostered by China (and excluding the United States) as the Conference on Interaction and Confidence Building in Asia (CICA) and the Regional Comprehensive Economic Partnership (RCEP) trade and economic agreement.

CHINESE ELITE AND POPULAR VIEWS OF THE UNITED STATES

The conditioning of Chinese elite and popular opinion for many years by government-controlled education and media has reinforced a strong sense of patriotism and suspicion of the United States. The conditioning often stresses the need to speed China's drive for comprehensive national power in order to ensure China's rightful interests in the face of US and other foreign pressures.[33] At times of cooperative China-US relations, Chinese government authorities play down the anti-US stance, but it emerges often and with surprising vehemence at times of Sino-US friction.[34]

Assessments by US, Chinese, and other specialists have continued to find that Chinese officials and the experts who advise them view US policy and behavior with a great deal of suspicion. Wang Jisi, one of the most prominent Chinese specialists on US-China relations and a frequent advisor to Chinese leaders, wrote in 2005 that despite some ups and downs in Chinese views of the United States since the end of the Cold War, "the official line continues to point to the United States as the mainstay of the 'hostile forces' that try to destabilize China and refers to the United States as the hegemonic power that threatens global security." He added, "To most Chinese observers, . . . the United States is an insatiable domineering country that believes only in its own absolute power, one that would never allow any other country to catch up with it." Given their perception of American intentions and hegemony, these Chinese elites tend not to trust US motives. Although they see China benefiting from and heavily dependent on economic and other ties with the United States, they continue to fear American manipulation of China in international strategic terms, exploitation in economic terms, and subversion in political and ideological terms. As Wang advised Chinese readers in an interview in October 2008, "Pax Americana" is an unjust international order "under power politics," and "China cannot accept being led by the United States" even as Beijing pursues cooperation with Washington for pragmatic reasons. Professor Wang teamed with a prominent American China specialist, Kenneth Lieberthal, to publish an important study in 2012 that reaffirmed the deep suspicions of Chinese and US official elites toward one another.[35]

Negative Chinese views of the United States showed in reaction to the widespread criticism of Chinese government policies and practices during the US 2016 presidential election campaign. The two main candidates, Democrat Hillary Clinton and Republican Donald Trump, were viewed negatively. Clinton was seen as rigid, committed to challenging China on a range of issues including the legitimacy of China's authoritarian Communist government—a very sensitive so-called core interest of the Chinese regime. There was some optimism that Donald Trump's critiques of China, which focused mainly on trade issues, could be addressed through pragmatic deals with the US leader.[36]

At the start of the twenty-first century, the list of Chinese charges and grievances against US hegemonism was long and involved many issues of direct concern to China and nearby Asia. They included the large and growing US defense budget; a strong tendency to use coercive measures in US foreign policy; allegedly wanton disregard of international institutions and rules when deemed inconvenient; an aggressive agenda in promoting Western values; unilateral decisions to build missile defenses; endeavoring to restrict high-technology information to China and others; arrogant violations of other countries' sovereignty; unjustified expansion of US alliances in Europe and Asia; and determination to contain emerging powers, notably China.[37]

To American policy makers and others interested in better US relations with China, the clear tendency of Chinese leaders to exaggerate the negatives in the US approach to China and to highlight the threat the United States posed to the key interests of the CCP leadership is a major obstacle to improved relations. Remedying these tendencies was difficult. Part of the problem was how deeply rooted the inclination was for leaders in China (and the United States) to exaggerate the power and influence—usually seen as negative—posed by the other side.[38]

Chinese strategists throughout the Cold War tended to focus on how the United States and/or the Soviet Union could or did use "power politics" and outright coercion to force China to compromise over key interests. The exaggerated Chinese claims that the United States was seeking to split up, hold back, and contain China in the 1990s and later echoed this approach. Adding to the tendency was the long-standing Chinese leadership practice of analyzing world politics in terms of "contradictions" derived from Marxism-Leninism and developed by Mao Zedong. As discussed in chapter 1, the Chinese international approach and worldview thus had a clear focus on the "main enemy" or danger to China and its interests. The United States played this role in the 1950s and 1960s; the Soviet Union was the main enemy in the 1970s and much of the 1980s. Beginning in the 1990s, despite China's strong need to promote advantageous economic and other relations with the United States, Chinese elite thinking and behavior showed that the United States again became the main target of Chinese international concern—that is, China's main "enemy."[39]

In order to mobilize domestic and international forces to deal with the main danger, Chinese leaders tended to portray the adversary in starkly negative terms. Often associated with this kind of international outlook was a "united front" policy. This involved Chinese efforts to win over other powers to assist in the focused attempts to counter the danger posed by the main adversary. Of course, China's dealings with the United States in the 1990s were not as clear-cut as its dealings with the Americans and the Soviets in the Cold War. The United States was not seen only as an adversary; it also was a competitor and a partner whose cooperation was essential to Chinese modernization. Thus, Chinese leaders endeavored to sustain a balanced approach to the United States that preserved a working relationship—especially economic relations—while continuing to view US power as threatening many important Chinese interests.[40]

The episodes of greater Chinese assertiveness against the United States, its Asian partners, and others in nearby Asia beginning in 2008 included a revival of exaggerated claims that the United States, now under the Obama administration, was using its avowed efforts to reengage with Asia-Pacific countries as a thinly veiled effort to contain and hold back China's rising influence in the region and throughout the world. Slow US recovery from the global economic crisis that started in 2008 and other perceived American weaknesses, contrasting with economic, military, and other Chinese advances, led many Chinese elite and popular observers to recalculate the international balance of power in China's favor. A weakened US superpower and the rise of China and other nations meant that a multipolar world was not far off, allowing, in the calculations of these Chinese opinion leaders, for a more assertive Chinese policy regarding a range of differences with the United States.[41] The Xi Jinping government's replacing Deng Xiaoping's low profile in foreign affairs with bold assertiveness seeking the China Dream appeared to reflect this recalibration of China's power vis-à-vis the United States.

CHINESE OPPOSITION TO SUPERPOWER DOMINANCE IN ASIA

Another legacy of the past that influences Chinese officials' contemporary worldview is the long record of Chinese policy and behavior in Asia, which shows repeated maneuvering to keep China's periphery as free as possible from hostile or potentially hostile great-power pressure. As noted earlier, Asia, especially the countries around China's periphery, has been the main arena of Chinese foreign relations. Efforts to keep this periphery free of potentially hostile great-power presence and pressure are seen as central to Chinese security, and China has long used both offensive and defensive measures to thwart perceived great-power ambitions in the region. This trend has persisted, along with the growing Chinese economic integration, increasing political and security cooperation, and active engagement with various multilateral organizations in the region.[42]

Some scholarship[43] shows a growing acceptance by PRC leaders of interdependence in international economic relations but continued wariness regarding close interaction with and dependence on others regarding political, security, and other concerns. It indicates that it is still too early to know if Chinese leaders are genuinely internalizing and embracing global norms and values that would argue for greater stability and moderation in Asian and world affairs. Alternatively, the recent Chinese actions under Xi Jinping suggest Chinese leaders have been adapting to some global norms to derive tactical benefits, biding their time to exert greater pressure and force to achieve Chinese goals as circumstances become more advantageous. While Chinese leaders have moved over time to see their interests best served by engagement with international economic norms, Chinese leaders generally seem to follow a case-by-case approach, doing cost-benefit analysis in making key foreign policy decisions. Interdependence with and moderation and accommodation toward powers involved in Asian and world affairs appear to prevail when the costs of a more assertive posture—one more consistent with Chinese nationalistic attitudes and evidenced in periodic recent assertive behavior toward Japan, India, Southeast Asian claimants to disputed territories in the South China Sea, and South Korea, as well as the United States, Taiwan, and others—outweigh the benefits. When the assessed cost-benefit calculus allows, China has appeared ready and willing to use coercion, intimidation, and violence to have its way in disputes in nearby areas.

Chinese foreign policy in the Maoist period strongly opposed US and Soviet power and pressure, especially along China's periphery. As reviewed in chapter 3, Moscow's persisting military buildup and search for greater political and military influence around China's periphery became the strategic focus of Chinese foreign policy in Asia and China's overall approach to world affairs in the late 1960s. At first under the leadership of Premier Zhou Enlai and Chairman Mao Zedong and later under Deng Xiaoping, China attempted to use US-Soviet differences pragmatically to China's advantage. Only at tremendous cost and great risk could China confront the Soviet Union on its own. It relied heavily on the United States and its allies and associates in Asia and elsewhere. And the end of US containment meant that it no longer posed a serious military threat to Chinese national security. Thus, Chinese leaders maintained a collaborative relationship with the United States and the West as a key link in its security policy against the Soviet Union.[44]

Post-Mao Chinese leaders gave high priority both to accomplish modernization and to maintain national security and internal order. The leaders were required repeatedly to assess their surroundings for changes that affected Chinese security and development interests. The result was repeated Chinese adjustments to take account of such changes.[45] At the same time, Chinese leaders had nationalistic and ideological objectives regarding irredentist claims (such as Taiwan) and a desire to stand independently in foreign affairs as a leading power among "progressive" developing nations of what was called the third world. These goals struck a responsive chord politically inside China. Deng Xiaoping's rise to power in the late 1970s saw the end of the acute debates over foreign policy during the Cultural Revolution. The Tiananmen crisis and crackdown of 1989 focused mainly on domestic issues, and China's foreign policy orientation toward strengthening national security and development was not altered fundamentally.[46]

In the 1970s and 1980s Chinese leaders saw the main danger of negative change in the surrounding environment posed by the Soviet Union. As discussed in chapter 3, they first perceived Soviet power as an immediate threat to its national security. Over time, they came to see the Soviet Union as more of a long-term threat, determined to use its growing military power and other sources of influence to encircle and pressure China into accepting its dominance in the balance of influence in Asia.[47]

China's strategy of deterrence and defense, therefore, aimed basically to exacerbate Soviet defense problems by enhancing the worldwide opposition to Soviet expansion in general and by raising the possibility of the Soviet Union confronting a multifront conflict in the event it attempted to attack or intimidate China in particular. Chinese leaders saw their nation's cooperation with the United States as especially important in strengthening deterrence of the Soviet Union and in aggravating Soviet strategic vulnerabilities. Chinese leaders also encouraged anti-Soviet efforts by developed countries—most of whom were formal allies of the United States—and by developing countries of the third world. At the same time, Chinese leaders used a mix of political talks, bilateral exchanges, and other forms of dialogue to help manage the danger posed by the Soviet Union.

Chinese leaders employed a varying mix of tactics to secure their interests, depending on international variables, such as the perceived strength and intentions of the superpowers, and Chinese domestic variables, such as leadership cohesion or disarray. When Chinese leaders judged that their strategic surroundings were at least temporarily stable, they had less immediate need for close ties with the United States and thus felt freer to adopt more insistent policies on Taiwan and other nationalistic issues that appealed to domestic constituencies but offended the United States. This type of calculus was in part responsible for China's tougher approach to the United States over Taiwan and other issues in 1981–83. But when the Chinese leaders judged that such tactics risked seriously alienating the United States and thereby endangered the stability of China's environment, they put them aside in the interest of preserving peaceful surroundings. Such reasoning undergirded China's moderation in approach toward the United States in 1983 and 1984, discussed in chapter 3.[48]

In the post–Cold War period, Chinese concerns over possible superpower dominance in Asia focused on the United States. In the 1990s, Chinese officials adopted a rhetorically confrontational approach, attacking the US alliance system in Asia and other reflections of what they saw as "Cold War thinking," "power politics," and "hegemonism" in US policies and behavior. The Chinese approach failed in the face of Asian states' unwillingness to side with China against the United States and in the face of strong US power and influence.[49]

Adjusting to rising US power and determination under George W. Bush, Chinese leaders changed policy. By 2003, they articulated a new policy that emphasized China's peaceful rise and peaceful development in Asian and world affairs. This policy continued strongly until the end of the Bush administration and the beginning of the Obama administration. Then episodes of Chinese assertive actions and strident rhetoric against the United States, its Asian partners, and other nearby states beginning in 2008 have raised questions about the policy's durability. The following years witnessed sometimes surprising assertiveness against the United States and its allies and partners in nearby Asia. Previous strong efforts to reassure America were put aside. Beijing was now prepared to risk rising tensions with the United States in pursuit of territorial and other ambitions at the expense of others. The Nineteenth CCP Congress in 2017 confirmed that China's low profile in foreign affairs was replaced by disruptive challenges, especially in nearby Asia.[50]

OUTLOOK IN ASIA: RISING CHINA-US COMPETITION AND TENSION

The pronouncements of the Nineteenth CCP Congress authoritatively confirmed to Asian neighbors and the United States their disappointment that post-Mao engagement with China had not resulted in China following a path of cooperation and accommodation in the region.[51] The China Dream of Xi Jinping underlined determination to control Taiwan and all other Chinese claimed territories and return China to Asia's leading position. There was little Chinese concern registered during the Congress or otherwise as to what the reaction would be of those neighboring countries whose interests were negatively impacted by Chinese intimidation, coercion, and expansion.

Meanwhile, President Xi spent more time than any other prominent world leader with Russian president Vladimir Putin. The two had broad common ground on the "threats" posed by Western-fostered color revolutions and the opportunities posed by perceived decline in the United States and its leading allies. Putin more aggressively, and China more cautiously, advanced their interests at the expense of the United States and its allies as well as partner countries, supporting one another against US and Western pressures and sanctions. They overlapped in their interests to sustain and strengthen the authoritarian regimes in their respective countries.[52]

In the "new era" of Xi Jinping, China was determined to march forward with its ambitious plans, while the United States, Japan, and India seemed prepared to defend their interests, compete actively with Beijing, and resist if necessary if China impinged seriously on their interests. Most other regional countries hedged their bets in this uncertain environment—seeking to preserve what they saw as the beneficial order of the prevailing status quo in the face of growing competition and tension resulting in particular from the conflicting goals of China and the United States.

NOTES

1. David M. Lampton, ed., *The Making of Chinese Foreign and Security Policy in the Era of Reform* (Stanford, CA: Stanford University Press, 2001); Evan Medeiros and Taylor Fravel, "China's New Diplomacy," *Foreign Affairs* 82, no. 6 (November–December 2003): pp. 22–35; People's Republic of China State Council Information Office, "China's Peaceful Development Road," *People's Daily Online*, December 22, 2005; Linda Jakobson and Dean Knox, *New Foreign Policy Actors in China* (Stockholm: SIPRI Policy Paper No. 26, September 2010); Robert Sutter, *Chinese Foreign Relations: Power and Policy since the Cold War* (Lanham, MD: Rowman & Littlefield, 2016), pp. 37–57; Yun Sun, *Chinese National Security Decision-making: Processes and Challenges*, Brookings Institution Press, May 2013, https://www.

brookings.edu/wp-content/uploads/2016/06/chinese-national-security-decisionmaking-sun-paper.pdf (accessed January 21, 2018); Yong Deng, "China: The Post-Responsible Power," *Washington Quarterly* 37, no. 4 (Winter 2015): pp. 117–32.

2. David M. Lampton, *Same Bed, Different Dreams* (Berkeley: University of California Press, 2001), pp. 59–61; Robert Sutter, *China's Rise in Asia: Promises and Perils* (Lanham, MD: Rowman & Littlefield, 2005), p. 29.

3. John Keefe, *Anatomy of the EP-3 Incident* (Alexandria, VA: Center for Naval Analysis, 2002); Michael Swaine and Zhang Tuosheng, eds., *Managing Sino-American Crises: Case Studies and Analysis* (Washington, DC: Carnegie Endowment, 2006).

4. James Przystup, "Japan-China Relations: No End to History," *Comparative Connections* 7, no. 2 (2005): pp. 119–32.

5. "China Placates Foes Abroad, Nationalists at Home," *Economist*, June 4, 2008; Wang Jisi, "China's Search for a Grand Strategy," *Foreign Affairs* 90, no. 2 (March/April 2011): pp. 68–79; Wang Jisi, "China-Southeast Asia Relations," *Comparative Connections* 13, no. 1 (May 2011), http://www.csis.org/pacfor; James Przystup, "Japan-China Relations," *Comparative Connections* 13, no. 3 (January 2013), http://www.csis.org/pacfor.

6. Personal consultations with US government officials, Washington, DC, 1999–2001; Swaine and Zhang, *Managing Sino-American Crises*.

7. "Friend or Foe? A Special Report on China's Place in the World," *Economist*, December 4, 2010, pp. 3–16.

8. Personal consultations with US government officials, Washington, DC, November 1999.

9. Personal interviews and consultations with Chinese officials and foreign policy specialists, Beijing and Shanghai, May–June 2006, Beijing, June 2010.

10. "Full Text of Chinese State Councilor's Article on Xi Jinping's Diplomacy Thought," *Xinhuanet*, July 19, 2017, http://news.xinhuanet.com/english/2017-07/19/c_136456009.htm (accessed January 21, 2018).

11. Lu Ning, "The Central Leadership, Supraministry Coordinating Bodies, State Council Ministries, and Party Departments," in *The Making of Chinese Foreign and Security Policy in the Era of Reform*, ed. David M. Lampton (Stanford, CA: Stanford University Press, 2001), pp. 39–60; Fei-Ling Wang, "Beijing's Incentive Structure: The Pursuit of Preservation, Prosperity, and Power," in *China Rising: Power and Motivation in Chinese Foreign Policy*, ed. Yong Deng and Fei-Ling Wang (Lanham, MD: Rowman & Littlefield, 2005), pp. 19–50; Javier Hernandez, "China's 'Chairman of Everything': Behind Xi Jinping's Many Titles," *New York Times*, October 25, 2017, https://www.nytimes.com/2017/10/25/world/asia/china-xi-jinping-titles-chairman.html (accessed January 21, 2018).

12. Alice Miller, "The CCP's Central Committee's Leading Small Groups," *China Leadership Monitor* 26 (Fall 2008), http://www.chinaleadershipmonitor.org; Alice Miller, "More Already on Central Committee's Leading Small Groups," *China Leadership Monitor* 44 (Fall 2013), https://www.hoover.org/sites/default/files/research/docs/clm44am.pdf; Cary Huang, "How Leading Small Groups Help Xi Jinping and Other Party Leaders to Exert Power," *South China Morning Post*, January 20, 2014, http://www.scmp.com/news/china/article/1409118/how-leading-small-groups-help-xi-jinping-and-other-party-leaders-exert (accessed January 21, 2018).

13. Miller, "The CCP's Central Committee's Leading Small Groups."

14. Joel Wuthnow, "China's Much Heralded NSC Has Disappeared," *Foreign Policy*, June 30, 2016, http://foreignpolicy.com/2016/06/30/chinas-much-heralded-national-security-council-has-disappeared-nsc-xi-jinping/ (accessed January 21, 2018).

15. See among others Chen Jian, *Mao's China and the Cold War* (Chapel Hill: University of North Carolina Press, 2001).

16. Barbara Barnouin and Yu Changgen, *Chinese Foreign Policy during the Cultural Revolution* (New York: Columbia University Press, 1997).

17. Ezra Vogel, *Deng Xiaoping and the Transformation of China* (Cambridge, MA: Harvard University Press, 2012), pp. 91–119.

18. Vogel, *Deng Xiaoping and the Transformation of China*, pp. 266–348, 640–63.

19. Vogel, *Deng Xiaoping and the Transformation of China*, pp. 266–348.

20. Immanuel Hsu, *The Rise of Modern China* (New York: Oxford University Press, 2000), pp. 763–980.

21. Bonnie Glaser and Matthew Funaiole, *Xi Jinping's 19th Party Congress Speech Heralds Greater Assertiveness in Chinese Foreign Policy*, CSIS, October 26, 2017, https://www.csis.org/analysis/xi-jinpings-19th-party-congress-speech-heralds-greater-assertiveness-chinese-foreign-policy (accessed January 21, 2018); Rush Doshi, "Xi Jinping Just Made It Clear Where China's Foreign Policy Is Heading," *Washington Post*, October 25, 2017, https://www.washingtonpost.com/news/monkey-cage/wp/2017/10/25/xi-jinping-just-made-it-clear-where-chinas-foreign-policy-is-headed/?utm_term=.58d4595c23cc (accessed January 21, 2018).

22. Lampton, *The Making of Chinese Foreign and Security Policy in the Era of Reform*, pp. 1–38.

23. Lu Ning, "The Central Leadership, Supraministry Coordinating Bodies, State Council Ministries, and Party Departments," in Lampton, ed., *The Making of Chinese Foreign and Security Policy in the Era of Reform*, pp. 39–60; Wang, "Beijing's Incentive Structure," pp. 19–50.

24. Lampton, *The Making of Chinese Foreign and Security Policy in the Era of Reform*; Medeiros and Fravel, "China's New Diplomacy," pp. 22–35.

25. "Priorities Set for Handling Foreign Affairs," *China Daily*, August 24, 2006, p. 1.

26. Jakobson and Knox, *New Foreign Policy Actors in China*; David Shambaugh, "Coping with a Conflicted China," *Washington Quarterly* 34, no. 1 (Winter 2011): pp. 7–27.

27. Suisheng Zhao, *A Nation-State by Construction: Dynamics of Modern Chinese Nationalism* (Stanford, CA: Stanford University Press, 2004); Peter Gries, *China's New Nationalism* (Berkeley: University of California Press, 2004); Anne-Marie Brady, *Marketing Dictatorship: Propaganda and Thought Work in Contemporary China* (Lanham, MD: Rowman & Littlefield, 2008), pp. 151–74.

28. John Garver, *Foreign Relations of the People's Republic of China* (Englewood Cliffs, NJ: Prentice Hall, 1993), pp. 1–28.

29. Sources for this historical review include Warren I. Cohen, *America's Response to China: A History of Sino-American Relations* (New York: Columbia University Press, 2010).

30. Yan Xuetong, "The Instability of China-US Relations," *Chinese Journal of International Politics* 3, no. 3 (2010): pp. 1–30; Suisheng Zhao, "China's Pragmatic Nationalism: Is It Manageable?" *Washington Quarterly* 29, no. 1 (Winter 2005–6): pp. 131–44.

31. Among foreign studies on this subject, see David Kang, *China's Rising: Peace, Power and Order in East Asia* (New York: Columbia University Press, 2007).

32. Glaser and Funaiole, *Xi Jinping's 19th Party Congress Speech*; Doshi, "Xi Jinping Just Made It Clear."

33. Hu Guocheng, "Chinese Images of the United States: A Historical Review," in *Chinese Images of the United States*, ed. Carola McGiffert (Washington, DC: CSIS, 2006), pp. 3–8; Jakobson and Knox, *New Foreign Policy Actors in China*; Shambaugh, "Coping with a Conflicted China."

34. Lampton, *Same Bed, Different Dreams*, p. 60.

35. Wang Jisi, "From Paper Tiger to Real Leviathan: China's Images of the United States since 1949," in McGiffert, ed., *Chinese Images of the United States*, pp. 12–18; Zhao Lingmin, "Optimistic View of Sino-US Relations—Exclusive Interview with Professor Wang Jisi," *Nanfeng Chuang* (Guangzhou), October 8, 2008, pp. 50–53; Kenneth Lieberthal and Wang Jisi, *Assessing U.S.-China Strategic Mistrust* (Washington, DC: Brookings Institution John Thornton China Center, 2012).

36. Robert Sutter and Satu Limaye, *America's 2016 Election Debate on Asia Policy and Asian Reactions* (Honolulu: East-West Center, 2016), p. 21.

37. Rosalie Chen, "China Perceives America," *Journal of Contemporary China* 12, no. 35 (2003): pp. 288–92.

38. Robert Ross and Jiang Changbin, *Re-Examining the Cold War: U.S.-China Diplomacy 1954–1973* (Cambridge, MA: Harvard University Press, 2001), pp. 19–21; Lieberthal and Wang, *Assessing U.S.-China Strategic Mistrust*.

39. Wang, "From Paper Tiger to Real Leviathan"; Gong Li, "The Official Perspective: What Chinese Government Officials Think of America," in McGiffert, ed., *Chinese Images of the United States*, pp. 9–32.

40. The mix of challenge and opportunity posed by the United States for Chinese interests and policies in Asian and world affairs prompted differing assessments by Chinese and foreign specialists. Some emphasize positive and cooperative aspects of US-China relations. See Medeiros and Fravel, "China's New Diplomacy"; Jia Qingguo, "Learning to Live with the Hegemon: Evolution of China's Policy toward the United States," *Journal of Contemporary China* 14, no. 44 (August 2005): pp. 395–407; and Stephanie Kleine-Ahlbrandt and Andrew Small, "China's New Dictatorship Diplomacy," *Foreign Affairs* 87, no. 1 (January–February 2008): pp. 38–56; others emphasize more negative and competitive aspects. See Joshua Kurlantzick, *Charm Offensive: How China's Soft Power Is Transforming the World* (New Haven, CT: Yale University Press, 2007); US-China Economic and Security Review Commission, *Report to Congress*, 2008, http://www.uscc.gov; US Department of State, *China's Strategic Modernization: Report from the Secretary's International Security Advisory Board (ISAB) Task Force*, 2008, http://video1.washingtontimes.com/video/ChinaStrategicPlan.pdf (accessed December 27, 2008); People's Republic of China State Council Information Office, "China's National Defense in 2006," Beijing, December 29, 2006; Michael Pillsbury, *The Hundred-Year Marathon* (New York: Henry Holt, 2015).

41. Thomas Christensen, "The Advantages of an Assertive China," *Foreign Affairs* 90, no. 2 (March–April 2011): pp. 54–67.

42. Yan, "The Instability of China-US Relations"; Lampton, *The Three Faces of Chinese Power*, 164–74; Zhang Liping, "A Rising China and a Lonely Superpower America," in *Making New Partnership: A Rising China and Its Neighbors*, ed. Zhang Yunlin (Beijing: Social Sciences Academic Press, 2008), pp. 324–55; Wu Xinbo, "The End of the Silver Lining: A Chinese View of the U.S.-Japanese Alliance," *Washington Quarterly* 29, no. 1 (Winter 2006): pp. 119–30; Denny Roy, *Return of the Dragon: Rising China and Regional Security* (New York: Columbia University Press, 2013); Robert Blackwill and Ashley Tellis, *Revising U.S. Grand Strategy toward China* (Washington, DC: Council on Foreign Relations, *Council Special Report*, April 2015).

43. Robert Sutter, *China's Rise in Asia: Promises and Perils* (Lanham, MD: Rowman & Littlefield, 2005), p. 35. Among differing perspectives, see Lampton, *The Three Faces of Chinese Power*; Alastair Iain Johnston, "Is China a Status Quo Power?" *International Security* 24, no. 4 (Spring 2003): pp. 5–56; and Yong Deng and Thomas Moore, "China Views Globalization: Toward a New Great-Power Politics," *Washington Quarterly* 27, no. 3 (Summer 2004): pp. 117–36.

44. Robert Sutter, *Chinese Foreign Policy: Developments after Mao* (New York: Praeger, 1986), p. 5.

45. Sutter, *Chinese Foreign Policy*, p. 9.

46. Garver, *Foreign Relations of the People's Republic of China*, pp. 70–109.

47. Sutter, *Chinese Foreign Policy*, pp. 10–12.

48. James Mann, *About Face* (New York: Knopf, 1999), pp. 128–54.

49. Sutter, *China's Rise in Asia*, pp. 10–17.

50. Martin Indyk, Kenneth Lieberthal, and Michael O'Hanlon, *Bending History* (Washington, DC: Brookings Institution Press, 2012), pp. 24–69; Glaser and Funaiole, *Xi Jinping's 19th Party Congress Speech*; Michael Swaine, *The 19th Party Congress and Chinese Foreign Policy*, Carnegie Endowment for International Peace, October 16, 2017, http://carnegieendowment.org/2017/10/16/19th-party-congress-and-chinese-foreign-policy-pub-73432 (accessed January 21, 2018).

51. Harry Harding, "Has U.S. China Policy Failed?" *Washington Quarterly* 38, no. 3 (2015): 95–122; Blackwill and Tellis, *Revising U.S. Grand Strategy toward China*; Orville Schell and Susan Shirk, Chairs, *US Policy toward China: Recommendations for a New Administration* (New York: Asia Society, 2017).

52. *Russia-China Relations: Assessing Common Ground and Strategic Fault Lines* (National Bureau of Asian Research, July 2017), http://www.nbr.org/publications/issue.aspx?id=349 (accessed January 21, 2018).

Chapter Six

China's Changing Importance in World Affairs

The review of Chinese foreign policies and behavior in chapters 2 through 4 shows enormous change. Not surprisingly, the People's Republic of China's impact on and role in world affairs has changed dramatically as well. The introductory pages in chapter 1 show how China's contemporary rise as a world power second only to the United States is based on China's rapidly growing economic importance, advancing military power, and increasing prominence in bilateral and multilateral diplomacy and global governance. These important changes support the widespread assessments that China has advanced to the point of challenging the existing international order in the Asia-Pacific region and more broadly. When combined with recent judgments of economic and international decline on the part of the United States and other developed countries on account of economic weaknesses and various external and internal failings and constraints, China's rise is commonly viewed to represent a fundamental power shift in regional and world politics.

As noted in chapter 1, this book judges that such forecasts of a power shift resulting in Chinese primacy and leadership in the Asia-Pacific and broader world affairs are premature and may be wrong. This chapter provides two areas of assessment that assist readers in understanding the more balanced and realistic examination of China's actual influence in regional and world affairs presented in the three following chapters.

The first area of assessment highlights instances of the People's Republic of China's past impact on regional and world affairs to show that China's strategic and political importance was often seen by major powers and states in Asia as intensely important. The perceived importance of China and its international influence loomed especially large in the Asia-Pacific region and as part of the competition for international leadership by the United States and the Soviet Union during the Cold War. At several junctures during this period, China's actual impact in the calculus of US, Soviet, and Asian leaders appeared more salient to their important interests than does the impact of rising China in recent years.

The second area of assessment involves examination in some detail of the key elements in China's contemporary regional and world influence: economic development, diplomacy and other involvement in global governance, and military power. Showing China's constraints and limitations as well as advances in these three areas provides a foundation for the more nuanced and sober view of Chinese influence in world relationships detailed in the three following chapters.

Today's China's greatest importance is as the world's second-largest and fastest-growing economy. China's modernization and economic advance spread and deepen throughout the vast country and into all corners of the world. They support active diplomacy in multilateral and bilateral relations. They also provide the basis for the fastest-growing military modernization of any country in the post–Cold War period, and thereby change the security calculus of China's neighbors and other concerned powers, notably the United States.

China's role in today's world has depended fundamentally on the success of the economic reforms and international outreach begun in the post-Mao period by Deng Xiaoping and his colleagues and their successors. China's growing international economic footprint has increased its heretofore limited importance to a wide range of countries in the developed and developing world as a trading partner, a recipient and source of investment, and a creditor.

Prior to that time, China exerted important influence in world affairs in different ways and for different reasons. As discussed in chapters 2 and 3, China's vast size, strategic location, revolutionary and nationalistic zeal, and broad popular mobilization made China a formidable opponent for both the United States and the Soviet Union and an important determinant in the foreign policy calculations of neighboring Asian countries. China's importance grew as it developed nuclear weapons and the ballistic missiles to deliver them to targets as far away as Washington, DC. Ironically, China's prevailing backwardness in economic development for much of this period made China more difficult for the US and Soviet superpowers to deter and to counter adverse Chinese moves, thereby increasing China's importance in their calculations.

Thus, one can argue that the Truman and early Eisenhower administrations' focus on China's importance in the Korean War, and President Lyndon Johnson's preoccupation with the protracted war in Vietnam, where hundreds of thousands of Chinese soldiers served in North Vietnam and Laos, gave more importance to managing relations with China than any US president in the post–Cold War period. Subsequently, with the establishment of a rough balance of power and influence between the United States and the Soviet Union after two decades of Cold War, China came to be seen by both superpowers as the most important independent source of international influence in world affairs. Beginning with the Nixon administration, the United States assiduously sought China's support, giving relations with China very high importance in US strategic calculations. The record seems to show that the importance US policy gave to relations with China during the late 1960s until the early 1980s was even more than the relatively high importance US policy has given to China in the contemporary period. For its part, the leadership in Moscow under the Soviet Union during this period clearly devoted more attention to relations with China than post-Soviet Russia has ever devoted to China. Details showing China's actual and often remarkable international impact during the forty years of the Cold War follow.

CHINA'S INITIAL COLD WAR INFLUENCE

US and Soviet competition for influence in Asia in the early years of the Cold War at first appeared secondary to their competition in Europe and the Middle East. The American support for Chiang Kai-shek against the Communist-led forces of Mao Zedong in the Chinese Civil War ended with Chiang's defeat and retreat to Taiwan in 1949. The failure of US policy in China, the so-called loss of China, fed into often partisan debates in American public opinion on how the United States should be positioned in dealing with Mao's government and new realities in China. Mao's leaning to the Soviet Union in the Cold War and the signing of the Sino-Soviet alliance in February 1950 added to growing concerns in America that the Soviet Union and its partners were posing direct threats to the United States. [1]

The North Korean attack on South Korea in June 1950, which had the backing of Moscow and Beijing, represented a tipping point in American calculations and behavior. The US-led ring of containment against Soviet-backed expansion in Europe and the Middle East was now expanded to Asia and concentrated on China. The upshot included two and a half years of hard combat with Chinese forces in Korea. Despite American advanced weaponry and control of air and sea access, China resorted to manpower-intensive battlefield and logistical measures that allowed their forces to fight the Americans to a standstill. The American commitment to protect Taiwan against China grew into a formal defense alliance as part of the various treaties, military deployments, and foreign assistance arrangements featured in the strong US presence along China's eastern flank. [2]

The United States countered two major episodes of military confrontation in the Taiwan Strait—in 1954 and again in 1958—with strong military measures and threats to use nuclear weapons against China. The Americans also supported the French against Communist forces backed by China in Indochina, and became more actively involved in the region following the French withdrawal in 1954. In the 1959 uprising against Chinese rule in Tibet the United States clandestinely supported the Tibetan resistance with training and weapons. The hidden American strategy in this period was for the United States to differentiate between the Soviet Union and China, seeking to exert heavy pressure on China while showing some moderation toward, and engaging in some pragmatic interchange with, post-Stalin Soviet leaders. The intent was to exacerbate differences between the Sino-Soviet partners on how to deal with the United States. [3]

While Stalin was in a position to dictate terms in the Sino-Soviet alliance, post-Stalin leaders headed by Nikita Khrushchev at various times sought Chinese support or sought to offset Chinese initiatives in policy areas of importance to the USSR. Khrushchev seemed confident enough in his struggle for top power in the post-Stalin leadership to spend two weeks in China on the occasion of the PRC's fifth anniversary in October 1954. He endeavored to appeal to China by lauding China's role in leading revolutionary forces in Asia, agreeing to return Soviet-held territory to China, and supporting China in an emerging military confrontation with Chiang Kai-shek's US-backed forces in the Taiwan Strait. [4]

After Khrushchev rose to undisputed leadership with the demotion of Georgy Malenkov in 1955, he found that China often complicated his policies and reforms. Mao opposed Khrushchev's denunciation of Stalin's excesses in his secret speech to the Soviet Party Congress in February 1956. The Chinese supported the leadership of Poland, where the Communist Party in October 1956 resisted pressure from Khrushchev to avoid what was deemed by Moscow as excessive nationalism and defiance of Soviet instructions. In contrast, Chinese leaders supported the intervention of Soviet troops into Hungary in November 1956 because the existing Communist regime was seen to be unable to contain burgeoning mass movements that were increasingly taking outright anti-Communist forms. [5]

Mao opposed Khrushchev's moderate approach to Yugoslavia's Josip Tito and his periodic pragmatic relations with the United States. And at the international gathering of Communist leaders in Moscow in 1957, Mao's call for a tougher stance against the United States stood in contrast to Khrushchev's policies. Mao later rebuffed Khrushchev's efforts to coordinate Sino-Soviet military operations, and his launching of the Great Leap Forward and the Taiwan Strait crisis in 1958 were seen by Khrushchev as reckless and involving gross misuse of massive Soviet material support to China. By 1960 aid relations were ended and polemics intensified over differences within the international communist movement, relations with the United States, and appropriate paths to development. China sided with dissidents in the international communist movement, notably Enver Hoxha of Albania, and took a high profile in support of newly formed nations and liberation movements in Africa and elsewhere in the developing world. As such, China competed with the Soviet Union as well as with the West for international influence.[6]

As discussed in chapter 2, China's Communist-led neighbors North Korea and North Vietnam maneuvered between Moscow and Beijing in order to support their interests in opposition to the United States and its allies and associates. Many other Chinese neighbors saw their interests best served by close alignment with the United States in opposition to China, though the most important US Asian ally, Japan, endeavored to reach out to China and became its major international trading partner after the collapse of the Sino-Soviet alliance. Leading nonaligned Asian countries, notably India and Indonesia, moved to establish closer ties with China before adverse developments in the 1960s caused them to reverse course and become deeply suspicious of China and its intentions.

THE "GREAT POWER TRIANGLE"

The opening of Chinese relations with the United States and many other countries beginning during a period of violent Chinese conflict with the Soviet Union in the late 1960s reflected contrasting views of China's international importance and influence. Scholarship shows that American strategists and other international observers saw China weakened by the massive economic disaster of the Great Leap Forward (1958–61) followed by years of violent and disruptive governance during the Cultural Revolution begun in 1966. China was isolated in international affairs. Its strident emphasis on economic self-reliance sharply limited foreign trade, and technology transfer, educational exchanges, and other interaction conducive to economic modernization were minimal, pushing China and its self-righteous and self-reliant leadership further behind in economic development compared with many of its neighbors in Asia. Most Chinese initiatives in support of newly emerging states in the developing world collapsed as a result of territorial and political differences, Chinese excesses during the so-called Red Guard diplomacy years of the Cultural Revolution, and Soviet and Western competition. By 1968 only a small handful of developing countries had workable foreign relations with China.[7]

Nevertheless, the prevailing perception of China during this period was one of great international influence. The reasons were predominantly strategic. A rough balance of influence emerged between the rising Soviet Union and the United States. America's failure in the massive and protracted war effort in Vietnam headed the list of its economic, social, and strategic problems. While the United States appeared in decline with no good answer to its predicament in Vietnam, the Soviet Union appeared to reach parity with US strategic weaponry. The more confident and assertive leadership of Leonid Brezhnev was expanding Soviet commitments and involvement into Asia and other parts of the world that further complicated US interests and was seen to pose a direct threat to Maoist China.[8]

As explained in chapter 3, the Soviet expansion and various US and Chinese weaknesses and vulnerabilities provided the foundation for the opening of China's relationship with the Nixon administration and a variety of other countries as well as the United Nations. For much of the next twenty years, US officials sought closer ties with China as a means to right the balance in Cold War competition with the USSR. American interest in the so-called US-Soviet-Chinese Great Power Triangle gave China high priority in US foreign policy calculations. The American interest was shared by many of its allies and associates, who also were anxious to work closely with China as a means to counter perceived dangers posed by Soviet expansion. Thus, US-aligned countries in Europe, the Asia-Pacific region, and the Western Hemisphere moved quickly to establish formal diplomatic relations with newly welcoming China. Companies in these countries and the international economic institutions supported by these countries prepared for what turned out to be an enormous increase in economic interchange once the post-Mao economic reforms took hold in China in the late 1970s.[9]

Moscow for its part endeavored to deal with an emerging international united front with the United States, its allies, and China at the center. On the one hand, it employed a thinly disguised containment effort directed against China in Asia, involving Soviet treaties and strategic agreements with Mongolia, Vietnam, and India, large Soviet military deployments in Mongolia and along the disputed Sino-Soviet border, close military cooperation and bases in Vietnam, active air and naval patrols along China's maritime periphery, and arms sales and military cooperation with India. On the other hand, Soviet leaders endeavored to seek common ground in détente efforts with the United States and Western countries as a means to reduce East-West tensions and undermine the Western-Chinese united front effort. The Soviet Union also periodically made efforts to ease tensions with China in ways that seemed to threaten US and Western interests.[10]

The overlap of US-Soviet and Sino-Soviet rivalry complicated the foreign policy calculations of China's Communist-ruled neighbors, North Korea and Vietnam. Vietnam decided to align with Moscow as it invaded Cambodia and expelled the Chinese-backed Khmer Rouge regime in 1978, setting the stage for China's limited invasion of Vietnam and ten years of confrontation and conflict in Sino-Vietnamese relations.[11] North Korea's Kim Il Sung was more flexible, as he continued to maneuver between China and the Soviet Union for assistance and other benefits that would strengthen North Korea against South Korea and its backer, the United States.[12]

America's non-Communist allies and associates in Southeast Asia were alarmed by the US decline and pullback from the region after the defeat in Vietnam in 1975. They shored up their security by reaching out to China, which was reaching out to them in order to deal with the common danger posed by the expansion of Soviet-backed Vietnam into Cambodia. With its interest in a common front against the USSR, China welcomed Japan's improvements of its military capabilities within the framework of the US-Japan alliance and the coordination of its foreign policies with both Washington and Beijing against perceived Soviet expansion. South Korea's closer ties with China developed slowly, focusing at first on mutually beneficial economic exchanges between dynamic South Korean enterprises and the newly opening Chinese economy. China was reluctant to develop closer political and security ties out of concern for its relations with North Korea. [13]

As discussed in chapter 3, the importance of China among the developing countries in Africa, the Middle East, and elsewhere in the so-called third world was more muted during this period. China's siding with the United States and its allies, including various right-wing regimes (e.g., the Shah of Iran; Chile's Augusto Pinochet; Zaire's Sese Mobutu) in the developing world alienated elite and public opinion in developing countries that remained friendly to Moscow and suspicious of the West. China's call for developing countries to resist the expansion of the Soviet Union into Africa, Southwest and Southeast Asia, and Latin America was not backed by much concrete Chinese support for these states. Beijing began to cut back its aid efforts and began directly competing with developing countries for international assistance provided by UN and regional financial and economic organizations.

CHINA'S RECENT ROLE IN THE WORLD ECONOMY, GOVERNANCE, AND DEFENSE

China's importance and engagement in the world economy and in international governance have grown dramatically in the post–Cold War period. Measuring the actual importance of China to the international economy and assessing the actual significance of Chinese involvement in international governing bodies remain difficult, however. Some specialists in China and abroad view Chinese leaders as increasingly confident as they use China's large economic power to exert influence in line with China's long-standing ambitions of greater regional and global power. [14] Others, myself included, view the Chinese leaders as continuing to follow contingent policies based on changing assessments of the costs and benefits for China that in turn depend on international and domestic circumstances. The amount of influence China exerts on the world economy is growing, but so is China's dependence on key variables in the world economy that the Chinese leadership does not control, including substantial decline in the growth of world trade, protectionist tendencies among developed and developing countries, secure sea lines of communication for China's wide-ranging foreign trade and access to oil and other vital commodities, and international disapproval of the environmental and other negative impacts of China's energy-intensive development at home and economic investments abroad.[15] Such dependence limits the amount of influence China actually exerts in international affairs.

Meanwhile, China's leaders use greater engagement in multilateral organizations defensively, notably to protect Chinese interests from unwanted US interventions, as they use such involvement to enhance China's international prominence and importance. In the second decade of the twenty-first century, the reality seems to be that China has become a major power with a large and growing economy that is heavily dependent on important international and internal variables. Against this background, China's leaders—despite massive self-promotion by Chinese publicists extolling China's international largesse—generally continue to eschew major risks, costs, or commitments involved in providing regional or international common goods or asserting international leadership unless they have direct bearing on carefully and usually narrowly defined Chinese national interests. Such practices limit the amount of influence China actually exerts in international affairs. Against this background, Xi Jinping at the Nineteenth Communist Party Congress in November 2017 indicated that countries should follow the Chinese development model, but soon after he disavowed China as such an international model.[16]

Thus, while China has a large footprint in world affairs and often seeks the limelight in international meetings and the councils of international governance, China also has been widely seen as a "free rider" or at least a "cheap rider" in undertaking costs and commitments for common regional and global goods. In general terms, China is strongly wedded to the "win-win" approach in international relations. If China is going to extend effort and resources for a common good, it has to be shown that such actions will result in tangible benefits for China defined in a fairly narrow Chinese win-set. For example, in providing funds for developing countries, Beijing is usually careful in assuring that the Chinese outlays will be paid back. The repayment methods vary, including monetary repayment or repayment in commodities. Several developing countries have been so burdened by repayment of Chinese loans that the arrangements they have worked out with China for repayment have involved China gaining direct control of factories, facilities, or other equity in the country or Chinese control of long-term leases involving large tracts of territory in the countries. Critics label this overall phenomenon as the "Chinese Debt Trap."[17]

Meanwhile, China repeatedly publicizes its role as the largest participant in UN peacekeeping efforts among the permanent members of the UN Security Council. It has rarely pointed out that its contributions are largely noncombatants, and thus generally its personnel are positioned out of harm's way. It has avoided highlighting the fact that the Chinese participants, like those from Bangladesh and other large contributors to UN peacekeeping missions, get paid from the UN peacekeeping budget. And China has rarely noted that the size of its peacekeeping budget contribution took many years to rise from a very low level to its level today, which is in line with China's economic importance. In 2012 China contributed the same small amount to UN peacekeeping as Italy. Also, China engaged in a similar approach, resisting for many years increases in its annual dues to the United Nations, even though China has long strongly supported the United Nations as the ultimate arbiter of international issues. In 2012, China paid the same level of UN dues as Spain. Against this background, UN observers were notably excited when President Xi Jinping announced during his first visit to the United Nations in 2015 that China would bear a much greater share in paying UN dues and peacekeeping funds and would provide additional special assistance for peacekeeping. Beijing has followed through with these commitments. [18]

Evidence of self-serving Chinese behavior carefully nurturing tangible benefits for China and eschewing risks and costs for regional and global goods includes China's continuing to receive more than $6 billion in foreign assistance annually from UN programs, the World Bank, the Asian Development Bank, and a variety of OECD (Organisation for Economic Co-operation and Development) countries. For example, China in 2008 renewed long-term agreements with the World Bank to provide continued loans to China for several years into the future, and in 2010 it renewed for five more years the generous contributions to Chinese development of the UN Development Program (UNDP) and more than twenty other UN-affiliated agencies offering assistance in China. Such reception comes at a time when China's economic condition is so flush with cash that it has more than $3 trillion in foreign exchange reserves. In 2015, the *Economist* reported that "as recently at 2010 it [China] was still a net recipient of foreign assistance." [19] In 2017, the Donald Trump administration reportedly balked at a World Bank effort to get more funds for development loans because China was the biggest recipient of World Bank development loans, valued at $2.4 billion. [20] A more generous China might be inclined to encourage some of this foreign assistance to go to more needy nations in a less advantageous economic position than China. [21]

The reasons for China's continued receipt of large amounts of foreign assistance and its reluctance to spend abroad in the interests of regional and global governance appear related to Chinese domestic requirements. The range of obligations inside China requiring resources seems wide and deep.

Chinese leaders appear disinclined to turn away foreign assistance that benefits these domestic requirements or to extend efforts and expenses abroad that
could be employed for domestic Chinese concerns.[22]

When one contrasts the Chinese cheap riding of recent years with Chinese
actions abroad in previous decades, one sees episodes of remarkable leadership by Mao Zedong and Deng Xiaoping that obviously added to Chinese
influence in world affairs. Mao undertook enormous commitments and risks
in confronting the United States in Korea, in supporting the Communist
insurgents in Indochina against the French and against the United States, and
in probing and wearing down the US containment. His commitment to the
international struggle against Soviet hegemonism showed a willingness to
endure great sacrifice while encouraging the United States and its allies and
associates to hold the line against the USSR. As explained earlier, Deng
Xiaoping followed in Mao's path in undertaking great costs and risking
Chinese national security in order to teach Vietnam a "lesson" over its invasion of Cambodia in 1978. The Chinese lesson also applied to the United
States and its allies and associates, showing them that China was prepared to
stand up to Soviet expansion and that they should do the same.

There are few instances in the post–Cold War period that compare to such
episodes demonstrating international influence and leadership under Mao
and Deng. In 2017, China's continued strong reluctance to take risks in
pressing its neighbor, North Korea, to halt its nuclear weapons program that
grossly endangered regional and international security showed clear limits on
Chinese willingness to take potentially costly actions for the sake of the
broader regional and global order. Xi Jinping's signature Belt and Road
Initiative (BRI) was still largely a vision in 2017 but there was plenty of
evidence that China's purported largesse in this multifaceted endeavor would
continue China's emphasis on "win-win" with the Chinese win-set involving
Beijing being repaid for loans and gaining economic and other tangible benefits in return for its loans and other avowed assistance. This gap in China
undertaking risks, costs, and commitments associated with other influential
great powers of the past and with the United States up to the present helps to
explain why China's recent big international footprint and expanding international activism often do not translate into international influence.[23]

China's Economic Importance

From 1979 to 2014, the average annual growth rate of China's gross domestic product (GDP) was about 10 percent. By 2010, China became the world's
second-largest economy, after the United States. In 2011, it became the largest manufacturer, surpassing the United States. In 2012, it became the
world's largest trader. China also has become the second-largest destination
of foreign investment, the largest holder of foreign exchange reserves, and

the largest creditor nation.[24] Several predictions said that China was on track to surpass the United States, the world's largest economy, in the next decade.[25]

Chinese growth rates declined steadily from 12.8 percent in 2012 to 6.7 percent in 2016. Chinese foreign-trade growth stopped and overall trade was less in 2016 than 2015. Trade levels grew again in 2017. In 2013, Chinese leaders began a wide range of over sixty sets of mainly economic reforms to deal with existing or anticipated economic weaknesses involving the inefficient practices of state-owned enterprises (SOEs) and the state banking system, resource and energy scarcities, massive environmental problems, and China's strong dependence on the health of the global trading economy, which stalled following the financial crisis and recession that began in 2008.[26] Active foreign direct investment (FDI) in China continued and growing Chinese investment abroad surpassed China's FDI in 2016.[27]

Trade continues to play a major role in China's rapid economic growth. It features strong dependence on foreign investment coming into China and China managing trade relations in ways that provide China with a large trade surplus each year. Foreign-invested enterprises (FIEs) are responsible for a significant level of China's foreign trade; FIEs accounted for 43.4 percent of Chinese exports and 45.9 percent of Chinese imports in January–April 2017. There were reportedly 445,244 FIEs registered in China in 2010, employing 55.2 million workers, or 15.9 percent of the urban workforce.[28]

According to the United Nations Conference on Trade and Development (UNCTAD), from 1990 to 2015, global annual FDI flows grew from $205 billion to $1,746 billion (up 752 percent), while the stock of FDI rose from $2,197 billion to $26,729 billion (up 1,116 percent). China's global FDI inflows grew rapidly after it began to liberalize its trade regime in 1979 and joined the World Trade Organization (WTO) in 2001. In 2016, China's FDI inflows were estimated by UNCTAD at $134 billion.[29]

The cumulative level of FDI in China from 1979 to the end of 2010 was over $1 trillion; about 40 percent of the FDI in China came from Hong Kong, 10 percent from the British Virgin Islands (a well-known tax haven), 8 percent from Japan, and 7 percent from the United States. The largest sector for FDI flows in China in recent years was manufacturing, which often accounted for over half of total annual FDI in China.[30] As noted above, a bit less than half of China's foreign trade is accounted for by foreign-invested firms in China.

The combination of trade surpluses and FDI added to China's foreign exchange reserves, the largest in the world, valued at $3 trillion in 2017. Against this background, China's outbound direct investment increased rapidly in recent years. According to UNCTAD, from 2007 to 2016, China's FDI outflows rose from $27 billion to $183 billion in 2016, a 578 percent increase (while inflows over this period grew by 60 percent). According to the UN, in 2016, China was the second-largest source of global FDI and the third largest FDI recipient.[31]

There are differing views among Chinese officials and international specialists about how important China is in international economic affairs. The views differ as well about what this means for overall Chinese foreign relations, especially China's expanding role in regional and global international organizations that deal with economic as well as political, security, environmental, and other matters of importance to the world community in the post–Cold War period.

According to many Chinese officials and international observers, China's growing economy and its burgeoning international trade and investment relationships provide a solid foundation for China to play an ever more important role in influencing and managing world affairs. In 2011, a debate emerged in mainstream Chinese media over whether or not China's economic success had reached a point where it provided a model to be followed by other countries. Many in the West in recent years saw the emergence of a "Beijing consensus" encompassing the main features of China's development approach; they judged that the Chinese government was in the process of spreading this development model throughout the world—a trend they viewed as adverse to Western values and goals, summed up as what they called the "Washington consensus."[32]

On the other hand, senior Chinese officials for many years tended to eschew association with a Beijing consensus or a China model that would oppose Western norms. The Chinese leaders duly criticized Western efforts to impose their values and development norms on other countries through conditions on foreign assistance, sanctions, and other means of interfering in other states' internal affairs. In their assessment foreign countries should be free to choose their desired development path, and should not feel obliged to follow one model or another. Some Chinese economic specialists were frank in highlighting the many shortcomings of the Chinese development model, suggesting that China had a long way to go before its economic development experience could provide a model for others to emulate.[33]

The above debate may be ending. Reflecting the rising Chinese government assertiveness in various aspects of foreign relations under the leadership of Xi Jinping, the Nineteenth Chinese Communist Party Congress marking the beginning of Xi's second five-year term as party leader featured commentary by Xi that the Chinese development model provided an important example for developing countries to follow. As noted earlier in this chapter, Xi a few weeks later clouded the situation by asserting that China was *not* such an international development model.[34]

Based on its status as the largest trading partner with Africa, Brazil, and most of its Asian neighbors; the top producer of steel and other metals, cement, ships, cars, electronic goods, and textiles; the leading consumer of many categories of international raw materials; and the world's largest creditor nation,[35] China is looked to increasingly as a leader in Asian and world affairs. A wide range of developing and developed countries that didn't consider China very important in the past, now give high priority to relations with China. As discussed in later chapters of this book, government leaders throughout the world often consult closely with Chinese leaders in bilateral exchanges and in international organizations, endeavoring to influence and govern international affairs to their mutual benefit.

Conforming to some of the significant norms of economic globalization, Chinese leaders notably put aside past Chinese government suspicion of Asian and international multilateral organizations.[36] They have embraced burgeoning Asian and international economic groupings, and they have shown sometimes more guarded cooperation with other international organizations dealing with political, security, and other issues. They implicitly and sometimes explicitly challenge existing international economic groupings; they led in the establishment of the Asian Infrastructure Investment Bank, the New Development Bank of the so-called BRICS countries (Brazil, Russia, India, China, and South Africa), and the massive China-led Belt and Road Initiative (BRI) involving scores of developing and developed countries. On balance, Chinese engagement has met with the general satisfaction of other regional and international participants.

Against this background, a number of foreign specialists and commentators in recent years have portrayed China as a leader in international economic affairs, surpassing Japan, India, and the European powers, as it closes the gap with the United States.[37] Thus, many commonly assert that China has become an economic superpower whose continuing rise will require perhaps painful and difficult adjustments on the part of the United States and other heretofore leading powers in the international economy. The latter will need to give way to China and its rising influence.

A contrasting view of China's international economic importance comes from foreign specialists and occasionally some Chinese officials who are diffident about Chinese economic power and influence in world affairs. They frequently emphasize important limitations and preoccupations at home and abroad that act as a brake on China's adopting a strong leadership role anytime soon in international economic and other world affairs. Indeed, a fundamental premise of the Chinese government for many years has been to stress China's adherence to the goals of peace and development; specialists see this emphasis flowing from the fact that Chinese authorities face many obstacles and problems at home and a variety of actual or potential obstacles abroad. Chinese leaders need to encourage and sustain a peaceful and harmonious world order as they deal with these concerns and pursue a longer-term goal of developing China's "comprehensive national power." I agree with this line of Chinese thinking. Supporting evidence includes significant obstacles in the path of China becoming an economic superpower or taking on the obligations of world leadership in the next decade. [38]

The arguments of the Chinese and foreign observers who are diffident about China's emerging power and influence in international economics and global governance start with the judgment that both China's future international role and the stability of the government led by the Chinese Communist Party (CCP) depend heavily on healthy growth of the Chinese economy. This in turn depends on the overall health of the world economy and on the Chinese government's effective implementation of reforms conducive to economic growth. The targets of economic and related reform in China are many, posing ongoing challenges for China's future economic growth and stability. [39]

The weaknesses and challenges include:

- *State-owned enterprises:* Accounting for about one-third of Chinese industrial production and employing a large part of China's urban workers, SOEs put a heavy strain on China's economy. Over half are believed to lose money and must be supported by subsidies, mainly through state banks.
- *Uneven economic growth:* The global economic crisis since 2008 demonstrated to the Chinese government the dangers of relying too heavily on foreign trade and investment for economic growth. Efforts to reform the economy to bring it more into line with international and domestic realities have stalled as Beijing—pursuing growth seen as needed for political stability—continues large production, causing gluts on the world market and sharp price declines.
- *An inflexible currency policy:* China does not allow its currency to float and therefore must make large-scale purchases of dollars to keep the exchange rate within certain target levels.
- *The banking system:* Banking in China faces several major difficulties because of its financial support of SOEs and its failure to operate solely on market-based principles. Results include excessive and wasteful production of unneeded goods and rising debt levels.
- *The agricultural system:* This system has been highly inefficient because of government policies that have sought to maintain a high degree of self-sufficiency in grains.
- *Rule of law:* The lack of the rule of law in China has led to widespread government corruption, financial speculation, and misallocation of investment funds.
- *Poor government regulatory environment:* China maintains a weak and relatively decentralized government structure to regulate economic activity.

- *Social issues:* A number of social problems have arisen from China's rapid economic growth and extensive reforms. These include a widening of income disparities between coastal and interior regions and between urban and rural parts of China and bankruptcies and worker layoffs.
- *Growing pollution:* The level of pollution in China continues to worsen, posing serious health risks for the population.

Internationally, economic growth and increased trade and investment enhance China's prominence, but increased trade and investment with neighbors in Asia does not automatically place China in a leadership position in Asia, much less in other areas farther from China's borders. Looking at China's profile in neighboring Asian areas, the growth in trade and South Korean investment in China provided the lead elements in improving China–South Korean relations, arguably one of the areas of greatest success in China's foreign policy in the first decade of the twenty-first century.[40] A similar pattern of Chinese trade and Southeast Asian investment in China has seen China advance markedly in relations with the countries of the Association of Southeast Asian Nations (ASEAN). Burgeoning Asian trade networks of processing trade involving Southeast Asia and China pushed China ahead of the United States as ASEAN's top trading partner. The Chinese government also set the pace in economic and other relations with the group of ten Southeast Asian states with initiatives involving a China-ASEAN free-trade agreement. China's BRI since 2014 has devoted special attention to Southeast Asia.[41]

Nevertheless, the strong economic links were not sufficient to prevent a serious downturn in China's relations with South Korea and with several Southeast Asian governments at various times over the past ten years. The disputes ranged from the North Korean threat to differences over territorial claims. That better economic ties sometimes do not automatically translate into good overall relations also showed graphically in China's relations with Japan. Booming trade with Japan and strong investment in China by Japanese businesses have helped to moderate political and security tensions between China and the neighboring government. Yet the Chinese government more often than not has had difficulty in improving strained relations with Japan, which feature periodic and hard-to-predict outbursts of intense Chinese pressure, including extralegal trade sanctions and violence directed at Japan and Japanese properties and people in China over sensitive issues of sovereignty and security between the two powers. Myanmar for many years was isolated from and sanctioned by the West and very dependent on economic interchange with China. Yet in 2011 the government sharply shifted course and reached out to developed countries, thereby undermining China's leading role in the country's economic development. Taiwan is by far the most dependent of China's neighbors on trade and economic relations with

China. Yet such dependence did not offset the landslide victory of Tsai Ing-wen and her party in the 2016 elections on a platform calling for less dependence on China.

International Governance: Increasing but Still Selective Involvement

China's growing involvement with and dependence on the world economy head the list of reasons explaining China's broadening and deepening involvement with various multilateral organizations. As noted in chapter 1, scholars and specialists have seen remarkable changes and increased Chinese activism in Asian regional multilateral organizations, with China in recent years taking a leading role in creating such structures as the China-ASEAN free-trade agreement and a regional security body that includes Russia and four central Asian states known as the Shanghai Cooperation Organization (SCO). The Chinese approach in these endeavors strives to meet the interests of the other participants while ensuring that Chinese interests of development and stability are well served. China also has participated actively in recent years in loosely structured global groups, notably the G-20, involving the world's twenty leading powers, and the BRICS—Brazil, Russia, India, China, and South Africa. The latter is one of several international groupings China has supported that compete with existing institutions led by Western powers and endorse state-directed policies and practices at odds with the liberal international order backed by the United States and its allies. [42]

China's approach to multilateralism has changed markedly since it became an active participant in such endeavors on entry into the United Nations in 1971. At one level of analysis, there has been a steady trend since then toward closer Chinese government cooperation with the United Nations and an ever wider range of multilateral organizations and the international norms they support. The record of Chinese adherence to multilateral guidelines and norms remains mixed, however. [43]

Chinese engagement with international economic organizations has been the most active and positive. These organizations provide numerous material benefits for China's development, and China's active participation ensures that China will play an important role in decisions affecting the world economy, on which Chinese development depends. There are some limits on Chinese cooperation with international economic institutions. For example, China does not cooperate closely with international organizations that seek to regulate scarcities in the global oil market. Rather than rely on the global energy market and international groups that seek to facilitate its smooth operation, China pursues an independent approach to ensure that it has the energy it needs for economic growth. China gave little attention to international complaints of rising energy prices and other negative results for the world oil market that resulted, for example, when at times in the past two decades China purchased foreign oil rights at high prices.[44]

China's recently more active and positive approach in Asian regional economic, security, and political organizations seemed for several years to reflect the Chinese leadership's goal not to be seen as a danger by its neighbors and the region's dominant outside power, the United States. As noted in chapter 4 and chapter 7, China's emphasis on its "peaceful rise," following the road of "peaceful development," and seeking of a "harmonious world" were part of its efforts to avoid actions that could prompt foreign measures that would work against the continuing rise of Chinese power. China's attentive diplomacy and periodic deference to the interests of its neighbors helped to reassure most of them about its intentions, giving rise to significant improvement in Chinese relations throughout its periphery. On the other hand, some saw the concurrent rise of Chinese military power and recent international assertiveness over territorial claims and other issues, along with the growth of China's economic power and active multilateral diplomacy, as inconsistent with China's avowed peaceful intentions and posing a possibly serious threat to the security of Asian states and regional stability.[45] At the Nineteenth Chinese Communist Party Congress in October 2017, Xi Jinping and his colleagues clarified this situation by making plain that China's power had reached a new stage and that the dictates of Deng Xiaoping urging keeping a low profile in foreign affairs no longer apply. China now seeks forthrightly to reunify and rejuvenate the country as Asia's leader and a global power. Those neighboring powers and others with an interest in preserving the regional status quo, notably including the United States, are adversely affected by China's plan. Beijing gives their concerns little attention, setting the stage for friction and tension.[46]

China has been reluctant to commit to international norms regarding regulation of environmental practices if they infringe on Chinese efforts to expand economic growth. As a result, media reports in late 2012 cited studies showing that China emits twice the carbon dioxide of the United States just three years after it overtook the United States as the world's largest greenhouse gas emitter.[47] More recently, China's stronger interest in domestic energy efficiency and curbing pollution in the country resulted in energy-use policies more in line with international climate-change ambitions. Notably, Beijing now saw its overall interests better served by putting aside China's past opposition to undertaking domestic economic changes to meet standards in proposals at the Copenhagen Climate Change Conference in 2009, and it supported the requirements of the Paris Climate Change agreement in 2016. With the incoming Trump administration threatening to withdraw from the Paris agreement, Xi Jinping and Chinese publicists positioned Beijing as the world leader in climate change efforts.[48] The Chinese government's approach to international human rights regimes has long focused on engaging in protracted dialogue and cooperating where possible or needed in order to avoid international sanction while nonetheless consistently avoiding significant commitments that would impede its ability to coerce those who are seen as challenging the Communist government.[49] Likewise with international arms control measures, China's cooperation has grown steadily in the past two decades, though it continues to avoid commitments that would impede its independence in certain areas sensitive to important Chinese interests.[50]

Specialists differed in assessing what this record of greater involvement actually meant for the Chinese government's attitude to international norms supported by the multilateral groups. A prevailing view held that Beijing at the start of the post–Cold War period was particularly reluctant to allow such participation to curb its freedom of action regarding key issues of security and sovereignty or to require costly economic or other commitments. Its participation involved maneuvering to pursue narrow national interests without great concern for international norms, primarily burnishing China's global image, deflecting international opprobrium, and securing Chinese interests more effectively.[51]

Over time, the Chinese government appeared truly to have accepted cooperative multilateralism as a means to take advantage of its strengths as an attractive economic and trading opportunity.[52] A more mixed picture has continued to prevail on human rights, environmental, energy, and international security questions, including arms control. While more cooperative in several instances, China remains concerned to defend narrow Chinese national interests, and it is particularly on guard in the face of possible US-led efforts to constrain Chinese power.[53]

Belt and Road Initiative (BRI)

While not a formal international organization, Xi Jinping's most important foreign policy program, the so-called Belt and Road Initiative (BRI), involves Chinese multifaceted interactions with over sixty countries and numerous regional organizations in Eurasia and parts of Africa. Chinese interactions with these countries are proceeding or are planned to take place around a vast network of transportation (railways, roads, port facilities, airports), energy (pipelines), and telecommunications infrastructure, linking Europe and Africa to Asia; they are to be accompanied by strengthened monetary cooperation and increased people-to-people exchanges.[54]

The advantages for Chinese interests noted by Chinese officials and commentary[55] are:

Economic: More profitable use of China's massive foreign exchange reserves previously invested in low-yield US and other securities; effective use abroad of China's massive excess capacity for infrastructure construction resulting from the completion of many of the main domestic building requirements in China; connecting poorer western and southern parts of China with neighbors and economic partners via modern transportation infrastructure; allowing Chinese industries with excess capacity or with negative environmental impacts to locate in nearby foreign locales and continue profitable production; growing trade that will involve more international use of China's currency; and developing overland transportation and trade routes that will be more secure than existing exposed sea-lanes.

Political: Demonstrate China's economic largesse and growing economic importance to neighboring states in order to encourage them to play down their differences with China over China's bullying of neighbors in pursuit of territorial interests in disputed areas and other problems around China's rim; demonstrate China's ability to muster resources and provide for regional needs in competition with China's main regional challenger, the United States, and its allies and associates, who are unable or unwilling to meet the needs of these many states with their poor creditworthiness, repressive governance, and/or unstable domestic situations.

Strategic: Position China at the center of the various webs of connectivity of increasing importance to its neighbors and to many other countries much farther from China that seek advantage in closer relations with Beijing.

The Chinese-proposed BRI effort remains very much in the initial stages of development even though more than three years have passed since it was announced by Xi Jinping and other leaders. Whether the effort succeeds will depend on how well the above advantages develop and whether they will offset dangers and risks seen by Chinese officials and commentators.[56] Those risks involve:

Economic: China made numerous poor investments in unstable or poor creditworthy developing countries during the "going out" investment movement begun early in the previous decade. China lost many billions of dollars as its assets were destroyed due to the wars in Iraq, Libya, and Syria. Whether or not the many high-risk investment countries involved in BRI will prove beneficial for Chinese investments is unclear. As a result, it remains to be seen how deeply China will become engaged in these countries. Those Chinese decision makers determined that China should be paid back for its large loans for infrastructure developments presumably would need some assurance of positive outcome for China's input before making commitments to risk-prone states.

Political: China's neighbors often are strongly wary of overdependence on China. The public wariness seen in Taiwan and Myanmar in recent years plays out privately among neighboring government decision makers. The highly publicized BRI in conjunction with Xi Jinping's China Dream of a unified and powerful China raises concerns that work against China achieving full success in its plans.

Strategic: A nascent China-centered order throughout Eurasia and adjacent seas is not in the interests of India, Japan, Australia, and the United States. China's grandiose ambitions appear threatening to their interests, making countermeasures by them more likely. President Vladimir Putin has aligned Russia ever more closely with China, but he may have a hard time sustaining close ties as China infringes more on Moscow's interests in the Russian "near abroad," involving countries neighboring Russia but also representing a key segment of China's planned BRI. Other neighboring states less willing to publicly stand against Beijing's wishes may seek ways to preserve their freedom of action by closer ties with the United States or others that work against China's perceived quest for regional dominance.

China's Growing Military Power: Mixed Implications for China's Foreign Influence

An important reason for international uncertainty about China's approach to world affairs involves the apparent disconnect between China's national development policy and China's national security policy. Chinese officials were the first to highlight that China in the recent past crafted and carried out a relatively clear national development policy. That Chinese approach was laid out authoritatively in the December 2005 Chinese government document "China's Peaceful Development Road," and was repeated in similar documents, most recently in late 2010. This approach was consistent with the thrust of Chinese leadership pronouncements since 2003, emphasizing Chinese leaders' determination to avoid trouble abroad and to seek international cooperation and a harmonious world order as China develops and rises peacefully in importance in Asian and world affairs in the twenty-first century.[57]

Unfortunately, the December 2005 document and the follow-on documents made little or no reference to military conflict, the role of the rapidly modernizing People's Liberation Army (PLA), and other key national security questions. When asked about this, one senior Chinese Foreign Ministry official said in May 2006 that China's national security policy was less clearly developed than China's national development policy.[58] In fact, however, the broad outlines of Chinese national security policy were and are fairly clearly laid out in official Chinese documents and briefings.[59] They—and the remarkable recent advances in China's military modernization in the post–Cold War period—are in the lead among Chinese statements and behaviors that have called into question just how peaceful and cooperative China's approach to Asia and the world actually will be.

In practice, as Chinese leader Xi Jinping and his colleagues moved toward what they called at the Nineteenth Communist Party Congress in October 2017 China's "new era" of rejuvenated national power and regional and global leadership, they put aside the reassuring low profile in foreign affairs followed by previous governments. The long-standing Chinese military view of suspicion of the United States became more prominent. A modern military was front and center in their plans for determining China's future international posture.[60]

During the past two decades, foreign specialists on the Chinese military pointed out seeming contrasts and contradictions in recent Chinese official pronouncements and actions dealing with trends in international security. Authoritative Chinese foreign policy pronouncements emphasized China's view of an emerging harmonious world order in which China was rising peacefully in national strength and international influence. China often was seen as occupying its most influential position in world affairs in the modern era. In contrast, white papers on national security,[61] public presentations by authoritative Chinese military representatives, and the continuation of an impressive buildup and modernization of the Chinese military forces revealed the Chinese leadership's strong concern about China's security in the prevailing regional and international order. This concern continued despite more than twenty years of double-digit-percentage increases in China's defense budgets and despite the view of many foreign specialists that China was becoming Asia's undisputed leading military power and an increasingly serious concern to American security planners as they sought to preserve stability and US leadership in Asia.[62]

Chinese military modernization programs have been under way for thirty years. They have reached the point where they strongly suggest that the objective of the Chinese leadership is to build Asia's most powerful defense force.[63] China's military growth complicated China's relations with the United States and some Asian neighbors, notably Taiwan, Japan, India, Vietnam, and South Korea, as well as such countries as Indonesia, the Philippines, Australia, and New Zealand. Leaders from the United States and some Asian countries were not persuaded by Chinese leadership pledges to pursue the road of peace and development. They saw Chinese national security policies and programs as real or potential threats to their security interests.[64]

Chinese national security pronouncements duly acknowledged that with the end of the Cold War, the danger of global war—a staple in Chinese warning statements in the 1970s and 1980s—ended. However, Chinese national security statements rarely highlighted the fact that Chinese defense policy was being formulated in an environment that was less threatening to China than at any time in the past 200 years. Typically, in the 2010 white paper on national defense, the international system was represented as stable, but "international strategic competition" was "intensifying," "security threats" were "increasingly" volatile, and "world peace" was "elusive." The carefully measured Chinese response to the Obama government's emphasis since 2011 on military as well as economic and political reengagement with

Asia under the rubric of the so-called rebalance policy reflected thinly disguised Chinese suspicion of a revival of American efforts to constrain and contain China's spreading influence.[65]

PLA pronouncements and Western scholarship made clear that the United States remained at the center of the national security concerns of Chinese leaders.[66] The 2004 white paper presented a widening military imbalance of grave concern to China caused by US military technological advances and doctrinal changes referred to as the "World Wide Revolution in Military Affairs (RMA)." Authoritative PLA briefings in 2008 presented growing US military power as the most serious complication for China's international interests, China's main security concern in the Asian region, and the key military force behind Chinese security concerns over Taiwan, Japan, and other neighbors. Explaining China's concerns in the Asia-Pacific region, the 2010 white paper warned that "the United States is reinforcing its regional military alliances, and increasing its involvement in regional security affairs."

Chinese statements and the PLA buildup opposite Taiwan underlined that Taiwan was the most likely area of military conflict. And the United States and its military allies were portrayed as the principal sources of potential regional instability in Asia. China responded harshly to indications of closer US-Japanese strategic cooperation over Taiwan, notably a statement supporting a peaceful resolution of the Taiwan issue that was released following the US-Japan Security Consultative Committee meeting in February 2005. The Chinese Foreign Ministry claimed that US Secretary of State Hillary Clinton's intervention concerning disputes in the South China Sea at the ASEAN Regional Forum (ARM) meeting in Hanoi in July 2010 represented an "attack on China."[67]

The PLA and other Chinese officials registered strong determination to protect Chinese territory and territorial claims, including areas having strategic resources such as oil and gas. As Chinese-Japanese and other territorial conflicts involving energy resources in the East and South China seas grew in scope and intensity, they intruded ever more directly on these PLA priorities. Chinese concerns increased over US and allied forces controlling sea lines of communication, which were essential for increasing oil flows to China. The Chinese government appeared uncertain as to the seriousness of the strategic danger posed by the vulnerability of China's energy flows from the Middle East and Africa through the Malacca Strait and other choke points in Southeast Asia and what should be done about it. Chinese national security officials openly debated these issues.[68] The solutions pursued included overland oil and gas pipelines that would bypass the Malacca Strait and the steady buildup of Chinese naval capabilities, including the development of Chinese aircraft carriers that would provide more military capability to protect Chinese trade, energy flows, and other maritime communications.[69]

Given the recent record of US policies and behavior regarding China, the concern Chinese leaders had over the strategic intentions of the United States regarding Taiwan, Japan, Asia, and world affairs was not unwarranted. The George W. Bush administration worked more closely with Taiwan's government in efforts to support Taiwan's defense against China than any US administration since the break in official US relations with Taiwan in 1979. It also worked more closely in defense collaboration with Japan, which focused on Taiwan and other possible contingencies regarding China, than at any time since the normalization of US and Japanese relations with China in the 1970s. Policy statements such as the National Security Strategy of the United States of 2002 and the Quadrennial Defense Report of 2006 made clear that the US military was able and willing to take steps to sustain Asian stability in the face of possible adverse consequences of China's rising military strength. Bush administration leaders emphasized US uncertainty over China's longer-term strategic intentions; they affirmed that they were not fully persuaded by Chinese pronouncements on peace and development and remained unsure if China would be a friend or a foe of the United States. They built up US forces in Asia and collaborated with Japan and other allies and partners, including India, in part to ensure that US interests and Asian stability would be sustained in the face of possible disruptive or negative actions by Chinese military forces.

The Barack Obama administration continued American resolve in the face of China's military buildup as it carried out the most significant US reengagement with the Asia-Pacific region in many years. Speaking to reporters on the way to Beijing in January 2011, Secretary of Defense Robert Gates publicly affirmed US determination to deal effectively with Chinese advancing military capabilities. [70]

In this context, it appeared reasonable for Chinese leaders to carry out the acquisition, development, and advancement of military capabilities specifically designed to defeat US forces, especially if they were to intrude in a confrontation regarding China's avowed top priority: restoring Taiwan to Chinese sovereignty. And as the Chinese leaders devoted ever greater effort to this military buildup, the US advancement of its military deployments and defense cooperation with Taiwan, Japan, Australia, India, and others also seemed logical in order to deter Chinese attack and preserve stability. Of course, the result was an escalating arms race and defense preparations that seemed very much at odds with the harmonious international environment Chinese leaders sought to nurture and sustain. In effect, the respective Chinese and US defense buildups and preparations regarding Taiwan demonstrated that Chinese leaders were not prepared to pursue uniformly "the road to peace and development" set forth in the document "China's Peaceful Development Road." The emphasis on peace and development and a harmonious international environment clearly were goals of Chinese foreign policy, but Chinese leaders at the same time were hedging their bets, notably with an impressive array of military acquisitions that provided capabilities they judged necessary.[71]

The Chinese emphasis on reassuring the United States and China's neighbors early in the twenty-first century did not last. On the one hand, the Xi Jinping leadership came to power in 2012–13 stressing a nonconfrontational and constructive framework for US-China relations known as a "new type of great power relationship." On the other hand, Beijing carried out a wide range of actions much bolder than under the previous Chinese president to advance the Xi government's avowed "China Dream," which involved policy choices that came at the expense of a broad range of American interests in the prevailing Asian and international order. Many Chinese and American observers saw the United States as weakened and in decline on account of the draining wars and security commitments involving Iraq, Afghanistan, Syria, and the Islamic State and the protracted economic recession brought on by the American financial breakdown in 2008. Under these circumstances, China was seen opportunistically advancing its interests through bolder actions and initiatives short of military confrontation that came at American expense.[72]

The Barack Obama government endeavored to counter China's moves in part through its signature "rebalance" policy. It also became concerned about China's perceived assertiveness and its repeated public threats and use of coercion and intimidation regarding territorial claims involving neighboring countries and US interests in unimpeded transit through Chinese-claimed air and sea spaces. Encouraged by China's neighbors, the US government embarked on a new military strategy, announced in January 2012 as part of the rebalance policy, that emphasized American security, economic, and diplomatic reengagement with the Asia-Pacific region.

Though initial US military advances remained modest, US leaders pledged robust US military interchange with allies and associates throughout China's eastern and southern periphery, from the Korean peninsula through Southeast Asia, Australia, New Zealand, and the Pacific Islands and into the Indian Ocean and its central power, India. They said that with the US military withdrawal from Iraq and planned withdrawal from Afghanistan, the United States would reposition military assets and expand defense ties with many of China's neighbors and the proportion of US warships in the Asia-Pacific region would rise from 50 percent to 60 percent of the US war fleet.[73]

China's criticism of the US initiatives made clear to specialists at home and abroad a forecast of greater strategic competition for influence between the United States and China that would deepen the security dilemma at the heart of pervasive distrust between Chinese and American leaders. Indeed, the bold and assertive initiatives of the Xi Jinping government beginning in 2012–13:

- departed from China's previous reassurance efforts under President Hu Jintao (2002–12);
- used wide-ranging coercive means short of direct military force to advance Chinese control in the East and South China Sea at the expense of neighbors and key American interests;
- advanced China's military buildup targeted mainly at the United States in the Asia-Pacific region;
- increased military, economic, and political pressure on Taiwan's government;
- rebuffed efforts for stronger pressure on North Korea's nuclear weapons development while sharply pressuring South Korea's enhanced US-supported missile defense efforts;
- cooperated ever more closely with Russia as both powers increasingly supported one another as they pursued through coercive and other means disruptive of the prevailing order their revisionist ambitions in respective spheres of influence, taking advantage of opportunities coming from weaknesses in the United States, Europe, the Middle East, and Asia;
- used foreign-exchange reserves and massive excess industrial capacity to launch the BRI and various self-serving international economic development programs and institutions that undermine US leadership and/or exclude the United States; and
- continued cyber theft of economic assets, notably intellectual property; employed grossly asymmetrical market access, investment and currency practices; and intensified internal repression and tightened political control—all with serious adverse consequences for US interests.[74]

In sum, the rebalance policy was widely welcomed by China's neighbors concerned with Beijing's new assertiveness in the region. Beijing reacted negatively and countered with various military, economic, and diplomatic initiatives undermining US interests. Beginning in 2014, the usually reserved President Obama complained often. President Xi tended to publicly ignore the complaints; he emphasized a purported "new great power relationship" with the United States. American critics were skeptical of Xi's intentions. China for the most part went ahead with offensive actions. Chinese strong reassurance of the United States in the first decade of this century was now privately seen as having been a mistake—a sign of weakness that would not be repeated.[75]

Recent Military Modernization: Foreign Policy Implications

Overall, Chinese defense acquisition and advancement showed broad ambitions for Chinese military power. While they appeared focused recently on dealing with US forces in the event of a Taiwan contingency, these forces can be used by Chinese leaders as deemed appropriate in a variety of circumstances.[76] Salient Chinese defense acquisitions and modernization efforts include the following:[77]

- Research and development in space systems to provide wide-area intelligence, surveillance, and reconnaissance and the development of antisatellite systems to counter the surveillance and related efforts of potential adversaries; development of electronic warfare capabilities
- Cruise missile acquisitions and programs that improve the range, speed, and accuracy of Chinese land-, air-, and sea-launched weapons
- Ballistic missile programs that improve the range, survivability (through mobile systems in particular), reliability, accuracy, and response times of tactical, regional, and intercontinental-range weapons to augment or replace current systems
- Development of ballistic missiles capable of targeting US or other naval combatants
- Construction and acquisition of advanced conventional-powered submarines with subsurface-launched cruise missiles and guided torpedoes and nuclear-powered attack and ballistic missile submarines to augment or replace older vessels in service
- Development and acquisition of more capable naval surface ships armed with advanced antiship, antisubmarine, and air defense weapons
- Air force advances, including hundreds of modern multirole fighters, advanced air-to-air missiles, airborne early warning and control system aircraft, aerial refueling capabilities, and unmanned aerial vehicles
- Air defense systems involving modern surface-to-air missiles and air defense fighters
- Improved power projection for ground forces, including more sea- and airlift capabilities, special operations forces, and amphibious warfare capabilities
- Research and development of defense information systems and improved command, control, communications, and computer systems
- Development of cyber warfare capabilities
- Increasing the tempo and complexity of exercises in order to make the PLA capable in joint interservice operations involving power projections, including amphibious operations

As noted in chapter 1, the Chinese advances mean that no single Asian power can come close to matching China's military power on continental Asia. With the possible exception of Japan, no Asian country will be capable of challenging China's naval power and airpower in maritime eastern Asia. Should Beijing choose to deploy naval and air forces to patrol the sea lines of communications in the Indian Ocean, only India conceivably would be capable of countering China's power.[78]

Looking to the future, it is possible to limit the scope of China's military buildup. Available evidence shows that it is focused on nearby Asia. The major possible exceptions include the long-range nuclear weapons systems that target outside Asia and cyber warfare and space warfare capabilities. China has used its long-range nuclear weapons to deter the United States and other potential adversaries by demonstrating a retaliatory, second-strike capability against them.[79]

The objectives of the Chinese military buildup seem focused first on Taiwan, preventing its move toward independence and ensuring that China's sovereignty will be protected and restored. More generally, Chinese forces can be deployed to defeat possible threats or attacks on China, especially China's economically important eastern coastline. Apart from conflict over Taiwan, they are designed to deal with a range of so-called local war possibilities. These could involve territorial disputes with Japan, Southeast Asian countries, or India or instability requiring military intervention in Korea.

Meanwhile, the Chinese military plays a direct role in Chinese foreign policy, which seeks to spread Chinese international influence, reassure neighboring countries and others of Chinese intentions, and nurture an international environment that will allow China to rise in power and influence without major disruption. This role likely will involve continued active diplomacy by Chinese military officials, increasing numbers of military exercises with Asian and other countries, some Chinese arms sales to and training of foreign military forces, and more active participation by Chinese national security officials in regional and other multilateral security organizations and agreements, some created and fostered by China.[80]

The Chinese military is on course to continue a transformation from its past strategic outlook, that of a large continental power requiring large land forces for defense against threats to borders. The end of the threat from the Soviet Union and the improvement of China's relations with India, Vietnam, and others have eased this concern. China is likely to move further away from a continental orientation requiring large land forces to a combined continental/maritime orientation requiring smaller, more mobile, and more sophisticated forces capable of protecting China's inland and coastal periphery. Unlike the doctrine of protracted land war against an invading enemy prevalent until the latter years of the Cold War, Chinese doctrine probably will continue its more recent emphasis on the need to demonstrate an ability to attack first in order to deter potential adversaries and to carry out first strikes in order to gain the initiative in the battlefield and secure Chinese objectives.

To fulfill these objectives, Chinese forces will need and will further develop the ability to respond rapidly, to take and maintain the initiative in the battlefield, to prevent escalation, and to resolve the conflict quickly and on favorable terms. Chinese military options will include preemptive attacks and the use of conventional and nuclear forces to deter and coerce adversaries. Chinese forces will expand power-projection capabilities, giving Chinese forces a solid ability to deny critical land and sea access (e.g., Taiwan Strait) to adversaries and providing options for force projection farther from Chinese borders.[81]

To achieve these objectives, Chinese conventional ground forces will evolve, consistent with recent emphasis, toward smaller, more flexible, highly trained, and well-equipped rapid reaction forces with more versatile and well-developed assault, airborne, and amphibious power-projection capabilities. Special operations forces will play an important role in these efforts. Navy forces will build on recent advances with more advanced surface combatants and submarines having better air defense, antisubmarine warfare, and antiship capabilities. Their improved weaponry of cruise missiles and torpedoes, an improved naval air force, and greater replenishment-at-sea capabilities will broaden the scope of their activities and pose greater challenges to potential adversaries. Air forces will grow with more versatile and modern fighters, longer-range interceptor/strike aircraft, improved early warning and air defense, and longer-range transport, lift, and midair refueling capabilities.

These forces will be used increasingly in an integrated way consistent with an emphasis on joint operations that involve more sophisticated command, control, communications, computers, intelligence, and strategic reconnaissance (C4ISR) early warning and battlefield management systems. Improved airborne and satellite-based systems will improve detection, tracking, targeting, and strike capabilities and enhanced operational coordination of the various forces.

Chinese strategic planners are sure to build on the advantages that Chinese strategic missile systems provide. Estimates vary, but it appears that Chinese plans call for over 1,500 short-, medium-, and intermediate-range solid-fueled, mobile ballistic missiles (with a range under 4,000 miles) and short-range cruise missiles with increased accuracy and some with both nuclear and conventional capabilities. China is also modernizing a small number of longer-range nuclear missiles capable of hitting the continental United States and seems likely to develop a viable submarine-launched nuclear missile that would broaden Chinese nuclear options. Chinese nuclear missiles will have smaller and more powerful warheads with multiple independently targeted reentry vehicles or multiple reentry vehicle capabilities. The emphasis on modern surveillance, early warning, and battle management systems with advanced C4ISR assets seen in Chinese planning regarding conventional forces also applies to nuclear forces.

These advances pose concerns for the United States, Taiwan, Japan, and many other neighbors of China, and they will build on China's existing military abilities. Those abilities include the following:

- The ability to conduct intensive, short-duration air and naval attacks on Taiwan as well as prolonged air, naval, and possibly ground attacks. China's ability to prevail against Taiwan is seen as increasing steadily, especially given less than robust defense preparedness and political division in Taiwan. Massive US military intervention is viewed as capable of defeating a Chinese invasion, but Chinese area denial capabilities could substantially impede and slow the US intervention.
- Power-projection abilities to dislodge smaller regional powers from nearby disputed land and maritime territories and the ability to conduct air and sea denial operations for two hundred miles along China's coasts.
- Strong abilities to protect Chinese territory from invasion, to conduct ground-based power projection along land borders against smaller regional powers, and to strike civilian and military targets with a large and growing inventory of ballistic missiles and medium-range bombers armed with cruise missiles.
- A limited ability to project force against the territory of militarily capable neighboring states, notably Russia, India, and Japan.
- Continued ability to deter nuclear and other attacks from the United States and Russia by means of modernized and survivable Chinese nuclear missile forces capable of striking at these powers.

As China's military capabilities continue to grow more rapidly than those of any of its neighbors, and as China solidifies its position as Asia's leading military power, the situation clearly poses serious implications for, and some complications in, China's foreign policy. Many neighboring officials and those in the United States, sometimes publicly but more often privately, remain concerned for several reasons.

The history of the use of force in Chinese foreign policy provides little assurance to Americans or others that China's avowed peaceful emphasis will be sustained. The Chinese government has resorted to the use of force in international affairs more than most governments in the modern period.[82] The reasons have varied.[83] China's growing stake in the international status quo and its dependence on smooth international economic interchange are seen to argue against Chinese leaders' resorting to military force to achieve international objectives. At the same time, the rapid development of Chinese military capabilities to project power and the change in Chinese doctrine to emphasize striking first to achieve Chinese objectives are seen to increase the likelihood of Chinese use of force to achieve the ambitions and objectives of the Chinese government. The major military reforms carried out by President

Xi Jinping are viewed as increasing the overall capabilities of the Chinese military, which continues to receive generous funding from the Chinese government.[84] Against this background, it is not surprising that an active debate continues in the United States and elsewhere about Chinese national security intentions and whether they will override the Chinese government's public emphasis on promoting peace and development in Chinese foreign affairs. Prudence argues for increased US defense preparations in the face of China's rise. As those American efforts continued, notably under the rubric of the Obama government's reengagement with the Asia-Pacific region, they strengthened long-standing Chinese suspicions that the positive hand of US engagement was accompanied by the negative hand of US containment. Deeply rooted Chinese suspicions of US intentions and policies were reinforced.

During the past decade, Chinese and American security officials have tended to register their reservations and concerns in dialogues or less prominent briefings and statements. Chinese concerns and differences with the United States on security issues involve a long list of US security activities that concern China and are seen to underline a US security posture opposed to China. They include:

- US statements and actions seen by China to show that the United States viewed China as a potential adversary, that it sought to change China's authoritarian political system, and that it endeavored to complicate and hold back China's rising international role;
- perceived US support for Taiwan independence, US refusal to support Taiwan's reunification with China, and US use of Taiwan as a "card," a source of leverage, in negotiations with China;
- US support for leaders and groups in Tibet and Xinjiang that undermine Chinese sovereignty;
- US force deployments and defense arrangements in the Asia-Pacific region that are seen to surround China with adverse strategic pressures and to prompt China's neighbors to more actively contest with China over territorial disputes;
- strengthened US-Japan alliance that is directed at countering rising China;
- US nuclear weapons strategy that sees China as a potential enemy;
- US, Japanese, and South Korean missile defense efforts that are or are seen as targeted against China's growing ballistic missile capabilities; and
- US-backed Western arms embargo against China.

Forecasts of Chinese military strengths and their challenges to the United States differ because of variables involving political, economic, and other developments and because of possible upturns or downturns in Sino-American relations. Nonetheless, the United States and China have become more competitive and China's economy is catching up with and is widely seen to surpass that of the United States in the next decade. Against that background, more attention is focused on China's robust military buildup targeted along its periphery and what forces the United States, still the world's largest military power, can bring to bear to offset negative impacts from China's military rise.

The debate in the United States on what to do about China's rise includes a range of specialists who see the implications of China's military strengthening as requiring substantial changes in US policy. On one side are those arguing in support of US Defense Department plans that in the event of an armed confrontation with China, the United States should be ready to attack China with air and sea forces that would destroy and disrupt Chinese forces that otherwise would strike at US and allied combatants in areas along China's periphery.[85] This so-called air-sea battle concept calls for US forces to be prepared to attack Chinese sensors, radars, targeting systems, and/or weapons in order to break links in the Chinese process of finding the US or allied targets and striking them. This offensive posture is seen as likely to lead to a broader and very destructive US-China war, and so other specialists call for an American response to a confrontation with China that would involve an American and allied blockade of major shipping routes to China that would seek to destroy Chinese shipping and supporting naval vessels but avoid direct attack on Chinese territory.

On the other side are specialists who judge that it is futile for the United States to endeavor to preserve its leading position in Asia through military primacy.[86] Given the rapid increase in Chinese military power and the worldwide commitments of US forces, the United States is advised to seek an agreement with China on a balance of power in the region that both find acceptable. A challenge facing this proposal is persuading China, which has in recent years seen significant advance in its control of contested territories and its related influence in Asia, to set aside its assertiveness in seeking its vision of the China Dream in favor of an accommodation with the United States, a power seen on the decline and thus far ineffective in checking China's advances along its periphery.

NOTES

1. Tang Tsou, *America's Failure in China, 1941–1950* (Chicago: University of Chicago Press, 1963); Zi Zhongyun, *No Exit? The Origin and Evolution of US Policy toward China, 1945–1950* (Norwalk, CT: Eastbridge, 2004).

2. William Stueck, *The Road to Confrontation: American Policy toward China and Korea, 1947–1950* (Chapel Hill: University of North Carolina Press, 1981).

3. Gordon Chang, *Friends and Enemies: The United States, China, and the Soviet Union, 1948–1972* (Stanford, CA: Stanford University Press, 1990); Su Ge, *Meiguo: Dui hua Zhengce*

yu Taiwan wenti [America: China policy and the Taiwan issue] (Beijing: Shijie Zhishi Chuban-she, 1998).

4. Robert Sutter, *China-Watch* (Baltimore: Johns Hopkins University Press, 1978), pp. 40–42.

5. John Garver, *Foreign Relations of the People's Republic of China* (Englewood Cliffs, NJ: Prentice Hall, 1993), pp. 125–27.

6. Alice Lyman Miller and Richard Wich, *Becoming Asia* (Stanford, CA: Stanford University Press, 2011), pp. 122–36; Robert Sutter, *Historical Dictionary of Chinese Foreign Policy* (Lanham, MD: Scarecrow, 2011), pp. 117–18, 242.

7. Evelyn Goh, *Constructing the U.S. Rapprochement with China* (New York: Cambridge University Press, 2005).

8. Luella Christopher, *United States–Soviet Union–China: The Great Power Triangle* (Summary of hearings conducted by the Subcommittee on Future Foreign Policy Research and Development of the Committee on International Relations, October–December 1975, March–June 1976) (Washington, DC: US Government Printing Office, 95th Congress, 1st session, Committee print, 1997).

9. Robert S. Ross, ed., *China, the United States and the Soviet Union: Tri-Polarity and Policy Making in the Cold War* (Armonk, NY: M. E. Sharpe, 1993).

10. Miller and Wich, *Becoming Asia*, pp. 174–202.

11. David W. P. Elliott, ed., *The Third Indochina Conflict* (Boulder, CO: Westview, 1981); Miller and Wich, *Becoming Asia*, pp. 191–93.

12. Robert Sutter, *Chinese Foreign Policy: Developments after Mao* (New York: Praeger, 1986), pp. 162–64, 189–91.

13. Ezra Vogel, *Deng Xiaoping and the Transformation of China* (Cambridge, MA: Harvard University Press, 2011), pp. 266–93.

14. Hugh White, *The China Choice* (Oxford: Oxford University Press, 2013); Kishore Mahbubani, "Asia Is on the Brink of a Golden Era. Here's Why," *HuffPost*, October 1, 2017, https://www.huffingtonpost.com/kishore-mahbubani/asia-golden-era_b_6219866.html (accessed January 21, 2018); "The Dimensions of Chinese Influence," *East Asia Forum*, December 11, 2017, http://www.eastasiaforum.org/2017/12/11/the-dimensions-of-chinese-influence (accessed January 21, 2018); Wang Yi, "A New Era in China's Foreign Policy," *ChinaUSfocus*, December 18, 2017, https://www.chinausfocus.com/foreign-policy/chinas-diplomacy-breaking-new-ground (accessed January 21, 2018).

15. David Shambaugh, *China Goes Global* (New York: Oxford University Press, 2013); Wayne Morrison, *China's Economic Rise*, Congressional Research Service Report RL33534 (Washington, DC: Library of Congress, September 15, 2017); Elizabeth Economy, "Beijing Is No Champion of Globalization," *Foreign Affairs*, January 22, 2017, https://www.foreignaffairs.com/articles/china/2017-01-22/beijing-no-champion-globalization (accessed January 21, 2018); Damien Ma, *Rebalancing China's Energy Strategy* (Paulson Institute, January 2015); Zhong Nan, "Trade Volume Up Sharply, Ending a Two-Year Dip," *China Daily*, January 13, 2018, http://usa.chinadaily.com.cn/a/201801/13/WS5a59666ea3102c394518ef5d.html (accessed January 21, 2018); Michael Swaine, "Chinese Views of Global Governance since 2008-2009: Not Much New" (Carnegie Endowment for International Peace, February 8, 2016), http://carnegieendowment.org/2016/02/08/chinese-views-on-global-governance-since-2008-9-not-much-new-pub-62697 (accessed January 21, 2018); Elizabeth Economy, "Why China Is No Climate Leader," *Politico*, June 12, 2017, https://www.politico.com/magazine/story/2017/06/12/why-china-is-no-climate-leader-215249 (accessed January 21, 2018).

16. See debates and differing views of China's international economic importance in "'China Model' 30 Years On: From Home and Abroad," *People's Daily Online*, April 21, 2011, http://en.people.cn/90001/90780/91342/7357862.html; Evan Medeiros, "Is Beijing Ready for Global Leadership?" *Current History* 108, no. 719 (September 2009): pp. 250–56; Qu Xing, "China's Real Responsibilities," *China Daily*, February 18–20, 2011, p. 12; Stefan Halper, *The Beijing Consensus* (New York: Basic Books, 2010); Martin Jacques, *When China Rules the World* (London: Penguin, 2009); C. Fred Bergsten et al., *China's Rise: Challenges and Opportunities* (Washington, DC: Peterson Institute/CSIS 2008); David M. Lampton, *The Three Faces of Chinese Power* (Berkeley: University of California Press, 2008); US Senate, Committee on

Foreign Relations, *China's Foreign Policy and "Soft Power" in South America, Asia, and Africa* (Washington, DC: US Government Printing Office, 2008); Shambaugh, *China Goes Global*; Robert Sutter, *Chinese Foreign Relations: Power and Policy since the Cold War* (Lanham, MD: Rowman & Littlefield, 2016); Thomas Christensen, *The China Challenge* (New York: W. W. Norton, 2016). On Xi Jinping and the recent discussion of the China development model, see Bonnie Glaser, "Is China Proselytizing Its Path to Success?" *East Asia Forum*, January 11, 2018, http://www.eastasiaforum.org/2018/01/11/is-china-proselytising-its-path-to-success (accessed January 21, 2018).

17. Veasna Vir and Sovinda Po, "Cambodia, Sri Lanka and the Chinese Debt Trap," *East Asia Forum*, March 18, 2017, http://www.eastasiaforum.org/2017/03/18/cambodia-sri-lanka-and-the-china-debt-trap; see also William J. Norris, *Chinese Economic Statecraft: Commercial Actors, Grand Strategy and State Control* (Ithaca, NY: Cornell University Press, 2016).

18. "Nation to Chip In More for UN Kitty," *China Daily*, December 31, 2009, p. 2; Sutter, *Chinese Foreign Relations* (2016), pp. 97–98; Jane Parlez, "China Surprises UN with $100 Million and Thousands of Troops for Peacekeeping," *New York Times*, September 28, 2015, https://www.nytimes.com/interactive/projects/cp/reporters-notebook/xi-jinping-visit/china-surprisesu-n-with-100-million-and-thousands-of-troops-for-peacekeeping; "China, Japan and the Future of UN Peacekeeping," *Diplomat*, July 21, 2017, https://thediplomat.com/2017/07/china-japan-and-the-future-of-un-peacekeeping (accessed January 26, 2018).

19. "China's Financial Diplomacy: Rich but Rash," *Economist*, January 31, 2015, http://www.economist.com/news/finance-and-economics/21641259-challenge-world-bank-and-imf-china-will-have-imitate-them-rich.

20. Bethany Allen-Ebrahimian, "Trump Takes Aim at World Bank over China Loans," *Foreign Policy*, October 1, 2017, http://foreignpolicy.com/2017/10/13/trump-takes-aim-at-world-bank-over-china-loans (accessed November 1, 2017).

21. See Sutter, *Chinese Foreign Relations*, pp. 74–76; Xin Zhiming, "Government Clears $5.4b World Bank Loan," *China Daily*, July 25, 2008, p. 13; Asian Development Bank, *Asian Development Bank and the People's Republic of China: 2008, A Fact Sheet*, http://www.adb.org; Asian Development Bank, *Asian Development Bank and the People's Republic of China: 2017, A Fact Sheet*, http://www.adb.org; Fu Jing and Hu Haiyan, "China, UN Jointly Unveil Five-Year Aid Framework," *China Daily*, April 2, 2010; Gillian Wong, "China Rises and Rises, Yet Still Gets Foreign Aid," Associated Press, September 27, 2010, http://www.ap.com; Antoine Dechezlepretre et al., "Technology Transfer by CDM Projects," *Energy Policy* 37, no. 2 (2009): p. 1; World Bank, "Global Environmental Facility (GEF) Projects in China," July 2009; World Bank, "World Bank, GEF-Backed Energy Efficiency Program Expands in China," January 2008.

22. Qu Xing, "China's Real Responsibilities," *China Daily*, February 18, 2011, http://www.chinadaily.com.cn/opinion/2011-02/18/content_12036780.htm (accessed January 21, 2018).

23. Bates Gill, "US, China and the Balance of Influence in and around Asia," Stanford University, March 3, 2016, https://aparc.fsi.stanford.edu/sites/default/files/160303_stanford_fsi.pdf (accessed January 21, 2018).

24. Morrison, *China's Economic Rise*, summary page; Yu Yongding, "An Opportunity for China," *Japan Times*, April 12, 2015, http://www.japantimes.co.jp/opinion/2015/04/12/commentary/world-commentary/opportunity-china/#.VXLETdJViko.

25. "Catching the Eagle," *Economist*, August 22, 2014, http://www.economist.com/blogs/graphicdetail/2014/08/chinese-and-american-gdp-forecasts.

26. US China Business Council, *China Economic Reform Scorecard*, February 2015, https://www.uschina.org/reports/china-economic-reform-scorecard-february-2015 (the reviews are published four times a year). Dan Blumenthal and Derek Scissors, "China's Great Stagnation," *National Interest*, October 16, 2017, http://nationalinterest.org/feature/chinas-great-stagnation-18073.

27. "China's Outward Investments Tops $161 Billion in 2016," Reuters, December 26, 2016, http://www.reuters.com/article/us-china-economy-investment-idUSKBN14F07R.

28. Morrison, *China's Economic Rise*, p. 13.

29. Morrison, *China's Economic Rise*, p. 15.

30. Morrison, *China's Economic Conditions*, p. 15; "Foreign Investment in China Hits Record in 2010," Agence France-Presse, January 18, 2011, http://www.afp.com; Ding Qingfen, "ODI Set to Overtake FDI 'within Three Years,'" *China Daily*, May 6, 2011, p. 1; Xin Zhiming, "Trade Surplus Reaches New Peak," *China Daily*, September 11, 2008, p. 13; Morrison, *China's Economic Conditions* (2009), pp. 4–9; Diao Ying, "Firms Urged to Diversify Export Markets," *China Daily*, December 24, 2008, p. 1.

31. Morrison, *China's Economic Rise*, p. 15.

32. "'China Model' 30 Years On"; Halper, *The Beijing Consensus*.

33. Yu Yongding, "A Different Road Forward," *China Daily*, December 23, 2010, p. 9.

34. "Xi Jinping: Time for China to Take Center Stage," *BBC News*, October 18, 2017, http://www.bbc.com/news/world-asia-china-41647872; Glaser, "Is China Proselytizing Its Path to Success?"

35. Morrison, *China's Economic Conditions*, p. 1; Lampton, *The Three Faces of Chinese Power*, pp. 78–116; Morrison, *China's Economic Rise*.

36. Zhang Yunling, "China and Its Neighbors: Relations in a New Context," in *Making New Partnership: A Rising China and Its Neighbors*, ed. Zhang Yunling (Beijing: Social Science Academic Press, 2008), pp. 1–18.

37. See varying perspectives on these points in Arvind Subramanian, "The Inevitable Superpower: Why China's Rise Is a Sure Thing," *Foreign Affairs* 90, no. 5 (September–October 2011): pp. 66–78; Carl Dahlman, *The World under Pressure: How China and India Are Influencing the Global Economy and Environment* (Stanford, CA: Stanford University Press, 2011); Bates Gill, *Rising Star: China's New Security Diplomacy* (Washington, DC: Brookings Institution Press, 2007); Joshua Kurlantzick, *Charm Offensive* (New Haven, CT: Yale University Press, 2007); David Kang, *China Rising: Peace, Power and Order in East Asia* (New York: Columbia University Press, 2007); and David Shambaugh, "China Engages Asia: Reshaping the Regional Order," *International Security* 29, no. 3 (Winter 2004–5): pp. 64–99; Shambaugh, *China Goes Global*; Sutter, *Chinese Foreign Relations*.

38. Zheng Bijian, "China's 'Peaceful Rise' to Great-Power Status," *Foreign Affairs* 84, no. 5 (2005): pp. 18–24; People's Republic of China State Council Information Office, "China's Peaceful Development Road," *People's Daily Online*, December 22, 2005, http://english.peopledaily.com.cn (accessed July 7, 2006); Rosemary Foot, "Chinese Strategies in a U.S.-Hegemonic Global Order: Accommodating and Hedging," *International Affairs* 82, no. 1 (2006): pp. 77–94; Susan Shirk, *China: Fragile Superpower* (New York: Oxford University Press, 2007); Yu, "A Different Road Forward"; Qu, "China's Real Responsibilities"; Sutter, *Chinese Foreign Relations*, pp. 78–87.

39. Morrison, *China's Economic Conditions*, 26–32; Arthur Kroeber, *China's Economy: What Everyone Needs to Know* (New York: Oxford University Press, 2016); Morrison, *China's Economic Rise*, pp. 29–45.

40. Samuel Kim, *The Two Koreas and the Great Powers* (New York: Cambridge University Press, 2006).

41. Michael Glosny, "Heading toward a Win-Win Future? Recent Developments in China's Policy toward Southeast Asia," *Asian Security* 2, no. 1 (2006): pp. 24–57; Evelyn Goh, ed., Rising China's Influence in Developing Asia (New York: Oxford University Press, 2016); Nadege Rolland, *China's Eurasian Century?* (Seattle: National Bureau of Asian Research, 2017).

42. Michael Yahuda, *The International Politics of the Asia-Pacific* (London: RoutledgeCurzon, 2004), pp. 298–305; Jing-Dong Yuan, "China's Role in Establishing and Building the Shanghai Cooperation Organization (SCO)," *Journal of Contemporary China* 19, no. 67 (November 2010): pp. 855–70; Wu Xinbo, "Chinese Perspectives on Building an East Asian Community in the Twenty-First Century," in *Asia's New Multilateralism*, ed. Michael Green and Bates Gill (New York: Columbia University Press, 2009), pp. 55–77; Rosemary Foot and Andrew Walter, *China, the United States and the Global Order* (New York: Cambridge University Press, 2011); Swaine, *Chinese Views on Global Governance since 2008–2009: Not Much New*; Rolland, *China's Eurasian Century*; Shambaugh, *China Goes Global*; Robert Sutter, *Historical Dictionary of Chinese Foreign Policy* (Lanham, MD: Scarecrow, 2011), pp. 54, 111.

43. Jianwei Wang, "China's Multilateral Diplomacy in the New Millennium," in *China Rising: Power and Motivation in Chinese Foreign Policy*, ed. Yong Deng and Fei-Ling Wang (Lanham, MD: Rowman & Littlefield, 2005), pp. 159–66; Ellen Frost, *Rival Regionalisms and the Regional Order*, National Bureau of Asian Research Special Report no. 48, December 2014, http://www.nbr.org/publications/specialreport/pdf/free/021115/SR48.pdf (accessed November 1, 2017).

44. David Zweig and Bi Jianhai, "China's Global Hunt for Energy," *Foreign Affairs* 84, no. 5 (September–October 2005): 25–38. Mike Mochizuki and Deepa Ollapally, *Energy Security in Asia and Eurasia* (New York: Routledge, 2017), pp. 36–59.

45. Jianwei Wang, "China's Multilateral Diplomacy," pp. 166–77; Yahuda, *The International Politics of the Asia-Pacific*, pp. 298–305; Sutter, *Chinese Foreign Relations*, pp. 88–93.

46. "Xi Jinping: Time for China to Take Center Stage."

47. Shi Jiangtao, "China's Carbon Pollution Could Match US on Per Capita Basis by 2017," *South China Morning Post*, September 20, 2012, http://www.scmp.com (accessed October 9, 2012).

48. Carolyn Beeler, "Is China Really Stepping Up as the World's New Climate Leader," *PRI*, November 9, 2017, https://www.usatoday.com/story/news/world/2017/11/09/china-really-stepping-up-worlds-new-climate-leader/847270001 (accessed December 1, 2017).

49. Ming Wan, "Democracy and Human Rights in Chinese Foreign Policy," in Deng and Wang, eds., *China Rising*, pp. 279–304.

50. Evan Medeiros, *Reluctant Restraint: The Evolution of China's Nonproliferation Policies and Practices, 1980–2004* (Stanford, CA: Stanford University Press, 2007); Ann Kent, *Beyond Compliance* (Stanford, CA: Stanford University Press, 2007); Nicola Horsburgh, *China and Global Nuclear Order* (New York: Oxford University Press, 2015); Eric Heginbotham et al., *China's Evolving Nuclear Deterrent* (Santa Monica, CA: RAND Corporation, 2017).

51. Bates Gill, "Two Steps Forward, One Step Back: The Dynamics of Chinese Nonproliferation and Arms Control Policy-Making in an Era of Reform," in *The Making of Chinese Foreign and Security Policy in the Era of Reform*, ed. David M. Lampton (Stanford, CA: Stanford University Press, 2001), pp. 257–88; Alastair Iain Johnston and Paul Evans, "China's Engagement," in *Engaging China*, ed. Alastair Iain Johnston and Robert Ross (New York: Routledge, 1999), p. 253.

52. Margaret Pearson, "China in Geneva: Lessons from China's Early Years in the World Trade Organization," in *New Directions in the Study of China's Foreign Policy*, ed. Alastair Iain Johnston and Robert S. Ross (Stanford, CA: Stanford University Press, 2006), pp. 242–75.

53. Samuel Kim, "Chinese Foreign Policy Faces Globalization Challenges," in Johnston and Ross, eds., *New Directions in the Study of China's Foreign Policy*, pp. 276–308; Frost, *Rival Regionalisms.*

54. Rolland, *China's Eurasion Century,* p. 2; Xue Gong, "China's Belt and Road Forum: What Now?" Singapore: *RISS Commentary* No. 096/2017, May 17, 2017; Peter Cai, *Understanding the Belt and Road Initiative* (Sydney: Lowy Institute, March 2017).

55. See among other sources the review in "Ambitious Economic Initiatives amid Boundary Disputes," *Comparative Connections* 17, no. 1 (May 2015): pp. 57–61.

56. Ibid.

57. People's Republic of China State Council Information Office, "China's Peaceful Development Road"; "Full Text of Chinese President Hu Jintao's Speech at Opening Session of Boao Forum," *China Daily*, April 15, 2011, http://www.chinadaily.com.cn.

58. Interview, Chinese Foreign Ministry, Beijing, May 30, 2006.

59. I benefited notably from comprehensive briefings on China's national security policy given by leaders of the PLA's Academy of Military Science in Beijing in June 2008 and June 2011 and briefings by senior representatives of the academy at a public meeting at Georgetown University, Washington, DC, in October 2008.

60. Charlotte Gao, "Three Major Take-Aways from Xi Jinping's Speech at the 19th Party Congress," *Diplomat*, October 18, 2017, https://thediplomat.com/2017/10/3-major-takeaways-from-xi-jinpings-speech-at-the-19th-party-congress.

61. People's Republic of China State Council Information Office, "China's National Defense in 2004" (Beijing, December 27, 2004); People's Republic of China State Council Infor-

mation Office, "China's National Defense in 2006" (Beijing, December 29, 2006); People's Republic of China State Council Information Office, "China's National Defense in 2008" (Beijing, January 2009); People's Republic of China State Council Information Office, "China's National Defense in 2010" (Beijing, March 2011); "Document: China's Military Strategy," *USNI News*, May 26, 2015, http://news.usni.org/2015/05/26/document-chinas-military-strategy.

62. Paul Godwin, "China as a Major Asian Power: The Implications of Its Military Modernization (A View from the United States)," in *China, the United States, and Southeast Asia: Contending Perspectives on Politics, Security, and Economics*, ed. Evelyn Goh and Sheldon Simon (New York: Routledge, 2008), pp. 145–66; Aaron Friedberg, *Beyond Air-Sea Battle* (London: Routledge 2014).

63. Chu Shulong and Lin Xinzhu, "It Is Not the Objective of Chinese Military Power to Catch Up and Overtake the United States," *Huanqiu Shibao* (Beijing), June 26, 2008, p. 11; Andrew Nathan and Andrew Scobell, *China's Search for Security* (New York: Columbia University Press, 2012); Ashley J. Tellis and Travis Tanner, eds., *Strategic Asia 2012–13: China's Military Challenge* (Seattle: National Bureau of Asian Research, 2012); Ian Rinehart, *The Chinese Military: Overview and Issues for Congress*, CRS Report 44196 (Washington, DC: Congressional Research Service, Library of Congress, March 24, 2016).

64. US Department of Defense, *Annual Report to Congress: Military and Security Developments Involving the People's Republic of China 2012* (Washington, DC: US Department of Defense, May 2012).

65. People's Republic of China State Council Information Office, "China's National Defense in 2010," p. 4; Martin Indyk, Kenneth Lieberthal, and Michael O'Hanlon, *Bending History: Barack Obama's Foreign Policy* (Washington, DC: Brookings Institution Press, 2012), pp. 61–62; Kurt Campbell, *The Pivot* (New York: Twelve, 2016).

66. David Shambaugh, "Coping with a Conflicted China," *Washington Quarterly* 34, no. 1 (Winter 2011): pp. 7–27; M. Taylor Fravel, "China's Search for Military Power," *Washington Quarterly* 33, no. 3 (Summer 2008): pp. 125–41; briefings by Major General Luo Yuan and Senior Colonel Fan Gaoyue of the Academy of Military Science, Georgetown University, Washington, DC, October 2, 2008; People's Republic of China State Council Information Office, "China's National Defense in 2010," p. 4.

67. Hu Xiao, "Japan and U.S. Told, Hands Off Taiwan," *China Daily*, March 7, 2005, p. 1; Academy of Military Science briefings, June 2008, October 2008; People's Republic of China State Council Information Office, "China's National Defense in 2004"; "Chinese FM Refutes Fallacies on the South China Sea Issue," *China Daily*, July 25, 2010, p. 1.

68. "China-Southeast Asia Relations," *Comparative Connections* 9, no. 3 (October 2007): 75, http://www.csis.org/pacfor; Mochizuki and Ollapally, *Energy Security in Asia*, pp. 38–54.

69. "China–Southeast Asia Relations," *Comparative Connections* 10, no. 4 (January 2009), http://www.csis.org/pacfor.

70. Evan Medeiros, "Strategic Hedging and the Future of Asia-Pacific Stability," *Washington Quarterly* 29, no. 1 (2005–6): pp. 145–67; Elizabeth Bumiller, "U.S. Will Counter Chinese Arms Buildup," *New York Times*, January 8, 2011.

71. Richard Bush and Michael O'Hanlon, *A War Like No Other: The Truth about China's Challenge to America* (Hoboken, NJ: Wiley, 2007).

72. Jeffrey Bader, *Obama and China's Rise* (Washington, DC: Brookings Institution Press, 2012).

73. On the military aspects of the Obama government's reengagement policies, see *Pivot to the Pacific? The Obama Administration's "Rebalancing" Toward Asia*, CRS Report 42448 (Washington, DC: Congressional Research Service, Library of Congress, March 28, 2012). See also Campbell, *The Pivot*.

74. Reviewed in Robert Sutter, *US-China Relations*, 3rd ed. (Lanham, MD: Rowman & Littlefield, 2017), pp. 145–64.

75. Evan Medeiros, *China's International Behavior: Activism, Opportunism, and Diversifications* (Santa Monica, CA: RAND Corporation, 2009), 48–53; Bonnie Glaser and Brittany Billingsley, "Creating a New Type of Great Power Relations," *Comparative Connections* 14,

no. 2 (September 2012): 25–32. Author's consultations with Chinese specialists, Beijing, March 25, 2015.

76. Dan Blumenthal, "Fear and Loathing in Asia," *Journal of International Security Affairs* (Spring 2006): pp. 81–88.

77. Paul Godwin, "China as a Major Asian Power"; U.S. Department of Defense, *Annual Report to Congress: Military and Security Developments Involving the People's Republic of China 2012*; Andrew Erickson and David Yang, "On the Verge of a Game-Changer," *Proceedings* (May 2009): pp. 26–32; Department of Defense, *Annual Report to Congress: Military and Security Developments Involving the People's Republic of China 2017*, https://www.defense.gov/Portals/1/Documents/pubs/2017_China_Military_Power_Report.PDF (accessed November 11, 2017); Nathan and Scobell, *China's Search for Security*; Tellis and Tanner, eds., *Strategic Asia 2012–13*; Rinehart, *The Chinese Military*.

78. Tellis and Tanner, eds., *Strategic Asia 2012–13*.

79. Michael Swaine, "China's Regional Military Posture," in *Power Shift: China and Asia's New Dynamics*, ed. David Shambaugh (Berkeley: University of California Press, 2005), p. 266; Lampton, *The Three Faces of Chinese Power*, pp. 40–42.

80. David Shambaugh, "China's Military Modernization: Making Steady and Surprising Progress," in *Strategic Asia 2005–2006*, ed. Ashley Tellis and Michael Wills (Seattle: National Bureau of Asian Research, 2005), pp. 67–104; Bates Gill, *Rising Star: China's New Security Diplomacy* (Washington, DC: Brookings Institution Press, 2007); Phillip Saunders and Andrew Scobell, eds., *PLA Influence on China's National Security Policymaking* (Stanford, CA: Stanford University Press, 2015).

81. The discussion here and in the following several paragraphs is adapted from Swaine, "China's Regional Military Posture," pp. 268–72; see also the annual assessments in US Department of Defense, *Annual Report to Congress: Military and Security Developments Involving the People's Republic of China*.

82. Garver, *Foreign Relations of the People's Republic of China*, 249–64.

83. Robert Suettinger, *Beyond Tiananmen: The Politics of U.S.-China Relations, 1989–2000* (Washington, DC: Brookings Institution Press, 2003), pp. 200–263; Twomey, "The Military-Security Relationship"; Lawrence and MacDonald, *U.S.-China Relations*, 8–24; Robert Ross, "The Problem with the Pivot," *Foreign Affairs* (November–December 2012).

84. Joel Wuthnow and Phillip Saunders, *Chinese Military Reforms in the Age of Xi Jinping* (Washington, DC: National Defense University, March 2017).

85. Reviewed in Friedberg, *Beyond Air-Sea Battle*.

86. Michael Swaine, *Creating a Stable Asia* (Washington, DC: Carnegie Endowment for International Peace, 2016).

Chapter Seven

Relations with the United States

The record of Sino-American relations discussed in this chapter shows the continued central role of the United States in the foreign policy of the People's Republic of China. The discussion acknowledges that there have been periods of intense Chinese preoccupation with domestic matters, as during the early years of the Cultural Revolution, when foreign policy in general and China's relations with the United States seemed secondary. It demonstrates that there have been periods when China's leaders saw others, notably the Soviet Union, as more threatening and thereby more important to China's interests than the United States. And it shows that there have been periods, as during the Ford and Carter administrations and in recent years, when China saw US power and influence in decline.

Nevertheless, the overall record makes clear the sustained central role of the United States in the changing foreign policy calculations of Chinese leaders. Since the radical phase of the Cultural Revolution, Chinese leaders have viewed appropriate management of relations with the United States as a top priority in order to sustain China's security, preserve and enhance China's sovereignty, and advance China's economy. For its part, the United States focused on the PRC as a danger and gave a high priority to trying to isolate and contain it for twenty years in the 1950s and 1960s. With Nixon's opening, American officials for the next two decades devoted often extraordinary efforts to developing closer ties with China, initially for security reasons having to do with the threat seen posed by the Soviet Union. The 1989 Tiananmen crackdown and the end of the Cold War initiated several years when US leaders, with some notable exceptions, viewed American interests in China as best served by restricting contacts and isolating China. That phase ended with the ascendance of the Chinese economy in American international calculations and the Taiwan Strait crisis of 1995–96, which provided a wake-up call to US officials who thought they could infringe on important Chinese interests without serious consequence. Since then, US administrations have given a high priority to managing increasingly multifaceted and complicated relations with China.

CONFLICT AND CONTAINMENT

As noted in chapter 2, Mao Zedong and his Communist Party–led fighters faced serious challenges as they endeavored to consolidate their rule after defeating Chiang Kai-shek's Nationalist forces in the Chinese Civil War and establishing the People's Republic of China on the Chinese mainland in 1949. China had been war ravaged for decades and arguably had been without effective governance for over a century. The Communists were a rural-based movement with decades of experience in guerrilla war and supporting administrative efforts in the countryside, but with little experience in managing the complicated affairs of China's cities, its urban economy, or its national administration. Seeking needed technical and economic backing as well as guarantees and support for China's national security, the Maoist leadership endeavored to consolidate relations with the Soviet Union in an international environment heavily influenced by the United States, the main international supporter of its Chinese Nationalist adversary, and American-associated states influential in Asian and world politics. Communist China's approach toward American power also demonstrated determination to challenge the United States and its allies and associates in Asia as the Maoist leadership sought to promote revolutionary changes at home and abroad. A related tendency was to exploit episodes of confrontation with America as a means of mobilizing greater national support for those revolutionary changes.[1]

Chairman Mao Zedong and President Harry Truman did not foresee war between the United States and China in early 1950. The Americans were surprised when North Korean forces, with the support of Soviet and Chinese leaders, launched an all-out military attack against South Korean forces in June of that year. Likewise, the Chinese Communist leaders and their Korean and Soviet Communist allies were surprised when the United States quickly intervened militarily, and also sent the US Seventh Fleet to prevent a Chinese Communist attack on Taiwan. By early fall, US and South Korean forces with growing international support had destroyed the North Korean armies, setting the stage for new miscalculations and a wider war.[2] Ignoring Chinese warnings, US and South Korean forces proceeded into North Korea, and by November hundreds of thousands of Chinese Communist forces were driving them south in full retreat. Eventually, the Americans and their allies were able to sustain a line of combat roughly in the middle of the peninsula, as the two armies faced off for over two more years of warfare.[3]

Chinese Communist leaders took the opportunity to initiate campaigns to root out domestic pro-American influence and seize control of US cultural, religious, and business organizations that remained in China. For its part, the United States began a wide-ranging strategic effort to contain the expansion of Chinese power and Chinese-backed Communist expansion in Asia. A strict US economic and political embargo against China, large US force deployments eventually numbering between five hundred thousand and one million troops, massive aid allocations to Asian allies and supporters, and a ring of US defense alliances around China were used to block Chinese expansion and to drive a wedge between China and its Soviet ally.

Employing the advantage of possessing nuclear weapons, the Eisenhower administration used threats and negotiations to reach an armistice agreement that stopped the fighting in Korea in 1953. Meanwhile, it advanced American efforts to strengthen military alliances and deployments to contain Chinese Communist–backed expansion in the region. Defeat of US-backed French forces in Indochina led to the 1954 Geneva Conference and Accords that formalized French withdrawal. US policy worked to support a non-Communist regime in South Vietnam, backing the regime when it resisted steps toward reunification set forth in the Geneva Accords.[4]

Although President Eisenhower and Secretary of State John Foster Dulles were wary of Chiang Kai-shek and Chinese Nationalist maneuvers that might drag the United States into a war with the Chinese Communists, they dramatically expanded US military and economic assistance to Taiwan, and Washington signed a bilateral defense treaty with Taipei in December 1954.[5] Mao reacted with harsh rhetoric and military assaults against Nationalist-controlled islands off the coast of the Chinese mainland. US forces helped Nationalist forces on some exposed islands to withdraw. This Taiwan Strait crisis of 1955 raised fears of renewed war between the United States and China.[6]

Chinese premier Zhou Enlai used the Afro-Asian Conference in Bandung, Indonesia, in 1955 to ease tensions and call for high-level talks with the United States. Secretary of State Dulles was wary that direct talks with the PRC would undermine Chiang Kai-shek's Nationalist government on Taiwan, but facing congressional and allied pressures to meet with the Chinese, Dulles agreed to low-level ambassadorial talks that began in Geneva in 1955. The two sides reached an agreement on repatriating detained personnel, but the agreement was soon disputed. The US side also pressed hard for a Chinese renunciation of force regarding Taiwan, effectively stopping all progress in the talks, which were suspended for a time before resuming in Warsaw in 1958. There the two sides met periodically without much result. The talks did at least provide a useful line of US-PRC communication during times of crisis, as both sides strove to avoid direct military conflict.[7]

Dulles vigorously pursued a US containment policy against China, favoring a tougher policy toward China than toward the Soviet Union. He endeavored thereby to force Beijing to rely on Moscow for economic and other needs that the Soviet Union could not meet. In this and other ways, he hoped to drive a wedge between China and the USSR.[8]

The Chinese-Soviet alliance in fact began to unravel by the late 1950s, and 1960 saw a clear public break, with the withdrawal of Soviet economic aid and advisors. US policy makers were slow to capitalize on the situation, however, as China remained more hostile than the Soviet Union to the United States and deepening US military involvement in Vietnam exacerbated US-China frictions.[9]

During the 1960 presidential election campaign, Senator John F. Kennedy criticized the "tired thinking" of the outgoing administration on issues regarding China, but said little about China once he assumed office in 1961. US domestic opposition, Chinese nuclear weapons development, Chinese aggression against India, and Chinese expansion into Southeast Asia were among factors that blocked meaningful US initiatives toward China. Kennedy took firm action in 1962 to stop plans by Chiang Kai-shek to attack the Chinese mainland at a time of acute economic crisis in China, but continued strong US backing of Chiang in the United Nations.[10]

During the administration of Lyndon Johnson, 1963–69, escalating American military commitment and related difficulties in Vietnam dominated US Asian policy. There was some movement within the US government for a more flexible approach to China, consistent with growing signs of congressional and US interest-group advocacy in favor of a US policy of containment without isolation toward China. But it came to little, as China entered the throes of the violent and often xenophobic practices of the Cultural Revolution, and American forces in Vietnam faced hundreds of thousands of Chinese support troops sent to Vietnam and Laos. Johnson was anxious to avoid prompting a full-scale military involvement of China in the Vietnam conflict, and American diplomats signaled these intentions using the otherwise moribund ambassadorial talks in Warsaw. Chinese officials made it clear that China would restrain its intervention accordingly.[11]

By early 1968, the bitter impasse in US-Chinese relations had lasted two decades and seemed unlikely to change soon. Chinese leaders were in the midst of life-or-death struggles for power and attendant violent mass campaigns that brought conventional Chinese diplomacy to a halt and required martial law to restore order in Chinese cities. Militant Chinese policies in support of the Vietnamese and other Communist insurgencies in Southeast Asia complemented a rigid Chinese stance on Taiwan, Korea, and other issues that had divided China and the United States. US leaders saw little prospect for any significant movement in relations with the PRC as they grappled with consuming preoccupations associated with the failing American effort against Communist insurgents in Vietnam. [12]

RAPPROCHEMENT AND NORMALIZATION

Despite deeply rooted differences between the US government and Chinese Communist leaders on ideological, economic, and international issues, their relations since the start of World War II witnessed a few instances where one side or the other saw its interests served by reaching out and seeking reconciliation and better ties with the other party. The Chinese Communists in particular tried a moderate and accommodating approach to the United States in greeting the American Military Observer Group to Yenan in 1944, and in the initial ambassadorial talks following Zhou Enlai's moderate overture at Bandung in 1955. The Americans tried more tentative overtures to Beijing in 1949, and showed interest in more flexibility toward China by the 1960s. Unfortunately, these initiatives and overtures failed, as there were never occasions when both sides sought improved relations at the same time, until internal and international weaknesses in 1968 and 1969 drove the United States and China closer together in a pragmatic search for ways to deal with difficult circumstances. [13]

Difficulties in the United States in 1968 began in January when the Communist Tet offensive throughout South Vietnamese cities shattered the Johnson administration's predictions of progress in the Vietnam War and prompted American commanders to call for two hundred thousand more troops in addition to the over half a million already in the country. Antiwar demonstrations in the United States grew in size and frequency. President Johnson's mandate collapsed when he did poorly in the March 12 New Hampshire primary, running against an otherwise unexceptional opponent who emphasized an antiwar platform. Johnson pulled out of the race and redoubled peace efforts in talks with the Vietnamese Communists in Paris. [14]

The assassination of Martin Luther King on April 4 set off a rampage of urban looting and burning that afflicted several American cities and notably closed Washington, DC, for days as the city burned and fire-fighting was prevented by snipers and mob violence. Order was restored only after the imposition of martial law by US Army combat troops. The contentious Democratic primaries reached a conclusion in California, where Senator Robert Kennedy won, only to be assassinated on June 5 just after the victory was secured.

With Kennedy dead, antiwar advocates gathered in Chicago in August to protest the likely selection of Johnson's vice president, Hubert Humphrey, as the Democratic standard bearer. Chicago's Mayor Richard Daley and his police officers promised tough measures to deal with unauthorized demonstrations. They delivered on their promise as American television audiences watched in shock as police officers clubbed and beat demonstrators, reporters, and others they deemed obstructing the smooth flow of the convention and nearby hotel receptions.

The Republicans at their convention in August nominated Richard Nixon. On a political comeback after retreating from public life in the early 1960s, Nixon said he had a plan to deal with the Vietnam morass. He did not speak very much about an opening to China. Upon entering office, Nixon moved quickly to begin what would turn out to be the withdrawal of over six hundred thousand US troops from around China's periphery in Asia. In his first year in office, he announced a broad framework for Asia's future without massive American troop deployments. He also made several mainly symbolic gestures to the Chinese government while pursuing vigorous efforts in secret to develop communications with the Mao Zedong leadership.

As explained in chapter 3, China was in turmoil. Mao succeeded in removing political rivals in the early years of the Cultural Revolution, but at tremendous cost. Two of the three pillars of control in the PRC, the Communist Party and the government administration, were seriously disrupted. The third pillar, the army, was called in to rule the cities with de facto martial law. Under these circumstances, China was not prepared for a national security shock.

The Soviet Union invaded Czechoslovakia in August 1968 and removed its leadership, putting in power a regime more compatible with Soviet interests. Under the so-called Brezhnev doctrine, the Soviet Union made clear that it reserved the right to take similar actions in other deviant Communist states. Chinese leaders well knew that, from the Soviet perspective, there was no Communist state more deviant than China. Some in China also were alarmed over Moscow's deploying ever-larger numbers of modern and mobile forces along the Manchurian and Sino-Mongolian borders.

The crisis and debate in the Chinese leadership saw some reaching out to the United States as a means to offset the Soviet threat. The Chinese Foreign Ministry under Zhou Enlai's direction called for renewed ambassadorial talks with the newly elected Nixon administration. Others strongly opposed an opening to the United States, with Lin Biao and his lieutenants, along with the radically Maoist leadership faction, the Gang of Four, arguing in favor of continued strong Chinese opposition to both the United States and the Soviet Union.[15]

The latter leaders held the upper hand in Chinese leadership councils during much of 1969. Chinese media rebuked and ridiculed the new US president and at the last moment Chinese leaders canceled the slated ambassadorial talks in February. The Chinese army took the offensive in the face of Soviet military pressure along the border, ambushing a Soviet patrol on a disputed island in early March and publicizing the incident to the world. The

Soviets responded with greater force, resulting in a series of escalating military clashes along the frontier. By late summer, Soviet officials were warning Americans and others abroad that the Soviet Union was in the process of consulting with foreign powers to be assured they would stand aside as the Soviet Union prepared an all-out attack on China, including the possible use of nuclear weapons.[16]

Zhou Enlai eased the tension in negotiations with Soviet leaders. China was buying time as it refused to accept Soviet demands and prepared for protracted confrontation with its new number one enemy. Zhou and others in the Chinese leadership argued for an opening to the United States to assist China against the Soviet Union, but Lin Biao and others argued that both superpowers were enemies of China and in the end they would cooperate together to isolate and control China.[17]

Mao Zedong came to side with the view associated with Zhou Enlai. Repeated initiatives by the Nixon administration ultimately succeeded and Sino-US ambassadorial talks were resumed in Warsaw in early 1970. The Nixon administration's expansion of the Vietnam War by invading Cambodia in 1970 caused China to cancel the talks, however, and slowed forward movement. Nonetheless, clandestine US-China communication continued, as did the withdrawal of US forces from Vietnam and other parts of Asia.[18]

The July 1971 announcement of Nixon's trip to China came as a surprise to most Americans, who watched with general approval and interest the president's visit to China in February 1972. Nixon privately indicated to Chinese leaders he would break US ties with Taiwan and establish diplomatic relations with China in his second term. In the Shanghai Communiqué signed at the end of President Nixon's historic visit to China, both sides registered opposition to "hegemony," a code word for Soviet expansion; laid out differences on a variety of Asian and other issues; and set forth the US intention to pull back militarily from Taiwan and to support a "peaceful settlement of the Taiwan question by the Chinese themselves." Subsequently, both sides agreed to establish US-Chinese liaison offices staffed with senior diplomats in Beijing and Washington in 1973, despite the fact that the United States still maintained official relations with the Chinese Nationalist government in Taipei.[19]

Progress toward establishing formal US-Chinese relations, the so-called normalization of relations, was delayed in the mid-1970s on account of circumstances mainly involving the United States. A politically motivated break-in at the Watergate office complex in Washington, DC, and cover-up of the crime involved President Nixon in criminal activity. As the congressional investigation led toward impeachment, Nixon resigned in August 1974. His promise to normalize relations with China in his second term ended with his resignation. President Gerald Ford privately reaffirmed Nixon's pledge to shift diplomatic recognition from Taiwan to China, but then he backtracked in the face of US domestic opposition and international circumstances.[20]

Chinese leaders did not register great dissatisfaction in the delay, as they were preoccupied with Mao's death and the most important leadership succession struggle in the history of the People's Republic of China. The struggle involved the arrest and detention of the four radical senior leaders known as the Gang of Four a few weeks after Mao's death in September 1976. The radicals were held until they were put on public trial and sentenced to prison terms in 1980. In 1977, senior leader Deng Xiaoping—who had been removed from power at the start of the Cultural Revolution, restored to a leadership position in 1973, and then removed again in 1976—resumed a leadership position; Deng began a rapid comeback to power that would make him China's most important leader by 1978. While interested in establishing official diplomatic relations with the United States, Chinese leaders at this time also were preoccupied with efforts to counter strong moves by the Soviet Union to use military power and relations with allies around China's periphery like Vietnam and India to contain and pressure China, imitating the US-led containment effort against China earlier in the Cold War. Under these circumstances, Chinese leaders were prepared to wait for the United States to meet their conditions on breaking all official ties with Taiwan, including the US-Taiwan defense treaty, before moving ahead with full normalization of PRC relations with the United States.[21]

Desiring to complete the normalization of US-China relations begun by President Nixon, President Jimmy Carter felt compelled to wait until after his success in spring 1978 in gaining Senate passage of a controversial treaty transferring control of the Panama Canal to Panama. A visit by Secretary of State Cyrus Vance to China in 1977 showed that Chinese leaders were not prepared for significant compromise on Taiwan. President Carter was aware that a complete ending of US official relations with Taiwan would alienate many in the US Senate, and he needed the support of many of these senators for the two-thirds Senate vote of ratification on the Panama Canal treaty. Once the Senate approved the Panama treaty in spring 1978, Carter moved forward expeditiously with normalization with China.[22]

National Security Advisor Zbigniew Brzezinski was in the lead in seeking rapid progress in normalizing US-China relations in 1978, and in subsequent steps, as a means to counter Soviet power and expansion. Carter followed Brzezinski's advice against that of Secretary of State Cyrus Vance, who gave a higher priority to US-Soviet arms control agreements. The United States–China communiqué announced in December 1978 established official US relations with the People's Republic of China under conditions whereby the United States recognized the PRC as the government of China, acknowledged that Taiwan was part of China, ended official US relations with the Republic of China (ROC) government on Taiwan, and terminated the US defense treaty with the ROC on Taiwan. Official US statements underlined American interest that Taiwan's future be settled peacefully and that the United States would continue sales of defensive arms to Taipei.[23]

US and especially Chinese leaders used the signs of their improved relations in the communiqué and during Chinese leader Deng Xiaoping's widely publicized visit to the United States in January 1979 to underline Sino-US cooperation against "hegemony," notably a Soviet-backed Vietnamese military assault against Cambodia beginning in late December 1978. In February 1979, Deng launched a large-scale Chinese military offensive into Vietnam's northern region. Chinese forces withdrew after a few weeks; however, they maintained strong artillery attacks and other military pressure against Vietnamese border positions until the Vietnamese eventually agreed to withdraw from Cambodia ten years later. Carter administration officials voiced some reservations about Deng's confrontational tactics against Soviet and Vietnamese expansionism, but Sino-US cooperation against the USSR and its allies increased.[24]

In pursuing normalization of relations with China, President Carter and National Security Advisor Brzezinski followed the pattern of secret diplomacy used successfully by President Nixon and National Security Advisor Henry Kissinger in early interactions with China. Thus, there was very little consultation with Congress, key US allies, or the Taiwan government regarding the conditions and timing of the 1978 normalization agreement. In contrast to general US congressional, media, and popular support for the surprise Nixon opening to China, President Carter and his aides notably were less successful in winning US domestic support for their initiatives. Many in Congress were satisfied with the stasis that had developed in US-PRC-ROC relations in the mid-1970s and were unconvinced that the United States needed to end defense and other official ties with Taiwan. They resisted the president's initiatives and passed the Taiwan Relations Act (TRA) and other laws that blocked a full break in American defense and other sensitive relations with Taiwan.[25]

The Taiwan Relations Act was passed by Congress in March 1979 and signed by President Carter on April 10, 1979. The initial draft of the legislation was proposed by the Carter administration to govern US relations with Taiwan once official American ties were ended in 1979. Congress rewrote the legislation, notably adding or strengthening provisions on US arms sales, opposition to threats and use of force, economic relations, human rights, and congressional oversight. Treating Taiwan as a separate entity that would continue to receive US military and other support, the law appeared to contradict the American stance in the US-PRC communiqué of 1978 establishing official US-PRC relations. Subsequently, Chinese and Taiwan officials and their supporters in the United States competed to incline American policy toward the commitments in the US-PRC communiqué or the commitments in the TRA. US policy usually supported both, though it sometimes seemed more supportive of one set of commitments than the other.[26]

Running against President Carter in 1980, California governor Ronald Reagan criticized Carter's handling of Taiwan. Asserting for a time that he would restore official relations with Taipei, Reagan later backed away from this stance but still claimed he would base his policy on the Taiwan Relations Act. The Chinese government put heavy pressure on the Reagan administration. It threatened serious deterioration in relations over various issues, but especially continuing US arms sales to Taiwan. Viewing close relations with China as a key element in American strategy against the Soviet Union, Secretary of State Alexander Haig led those in the Reagan administration who favored maintaining those relations and opposed American arms sales to Taiwan that might provoke China. For a year and a half, Haig and his supporters were successful in leading US efforts to accommodate PRC concerns over Taiwan, especially arms sales to the ROC, in the interest of fostering closer American-Chinese cooperation against the Soviet Union. The United States ultimately signed the August 17, 1982, communiqué with China. In the communiqué, the United States agreed gradually to diminish arms sales and China agreed it would seek peaceful reunification of Taiwan with the mainland. Subsequent developments showed that the vague agreement was subject to varying interpretations. President Reagan registered private reservations about this arrangement, and his administration also took steps to reassure Taiwan's leader of continued US support.[27]

As explained in chapter 3, American policy shifted with Haig's resignation in 1982 and the appointment of George Shultz as secretary of state. American policy moved toward a less solicitous and accommodating stance toward China, while giving much higher priority to US relations with Japan. There was less emphasis on China's strategic importance to the United States in American competition with the Soviet Union, and there was less concern among US policy makers about China possibly downgrading relations over Taiwan and other disputes.

The Chinese leaders grudgingly adjusted to the new US stance, viewing their interests best served by less pressure and more positive initiatives to the Reagan administration, seen notably in their warm welcome for the US president on his visit to China in 1984. Cooperative relations with the United States were critically important to the Chinese leadership in maintaining the flow of aid, investment, and trade essential to the economic development and modernization under way in China—the linchpin of the Communist leadership's plans for sustaining their rule in China. Meanwhile, the Reagan leadership learned not to confront the Chinese over issues like Taiwan overtly, seeking to continue US military and other support for Taiwan in ways less likely to provoke strong Chinese reaction. As shown in chapter 3, Reagan's second term in office did not see repetition of the controversies that had marked Reagan's relations with China in his first term.

TIANANMEN, TAIWAN, AND POST–COLD WAR REALITIES

Unexpected mass demonstrations centered in Beijing's Tiananmen Square and other Chinese cities in spring 1989 represented the most serious challenge to China's post-Mao leadership. Deng Xiaoping was decisive in resolving Chinese leadership differences in favor of hard-liners who sought a crackdown on the demonstrators and a broader suppression of political dissent. The crackdown began with the bloody attack on Tiananmen Square on June 4, 1989. Reform-minded leaders were purged and punished.[28]

Anticipating shock and disapproval of the Tiananmen crackdown from the United States and the West, Deng nonetheless argued that the negative reaction would have few prolonged negative consequences for China. The Chinese leader failed to anticipate the breadth and depth of US disapproval, which would profoundly influence American policy into the twenty-first century. The influence was compounded by the unanticipated and dramatic collapse of Communist regimes in the Soviet bloc and other areas, leading to the demise of the Soviet Union by the early 1990s. These developments undermined the perceived need for the United States to cooperate pragmatically with China against the Soviet Union. Meanwhile, Taiwan's authoritarian government was moving steadily at this time to promote democratic policies and practices, marking a sharp contrast to the harsh political authoritarianism in mainland China and greatly enhancing Taiwan's popularity and support in the United States.[29]

Taken together, these circumstances generally placed the initiative in US-Chinese relations with American leaders. Chinese leaders at first focused on maintaining internal stability as they maneuvered to sustain workable economic relations with the United States while rebuffing major US initiatives that infringed on Chinese internal political control or territorial and sovereignty issues involving Taiwan and Tibet. As the Chinese government presided over strong economic growth beginning in 1993, Chinese leaders reflected more confidence as they dealt with American pressures for change. However, they generally eschewed direct confrontation that would endanger the critically important economic relations with the United States.[30]

Effective US policy toward China proved elusive amid contentious American domestic debate over China policy during the 1990s. That debate was not stilled until the September 11, 2001, terrorist attacks on America muffled continued US concerns over China amid an overwhelming American concern to deal with the immediate and broad consequences of the global war on terrorism.[31]

RELATIONS DURING THE
GEORGE H. W. BUSH ADMINISTRATION

President George H. W. Bush, with strong personal conviction in the importance of cooperative American relations with China, at first tried to preserve
cooperative ties amid widespread American outrage and pressure for retribu-
tion after the Tiananmen Square crackdown.[32] President Bush was the most
experienced US chief executive in dealing with China. He had served as the
head of the American liaison office in China in the mid-1970s. Bush took the
lead in his own administration, 1989–93, in dealing with the severe problems
in China-US relations and the decline in US strategic interest in China as a
result of the collapse of the Soviet bloc.

The US Congress, most American media, and broad public opinion favored sanctions and other pressures on China's rulers. They focused particularly on the annual requirement for the president to notify Congress of his
decision to renew "most favored nation" (MFN) tariff treatment for China's
trade with the United States. As with other presidents since the normalization
of relations with China, President Bush favored the renewed trade status for
China; without the renewal, tariffs on Chinese imports would rise dramatically and halt most Sino-American trade. Congress annually considered legislation to disapprove or strongly condition the continuing MFN trade status for
China. Bush rejected such congressional moves, and Congress, in often heat-
ed debate, was unable to muster the two-thirds vote in each house of Congress needed to overcome the actual or threatened presidential veto of such
legislation.

Although Bush told Congress that he had cut off senior contacts with
China after the Tiananmen crackdown, in following months he resorted to
secret diplomacy and sent his national security advisor and the deputy secretary of state on two clandestine missions for talks in Beijing. When the
missions were publicly disclosed in late 1989, an uproar in Congress and
among US media soured the president's already poor standing with the US
Congress, media, and interest groups.

Senior Chinese leaders remained fairly rigid against Bush's efforts to
maintain constructive communication. Uncertain of their ability to maintain
control and promote economic and other development inside China, as well
as facing strong negative reactions from most developed countries, the Chinese leaders were unable or unwilling to make many gestures to help Bush
justify a continued moderate stance toward China.[33]

Bush eventually became frustrated with the Chinese leadership's intransi-
gence and took a tough stance on trade and other issues, though he made
special efforts to ensure that the United States continued MFN tariff status
for China, despite opposition by a majority of the US Congress and much of
the American media. Reflecting more positive US views of Taiwan, the Bush

administration upgraded American interchange with the ROC by sending a cabinet-level official to Taipei in 1992, the first such visit since official relations were ended in 1979. He also seemed to abandon the limits on US arms sales set in accord with the US communiqué with China on August 17, 1982, by agreeing in 1992 to a sale of 150 advanced F-16 jet fighters to Taiwan worth over $5 billion.[34]

RELATIONS DURING THE BILL CLINTON ADMINISTRATION

Presidential candidate Bill Clinton used sharp attacks against Chinese government behavior, notably the Tiananmen crackdown, and President Bush's moderate approach to China to win support in the 1992 election. The presidential candidate's attacks, though probably reflecting sincere anger and concern over Chinese behavior, also reflected a tendency in the American China debate in the 1990s to use China issues, particularly criticism of China and US policy toward China, for partisan and other ulterior purposes. The president-elect, and US politicians in following years, found that criticizing China and US policy toward China provided a convenient means to pursue political and other ends. For candidate Clinton and his aides, using China issues to discredit the record of the Republican candidate, George H. W. Bush, proved to be an effective way to take votes from the incumbent. Once he won the election and was in office, President Clinton showed little interest in China policy, leaving the responsibility to subordinates.[35]

In particular, Assistant Secretary of State for East Asia Affairs Winston Lord in 1993 played the lead administration role in working with congressional leaders—notably Senate Majority Leader George Mitchell and a House of Representatives leader on China and human rights issues, Representative Nancy Pelosi—and others to establish the human rights conditions the Clinton administration would require before renewing MFN tariff status for China. The terms he worked out were widely welcomed in the United States at the time. However, the Chinese government leaders were determined not to give in on several of the US demands, and they appeared to calculate that US business interests in a burgeoning Chinese economy would be sufficient to prevent the United States from taking the drastic step of cutting MFN tariff treatment for China and risking the likely retaliation of the PRC against American trade interests. US business pressures pushed Clinton to intervene in May 1994 to reverse existing policy and allow for unimpeded US renewal of MFN status for China.[36]

Pro-Taiwan interests in the United States, backed by American public relations firms in the pay of entities and organizations in Taiwan, took the opportunity of congressional elections in 1995 that gave control of the Congress to pro-Taiwan Republican leaders to push for greater US support for

Taiwan, notably a visit by ROC President Lee Teng-hui to his alma mater, Cornell University. President Clinton was privately urged by his administration's China policy advisors not to depart from understandings with China that required restricting access by the Taiwan president to the United States. Nevertheless, Clinton allowed Taiwan's president to visit, as he was under heavy domestic political pressure from Congress, which was almost uniform in supporting the administration granting a visa to the Taiwan president. The congressional view also was reflected strongly in American media.[37]

A military confrontation with China in the Taiwan Strait eventually involving two US aircraft carrier battle groups resulted, and the Clinton administration moved to a much more coherent engagement policy toward China that received consistent and high-level attention from the president and his key aides. Marked by two US-China summit meetings in 1997 and 1998, the administration's new and intense focus of developing positive engagement with China was premised in part on the high priority administration officials now gave to insuring no repetition of the dangerous confrontation between US and Chinese military forces in the Taiwan area in 1996. The change in policy also reflected and relied on the growing interest of US businesses that had an increasingly important stake in improving profitable economic relations with China. For their part, the Chinese leaders welcomed the summits with the American leader, which signaled to audiences at home and abroad that Chinese leaders were now accepted as legitimate among developed countries despite the bloody crackdown at Tiananmen and the now waning international sanctions against China.

Progress in the avowed process of building a "strategic partnership" between the United States and China was difficult. Negotiations between representatives of the two powers often were tense and acrimonious, reflecting in particular deep Chinese suspicions and the negative experiences in the years after Tiananmen. Apart from the summits, an agreement in 1999 led to China's entry into the World Trade Organization in 2001 and US passage of legislation in 2000 agreeing to provide permanent normal trade status for China. The latter US move ended the annual requirement to renew MFN tariff treatment for China, which had proven to be the focal point of congressional debate on China for ten years. However, the newly positive Clinton administration approach to China failed to still the vigorous US debate against forward movement in US relations with China on a wide range of strategic, economic, and political issues.[38]

As in the case of Clinton's attacks on George H. W. Bush, many of the attacks on Clinton's engagement policy with China after 1996 were not so much focused on China and China issues for their own sake as on partisan concerns. Most notably, as congressional Republican leaders sought to impeach President Clinton and tarnish the reputation of his administration, they endeavored to dredge up a wide range of charges regarding issues such as

China's illegal involvement in US political fund-raising; espionage; and deviations from international norms regarding human rights, nuclear weapons, and ballistic missile proliferation in order to discredit President Clinton's moderate engagement policy toward China, and in so doing cast doubt on the moral integrity and competence of the president and his aides.[39]

The Clinton policy of engagement with China also came under attack from organized labor interests within the Democratic Party, some of whom used the attacks on the administration's China policy as a means to get the administration to pay more attention to broader labor interests within the Democratic Party. In a roughly similar fashion, social conservatives in the Republican Party used sharp attacks against continuation of US MFN tariff status for China (a stance often supported by congressional Republican leaders) as a means to highlight Chinese coercive birth control policies and embarrass and pressure the Republican leaders to pay more attention to the various agenda issues of social conservatives.

During the 1990s, congressional criticism of China and the moderate US policy toward China was easy to do and generally had benefits for those doing the criticism. The criticism generated positive coverage from US media strongly critical of China. It generated support and perhaps some fund-raising for the congressional critics from the many interest groups in the United States that focused criticism on Chinese policies and practices. The Chinese government, anxious to keep the economic relationship with the United States on an even keel, was disinclined to take substantive action against such congressional critics. More likely were Chinese invitations to these members of Congress for all-expenses-paid trips to China in order to persuade them to change their views by seeing actual conditions in China. Finally, President Clinton, like President George H. W. Bush, often was not in a position to risk other legislative goals by punishing members critical of his China policy. In short, from a congressional perspective and a broader perspective in American politics, sharp congressional criticism of China in the 1990s became a "free ride" with many benefits for those doing the criticizing and few perceived drawbacks.

As President Clinton and his staff took more control over China policy after the face-off with Chinese forces in the Taiwan Strait in 1996, they emphasized—like George H. W. Bush—a moderate policy of engagement, seeking change in offensive Chinese government practices through a gradual process involving closer Chinese integration with the world economic and political order. The US-China relationship improved but also encountered significant setbacks and resistance. The president's more activist and positive policy of engagement with China brought such high points as the China-US summits in 1997 and 1998, the Sino-American agreement on China's entry into the WTO in 1999, and passage of US legislation in 2000 granting China permanent normal trade relations status. Low points in the relationship during this time included strong congressional opposition to the president's stance against Taiwan independence in 1998; the May 1999 bombing of the Chinese embassy in Belgrade and Chinese demonstrators trashing US diplomatic properties in China; strident congressional criticism in the so-called Cox Committee report of May 1999 charging administration officials with gross malfeasance in guarding US secrets and weaponry from Chinese spies; and partisan congressional investigations of Clinton administration political fund-raising that highlighted some illegal contributions from sources connected to the Chinese regime and the alleged impact they had on the administration's more moderate approach to the PRC.[40]

Chinese leaders had long sought the summit meetings with the United States. Coming in the wake of Chinese meetings with other world leaders in the aftermath of the international isolation of China caused by the Tiananmen crackdown, the summit meetings with the American president were a clear signal that the Communist administration of China had growing international status and that its position as the legitimate government of China now was recognized by all major world powers.[41]

The benefits for the United States in the summit meetings were more in question, though the Clinton administration justified these steps as part of its efforts to use engagement in seeking change in offensive Chinese government practices through a gradual process involving closer Chinese integration with the world economic and political order. American and other critics failed to accept this rationale and honed their criticism of what they viewed as unjustified US concessions to Chinese leaders. Heading the list were perceived concessions in the US president articulating limits on American support for Taiwan in the so-called three nos. Speaking in Shanghai in June 1998 during his visit to China, President Clinton affirmed that the United States did not support Taiwan independence, two Chinas, or one Taiwan and one China, and that the United States did not believe Taiwan should be a member of an organization where statehood is required. The Clinton administration claimed the three nos were a reaffirmation of long-standing US policy, but the president's action was roundly criticized in Congress and the US media as a new gesture made to accommodate Beijing and undermine Taipei.[42]

Progress in US negotiations leading to eventual agreement on China's entry into the WTO was not without serious difficulties and negative consequences. The United States took the lead among the organization's contracting parties in protracted negotiations (1986–99) to reach agreements with China on a variety of trade-related issues before Chinese accession could move forward. Chinese premier Zhu Rongji visited Washington in April 1999 hoping to reach agreement with the United States on China's entry into the World Trade Organization. An agreement was reached and disclosed by the Americans, only to be turned down by President Clinton. The setback embarrassed Zhu and raised serious questions in the Chinese leadership about the intentions of President Clinton and his administration. Recovering from the setback, Zhu was able to complete the US-China negotiations in November 1999, paving the way for China's entry into the WTO in 2001. After the United States agreed in late 1999 to China joining the World Trade Organization, US legislation was passed granting China permanent normal trade relations (PNTR) in 2000. This ended the need for annual presidential requests and congressional reviews regarding China keeping normal trade relations (NTR) tariff status, previously known as most favored nation tariff status.[43]

Making such progress in Sino-American relations was difficult because of incidents and developments affecting US-China relations and vitriolic American debate over the Clinton administration's China policy. In particular, the accidental US bombing of the Chinese embassy in Belgrade was the most important incident in US-China relations after the Tiananmen crackdown. The reaction in China included mobs stoning the US embassy in Beijing and burning US diplomatic property in Chengdu. Both governments restored calm and dealt with some of the consequences of the bombing, but China and the United States never came to an agreement on what happened and whether the United States explained its actions appropriately.[44]

Taiwan President Lee Teng-hui added to Taiwan Strait tension that worried American policy makers when he asserted in July 1999 that Taiwan was a state separate from China and that China and Taiwan had "special state-to-state relations." Chinese leaders saw this as a step toward Taiwan independence and reacted with strong rhetoric, some military actions, and by cutting off cross-strait communication links.[45]

Complementing difficulties abroad were the many challenges at home to the Clinton administration's moderate policy of engagement toward China. The US media ran repeated stories in the second term of the Clinton administration linking the president, Vice President Al Gore, and other administration leaders with illegal political fund-raising involving Asian donors, some of whom were said to be connected with the Chinese government. Congressional Republican Committee Chairmen, Senator Fred Thompson and Representative Dan Burton, held hearings, conducted investigations, and produced information and reports regarding various unsubstantiated allegations of illegal contributions from Chinese backers in return for the Clinton administration turning a blind eye to Chinese illegal trading practices and Chinese espionage activities in the United States.[46]

More damaging to the administration and its engagement policy toward China was the report of the so-called Cox Committee. Formally known as the Select Committee on US National Security and Military/Commercial Concerns with the People's Republic of China, and named for its chairman, Republican congressman Christopher Cox, the committee released in May 1999 an eight-hundred-page unclassified version of a larger classified report.

It depicted long-standing and widespread Chinese espionage efforts against US nuclear weapons facilities, allowing China to build advanced nuclear warheads for use on missiles that were made more accurate and reliable with the assistance of American companies. It portrayed the Clinton administration as grossly negligent in protecting such vital US national security secrets. The report added substantially to concerns that the United States faced a rising security threat posed by China's rapidly expanding economic and military power.[47]

DEVELOPMENTS DURING THE
GEORGE W. BUSH ADMINISTRATION

George W. Bush became president in 2001 with a policy toward China tougher than the policy of his predecessor. Seeking to sustain economic relations with China, the new president was wary of China's strategic intentions and took steps to deter China from using military force against Taiwan. Most notably, he departed sharply from past US practice since the US normalization of relations with China by announcing in April 2001 that the United States would do "whatever it takes" to help defend Taiwan in the face of military attack from China. Relations deteriorated when on April 1, 2001, a Chinese jet fighter collided with a US reconnaissance plane, an EP-3, in international waters off the coast of China. The jet was destroyed and the pilot killed. The EP-3 was seriously damaged but managed to make an emergency landing on China's Hainan Island. The US crew was held for eleven days and the US plane much longer by Chinese authorities. Weeks of negotiations produced compromises that allowed the crew and plane to return to the United States, but neither side accepted responsibility for the incident.[48]

Many specialists predicted continued deterioration of relations, but both governments worked to resolve issues and establish a businesslike relationship that emphasized positive aspects of the relationship and played down differences. The terrorist attack on America on September 11, 2001, diverted US attention away from China as a potential strategic threat. Chinese officials privately indicated that they sought a constructive relationship with the new US government, and in the process they publicly showed remarkable deference in the face of the Bush government's uniquely assertive stance on Taiwan as well as its strong positions on regional and national ballistic missile defense, expansion of US-Japanese defense cooperation, NATO expansion, and other sensitive security issues that had been focal points of Chinese criticism of the United States in the recent past. The Chinese leaders seemed preoccupied at home, notably focusing on a very important and somewhat irregular leadership transition and related issues of power sharing and development policy. Against this background, Chinese leaders worked hard to moderate previous harsh rhetoric and pressure tactics in order to consolidate relations with the United States.

Specialists offered different explanations for what they viewed as a surprising improvement in American-Chinese relations during the administration of President George W. Bush. Some focused on greater Chinese leadership confidence and maturity as the cause for the turnabout in relations, arguing that such confidence and maturity prompted the Chinese government to deal more moderately and with restraint regarding some of the challenges posed by the new US administration and its assertive policies. [49]

Another group of specialists was less convinced that US-China relations were destined to converge substantially over Asian and world affairs. These specialists emphasized the importance of what they saw as the Bush administration moving fairly rapidly from an initial toughness toward China to a stance of accommodation and compromise. In their judgment, the shift toward a moderate US stance prompted Chinese leaders to pursue greater moderation in turn in their overall approach to Asian and world affairs. [50]

A third view involved specialists, including this writer, who gave more weight to the Bush administration's initially firm and effective policies toward China, which were seen to have curbed assertive and potentially disruptive Chinese tendencies and served to make it in China's interests to avoid confrontation, seek better US ties, and avoid challenge to US interests in Asian and world affairs. This view held that it was more China than the United States that took the lead in seeking better ties in 2001, and that greater US-China cooperation in Asian affairs depended not so much on Chinese confidence and maturity as on effective US use of power and influence to keep Chinese tendencies in check and to prevail upon China to limit emphasis on differences with the United States. [51]

All three schools of thought judged that the improvement in US-China relations reinforced generally moderate Chinese tendencies in Asian and world affairs, but their differences over the causes of the American-Chinese thaw had implications for assessing future Chinese policy and behavior. In the first instance, the key variable seemed to be Chinese confidence and maturity, which presumably would continue to grow along with Chinese development and moderation, suggesting a continued moderate Chinese approach for the next several years if not longer. The latter two views depended heavily on the United States, with the first view arguing that continued US moderation and accommodation of Chinese interest was required, as a more firm American stance presumably could lead to a more assertive and aggressive Chinese stance in the region. The second of the latter two views indicated that much depended on continued US resolve, power, and effectiveness in dealing with China. Weakness or extremism in the American stance could reverse the prevailing trend of Chinese moderation in the region and lead to a more assertive and disruptive approach.

In any event, the course of US-China relations was smoother than at any time since the normalization of US-China relations. American preoccupation with the wars in Afghanistan and Iraq and the broader war on global terrorism meant that US strategic attention to China as a threat remained a secondary consideration for American policy makers. Chinese leaders for their part continued to deal with an incomplete leadership transition and the broad problem of trying to sustain a one-party authoritarian political regime amid a vibrant economy and rapid social change. In this context, the two powers, despite continuing differences ranging from Taiwan and Tibet to trade issues and human rights, managed to see their interests best served by generally emphasizing the positive. In particular, they found new common ground in dealing with the crisis caused by North Korea's nuclear weapons program beginning in 2002, and the Chinese appreciated Bush's warning in December 2003 to Taiwan's leader Chen Shui-bian to avoid steps toward independence for Taiwan that could lead to conflict in the Taiwan Strait.

It is easy to exaggerate the speed and consistency of growing Sino-American convergence during the Bush administration. The antiterrorism campaign after September 11, 2001, saw an upswing in US-China cooperation, though China was somewhat tentative and reserved in supporting the US war against Afghanistan. President Bush's visits to Shanghai in October 2001 and Beijing in February 2002 underlined differences as well as common ground. The US president repeatedly affirmed his strong support for Taiwan and his firm position regarding human rights issues in China. His aides made clear China's lower priority in the administration's view of US interests as the Bush administration continued to focus on relations with Japan and other allies in Asia and the Pacific. In its first year, the Bush administration imposed sanctions on China over issues involving China's reported proliferation of weapons of mass destruction more times than during the eight years of the Clinton administration. The Defense Department's Quadrennial Defense Review unmistakably saw China as a potential threat in Asia. American ballistic missile defense programs, opposed by China, went forward, and rising US influence and prolonged military deployments were at odds with Chinese interest to secure China's western flank.[52] The Defense Department's annual reports on the Chinese military pulled few punches in focusing on China's military threat to Taiwan and to US forces that might come to Taiwan's aid in the event of a conflict with the PRC. The Bush administration's September 2002 National Security Strategy Report called for better relations with China but clearly warned against any power seeking to challenge US interests with military force.[53]

It was notable that China's increased restraint and moderation toward the United States came even in the face of these new departures in US policy and behavior under the Bush administration, particularly presidential pledges along with military and political support for Taiwan, strong missile defense programs, and strong support for alliance strengthening with Japan and expanded military cooperation with India. In the recent past, such US actions would have prompted strong Chinese public attacks and possibly military countermeasures.

American leaders showed an increased willingness to meet Chinese leaders' symbolic needs for summitry, and the US president pleased his Chinese counterpart by repeatedly endorsing a "constructive, cooperative, and candid" relationship with China. Amid continued Chinese moderation and concessions in 2002 and reflecting greater US interest in consolidating relations and avoiding tensions with China at a time of growing US preoccupation with the war on terrorism, Iraq, and North Korea, the Bush administration broadened cooperation with China and gave US relations with China a higher priority as the year wore on. An October 2002 meeting between President Bush and President Jiang Zemin at the US president's ranch in Crawford, Texas, highlighted this trend. Concessions and gestures, mainly from the Chinese side, dealing with proliferation, Iraq, the release of dissidents, US agricultural imports, Tibet, and Taiwan, facilitated the positive Crawford summit.[54] Meanwhile, senior US leaders began to refer to China and Jiang Zemin as a "friend."[55] They adhered to public positions on Taiwan that were acceptable to Beijing, and they sanctioned an anti-PRC terrorist group active in China's Xinjiang region. The Defense Department was slow to resume high-level contacts with China, reflecting continued wariness in the face of China's ongoing military buildup focused on dealing with Taiwan and US forces that might seek to protect Taiwan, but formal relations at various senior levels were resumed by late 2002.[56]

Looking back, it appears that patterns of Bush administration policy and behavior toward China began to change significantly in 2003. American officials sometimes continued to speak in terms of "shaping" Chinese policies and behavior through tough deterrence along with moderate engagement. However, the thrust of US policy and behavior increasingly focused on positive engagement. China also received increasingly high priority in US foreign policy.

The determinants of the US approach appeared to center on the Bush administration's growing preoccupations with the war in Iraq, its mixed record in other areas of the war on terror and broader complications in the Middle East, and growing international and domestic disapproval of Bush administration policies. The North Korean nuclear program emerged as a major problem in 2003, and the US government came to rely heavily on China to help manage the issue in ways that avoided major negative fallout for the interests of the US government. Although Asian policy did not figure prominently in the 2004 presidential campaign, Senator John Kerry, the Democratic candidate, used a televised presidential debate to challenge President Bush's handling of North Korea's nuclear weapons development. President Bush countered by emphasizing his reliance on China in order to manage the issue in accord with US interests.[57]

With the Bush administration's determination to avoid trouble with China at a time of major foreign policy troubles elsewhere, the president strongly pressured Taiwan's government to stop initiating policies seen as provocative by China and possible causes of confrontation in US-China relations.[58] The strong rhetorical emphasis on democracy promotion in the Bush administration's second term notably avoided serious pressures against China's authoritarian system.

The US government's emphasis on positive engagement with China did not hide the many continuing differences or US efforts to plan for contingencies in case a rising China turned aggressive or otherwise disrupted US interests. The United States endeavored to use growing interdependence, engagement, and dialogues with China to foster webs of relationships that would tie down or constrain possible Chinese policies and actions deemed negative to US interests.[59]

On the whole, the government of President Hu Jintao welcomed and supported the new directions in US-China policy. The Chinese leaders endeavored to build on the positives and play down the negatives in relations with the United States. This approach fit well with the Chinese leadership's broader priorities of strengthening national development and Communist Party legitimacy that were said to require China to use carefully the "strategic opportunity" of prevailing international circumstances seen as generally advantageous to Chinese interests. As in the case of US policy toward China, Chinese engagement with the United States did not hide Chinese contingency plans against suspected US encirclement, pressure, and containment and the Chinese use of engagement and interdependence as a type of Gulliver strategy to constrain and tie down possible US policies and actions deemed negative to Chinese interests.[60]

As China expanded military power along with economic and diplomatic relations in Asian and world affairs at a time of US preoccupation with the war in Iraq and other foreign policy problems, debate emerged inside and outside the US government about the implications of China's rise for US interests. Within the Bush administration, there emerged three viewpoints or schools of thought, though US officials frequently were eclectic, holding views of the implications of China's rise from various perspectives.[61]

On one side were US officials who judged that China's rise in Asia was designed to dominate Asia and in the process to undermine US leadership in the region.[62] A more moderate view of China's rise in Asia came from US officials who believed China's focus in the region was to improve China's position in Asia mainly in order to sustain regional stability, promote China's development, reassure neighbors and prevent balancing against China, and isolate Taiwan. Officials of this school of thought judged that China's intentions were not focused on isolating and weakening the United States in Asia. Nevertheless, the Chinese policies and behavior, even though not targeted against the United States, contrasted with perceived inattentive and maladroit US policies and practices. The result was that China's rise was having an indirect but substantial negative impact on US leadership in Asia.

A third school of thought was identified with US Deputy Secretary of State Robert Zoellick, who by 2005 publicly articulated a strong argument for greater US cooperation with China on Asian and other issues as China rose in regional and international prominence.[63] This viewpoint held that the United States had much to gain from working directly and cooperatively with China in order to encourage the PRC to use its rising influence in "responsible" ways in accord with broad US interests in Asian and world affairs. This viewpoint seemed to take account of the fact that the Bush administration was already working closely with China in the six-party talks to deal with North Korea's nuclear weapons development and that US and Chinese collaboration or consultations continued on such sensitive topics as the war on terror, Afghanistan, Pakistan, Iran, Sudan, Burma, and even Taiwan as well as bilateral economic, security, and other issues. Thus, this school of thought gave less emphasis than the other two on competition with China and more emphasis on cooperation with China in order to preserve and enhance US leadership and interests in Asia as China rises.

Bush administration policy came to embrace the third point of view. Senior US leaders reviewed in greater depth the implications of China's rise and the strengths and weaknesses of the United States in Asia. The review showed that US standing as Asia's leading power was basically sound. American military deployments and cooperation throughout the Asia-Pacific region were robust. The US economic importance in the region was growing, not declining. Overall, it was clear that no other power or coalition of powers was even remotely able or willing to undertake the costs, risks, and commitments of the United States in sustaining regional stability and development essential for the core interests of the vast majority of regional governments.[64] Thus, China's rise—while increasingly important—posed a less substantial and significant challenge for US interests than many of the published commentaries and specialists' assessments might have led one to believe.

On this basis, the US administration increasingly emphasized positive engagement and dialogues with China, encouraging China to act responsibly and building ever-growing webs of relationships and interdependence. This pattern fit well with Chinese priorities regarding national development in a period of advantageous international conditions while building interdependencies and relationships that constrain possible negative US policies or behaviors.

BARACK OBAMA, DONALD TRUMP, AND XI JINPING: PRAGMATISM FALTERS, TENSIONS RISE

With incoming President Barack Obama in January 2009, it appeared that the crisis in US-China relations after the Cold War and the Tiananmen crackdown had evolved during the first decade of the twenty-first century into a positive relationship that for a time seemed likely to continue. Converging US and Chinese engagement policies broadened common ground while the governments dealt with differences through dialogues. Neither side sought trouble with the other; both were preoccupied with other issues, notably the massive negative consequences of the international economic crisis and deep recession that began in 2008.

However, long-standing differences were not significantly changed as a result of pragmatic engagement. In general terms, four categories of Chinese differences with the United States have remained salient for decades. They are (1) opposition to US support for Taiwan and involvement with other sensitive sovereignty issues, including Tibet and disputed islands and maritime rights along China's rim; (2) opposition to perceived US efforts to change China's political system; (3) opposition to the United States playing the dominant role along China's periphery in Asia; and (4) opposition to many aspects of US leadership in world affairs.[65]

The risk-averse Hu Jintao leadership appeared to have little incentive to accommodate the United States on sensitive questions. Rather, his government took steps beginning in 2009 that challenged and tested the resolve of the new US administration.

Explanations varied as to why China put aside past efforts to reassure the United States and instead undertook more assertive and often coercive actions in areas of difference with the United States. Chinese commentators tended to see a starting point in the rising challenges in US-China relations as the Obama government's rebalance policy announced in late 2011. The new US approach emphasized strong and positive US engagement with China, but it also called for stronger American diplomatic, security, and economic relationships throughout the region, which many Chinese commentators saw as encircling and designed to contain and constrain China's rising influence in Asia.[66]

Obama government officials and many other Americans tended to see the origins of Chinese greater assertiveness and challenges to the United States coming from altered Chinese views of power realities between the two countries and in Asian and world affairs. After the start of the economic crisis amid protracted military engagement in Southwest Asia, America appeared in decline. In contrast, China's economy rebounded quickly. Chinese elite and public opinion disapproved of the cautious and reactive approach of the

Hu Jintao government, favoring a more robust and prominent Chinese international approach.[67]

What followed over the next decade showed to this writer and many but certainly not all American specialists that China's repeated policy choices sought advantage at the expense of the United States and others as China rose in regional and global prominence. The main counterarguments came from American officials and specialists who judged that the recent offensive actions by China were exaggerated; US observers needed to consider more China's legitimate concerns and weigh differences against the many benefits of the Sino-American relationship. As Obama government officials left office, they offered private assessments to American specialists that the administration had been remarkably successful in charting a course between US-China differences and common ground. Other American specialists bemoaned that American myopia about China's "threats" obscured what they saw as needed compromise where the United States would "meet China halfway" in seeking mutually advantageous outcomes.[68]

What the recent record does show clearly is that at times in the past, even as recently as the first two years of the George W. Bush administration, assertive Chinese proclivities to seek rectification of differences with America and others were held in check by effective and resolute US countermeasures. US economic, military, and political strength and determination to use it at that time influenced Chinese leaders to shift to reassuring the United States that China's rise would not challenge the United States. The Bush government's ability to employ such countermeasures declined as it came to depend heavily on China and faced enormous preoccupations at home and abroad.

Also preoccupied with other problems at home and abroad, the Obama government gave a high priority to sustaining smooth relations with China despite growing differences. It stressed transparency and predictability, with any change coming only after careful deliberations that usually resulted in incremental adjustments in policy. Linkage—using US policy in one area to influence Chinese policy in another—was not used. The result was that Chinese leaders could easily assess the likely reaction of the United States to China's increased assertiveness and probes seeking to advance control in disputed territory, economic advantage at US expense, cooperation with Russia against American concerns, and other initiatives sensitive to US interests. The likelihood of substantial changes in US policy adverse to Chinese interests seemed low.[69]

The 2016 American election campaign showed that American discourse was shifting away from the optimistic outlook of the Obama government. Democrat Hillary Clinton registered the broadest-ranging indictment of Chinese infringements on American interests. She promised to confront Beijing as it maneuvered in duplicitous ways and "gamed" the United States over various issues. Her rhetoric captured growing frustrations in the United States as China advanced its influence at American expense. Republican Donald Trump had a narrower set of complaints against China, giving a high priority to negotiating more advantageous economic deals for America.[70]

During the election campaign, officials and specialists in China also adopted a more negative view of relations. They disliked both candidates but judged that Beijing would be better off with a Trump government.[71] They were taken up short when President-elect Trump accepted a phone call from Taiwan's president, questioned the US one-China policy, and criticized Chinese economic policies and expansion in the disputed South China Sea. After inauguration, the president reaffirmed the American one-China policy and conducted a businesslike series of meetings with President Xi Jinping in Florida in April 2017. They set negotiation frameworks for advancing relations and dealing with problems. Xi reciprocated with a lavish welcome for Mr. Trump in Beijing in October. Problems remained unresolved and highly prominent; there were frequent tense episodes, notably over what to do about North Korea's nuclear-weapons program.[72]

Early Chinese probes of the Obama government's resolve on differences with China included the following:

- Chinese government patrol boats confronted US surveillance ships in the South China Sea.[73]
- China challenged US and South Korean military exercises against North Korea in the Yellow Sea.[74]
- Chinese treatment of US arms sales to Taiwan and President Obama's meeting with the Dalai Lama in 2010 was harsher than in the recent past.[75]
- Chinese officials threatened to stop investing in US government securities and to move away from using the US dollar in international transactions.
- The Chinese government for a time responded very harshly to American government interventions in 2010 that (1) urged collective efforts to manage rising tensions in the South China Sea, and (2) affirmed, during Sino-Japanese disputes over East China Sea islands, that the US-Japan alliance covered all areas under Japanese government control, including the disputed islands in the East China Sea controlled by Japan but claimed by China.[76]

The Obama administration's rebalance policy came partly in response to Chinese assertiveness. It said:

- The Obama government's priority international attention would focus on Asia-Pacific following US military pullbacks from Iraq and Afghanistan.

- US force levels and military capabilities in the Asia-Pacific region would increase modestly despite expected substantial cutbacks in US defense spending.
- More widely dispersed US forces and basing/deployment arrangements would be used, indicated rising importance of Southeast Asia and the Indian Ocean in support of long-standing American priorities, including those in Northeast Asia.
- The dispersal of US forces and a developing US air/sea battle concept provided means to counter growing "area denial" efforts in the Asia-Pacific region, used mainly by China.
- Strong emphasis on free trade and open economic interchange, notably through the multilateral Trans-Pacific Partnership (TPP) arrangements, was in competition with less liberal regional arrangements supported by China that excluded the United States.
- Significantly enhanced and flexible US diplomatic activism both bilaterally and multilaterally would advance American interests in regional security and stability, free and open economic exchange, and political relations and values involving human rights and accountable governance.

At the same time, the US government took pains to reemphasize repeatedly the importance of across-the-board close and positive US engagement with China. US officials well understood that a zero-sum competition with China in the Asia-Pacific would fail, as the vast majority of those countries did not want to choose between good relations with China and good relations with the United States.[77]

The prominence and initial success of the rebalance almost certainly influenced the Chinese leadership's most significant changes in Chinese foreign relations since the death of Deng Xiaoping. Beijing shifted to an assertive foreign policy exacerbating long-standing Chinese differences with the United States and others that was more in line with the China-centered nationalism prevalent in Chinese elite and public opinion. The shift gained momentum with the transition to the strong-man rule carried out by Xi Jinping in 2012.[78] Specifically:[79]

- The government orchestrated the largest mass demonstration against a foreign target ever seen in Chinese history (against Japan over disputed islands in September 2012). It followed with intense political, economic, and security pressure on Japan unseen since World War II.
- China coerced neighbors in order to extend control of disputed territory.
- Chinese ever-expanding coercive capabilities were backed by the impressive and growing economic and military power of China.
- Steadily advancing Chinese military capabilities were arrayed against and focused on the American forces in the Asia-Pacific region.

- Russian president Putin's shift against the United States and the West coincided with Xi's rise to power. The two cooperated closely against US interests.[80]
- Despite increasing US complaints, the new Chinese government continued manipulative economic practices, cyber theft, and reluctance to contribute regional and global common goods.
- China used its large foreign exchange reserves, massive excess construction capacity, and strong trading advantages to develop international banks and to support often grandiose Chinese plans for Asian and global infrastructure construction, investments, loans, and trade areas that excluded the United States and/or countered American initiatives and support for existing international economic institutions.
- Xi Jinping tightened political control domestically in ways grossly offensive to American representatives seeking political liberalization and better human rights conditions in China.[81]

President Obama proved to be less than fully effective in dealing with the various challenges posed by Xi Jinping's policies and practices.[82] The administration tended to focus on the success of US-China cooperation on such global issues as climate change, where recent shifts in Chinese domestic energy efficiency and pollution policies made Chinese priorities more in line with those of the Obama government and thus facilitated US-China agreement. Meanwhile, various American government department representatives had a wide range of cooperative interactions with their Chinese counterparts. They understood that these would be in jeopardy if China chose to retaliate against US actions deemed offensive by Beijing. To avoid this, US officials reportedly favored the Obama government's approach of giving top priority to the positive overall relationship and managing differences within narrow channels and usually with private talks.[83]

Critics of the Obama government's approach argued that its reticence failed to dissuade China to stop offensive behavior undermining important American interests. They averred that Beijing could easily read the US government's caution and take incremental steps forward and at odds with US interests without much worry about negative consequences.[84]

The Obama government's reticence, despite deepening frustration with China's advances at American expense, showed during summit meetings in Washington in September 2015 and March 2016.[85] The international nuclear security summit in Washington from March 31 to April 1, 2016, featured positive interaction between President Obama and President Xi. Both leaders pledged increased international nuclear security, and both promised to sign the Paris Agreement on climate change. The agreements were central elements of the outgoing US president's historical legacy. Consistent with past practice, other issues, including growing differences over the South China Sea, were handled largely behind closed doors.

The cooperative atmosphere in US-China relations had deteriorated in the previous two years, and forecast tensions over key differences seemed accepted in Washington as unavoidable consequences of America's need to protect important interests from negative Chinese practices.[86] However, President Obama showed the priority he gave to South China Sea disagreements with China; his actions demonstrated that the president judged that this most prominent area of bilateral differences had not reached a level where it would be allowed to spill over and negatively affect other sensitive areas in the relationship, or jeopardize the cooperation with China that the United States sought. This situation allowed China to continue to advance its South China Sea control.[87] Relevant developments came in the wake of the strained summit of September 2015. They were:

- Much stronger US pressure than seen in the past to compel China to rein in rampant cyber theft of American property.
- Much stronger pressure than seen in the past to compel China to agree to international sanctions against North Korea.
- China's continued militarization of disputed South China Sea islands followed President Xi's seemingly duplicitous promise, made during the September summit, not to do so. In tandem came much more active US military deployments in the disputed South China Sea, along with blunt warnings by US military leaders of China's ambitions.
- More prominent cooperation with allies Japan, the Philippines, and Australia, along with India and concerned Southeast Asian powers, that strengthened regional states and complicated Chinese bullying.
- US action in March 2016 halted access to American information technology that impacted China's leading state-directed electronics firm, ZTE. The company reportedly had earlier agreed, under US pressure, to halt unauthorized transfers to Iran of US-sourced technology, but it then clandestinely resumed them.
- The US rebuked negative Chinese human rights practices in an unprecedented statement to the UN Human Rights Council in March 2016 that was endorsed by Japan, Australia, and nine European countries.

However, the impact of the actions was less than it appeared at first. The public pressure regarding cyber theft and Chinese support for sanctions against North Korea subsided once bilateral talks on cyber theft began and China went along with tougher UN sanctions against North Korea. Cutting off ZTE was reversed after a few days of secret consultations. Much later, during the early Trump administration, came the news that the United States had negotiated a punishment with ZTE that required payment of a fine of more than $1 billion.[88] The rebuke in the Human Rights Council turned out to be a one-time public occurrence.[89]

Overall, the Obama government's greater resolve against China's challenges seemed to end up focusing on one issue area: the South China Sea disputes and related American maneuvering with Japan, Australia, India, and some Southeast Asian nations, in response to China's destabilizing and coercive measures. Defense Secretary Ashton Carter and Pacific Commander Admiral Harry Harris repeatedly spoke of China's "aggressive" actions and what Harris called Chinese "hegemony in East Asia." They and other defense officials pointed to US military plans "to check" China's advances through deployments, regional collaboration, and assistance to Chinese neighbors. American officials also expected a Chinese defeat in a ruling later in the year by the arbitral tribunal at the Permanent Court of Arbitration in The Hague, which undermined the broad and vague Chinese claims used to justify expansion in the South China Sea.

Nevertheless, the opportunistic and incremental Chinese expansion in the South China Sea continued. From China's perspective, the benefits of Xi's challenges continued to appear to outweigh the costs. Notably, President Xi was viewed in China as a powerful international leader, while President Obama appeared weak. The opportunities for expansion in the South China Sea were promising, especially given the weaknesses of governments there. An adverse judgment in July 12 in the case at The Hague was effectively dismissed by Beijing, with the United States offering few public objections to China's flaunting its egregious opposition to the legally binding ruling.

In sum, it was obvious to Beijing and anyone else paying attention that US counters to China's expansionism were carefully measured to avoid serious disruption in the broader and multifaceted US-China relationship. The American government signaled that such measured resolve was likely to continue to the end of the Obama government, and it did. The Obama administration favored transparency and predictability in Sino-American relations. Unpredictability was generally not favored, notably by US officials responsible for managing US-China relations, in part because of all the work involved in managing uncertainty. Unfortunately, smooth policy management seen as fostered by the predictability and transparency of Obama policy allowed the opportunistic expansionism of China to continue without danger of serious adverse consequences for Chinese interests.

DISCERNING THE TRUMP ADMINISTRATION'S APPROACH TO CHINA

President-elect Trump's acceptance of the Taiwan president's phone call and subsequent questioning of the one-China policy and criticizing Chinese economic policy and policy in the South China Sea showed in a few comments and gestures how different he was from the deliberative, predictable, and undramatic Barack Obama. The new US leader was capable of a wide range of actions that could surprise Chinese counterparts with serious negative consequences.[90] Meanwhile, some elements of the administration's policy seemed to work strongly against Chinese interests. President Trump and his administration's defense and foreign policy leaders went to extraordinary measures to show solidarity with Japanese prime minister Shinzo Abe, who was treated to a summit meeting at the White House and a weekend of golf with the president at his Florida resort in February 2017.[91]

The Trump-Xi summit in April was followed by intense Trump government pressure on China to use its economic leverage to curb North Korea's nuclear weapons development. While stoking widespread fears of conflict on the peninsula, President Trump stressed his personal respect for President Xi. He promised Beijing easier treatment in negotiations on the two countries' massive trade imbalance and other economic issues. The crisis over North Korea for several weeks put a premium on US interaction with China. Planned arms sales to Taiwan, freedom of navigation exercises in the South China Sea, and other US initiatives that might complicate America's search for leverage to stop North Korea's nuclear weapons development were put on hold or delayed.[92] It was against this background that President Trump told the media in April 2017 that he would not accept another phone call from Taiwan's president until he had discussed the matter with President Xi.[93]

Showing a remarkable inclination to change American policy in ways that complicated Chinese efforts to seek the advantageous stability it desired in relations with the United States, President Trump in June expressed disappointment with China's efforts to curb North Korea's nuclear weapons. What followed were US freedom of navigation exercises in much faster sequence than in the recent past in the disputed South China Sea; an announced major US arms sales package for Taiwan; strong public statements from Secretary of Defense James Mattis and Secretary of State Rex Tillerson in support of American military and other commitments to Taiwan; substantial US sanctions against a Chinese bank and Chinese individuals seen by the US as aiding North Korea to circumvent international sanctions of its nuclear weapons program; and sharper US government criticism of Chinese human rights practices. Administration officials privately indicated that tougher trade and other policy measures were to come, demonstrating American resolve against Chinese actions seen opposed to US security, economic, and other interests.[94]

A key element in the Republican Party platform that was strongly supported by President Trump and his administration leaders was a major increase in defense spending that would allow for a marked increase in the presence of US forces in the Asia-Pacific. Such an increase is at odds with

China's avowed interests in the region. How much more money there will be for defense issues in the Asia-Pacific depends on legislation restricting such discretionary funding by representatives in the administration and Congress who require offsetting cuts or using other means to allow for a rise in defense spending beyond available revenue.[95]

The new US administration's approach to trade, investment, and related issues toward China remained ambiguous and arguably conflicted. Officials appointed as leaders of the Commerce Department, the Special Trade Representative office, and the so-called National Trade Council were known to be sharply critical of China on economic issues, whereas the leaders of the Treasury and State Departments and the director of the White House Economic Council came from backgrounds strongly supporting globalization and openness in American trade and investment policies. The latter at times were reported to be backed by the president's advisor and son-in-law, Jared Kushner.[96]

Chinese officials expected Trump to be less ideological on human rights, democracy promotion, and related issues. The president played down these issues in his visit to China in November 2017.[97]

Looking out, the recent zigs and zags in US policy toward China foreshadowed greater uncertainty and probably greater tensions. For its part, the Xi Jinping government avoided for now the more egregious kinds of challenges (e.g., island building in the disputed South China Sea) that it posed for the Obama government. President Trump was distracted, but he had considerable power and he was proven to be much less restrained than President Obama in using American power against China in pursuit of his objectives. Xi Jinping's China still sought to advance its power and influence at American expense, but it seemed determined to avoid a confrontation of major consequence. How Beijing would balance between these objectives going forward and how the Trump government would manage its various imperatives in dealing with China were not at all clear. What was clear was that the long-standing differences between the two powers were getting more public scrutiny at the highest levels in both countries. Such scrutiny raised tensions without showing mutually accepted paths to resolution.

NOTES

1. Chen Jian, *Mao's China and the Cold War* (Chapel Hill: University of North Carolina Press, 2001); Thomas Christensen, *Useful Adversaries: Grand Strategy, Domestic Mobilization, and Sino-American Conflicts, 1949–1958* (Princeton, NJ: Princeton University Press, 1996).

2. Bruce Cumings, *The Origins of the Korean War* (Princeton, NJ: Princeton University Press, 1990); William Stueck, *The Korean War: An International History* (Princeton, NJ: Princeton University Press, 1997).

3. Warren Cohen, *America's Response to China* (New York: Columbia University Press, 2000), pp. 169–72.

4. Robert Sutter, *Historical Dictionary of United States–China Relations* (Lanham, MD: Scarecrow, 2006), pp. 65–66.

5. Michael Schaller, *The United States and China: Into the Twenty-First Century* (New York: Oxford University Press, 2002), pp. 144–46.

6. Ralph Clough, *Island China* (Cambridge, MA: Harvard University Press, 1978), pp. 10–14.

7. Steven Goldstein, "Dialogue of the Deaf? Sino-American Ambassadorial-Level Talks, 1955–1970," in *Re-examining the Cold War: U.S.-China Diplomacy, 1954–1973*, ed. Robert Ross and Jiang Changbin (Cambridge, MA: Harvard University Press, 2001), pp. 200–237; Zhang Baijia and Jia Qingguo, "Steering Wheel, Shock Absorber, and Diplomatic Probe in Confrontation: Sino-American Ambassadorial Talks Seen from the Chinese Perspective," in Ross and Jiang, eds., *Re-examining the Cold War*, pp. 173–99.

8. Nancy Bernkopf Tucker, *Strait Talk: United States–Taiwan Relations and the Crisis with China* (Cambridge, MA: Harvard University Press, 2009), pp. 14–17.

9. Alice Lyman Miller and Richard Wich, *Becoming Asia* (Stanford, CA: Stanford University Press, 2011), pp. 122–37.

10. Tucker, *Strait Talk*, pp. 17–21.

11. Cohen, *America's Response to China*, pp. 190–94; Goldstein, "Dialogue of the Deaf?" pp. 229–37.

12. Sutter, *Historical Dictionary of United States–China Relations*, p. lvii.

13. Robert Sutter, *China-Watch* (Baltimore: Johns Hopkins University Press, 1978), pp. 1–62.

14. These American events are recounted in Robert Sutter, *U.S.-Chinese Relations: Perilous Past, Pragmatic Present* (Lanham, MD: Rowman & Littlefield, 2010), pp. 67–69.

15. Thomas Gottlieb, *Chinese Foreign Policy Factionalism and the Origins of the Strategic Triangle* (Santa Monica, CA: RAND Corporation, 1977).

16. Thomas Robinson, "The Sino-Soviet Border Dispute: Background, Development and the March 1969 Clashes," *American Political Science Review* 66, no. 4 (December 1972): pp. 1175–78.

17. Sutter, *China-Watch*, pp. 78–102.

18. Robert Ross, *Negotiating Cooperation: The United States and China, 1969–1989* (Stanford, CA: Stanford University Press, 1995), pp. 28, 34–35.

19. Schaller, *The United States and China*, pp. 178–84; Tucker, *Strait Talk*, pp. 29–68; Ross, *Negotiating Cooperation*, pp. 17–54.

20. Cohen, *America's Response to China*, pp. 198–200.

21. John Garver, *Foreign Relations of the People's Republic of China* (Englewood Cliffs, NJ: Prentice Hall, 1993), pp. 166–77, 310–11.

22. Cohen, *America's Response to China*, p. 201.

23. James Mann, *About Face: A History of America's Curious Relationship with China, from Nixon to Clinton* (New York: Knopf, 1999), pp. 82–92.

24. Ross, *Negotiating Cooperation*, pp. 125–26; Mann, *About Face*, pp. 98–100.

25. House Committee on Foreign Affairs, *Executive-Legislative Consultations over China Policy, 1978–1979* (Washington, DC: US Government Printing Office, 1980).

26. Harry Harding, *A Fragile Relationship: The United States and China since 1972* (Washington, DC: Brookings Institution Press, 1992), pp. 86–87.

27. Tucker, *Strait Talk*, pp. 129–52.

28. Tony Saich, *Governance and Politics of China* (New York: Palgrave Macmillan, 2004), pp. 70–74.

29. David M. Lampton, *Same Bed, Different Dreams: Managing U.S.-China Relations, 1989–2000* (Berkeley: University of California Press, 2001), pp. 17–55.

30. Barry Naughton, *The Chinese Economy* (Cambridge, MA: MIT Press, 2007), pp. 98–100.

31. Michael Swaine, *Reverse Course? The Fragile Turnabout in U.S.-China Relations*, Policy Brief 22 (Washington, DC: Carnegie Endowment, February 2003).

32. Authoritative reviews of this complicated period include Lampton, *Same Bed, Different Dreams*, and Robert Suettinger, *Beyond Tiananmen* (Washington, DC: Brookings Institution Press, 2003).

33. Schaller, *The United States and China*, pp. 204–5.

34. Robert Sutter, *U.S. Policy toward China: An Introduction to the Role of Interest Groups* (Lanham, MD: Rowman & Littlefield, 1998), pp. 26–44.

35. Mann, *About Face*, pp. 274–78.

36. Cohen, *America's Response to China*, pp. 229–31.

37. Schaller, *The United States and China*, pp. 214–19.

38. Cohen, *America's Response to China*, pp. 234–39.

39. For this and the next two paragraphs, see Robert Sutter, *Historical Dictionary of United States–China Relations* (Lanham, MD: Scarecrow Press, 2006), pp. lxix–lxx.

40. Schaller, *The United States and China*, pp. 219–27.

41. Cohen, *America's Response to China*, pp. 235–36.

42. Tucker, *Strait Talk*, pp. 217–18, 231–43.

43. Sutter, *Historical Dictionary of United States–China Relations*, p. lxxi.

44. Suettinger, *Beyond Tiananmen*, pp. 369–77.

45. Tucker, *Strait Talk*, pp. 239–44.

46. Lampton, *Same Bed, Different Dreams*, pp. 95–97.

47. Jean Garrison, *Making China Policy: From Nixon to G. W. Bush* (Boulder, CO: Lynne Rienner, 2005), pp. 148–52.

48. For background, see Sutter, *U.S.-Chinese Relations*, pp. 147–68.

49. Kenneth Lieberthal, "Behind the Crawford Summit," *PacNet* 44 (October 24, 2002), http://www.csis.org/pacfor.

50. Swaine, *Reverse Course?*

51. Hugo Restall, "Tough Love for China," *Wall Street Journal*, October 21, 2002, p. A14.

52. "Concern over US Plans for War on Terror Dominate Jiang Tour," Reuters, April 7, 2002, http://www.taiwansecurity.org (accessed April 9, 2002); Willy Wo-Lap Lam, "US, Taiwan Catch Jiang Off-Guard," CNN.com, March 19, 2002.

53. Bonnie Glaser, "Playing Up the Positive on the Eve of the Crawford Summit," *Comparative Connections*, October 2002, http://www.csis.org/pacfor.

54. "U.S. Says China Regulations Should Free Up Soybean Exports," statement of the Office of the U.S. Trade Representative, October 18, 2002, http://www.ustr.gov; "Mainland Offers Taiwan Goodwill Gesture," *China Daily*, October 18, 2002, http://www.taiwansecurity.org (accessed October 20, 2002); "China Tightens Rules on Military Exports," Reuters, October 21, 2002, http://www.taiwansecurity.org (accessed October 23, 2002); "Ashcroft to Open China FBI Office," Reuters, October 22, 2002, http://www.taiwansecurity.org (accessed October 24, 2002); "US and China Seal Billion Dollar Deals," BBC, October 22, 2002, http://www.taiwansecurity.org (accessed October 24, 2002); "U.S. and China Set New Rights Talks," *Washington Post*, October 24, 2002, http://www.taiwansecurity.org (accessed October 26, 2002).

55. Lu Zhenya, "Jiang Zemin, Bush Agree to Maintain High-Level Strategic Dialogue," *Zhongguo Xinwen She* (Beijing), October 26, 2002 (online version).

56. Shirley Kan, *U.S.-China Military Contacts: Issues for Congress*, Report RL32496 (Washington, DC: Library of Congress, Congressional Research Service, June 19, 2012), pp. 2–4.

57. "Bush, Kerry Square Off in 1st Debate," *Japan Today*, October 1, 2004, http://www.japantoday.com (accessed March 21, 2008).

58. Robert Sutter, "The Taiwan Problem in the Second George W. Bush Administration—US Officials' Views and Their Implications for US Policy," *Journal of Contemporary China* 15, no. 48 (August 2006): pp. 417–42.

59. Secretary of State Condoleezza Rice, remarks at Sophia University, Tokyo, Japan, March 19, 2005, 2001–9. http://state.gov/secretary/rm/2005/43655.htm; Evan Medeiros, "Strategic Hedging and the Future of Asia-Pacific Stability," *Washington Quarterly* 29, no. 1 (2005–6): pp. 15–28.

60. Rosemary Foot, "Chinese Strategies in a US-Hegemonic Global Order: Accommodating and Hedging," *International Affairs* 82, no. 1 (2006): pp. 77–94; Wang Jisi, "China's Search for Stability with America," *Foreign Affairs* 84, no. 5 (September–October 2005): pp. 39–48; Yong Deng and Thomas Moore, "China Views Globalization: Toward a New Great-Power Politics," *Washington Quarterly* 27, no. 3 (Summer 2004): pp. 117–36.

61. Off-the-record interviews with US officials reviewed in Robert Sutter, "Dealing with a Rising China: US Strategy and Policy," in *Making New Partnership: A Rising China and Its Neighbors*, ed. Zhang Yunlin (Beijing: Social Sciences Academic Press, 2008), 370–74.

62. Among published sources, see US-China Economic and Security Review Commission, *2005 Report to Congress* (Washington, DC: US Government Printing Office, 2005), pp. 143–90.

63. Remarks of Deputy Secretary of State Robert Zoellick, "Whither China? From Membership to Responsibility," National Committee for US-China Relations, September 21, 2005, http://www.ncuscr.org/files/2005Gala_RobertZoellick_Whither_China1.pdf.

64. Victor Cha, "Winning Asia: Washington's Untold Success Story," *Foreign Affairs* 86, no. 6 (November–December 2007): pp. 98–133; Daniel Twining, "America's Grand Design in Asia," *Washington Quarterly* 30, no. 3 (2007): pp. 79–94; Robert Sutter, *The United States in Asia* (Lanham, MD: Rowman & Littlefield, 2008), pp. 270–76, 281–83.

65. See contrasting views of China's approach to the United States and of various differences in China-US relations in Michael Swaine, *America's Challenge: Engaging a Rising China in the Twenty-First Century* (Washington, DC: Carnegie Endowment, 2011); Aaron Friedberg, *A Contest for Supremacy: China, America, and the Struggle for Mastery in Asia* (New York: W. W. Norton, 2011); and Jeffrey Bader, *Obama and China's Rise* (Washington, DC: Brookings Institution Press, 2012).

66. See assessments of prominent Chinese specialists in Nina Hachigian, ed., *Debating China: The U.S.-China Relationship in Ten Conversations* (New York: Oxford University Press, 2014); and Wu Xinbo, "Chinese Visions of the Future of U.S.-China Relations," in *Tangled Titans: The United States and China*, ed. David Shambaugh (Lanham, MD: Rowman & Littlefield, 2013), 371–88.

67. Christopher Johnson, "Thoughts from the Chairman: Xi Jinping Unveils His Foreign Policy Vision," Center for Strategic and International Studies, December 8, 2014, https://www.csis.org/analysis/thoughts-chairman-xi-jinping-unveils-his-foreign-policy-vision; Yun Sun, "China's Peaceful Rise: Peace Through Strength?" *PacNet* 25 (Honolulu: CSIS Pacific Forum, March 31, 2014); Yong Deng, "China: The Post-Responsible Power," *Washington Quarterly* 37, no. 4 (Winter 2015): 117–32.

68. On the contrasting views, see Aaron Friedberg, *Beyond Air-Sea Battle: The Debate over US Military Strategy in Asia* (London: IISS/Routledge, 2014); Ashley Tellis and Robert Blackwill, "Revising U.S. Grand Strategy toward China," Council on Foreign Relations, April 2015; Thomas Christensen, *The China Challenge: Shaping the Choices of a Rising Power* (New York: W. W. Norton, 2016); Lyle Goldstein, *Meeting China Halfway* (Washington, DC: Georgetown University Press, 2015); Michael Swaine, *Creating a Stable Asia: An Agenda for a U.S.-China Balance of Power* (Washington, DC: Carnegie Endowment, 2016).

69. Robert Sutter, "Obama's Cautious and Calibrated Approach to an Assertive China," YaleGlobal Online, April 19, 2016, http://yaleglobal.yale.edu/content/obamas-cautious-and-calibrated-approach-assertive-china.

70. Robert Sutter and Satu Limaye, *America's 2016 Election Debate* (Honolulu: East West Center, 2016), pp. 19–20.

71. Ibid., 21.

72. Bonnie Glaser and Alexandra Viers, "China Prepares for Rocky Relations in 2017," *Comparative Connections* 18, no. 3 (January 2017): 21–22; Bonnie Glaser and Alexandra Viers, "Trump and Xi Break the Ice at Mar-a-Lago," *Comparative Connections* 19, no. 1 (May 2017): 21–32.

73. The Chinese government took the position, opposed by the United States and the majority of concerned world powers, that China had the right to regulate the movement of military naval and air vehicles in the exclusive economic zone (EEZ) along China's rim. A coastal

state's EEZ generally extends from the edge of its territorial sea (twelve nautical miles from its coast) to a distance of two hundred nautical miles from its coast.

74. Such exercises had occurred in the past and in 2010 they were initiated in response to North Korean provocations in the sinking of a South Korean warship that resulted in the deaths of forty-six sailors and the shelling of a South Korean island that resulted in South Korean military and civilian casualties.

75. In both cases the Obama government had delayed these US actions that conformed to past American practice until after the president's first visit to China in November 2009, hoping not to undermine the emerging cooperative atmosphere in the administration's relationship with China. The more strident Chinese response came as a surprise to the United States.

76. Bonnie Glaser and Brittany Billingsley, "Friction and Cooperation Co-exist Uneasily," *Comparative Connections* 13, no. 2 (September 2011): pp. 27–40; Minxin Pei, "China's Bumpy Ride Ahead," *Diplomat*, February 16, 2011, http://thediplomat.com/2011/02/chinas-bumpy-ride-ahead; Robert Sutter, *Positive Equilibrium in US-China Relations: Durable or Not?* (Baltimore: University of Maryland School of Law, 2010).

77. Kurt Campbell, *The Pivot* (New York: Twelve, 2016); Robert Sutter, *The United States and Asia: Regional Dynamics and Twenty-First-Century Relations* (Lanham, MD: Rowman & Littlefield, 2015).

78. Deng, "China: The Post-Responsible Power," pp. 117–32 ; Denny Roy, *Return of the Dragon: Rising China and Regional Security* (New York: Columbia University Press, 2013); Yun Sun, "China's New Calculations in the South China Sea," *Asia-Pacific Bulletin* 267, June 10, 2014.

79. Assessments of US-China relations in this period include Bader, *Obama and China's Rise*; Martin Indyk, Kenneth Lieberthal, and Michael O'Hanlon, *Bending History: Barack Obama's Foreign Policy* (Washington, DC: Brookings Institution Press, 2013), pp. 24–69; Aaron Friedberg, *A Contest for Supremacy*; Kenneth Lieberthal and Wang Jisi, *Addressing U.S.-China Strategic Distrust* (Washington, DC: Brookings Institution Press, 2012); Andrew Nathan and Andrew Scobell, *China's Search for Security* (New York: Columbia University Press, 2012); Roy, *Return of the Dragon*; Hachigian, ed., *Debating China*; Goldstein, *Meeting China Halfway*; Christensen, *The China Challenge*; Shambaugh, ed. *Tangled Titans*; Tellis and Blackwill, "Revising U.S. Grand Strategy toward China"; Campbell, *The Pivot*; Sutter, *The United States and Asia*.

80. Robert Sutter, "Foreword: Russia-China Relations," in *Russia-China Relations: Assessing Common Ground and Strategic Fault Lines* (Seattle: National Bureau of Asian Research, July 2017), http://nbr.org/publications/element.aspx?id=950. The Russian and Chinese leaders increasingly converged most prominently on the desire to serve as a counterweight to perceived US preponderant influence and to constrain US power. China saw Russia as a useful counterweight to US power, and Russia valued Sino-Russian cooperation for the same reason. They worked separately and together to complicate and curb US power and influence in world politics, economy, and security. They supported one another in their respective challenges to the United States, allies, and partners in Europe, the Middle East, and Asia. These joint efforts also involved diplomatic, security, and economic measures in multilateral forums and bilateral relations involving US adversaries in North Korea, Iran, and Syria. The two powers also supported one another in the face of US and allied complaints about Russian and Chinese coercive expansion and other steps that challenged regional order and global norms and institutions backed by the United States.

81. Shannon Tiezzi, "American Government Torn on How to Handle China," *Diplomat*, August 4, 2015, http://thediplomat.com/2015/08/americas-government-is-torn-on-how-to-handle-china; Robert Sutter, "Americans Speak to U.S.-China Policy: Let's Be Frank," National Bureau of Asian Research, September 18, 2015, http://xivisit.nbr.org/2015/09/18/americans-speak-to-u-s-china-policy-robert-sutter (site discontinued); Orville Schell and Susan Shirk, Chairs, *US Policy toward China: Recommendations for a New Administration*, Task Force Report (New York: Asia Society, 2017); Sutter, *The United States and Asia*, pp. 307–14; and Robert Sutter, *Chinese Foreign Relations: Power and Policy since the Cold War*, 4th ed. (Lanham, MD: Rowman & Littlefield, 2016), pp. 133–49.

82. His administration gave top priority to supporting the overall positive US approach to engagement with China. Differences usually were dealt with in private consultations. Even if they seemed important, they were kept within carefully crafted channels and not allowed to "spill over" and impact other elements in the relationship. Thus, the Obama government eschewed "linkage"—that is, the seeking of US leverage to get China to stop behavior offensive to the United States by linking the offensive Chinese behavior to another policy area where the United States would threaten actions adverse to important Chinese interests.

83. Author consultations with US administration officials, Washington, DC, August 2016.

84. The critics identified particularly with the 2016 US election campaign rhetoric and the admonitions of Hillary Clinton in her avowed determination to halt the incremental Chinese advances made by Beijing as it "gamed" the United States on economic, security, and political issues important to the United States. Sutter and Limaye, *America's 2016 Election Debate*, p. 20.

85. Sutter, "Obama's Cautious and Calibrated Approach to an Assertive China"; Jeffrey Bader, "A Framework for U.S. Policy toward China," Asia Working Group Paper 3, Brookings Institution Press, March 2016, https://www.brookings.edu/wp-content/uploads/2016/07/us-china-policy-framework-bader-1.pdf; Deputy Secretary Blinken Testimony on US-China Relations: Strategic Challenges and Opportunities, Senate Foreign Relations Committee, April 27, 2016.

86. David M. Lampton, "A Tipping Point in U.S.-China Relations Is upon Us," *US-China Perception Monitor*, May 11, 2015; Harry Harding, "Has U.S. China Policy Failed?" *Washington Quarterly* 38, no. 3 (2015): pp. 95–122.

87. Sutter, "Obama's Cautious and Calibrated Approach to an Assertive China."

88. "China's ZTE to Pay Massive U.S. Fine over Iran, North Korea Sanctions Busting," Euronews, March 7, 2017, http://www.euronews.com/2017/03/07/china-s-zte-to-pay-massive-us-fine-over-iran-north-korea-sanctions-busting.

89. Meanwhile, the so-called Taiwan issue in Sino-American relations became more sensitive following the landslide election in January 2016 of Democratic Progressive Party (DPP) candidate Tsai Ing-wen and a powerful majority of DPP legislators. Avoiding actions that might "rock-the-boat," the Obama government eschewed controversy and emphasized constructive cross-strait dialogue.

90. "Trump's Unpredictability on Foreign Policy Keeps the World Guessing," *Financial Times*, January 19, 2017, https://www.ft.com/content/31b5d958-ddc1-11e6-9d7c-be108f1c1dce.

91. Samuel Osbourne, "Japanese Prime Minister Shinzo Abe Says Donald Trump Encouraged Him to Improve Relations with Vladimir Putin," *Independent*, February 14, 2017, http://www.independent.co.uk/news/world/americas/us-politics/japan-prime-misiter-shinzo-abe-donald-trum-p-improve-russia-relations-valdimir-putin-us-president-a7579166.html.

92. Bonnie Glaser and Alexandra Viers, "Trump and Xi Break the Ice at Mar-a-lago," *Comparative Connections* 19, no. 1 (May 2017): pp. 21–32.

93. David Brown and Kevin Scott, "China-Taiwan Relations," *Comparative Connections* 19, no. 1 (May 2017): pp. 62–63.

94. Shi Jiangtao, "US Doubts over One-China Linchpin to Stalk Sino-US Security Talks," *South China Morning Post*, June 16, 2017, p. 1; Mark Landler, "Trump Takes More Aggressive Stance with U.S. Friend and Foes in Asia," *New York Times*, June 30, 2017, https://www.nytimes.com/2017/06/30/world/asia/trump-south-korea-china.html.

95. Emily Rauhala, "As Trump Pushes for Bigger U.S. Defense Budget, China Slows Growth Rate of Its Military Spending," *Washington Post*, March 4, 2017, https://www.washingtonpost.com/world/as-trump-pushes-for-bigger-us-defense-budget-china-slows-growth-rate-of-its-military-spending/2017/03/04/ace6105c-0094-11e7-a51a-e16b4bcc6644_story.html?utm_term=.489451bdd660.

96. Mark Landler and Michael Shear, "Trump Administration to Take a Harder Tack on Trade with China," *New York Times*, April 6, 2017, https://www.nytimes.com/2017/04/06/us/politics/trump-xi-jinping-china-summit-mar-a-lago.html.

97. Tracy Wilkinsen, "Human Rights Fade from U.S. Foreign Policy Agenda under Trump," *Los Angeles Times*, April 5, 2017, http://www.latimes.com/nation/la-fg-trump-human-rights-

20170405-story.html; "Human Rights and Playing the Crowds off the Agenda for Trump in China," *South China Morning Post*, November 9, 2017, http://www.scmp.com/news/china/diplomacy-defence/article/2119182/human-rights-and-playing-crowds-agenda-trump-china.

Chapter Eight

Relations with Neighboring Asian Countries

The history of the foreign relations of the People's Republic of China shows strong and generally consistent attention of China's leaders to international trends influenced heavily by the United States, and for a long period the Soviet Union, that could impact Chinese interests. Though China often has aspired to and in recent decades has attained considerable global prominence and influence, the main arena where Chinese foreign relations have focused remains the periphery of the PRC. Even in the recent period of China's wide international importance as the world's largest trader, manufacturer, creditor, and greenhouse gas emitter and the second-largest economy, it has been estimated by some experienced Chinese officials and reinforced by recent Chinese behavior that 70 percent of Chinese leaders' attention in foreign affairs remains focused on nearby Asia.[1]

The reasons for this priority seem obvious. Nearby Asia holds the areas of disputed territories that nationalistic Chinese officials and people are committed to return to Chinese rule. That commitment has been strengthened by the Xi Jinping government's determination to achieve the China Dream of a reunified and rejuvenated China, a primary goal strongly reinforced at the Nineteenth Chinese Communist Party Congress in 2017.[2] The many security threats China has faced throughout most of its recent history came from large powers building strategic forces and influence along China's periphery. With the opening to the United States under President Nixon and Chairman Mao and the demise of the Soviet Union at the end of the Cold War, the danger of superpower threat to and attack on China declined. Nevertheless, Chinese officials showed continued strong concern over perceived US-led efforts in the post–Cold War period to use strategic deployments as well as economic and political pressures, especially along China's periphery, in order to "encir-

205

cle" and "contain" China's rising influence in Asian and world affairs. China's negative assessment of the implications for China of the Obama administration's rebalance policy underlined such long-standing Chinese concerns with superpower influence along China's rim.[3]

Meanwhile, the stability of nearby Asia has a direct impact on the beneficial international environment China has been seeking in order to foster economic growth—the key determinant of Chinese Communist Party legitimacy in the post-Mao period. And nearby Asia is much more important to Chinese economic interests than world areas farther away from China. Thus, China receives wide publicity as it has risen to become the largest trader in Africa in recent years, but its trade with South Korea in recent years was often more than its trade with the entire African continent.[4]

The findings of this and earlier chapters show that the wide array of key Chinese territorial, security, economic, and other concerns in nearby Asia have prompted Chinese leaders repeatedly to take decisive actions to protect their interests, even in the face of strong and adverse international circumstances. This pattern has not been followed in other world regions, where Chinese interests are less important and willingness to stand against strong international opposition is weaker. Mao Zedong's repeated confrontations with nuclear-armed American and Soviet intervention and pressure focused on nearby Asia. Deng Xiaoping showed consistent support for the internationally abhorrent Khmer Rouge in Cambodia in the face of Soviet Union–backed Vietnamese opposition; Deng decided to invade Vietnam despite the danger of Soviet attack on China in order to counter the Vietnamese invasion of Cambodia. For many years, recent Chinese leaders were much less prone than Mao and Deng to undertake risky initiatives that would seriously complicate Chinese international relationships. However, they repeatedly pledged to put aside the benefits of the recent period and attack Taiwan if it declared independence. And in the past decade they have undermined China's image as a responsible and moderate rising power with repeated resort to coercion, intimidation, extralegal measures, and violence beyond the pale of international norms in support of territorial claims and ambitions around China's rim. They also at times have stood in the way of international pressure on North Korea, and to a lesser degree Myanmar, that would have jeopardized Chinese interests in sustaining a stable situation in these areas along China's periphery.

The wide range of international variables influencing Chinese interests in nearby Asia over the years have mixed with changing and often conflicting Chinese policy priorities. The result has been patterns of advancing relations compromised by negative legacies and inconsistent directions. An assessment in chapter 10 sees China's rising influence in Asia encumbered by these changing circumstances, negative legacies, and inconsistent imperatives.

RELATIONS WITH JAPAN

China's historic antipathy toward Japan on account of Japan's record as the most brutal imperialist power in China during the nineteenth and twentieth centuries and China's deep suspicion of Japan's close alignment with the United States in recent periods of tension between Beijing and Washington have been at the forefront in Chinese foreign relations in Asia. As in the case of Chinese disputes with Japan over the Senkaku/Diaoyu Islands during 2012, Chinese animosity toward Japan sometimes receives enormous publicity and is depicted as the unquestioned determinant in Sino-Japanese relations. Nevertheless, the salience of these negative historical Chinese legacies and ongoing strategic concerns in fact has waxed and waned over the decades. The negatives flowing from these legacies and concerns have been balanced with strong Chinese economic and strategic interests in cooperating closely with Asia's leading developed country. In particular, the Chinese leadership often has sought to keep open channels of beneficial foreign trade, investment, assistance, and other interchange with Japan, even when political and security relations have been tense and confrontational.

The balance moved toward greater bilateral antagonism and rivalry with the coming to power of the Xi Jinping government amid Chinese nationalistic outrage at Japan's purchase of the disputed Senkaku (Diaoyu) Islands in 2012. China subsequently pursued a confrontational posture over territorial disputes; Beijing gave higher priority to advancing its claims in the East China Sea and South China Sea. Strident official statements and commentary repeatedly attacked and sought to demonize Japanese prime minister Shinzo Abe (2012–), who had Japanese forces stand against Chinese intrusions in the Japanese-controlled islands. Trade and investment dropped sharply for a time. Japan did not buckle under Chinese pressure. It became China's main international opponent as it built defenses at home, maneuvered for advantage in Asia, and sought and received strong backing from US leaders increasingly concerned with Chinese assertiveness and expansion.[5]

Japan became the major base used by the United States in the policy of containment of China during the Cold War. China opposed the United States–Japan Security Treaty and the large presence of US military forces in Japan. At the same time, Chinese officials in the 1950s and 1960s engaged in active interchange with opposition politicians and opinion leaders in Japan. Public opinion in Japan tended to favor improved relations with China. Business interests there chafed at US-led efforts to restrict Japanese and other allied economic interchange with China.[6]

China toughened its public posture toward Japan as part of its broadly more radical approach to domestic and foreign policy issues during the period of the Great Leap Forward in the late 1950s. The collapse of the Sino-Soviet alliance coincided with more pragmatic economic policies in China during the early 1960s. Against this background, Chinese leaders came to welcome Japan's interest in developing trade and other economic relations. An agreement in 1962 governed five years of trade anticipated at a value of $100 million annually. In fact, the new arrangement and other channels of exchange saw Sino-Japanese trade grow from $137 million in 1963 to over $600 million in 1966 before declining during the violent period of China's Cultural Revolution and then recovering again to about $600 million in 1969. Japan became an increasingly important source for material needed for China's economic modernization; the pragmatic Sino-Japanese relationship continued even during the disruptions of the Cultural Revolution. Japan was the major developed country involved in the support of China's economy.[7]

While continuing to trade with Japan even during the most disruptive and violent years of the Cultural Revolution in the late 1960s, Beijing also strove to use its nascent opening to the Nixon administration and growing pro-PRC sentiment in Japan in order to isolate Japanese prime minister Eisaku Sato and his conservative Liberal Democratic Party (LDP) government over their refusal to break ties with Taiwan and establish ties with Beijing. Richard Nixon's surprise opening to China forced a change in government in Japan. Sato, with a tough policy toward China, was replaced and the new Japanese government quickly adjusted policy, setting the stage for improved political as well as economic relations for much of the rest of the Cold War. A highlight of progress was the establishment of official diplomatic relations in 1972 using an arrangement to deal with continued unofficial Japanese relations with Taiwan that became known as the Japanese formula, which was followed by the United States in its normalization of relations with China. Another highlight was the signing of the China-Japan Peace and Friendship Treaty in 1978, in which China pressed to include a clause opposing "hegemony," a reference to joint opposition to Soviet international expansion. As in the case of Chinese interaction with the United States and US allies, China at this time urged strong Japanese defense and other measures as part of an international united front to deal with the menace seen in expanding Soviet international power and influence. Chinese long-standing concerns with the historical legacies of Japan's aggression against China leading to World War II and the perceived potential revival of what China called Japanese militarism were played down in the interest of seeing stronger Japanese national security efforts against the Soviet danger.[8]

As post-Mao China developed an "open door" foreign economic policy in the late 1970s, Japan loomed large in China's development calculus. Japan was China's largest trading partner. Aid relations grew rapidly, and by 1982 China was the largest recipient of official Japanese development assistance. Nonetheless, Chinese discontent grew in the 1980s over what China's officials and opinion leaders perceived as asymmetrical aspects of the economic relationship. For example, China sold Japan coal, oil, and raw materials;

Japan sold China higher-value-added machinery, autos, and other equipment. Uncertain about the overall business climate in China, Japanese business and government representatives eschewed large-scale direct investment in China; Japan also shared less technology with China than with some other developing countries. Combined with Chinese irritation over the refusal of Japanese officials to take what Beijing saw as an appropriately contrite posture regarding Japan's negative war record in China, the seeming imbalance in economic benefits led to sharp criticisms and demonstrations against Japan by students, opinion leaders, and some officials. Both governments moved to minimize the disputes, with Japan notably stepping up its aid efforts in China and curbing official references to the war record that were likely to elicit a sharp Chinese response.[9]

There also was some ambivalence in China's attitude to growing US-Japan security relations, which became especially close during the rule of President Ronald Reagan and Prime Minister Yasuhiro Nakasone. As explained in chapter 3, China shifted in the early 1980s to a more evenhanded posture in dealing with the superpowers and was less supportive of strengthening US security measures around China's periphery in Asia; the phase didn't last long, and China eventually came to support American and Japanese approaches in the face of a continued Soviet hard line in Asia up to the mid-1980s.

A period of several years after the Tiananmen incident of 1989 was widely acknowledged as the most positive and cooperative period in Sino-Japanese relations since World War II. Japan's initial response to the incident was muted. Tokyo went along with the United States and other leading developed countries in the so-called Group of Seven (G-7) as it imposed sanctions against China. In July 1990, however, Tokyo diverged from the rest of the G-7 to announce a resumption of lending to China. The Chinese government strongly supported the Japanese move, which ushered in a three-year period of cooperation and cordiality.[10]

A visit to China by Prime Minister Toshiki Kaifu in 1991 confirmed that Tiananmen was no longer an obstacle to a cordial relationship. The change in Japanese policy coincided with a surge in Japanese investment in China; many Japanese business leaders judged that Chinese authorities had shown themselves to be capable of maintaining stability, and this and later rapid Chinese economic growth encouraged Japanese investment. In a notable departure from past Japanese practice emphasizing the primacy of relations with the United States and the US-Japan alliance, Japanese prime minister Morihiro Hosokawa declared in late 1991 that Japan's relationship with China was as important as its relationship with the United States. A successful visit to China by the Japanese emperor in 1992 indicated just how far the two sides were willing to go in order to put the past behind them, at least for the time being. More forthright expressions of regret by Japanese leaders, including Hosokawa's in 1993 for past Japanese aggression against China, also were appreciated by the Chinese. Economic relations developed rapidly, with China becoming Japan's second-largest destination for direct foreign investment, after the United States. Official dialogues and intergovernmental cooperation expanded, including cooperation in military and security matters.[11]

The broad trends in relations since the mid-1990s have featured serious differences over historical, territorial, diplomatic, and security issues, even though economic ties and interdependence continue to advance. Japanese elite and public opinion has turned against China, and Chinese opinion of Japan remains suspicious and largely negative. Both sides demonstrate a tendency to react in nationalistic ways in response to perceived affronts by the other. Chinese official interaction with Japan was the least forthcoming in the general Chinese efforts in the post–Cold War period to reassure China's neighbors that China's rise would not threaten their interests. Although some Japanese leaders tried to give greater priority to improving relations with China, more common was a defensive concern about rising Chinese power asserting leadership in Asia at odds with fundamental Japanese political, economic, and security interests. As a result, Japanese leaders sought closer security ties with the United States and broadened relationships with Australia, India, and other powers seen useful in securing an Asian environment that would support and protect the interests of Japan as its power diminishes in the face of China's rise.

Against this background, a range of specialists have foreseen Sino-Japanese rivalry and confrontation characterizing the order in Asia for many years to come.[12] They highlight negative changes in attitudes of Japanese and Chinese decision makers, opinion leaders, and popular opinion about the status and outlook of their mutual relations. They tend to see initiatives reflecting strong Sino-Japanese friction and rivalry. Signs of Sino-Japanese competition and rivalry include the following:

- A continuing face-off between Chinese maritime security forces challenging Japanese counterparts in the contested Senkaku (Diaoyu) Islands
- Repeated large-scale military shows of force by China along Japan's rim viewed as threatening in Japan
- Repeated strong Japanese-US demonstrations of military power and resolve, sometimes directed at North Korea and sometimes viewed in Beijing as directed at China
- US-Japanese efforts to shore up the defenses and resolve of Southeast Asian nations, Australia, and India in the face of rising assertiveness by China over territorial claims and other issues
- Separate and seemingly competing proposals by China and Japan to establish free-trade arrangements and other agreements influencing the future order in the Asia-Pacific and the ongoing rivalry between China and Japan

to lead in the region. Most recently, Japan in 2017 led efforts to create a modified version of the Trans-Pacific Partnership (TPP) economic agreement that was fostered by the Barack Obama government but abandoned by the Donald Trump government. The TPP was widely viewed as a counter to China's rising economic ascendance in the region. [13]

- Intense Sino-Japanese competition for control of energy and other resources and disputed territory in the East China Sea and sometimes intense competition to gain improved access to Russian oil in the Far East
- Repeated Chinese international lobbying against Japanese efforts to gain a permanent seat in the UN Security Council
- Greater Japanese support for Taiwan
- Significant cutbacks in Japanese aid to China
- Increased Japanese willingness to deploy military forces in Asia in support of US initiatives
- Increased Japanese efforts to solidify relations with South Korea and the United States to form a closer Japan-South Korea-US alignment in reaction to North Korea's nuclear threat and China's refusal to implement stronger sanctions against Pyongyang

Underlying changes in Japan said to foreshadow greater Japanese-Chinese rivalry involved (1) a focus by strategic thinkers in the Japanese government and elsewhere in Japan on China's rising power as the major long-term security concern for Japan after the collapse of the Soviet Union and the end of the Cold War; (2) an increasing view by the Japanese of China as a rival for regional influence; (3) a lessening of Japanese sensitivity and responsiveness to Chinese demands for special consideration on account of Japan's negative war record in China seventy years ago; (4) a strong sense of national pride and determination among Japanese leaders and the public to preserve Japanese interests in the face of Chinese charges and demands. [14]

Meanwhile, changes in China said to be leading to greater friction with Japan included (1) rising state-directed Chinese nationalism focused negatively on Japan;[15] (2) Chinese strategists' long-standing concerns about Japan's military capabilities, compounded by US forces in the Asia-Pacific;[16] (3) Chinese concerns about stronger Japanese strategic support for US regional deployments at odds with Chinese interests; (4) Chinese government specialists' awareness of hardening Japanese attitudes toward China.

A contrasting perspective—which I favored in the past but have been forced to modify in the face of the acute recent tensions in Sino-Japanese relations—gave greater weight to the common interests and forces that continue to bind Sino-Japanese relations and to limit the chances of serious confrontation or conflict. Mutual interests centered on strong, growing economic and strategic interdependence between Japan and China and the influence of the United States and other third parties, including other national powers in Asia—all of whom have favored and appeared ready to work to preserve Sino-Japanese stability. The argument against the development of serious Sino-Japanese confrontation involved the following elements: (1) Both the Japanese and the Chinese governments remained domestically focused and seemed at least until recently to give high priority to the economic development of their countries, which appeared to require peaceful and cooperative relationships with Asian neighbors, notably with each other. (2) China valued Japan for foreign investment and technology and as a market for Chinese goods; Japan was increasingly dependent on China as a market, source of imports, and offshore manufacturing base. (3) Exchanges between Japan and China grew markedly. This involved tourism, students, and other interchange. (4) Few if any governments active in Asian affairs benefited from or sought to promote greater Sino-Japanese friction.[17]

The deterioration in China's relations with Japan since 2012 shows that despite the above mitigating factors, strong rivalry and repeated confrontation prevail. The above factors appear sufficient to prevent war, but the Xi Jinping government's active foreign-policy assertiveness, strident nationalism, and revanchist territorial claims have focused strongly on an uncompromising Japan. This mix has driven Sino-Japanese relations to their worst state since 1945.

RELATIONS WITH TAIWAN

As discussed in chapter 2, Mao Zedong repeatedly probed US and Nationalist Chinese defenses in the Taiwan Strait during the 1950s. There were major episodes of military conflict during the so-called Taiwan Strait crises of 1954–55 and again in 1958. Mao's actions were in line with broader efforts to confront and counter American-backed security measures in the ring of containment established following the start of the Korean War. The actions concerned and sometimes alarmed Nikita Khrushchev and the other Soviet leaders who were linked with China and wary of getting dragged into a war with the United States over Taiwan or other issues. Aligned with Chiang Kai-shek's Nationalist forces on Taiwan, the US leadership also was wary of getting involved in direct combat with China, though it showed resolve and repeatedly used threats of nuclear war and thereby engaged in what was pejoratively called "nuclear blackmail" in order to get the Communists to stop their aggression.

Communist military probes subsided with the massive economic collapse of the failed Great Leap Forward and the public break between China and its superpower ally in Moscow. The United States worked to insure a stasis in the Taiwan Strait by curbing Chiang Kai-shek's ambitions to exploit the Chinese difficulties and launch an attack on the mainland. The Communists on the mainland arguably enjoyed more support than the Nationalists in Taiwan among the newly emerging former colonies obtaining independence in the 1950s and 1960s. Nevertheless, Taiwan competed actively through foreign assistance efforts and other measures to win support in the developing world. Beijing's attraction also was overshadowed by the frequent xenophobic outbursts evident during the radical stage of "Red Guard diplomacy" during the early years of China's Cultural Revolution.[18]

The opening of China to relations with the United States and its allies and associates fundamentally changed the cross-strait dynamic. China enjoyed broad international support as it took the China seat on the United Nations Security Council and related bodies and Taiwan lost official representation. Chinese leaders used negotiations on diplomatic relations with the United States, Japan, and dozens of other countries establishing official relations with Beijing at this time to require breaking official ties with Taiwan. Within a few years, Taiwan was isolated, with only two dozen states sustaining official relations. The loss of US official recognition and the ending of the US-Taiwan defense treaty and all other official connections placed the Nationalist Party government, now led by Chiang Kai-shek's son, Chiang Ching-kuo, under enormous pressure. Not only was Taiwan less secure vis-à-vis China and acutely isolated internationally, it was under attack domestically from large and growing numbers of Taiwan's citizens who were unsympathetic to the authoritarian regime and favored a greater voice for their ambitions for Taiwan to be an independent government separate from China.[19]

Building on its international advantages, China appealed to Taiwan to pursue a "peaceful" path to reunification and as part of the first steps to open links for direct trade, transportation, and other communication across the strait. Taiwan rebuffed the Chinese initiatives. It sustained close unofficial ties with the United States, including active arms sales, despite US-Chinese agreements ostensibly limiting such sales. Taiwan's economy was strong and deeply integrated with Japan, the United States, and other major trading powers. Politically, the Chiang Ching-kuo government moved toward liberalization and democracy, which eased the split between the "mainlanders," those who came from mainland China with Chiang Kai-shek and their descendants, and the "Taiwanese," those whose roots in Taiwan went back to before the Chiang Kai-shek government, which was imposed on them after World War II.[20]

As martial law and other features of the authoritarian regime in Taiwan ended in the late 1980s, Chiang Ching-kuo's successor, Lee Teng-hui, took power as president and chairman of the Nationalist Party. Lee encouraged an emerging two-party political system as his Nationalist Party government sought its legitimacy at the ballot box from the voters of Taiwan. Unlike Chiang Kai-shek and his son, who stayed in Taiwan during their presidencies, Lee sought international travel as a means to highlight his importance to

Taiwan's voters and to enhance Taiwan's international stature. As explained in chapter 4, international circumstances were favorable as China was isolated on account of the harsh crackdown after the Tiananmen incident, and Taiwan's emerging democracy and vibrant economy appeared very positive by comparison. Even the Clinton administration was persuaded to change policy and allow Lee to visit the United States in 1995.

Lee's American visit prompted an extraordinary Chinese response, with a string of live-fire military exercises including ballistic missile tests in sensitive areas of the Taiwan Strait for the next nine months. The exercises were designed to deter Lee and others in Taiwan whom China suspected of working toward Taiwan independence. They also seemed designed to influence and perhaps intimidate the Taiwan voters in the lead-up to the first direct election of the Taiwan president in March 1996. And they demonstrated to the United States the risks and costs it would bear in the event that it supported Lee in further moves toward Taiwan independence. [21]

The Clinton administration delayed reaction to the Chinese military exercises for seven months. As the exercises continued and reached a crescendo prior to the Taiwan presidential election, the US government sent two aircraft carrier battle groups to the Taiwan area, marking the most serious US-China military face-off over Taiwan since the 1950s. [22]

Subsequently, cross-strait dynamics changed markedly. [23] An important area of continuity was that China continued to encourage cross-strait economic and social exchanges, and these were attractive to many businesspeople and others in Taiwan who pressed their government to allow for closer economic and other advantageous relations with China.

Significant change came as China increased diplomatic pressure to isolate and punish Taiwan for its efforts to seek greater international representation through presidential visits and other means. In the wake of China's show of resolve in the Taiwan Strait following the Lee Teng-hui visit to the United States, few nations—including the United States—were prepared to bear the responsibility and costs associated with hosting the Taiwan president. Many nations that had been open to informal contacts with Taiwan's leaders pulled back in the face of intense pressure from China.

Perhaps the most important change came in military preparations. The US deployment of aircraft carriers showed China that its military preparations would need to be sufficient to offset US military intervention to support Taiwan. The double-digit increases in the Chinese defense budgets for the next two decades focused importantly on building capabilities not only to intimidate Taiwan but to deter American intervention.

A new political order in Taiwan under President Chen Shui-bian began in May 2000, ending fifty years of rule by the Nationalist Party. Many in Taiwan, the PRC, and the United States linked Chen with the past strongly pro-independence stance of his party, the Democratic Progressive Party

(DPP). There were widespread predictions of an imminent crisis in cross-strait relations when Chen was elected. In fact, Chen initially appeared more moderate than was widely anticipated.[24]

A turn for the worse in cross-strait relations came with Chen Shui-bian's shift to a much more assertive and pro-independence stance in 2003–4, which Chinese officials watched with dismay. Chen's government rejected the principle of one China, condemned China's pressure tactics, and pushed hard for broad-ranging legal and institutional reforms in civil service practices, education, cultural support, public information, diplomacy, and other areas. The reforms, which included major constitutional changes, sought to end past government practices that identified Taiwan with China and reinforced Taiwan's identity as a country permanently separate from China.[25]

Chinese and US officials viewed the reforms as steps toward independence and as making it increasingly unlikely that Taiwan ever would voluntarily agree to be part of China.[26] Chinese officials focused on possible changes in provisions in the Republic of China constitution that identified Taiwan with China. They warned that removing those provisions and establishing a formal and legally binding status for Taiwan as a country permanently separate from China would result in China's use of force. Officials from the United States were anxious to avoid this outcome. Overall, the situation in the Taiwan Strait became tenser. China's leaders found that their mix of economic incentives, proposals for talks, military threats, and coercive diplomacy had obviously failed to stop Taiwan's moves toward greater separation.[27]

Seeing the rise of instability and an increased danger of conflict in the Taiwan area, US president George W. Bush publicly rebuked Taiwan's president on December 9, 2003. Chinese officials urged US and international pressure to rein in Chen. They judged that a strident public Chinese stance probably would increase support for him in the prevailing atmosphere in Taiwan and thus be counterproductive for China's purposes.[28]

Chen's narrow reelection victory in March 2004 showed Chinese and other observers how far the Taiwan electorate had moved from the 1990s, when pro-independence was a clear liability among the Taiwanese voters. Chinese officials were pleased that US pressure sought to curb Chen's more ambitious reform efforts that flirted with de jure independence, but they pushed for more overt US pressure, including curbs on US arms sales.[29]

Officials from the United States continued to press Chen to avoid provocative actions but remained firm in maintaining military support for Taiwan as a means to deter China from using force against Taiwan. They intervened repeatedly in the lead-up to the 2004 legislative elections to highlight differences between US policy and the assertive positions of President Chen and his supporters.[30]

In the end, the turmoil in Taiwan's relations with China and with the United States caused by Chen's maneuvers and their negative consequences for cross-strait and US-Taiwan relations, along with Chen's apparent deep personal involvement in corruption scandals, seemed to undermine the attractiveness of DPP candidates in Taiwan's legislative elections in January 2008 and the presidential election in March 2008. The result was a landslide victory for the Nationalist Party (Kuomintang, KMT) candidates. The party gained overwhelming control of the legislature; the new president, Ma Ying-jeou, had a strong political mandate to pursue policies of reassurance and moderation in cross-strait relations. [31]

PRESIDENTS MA YING-JEOU (2008–16) AND TSAI ING-WEN (2016–): STABILITY, THEN UNCERTAINTY

President Ma came to power with an agenda emphasizing that his government would not move Taiwan toward independence and stressing closer economic, social, and other contacts across the strait. Ma and his colleagues in Taiwan and their counterparts in China emphasized that progress would be easier in building closer and mutually advantageous economic and social ties; however, issues of security and sovereignty posed by the growing Chinese military buildup opposite Taiwan and reaching agreement on Taiwan's desired greater international participation were harder to deal with. [32]

On the whole, the improvements in cross-strait relations were rapid and impressive. The security situation in the Taiwan Strait entered a period of relaxing tensions. Both Beijing and Taipei emphasized enhancing people-to-people contacts and expanding economic ties. A major development was an agreement in 2010 establishing free trade between China and Taiwan known as the Economic Cooperation Framework Agreement (ECFA), which provided privileged access to Chinese markets and other economic benefits for various important constituencies in Taiwan. [33] On balance, Taiwan's voters saw the benefits as sufficient and supported President Ma's reelection in 2012. Also, the opposition DPP gradually moved its cross-strait policies away from past challenges to China and toward a more cooperative approach favored by the Taiwan electorate. [34]

There was no significant action on the part of the Chinese government to reduce its military presence directly opposite Taiwan. President Ma also was reluctant to engage in talks with China on a possible peace agreement, and he argued that discussion on possible reunification between Taiwan and China would have to await developments after his term in office.

The numerous cross-strait agreements brought burgeoning face-to-face interaction between Taiwan's and China's governments after decades of no direct dealings. The agreements were between ostensibly unofficial organizations—Taiwan's Straits Exchange Foundation (SEF) and China's Association for Relations across the Taiwan Strait (ARATS)—but they required officials of the two governments to deal with each other on a host of transportation, food safety, financial regulation, and law enforcement issues. In effect, three channels of communication were now active between Taiwan and China: the SEF-ARATS exchanges; exchanges between the leaders of the Chinese Communist Party (CCP) and Taiwan's KMT; and widening government-to-government coordination and cooperation on a variety of cross-strait issues. Many of the agreements, interactions, and understandings focused on managing the large-scale trade and investment between Taiwan and China.[35]

Meanwhile, the Ma Ying-jeou government achieved a breakthrough in getting China to allow Taiwan to participate in the annual World Health Assembly (WHA) meeting as an observer using the name "Chinese Taipei." Other evidence of progress in China-Taiwan relations over issues regarding Taiwan's participation in international affairs was the diminishment of what had been intense Taiwan-China competition for international recognition.[36]

US reaction to the developments in China-Taiwan relations was positive. The Bush administration welcomed the efforts of the Ma government and China's positive response as stabilizing and beneficial for all parties concerned. It turned aside an initiative by President-elect Ma to visit the United States for talks with US officials prior to his inauguration. Ma made no other such requests to the US government; he worked hard to keep his transit stops in the United States discreet in ways that would not complicate US relations with China. High-level contacts occurred between the United States and Taiwan in quiet and private ways that avoided upsetting China, and ongoing US military consultations with and advice to Taiwan's armed forces continued.[37]

The Bush administration delayed until close to the last minute approval of a large arms sales package for Taiwan. The approved package worth $6.5 billion was the largest during the tenure of the Bush government. Initial generous offers from the United States during Bush's first year in office were repeatedly delayed and whittled down on account of partisan bickering and funding delays for many years in Taiwan; this was followed by US reluctance to provide arms that would appear to support President Chen Shui-bian's provocative stance toward China. In the end, the package in 2008 represented about half of what Taiwan said it wanted, and it did not include sixty-six F-16 fighters that Taiwan had been trying for years to get the US government to consider selling to Taiwan. China reacted to the sale with strong criticism and suspension of military contacts with the United States. Those contacts were resumed in mid-2009.[38]

The Barack Obama government welcomed the new stability in cross-strait ties. Like the outgoing Bush government, the Obama administration appeared to be relying on President Ma and his team to continue to manage cross-strait ties in positive ways that would not cause the Taiwan "hot spot" to reemerge on the already crowded list of policy priorities needing urgent attention by the new US leader.[39] The Obama government followed through with a $6 billion arms package for Taiwan in 2010 and a similarly large package in 2011. The packages did not include F-16 fighters; they prompted sometimes strident public complaints from China, along with limited substantive retaliation.[40]

Unfortunately for Chinese leaders seeking to bring Taiwan closer to Beijing's desired reunification of Taiwan with the People's Republic of China, the domestic foundations of President Ma Ying-jeou's positive engagement with China remained unsteady. Vocal oppositionists in the Democratic Progressive Party (DPP) and other critics continued attacking as they grew in political prominence. Domestic opinion in Taiwan turned against closer ties with China, and mass demonstrations opposed agreements seen as making Taiwan more dependent on China. Ma's overall approval rating plummeted and his Nationalist (or Kuomintang, KMT) party lost the presidential and legislative elections in January 2016 by such wide margins that it was questionable how soon it would revive as a leading force in Taiwan politics.

The incoming DPP administration of President Tsai Ing-wen promised to sustain the status quo in cross-strait relations as it refused Chinese demands and pressures to accommodate Chinese interests. Beijing insisted that the new government had to endorse a vague notion of the China-favored "one-China principle" it saw in the so-called 1992 consensus reached by mainland China and Taiwan representatives meeting at that earlier time. China's insistence came notably in the first summit meeting between the leader of the Beijing government and the government in Taiwan as Xi Jinping and Ma Ying-jeou held talks in Singapore in November 2015, two months before the January 2016 Taiwan presidential and legislative elections. At that meeting, both Xi and Ma stressed the importance of the 1992 consensus.[41]

President Tsai sought to avoid trouble with Beijing but viewed the 1992 consensus as undermining Taiwan's sovereignty. To coerce deference to its demands, Beijing gradually increased negative military, diplomatic, and economic pressures with an eye to weakening Taiwan and thereby eroding domestic support for the Tsai government.[42] The Barack Obama government urged restraint. President-elect Donald Trump upset Beijing by accepting a congratulatory phone call from President Tsai in December 2016 and raising questions about deferring to Beijing on Taiwan, but within two months he endorsed the traditional and ambiguous American "one-China policy," which President Xi required before the Trump government could move forward with China's government. Given the controversy over the Trump-Tsai phone conversation, President Obama halted a planned sale of over $1 billion in arms to Taiwan at the end of his tenure. The Trump government went forward with the sale in mid-2017.[43]

RELATIONS WITH THE KOREAN PENINSULA

In the wake of the Korean War, discussed in chapter 2, China had a strong advantage over the Soviet Union in relations with Kim Il Sung and his Communist government in North Korea. At enormous cost in manpower and resources, China's military rescued the North Korean regime from annihilation at the hands of the United States and provided secure "rear area" support against a strengthening South Korea and the United States building the sinews of containment on the peninsula. Solicitous of Chinese assistance and maintaining close North Korean–Chinese relations, Kim Il Sung nonetheless established a position as the sole major Communist leader in Asia able to sustain a balanced position without taking sides in what emerged as intense Sino-Soviet competition for international support. As the Soviet leadership of Leonid Brezhnev expanded involvement in Asia in competition with China for influence in the region, Kim maneuvered between Moscow and Beijing.[44]

China's Cultural Revolution featured Red Guard attacks against Kim Il Sung as a "fat revisionist," and normal Sino–North Korean interchange was disrupted with the collapse of regular lines of communication and command. There was possible danger to China caused by the so-called *Pueblo* incident, involving North Korean capture in January 1968 of a US ship and crew engaged in gathering electronic intelligence off the coast of North Korea. However, the impact of the incident was overshadowed in the United States by the Communist Tet offensive in Vietnam. China meanwhile was in the throes of violent internal turmoil during this phase of the Cultural Revolution.[45]

Chinese leaders endeavored to reach out to international leaders including Kim Il Sung as they sought to build leverage and avoid isolation in the face of burgeoning pressure and threat from the Soviet Union in 1969. Kim disapproved of China's opening to the United States, though he came to engage in talks and reach agreements with South Korea, temporarily easing tensions on the peninsula. Chinese leader Deng Xiaoping reportedly counseled Kim Il Sung at the time of the US retreat from Vietnam in 1975 that North Korea should not use the occasion to attack South Korea.[46]

After Deng was again purged in early 1976 and then returned to power beginning in 1977, the Chinese reformer pursued closer relations with the United States and Japan in opposition to what China called Soviet "hegemonism." Deng worked hard, notably during a five-day visit to North Korea in 1978, to prevent Kim Il Sung's strong disagreement with China's pro-US and pro-Japan positions from driving North Korea to the Soviet side in the intense Sino-Soviet rivalry.[47] As discussed in chapter 3, China in 1981 came to play down ties with the United States and Japan while opening to more exchanges with the Soviet Union in a brief period of "independent" foreign policy. The Chinese change opened greater common ground between China and North Korea. Improvement in North Korean–Chinese relations continued during the visit to China of Kim Il Sung's son and heir apparent, Kim Jong Il, in mid-1983. China's relations with North Korea then declined after North Korea's assassination of South Korean leaders in a bombing in Rangoon, Burma, in October 1983. Continuing to play both sides of the street in a continuing strong Sino-Soviet competition for influence, Kim Il Sung in 1984 made his first visit to the Soviet Union in over twenty years.[48]

Mikhail Gorbachev's Soviet Union steadily withdrew the expensive support the USSR had been providing to North Korea and began reciprocating strong South Korean interest in improving relations with Moscow as well as Beijing. The Soviet Union and South Korea established diplomatic relations in 1990. Post-Mao China also was interested in closer relations with South Korea and its vibrant economy. Trade grew rapidly in the 1980s despite the absence of official relations between the two governments. China endeavored to sustain good relations with North Korea while moving forward incrementally with South Korea, eventually establishing official diplomatic relations in 1992.[49]

Chinese policy and practice toward North and South Korea following the end of the Cold War showed China endeavoring to sustain a leading position in relations with both North and South Korea as it reacted to changing circumstances on the Korean peninsula. Growing Chinese frustration with the twists and turns of North Korean behavior, especially Pyongyang's nuclear weapons development, has not resulted in a fundamental change in China's reluctance to pressure North Korea to conform more to international norms and eschew provocations and confrontation. China's focus has been to preserve stability in an uncertain environment caused by internal pressures and international provocations of North Korea and erratic policies by the United States and South Korea. China has a history of following practices that give priority to positive incentives rather than pressure in order to elicit North Korean willingness to avoid further provocations and to return to negotiations on eventual denuclearization.

Developments in the two decades after the end of the Cold War can be divided into three periods up to recent years:[50]

- 1989–2000 featured Chinese angst over North Korean leadership transition and instability and economic collapse as well as a crisis with the United States prompted by North Korea's nuclear weapons development. China supported US efforts to negotiate the Agreed Framework of 1994, which eased tensions over North Korea's suspected nuclear weapons program; it provided measured material support for North Korea in a period of economic collapse; and it markedly improved economic and political ties with South Korea.

- 2000–2001 featured a period of unprecedented détente, where China facilitated North Korean outreach and endeavored to keep pace with expanding North Korean contacts with South Korea, the United States, Russia, and others.
- 2002–9 featured periodic and intense North Korean provocations and wide swings in US policy ranging from thinly disguised efforts to force regime change in North Korea to close collaboration with Pyongyang negotiators. South Korean policy also shifted markedly from a soft to a harder line in dealing with North Korea.

A careful review of the gains China has made in improving relations with Asian neighbors and elsewhere in recent years shows South Korea to have been an area of considerable achievement, until recent years. The Chinese advances with South Korea also coincided with the most serious friction in US–South Korean relations since the Korean War during the first term (2001–5) of the George W. Bush administration. Thus, China's influence relative to the United States grew on the Korean peninsula.

Meanwhile, US policy evolved in dealing with North Korea. By 2003 the George W. Bush administration was working much more closely with China in order to facilitate international talks on North Korea's nuclear weapons program. North Korea at that time seemed to prefer to deal directly with the United States on this issue. While such bilateral interchange with North Korea presumably would have boosted US influence relative to that of China in peninsula affairs, the US government tended to see such US–North Korean contacts as counterproductive for US interests in securing a verifiable end of North Korea's nuclear weapons program. Thus, China's influence grew as it joined with the United States in the multilateral efforts to deal with the North Korean nuclear weapons issue on the one hand, while Beijing sustained its position as the foreign power having the closest relationship with the reclusive North Korean regime on the other.[51]

Against this background, China's relations with South Korea improved markedly.[52] China became South Korea's leading trading partner, the recipient in some years of the largest amount of South Korean foreign investment, and the most important foreign destination for South Korean tourists and students. For many years, it was a close and often like-minded partner in dealing with issues posed by North Korea's nuclear weapons program and related provocations on the one hand, and dealing with the Bush administration's hard-line policy toward North Korea on the other.

South Korea's trade with China grew rapidly. Despite the global economic crisis of 2008–9, the two countries met a goal of $200 billion in trade in 2010, according to Chinese figures. Chinese trade figures showed that about 30 percent of South Korean exports went to China and that China ran a $70 billion trade deficit with South Korea in 2010. South Korea became the third largest source of foreign investment in China, and China became the largest destination of foreign investment from South Korea. Meanwhile, in the face of the Bush administration's tough stance toward North Korea, 2001–6, South Korea and China were close partners in dealing more moderately than the United States with issues posed by North Korea's nuclear weapons program and related provocations.[53]

As relations developed, however, China's economic importance for South Korea was seen by South Koreans more in both negative and positive ways. Periodic trade disputes came with growing concerns by South Korean manufacturers, political leaders, and public opinion about competition from fast-advancing Chinese enterprises. China's economic attractiveness to South Korean consumers declined markedly as a result of repeated episodes of Chinese exports of harmfully tainted consumer products to South Korean and other markets. South Korean leaders strove to break out of close dependence on economic ties with China through free-trade agreements and other arrangements with the United States, Japan, and the European Union that would ensure inputs of foreign investment and technology needed for South Korea to stay ahead of Chinese competitors.

Other differences between the two countries focused on competing Chinese and Korean claims regarding the scope and importance of the historical Goguryeo kingdom, China's longer-term ambitions in North Korea, and Chinese treatment of North Korean refugees in China and of South Koreans endeavoring to assist them there. The disputes had a strong impact on nationalistic South Korean political leaders and public opinion. Public opinion polls showed a significant decline in South Korean views of China and its policies and practices since earlier in the past decade.[54]

Regarding Chinese relations with North Korea, China's frustration followed the North Korean nuclear weapons tests in 2006 and 2009 and other provocations.[55] The evidence of growing Chinese frustration with North Korea was strong; contrary to past practice, the Chinese government allowed a public debate where relations with North Korea often were depicted as a liability for China, requiring serious readjustment in Chinese policy. On balance, the overall record of Chinese policy and practice demonstrated continuing caution; China endeavored to preserve important Chinese interests in stability on the Korean peninsula through judicious moves that struck an appropriate balance among varied Chinese relations with concerned parties at home and abroad. China remained wary that North Korea, the United States, and others could shift course, forcing further Chinese adjustments in response.

Chinese leaders recognized that their cautious policies had failed to halt North Korea's nuclear weapons development; they probably judged that they would be living with a nuclear North Korea for some time to come, even as they emphasized continued diplomatic efforts to reverse North Korea's nuclear weapons development and create a nuclear-free peninsula. They appeared resigned to joining with US and other leaders in what was characterized as "failure management" as far as North Korean nuclear weapons development was concerned.[56] They endeavored to preserve stability and Chinese equities with concerned powers. As in the recent past, they avoided pressure or other risky initiatives on their own, waiting for the actions of others or changed circumstances that would increase the prospects of curbing North Korea's nuclear challenge and allow for stronger Chinese measures to deal with nuclear North Korea.

Recent Developments—Setbacks for China

China continued to make gains since the start of 2010 in solidifying its position as the most important and avid supporter of the North Korean leadership as North Korea underwent the most significant leadership transition in a generation amid poor domestic conditions and generally unfriendly international circumstances.[57] China also deepened economic relations with both North and South Korea. Though discussions between China and North Korea remained secret, it appeared that bilateral relations registered significant improvement despite differences over North Korea's proliferation and military provocations.

The same was not true about China's relations with South Korea. In 2010, those ties reached the lowest point since the establishment of diplomatic relations. Contacts designed to improve relations, notably a visit of one of China's rising "fifth generation" leaders, Vice Prime Minister Li Keqiang, to Seoul in 2011 and a visit by President Lee Myung-Bak to Beijing in 2012, barely hid deep differences. China's refusal to criticize egregious North Korean military attacks against South Korea in 2010 left a lasting and widespread impression of where China's priorities were when choosing between North and South Korea. In particular, China refused to join strong international condemnation of North Korea's sinking in March 2010 of the South Korean warship *Cheonan*, which killed forty-three South Korean military personnel, and the North Korean artillery barrage in November 2010 attacking South Korean soldiers and civilians on a coastal island, killing four and injuring others. China also blocked or weakened efforts in the United Nations against the North Korean aggression. Against this background, and contrary to China's longer-term objective to diminish US and Japanese influence on the Korean peninsula, China faced strengthened US–South Korean and US–Japanese alliance relationships, and off-again on-again efforts to forge closer strategic coordination between South Korea and Japan over North Korean issues. Adding to South Korean and US differences with China was Beijing's unexpectedly strong public opposition in 2010 to US-ROK military exercises in the Yellow Sea that were targeted at showing allied resolve and deepening deterrence against further North Korean military provocations.[58]

In following years, China's approach to North and South Korea continued to be driven by a broad, albeit slow-moving and low-risk, drive to establish an order in the Korean peninsula more influenced by China and less influenced by foreign and other elements seen as adverse to Chinese interests. In this context, growing Chinese frustration with the twists and turns of North Korean behavior, especially Pyongyang's nuclear weapons development, did not result in a major change in China's reluctance to pressure North Korea to conform to international norms and eschew provocations and confrontation. China's focus was to preserve stability in an uncertain environment caused by internal pressures and international provocations of North Korea, and sometimes erratic policies by the United States and South Korea. China continued to follow practices that gave priority to renewed negotiations in the six-party talks. At least until recently, it tried to use positive incentives rather than pressure in order to elicit North Korean willingness to avoid further provocations and to return to negotiations on eventual denuclearization.

Even though the Xi Jinping government is more assertive and demanding on key issues, at bottom, Xi Jinping's international activism thus far has not changed fundamentally China's overall approach to the difficult choices Beijing faces in dealing with North Korea and preserving stability on the Korean peninsula. Beijing was more forthright in pressuring South Korea in 2016 and 2017 against the US deployment in South Korea of the advanced antiballistic missile system known as THAAD to defend against North Korean ballistic missiles. Seeing the system as a threat to China, Beijing employed a range of pressure tactics that negatively impacted trade, tourist exchanges, and other interaction with South Korea. The incoming South Korean government of President Moon Jae In (2017–) reached an agreement with China, easing the dispute. Compounding China's difficulty in managing recalcitrant North Korea has been the unprecedented public US pressure being applied by the Donald Trump government on North Korea to end its nuclear weapons program and on China to do more to pressure the North Koreans to stop.[59]

RELATIONS WITH SOUTHEAST ASIA AND THE ASIA-PACIFIC

It has not been easy for the People's Republic of China to sustain an approach or approaches to Southeast Asia that allow for steady progress for China in this important neighboring region. The 1950s featured strong Chinese political, military, and economic support for the Vietnamese and other Communist-led forces in Indochina battling US-backed French forces up to 1954 and then American-backed indigenous leaders. China was generally critical of regional governments that sided with the United States and established formal security relationships with the United States.[60]

The mid-1950s featured an interlude of "peaceful coexistence" consistent with the efforts of the Soviet Union to ease international tensions and advance relations with independent-minded governments emerging in the developing world. As discussed in chapter 2, China became more radical in foreign affairs as its domestic policies swung to extremes in the Great Leap Forward and disagreements with the Soviet Union led to an open Sino-Soviet rift by 1960. In Southeast Asia, China continued overt support for Communists in Vietnam and Laos. Thinly disguised Chinese propaganda, financial, and military support grew for Communist-led insurgencies targeting several pro-Western governments (Thailand, Malaysia, and the Philippines). Better hidden—even from the pro-China leader of Cambodia at the time, Prince Norodom Sihanouk—was Chinese support for Pol Pot and other Cambodian Communists who would form the Khmer Rouge. In 1960, China settled its disputed border with Burma—which until then had seen Chinese military forces cross into Burma repeatedly to deal with remnants of Chiang Kai-shek Nationalist forces operating there as well as other concerns for China.[61]

As noted in chapter 2, China for several years in the 1960s placed great emphasis on its ever-closer relationship with Indonesia and its leader, Sukarno, who increasingly favored left-leaning policies. China supported President Sukarno in his radical nationalist policies of confrontation with Malaysia, which was backed by Great Britain, over whether Malaysia or Indonesia should control the disputed regions of Sarawak and Sabah. China also cooperated closely with the Indonesian Communist Party (PKI), the world's largest nonruling Communist party, which was growing rapidly in influence under Sukarno's policies.

In September 1965, radical officers attempted a coup against the top-level, anti-Communist leadership of the army. Several army leaders were assassinated. General Suharto took control of the army and put down the abortive coup. The army blamed the coup attempt on the PKI and instigated an Indonesia-wide anti-Communist propaganda campaign. An anti-Communist reign of terror developed. Hundreds of thousands of Communists, ethnic Chinese, and others were killed; the PKI was crushed. General Suharto sidelined Sukarno and took power as president in 1968, consolidating his influence over the military and government. Indonesian relations with China were suspended and would not be resumed for over twenty years. [62]

Faced with the deepening American military involvement in Vietnam and among Western-leaning Southeast Asian governments in the 1960s, China expanded its support and involvement in backing North Vietnam and Communist-led fighters against the Americans. China also upped the ante in supporting the Communist-led insurgencies targeting Southeast Asian states with pro-US leanings. Meanwhile, Red Guard diplomacy beginning in 1966 alienated several Southeast Asian governments that had been favorable to China, notably Cambodia and Burma.

In Burma, relations deteriorated seriously in 1967 when clashes inspired by Cultural Revolution zealots led to full-scale anti-Chinese riots leaving over one hundred Chinese dead. China subsequently organized, armed, and trained a large (twenty thousand fighters) insurgency against the Burmese government under the rubric of the Burmese Communist Party, which posed the major security threat to the Burmese government for the next twenty years. [63]

Cambodia's Prince Sihanouk overcame difficulties with China during the early years of the Cultural Revolution. When he was toppled from power in 1970 by generals backed by the United States, Sihanouk was supported by Chinese leaders who encouraged him to align with the Chinese-backed Khmer Rouge guerrillas in Cambodia. China continued support for Sihanouk and the Khmer Rouge regime that followed the defeat of the US-backed government in 1975 with such egregious misrule and terror that over one million Cambodians died. [64]

As discussed in chapter 3, China's strong equities with the Vietnamese Communists and their associates in Laos were undermined as a result of China's alignment with the United States in the early 1970s against the USSR and the latter's strengthening relationship with Communist Vietnam. Le Duan, the Communist leader of Vietnam at the time, directed deliberations that decided to rely more closely on the Soviet Union and seek a military solution of Vietnamese reunification at odds with the Paris Peace Agreement of 1973. The decision strongly alienated China. After the Communist takeover of South Vietnam in 1975, Le Duan became leader of a unified Vietnamese state. He aligned Vietnam formally with the Soviet Union and then approved a Vietnamese invasion of Cambodia late in 1978 to overthrow the Chinese-backed Khmer Rouge government of that country. The movement toward this invasion caused a major disruption in relations between Vietnam and China; Vietnam expelled ethnic Chinese residents of the country as it cultivated a closer alliance with the Soviet Union. China launched a retaliatory invasion of Vietnam in February 1979 and maintained strong military pressure along the Sino-Vietnamese border throughout the 1980s; China also supported Khmer Rouge and other armed guerrillas resisting Vietnamese forces in Cambodia until the Vietnamese forces withdrew and peace was restored in Cambodia as a result of the Paris Peace Agreement of 1991.[65]

Against the background of the demise of the USSR in 1991 at the end of the Cold War, Chinese foreign relations with Southeast Asian neighbors went through distinct phases in the following decades. In the shifts from one phase to the next Chinese leaders reversed or revised policy actions and goals seen as having failed or otherwise become counterproductive for Chinese interests, and added policy actions and goals better suited to advancing Chinese interests.[66]

1989–96: The first phase witnessed strong Chinese efforts to break out of the post-Tiananmen isolation and pressure imposed by the United States and Western-aligned countries by means of more active Chinese diplomacy. Chinese diplomacy focused on neighboring countries and other developing states that were more inclined to deal with China pragmatically and without pressure regarding China's political system or other internal affairs. The Chinese government emphasized sovereignty and nationalism and passed a territorial law in 1992 strongly asserting claims to disputed territories, especially along China's eastern and southern maritime borders. The Chinese military backed efforts by Chinese oil companies, fishing enterprises, and others to advance Chinese claims in the Spratly Islands of the South China Sea against the expansion of such activities by Vietnam, the Philippines, Malaysia, and other claimants. A major incident in 1995 brought the leading states of ASEAN together to stand against Chinese territorial expansion, and the United States also publicly weighed in in support of peaceful resolution of regional disputes. During the nine months of off-and-on large-scale Chinese military exercises against Taiwan in 1995–96, few of China's neighbors explicitly sided either with China or the United States. But many were seriously concerned with the implications of China's assertiveness and ambitions.

1996–2001: Chinese leaders in this period played down military actions and assertive commentary as they demonstrated more concern to reassure neighbors in Southeast Asia and other countries that China was not a threat. They propounded principles related to a "new security concept" that built on the moderate approach China had adopted sometimes in the past regarding the so-called Five Principles of Peaceful Coexistence in international affairs. Chinese diplomacy was very active in bilateral relations, establishing various types of special partnerships and fostering good-neighbor policies. China also increased interaction with the Association for Southeast Asian Nations (ASEAN), the ASEAN Regional Forum, and other Asian regional organizations. Chinese trade relations with neighboring countries generally grew at twice the rate of China's rapidly growing economy, which remained stable amid the Asian economic crisis of 1997–98. China did not devalue its currency, it sustained economic growth, and it supported some international efforts to assist failing regional economies—developments that boosted China's stature in the region.

The Chinese government continued strong public opposition to perceived US efforts to pressure and weaken China and strong public opposition to US domination and "hegemonism" in various world areas, notably including Southeast Asia. Beijing told neighboring states that its "new security concept" was in opposition to the archaic "Cold War thinking" seen in US efforts to sustain and strengthen alliance relations, including US alliances in Asia, notably with Japan, South Korea, Australia, and some Southeast Asian nations. Beijing indicated that these states would be wise to follow China's approach and to eschew closer alliance and military ties with the United States.

2001–9: The coming to power of the George W. Bush administration coincided with a further demonstrated shift in China's policy in Asia and elsewhere. As discussed in chapter 7, the initially tough Bush administration approach on supporting Taiwan, and opposing China's military buildup and Chinese proliferation practices, as well as other Bush administration initiatives on issues sensitive for China, such as strengthening US-Japanese alliance relations and developing ballistic missile defenses in Asia and the United States, did not elicit strident criticism by Chinese officials and in official Chinese media. In the recent past, even less serious US steps against Chinese interests had been routinely denounced as perceived manifestations of US hegemonism and Cold War thinking.

Over time, it became clear that China was endeavoring to broaden the scope of its ongoing efforts to reassure its neighbors that China was not a threat. The broadened efforts now included and focused on the United States. The previous Chinese efforts attacking US policies and alliance structures in order to get Asian governments to choose between closer relations with China and closer relations with the United States had failed and were put aside. In their place emerged a new and evolving Chinese emphasis focused on Washington as well as on Asian and other powers that China's "rise" would be a peaceful one that represented many opportunities and no threat to concerned powers. China's initial emphasis on "peaceful rise" eventually evolved into the even more moderate rubrics focused on "peaceful development" and seeking "harmony" in relations with all powers. The shift in China's approach reinforced the positive momentum in China's relations with Asian neighbors, notably in Southeast Asia and South Korea.

2009–18: As in the case of Chinese relations with South Korea, the gains in Chinese relations with Southeast Asia proved difficult to sustain. China in 2009–10 adopted what many outside of China and some in China assessed as "assertive" practices particularly regarding territorial claims with its Southeast Asian and other neighbors and the United States. The Chinese actions helped to forge common ground between US efforts to reengage with Southeast Asia and Southeast Asian efforts to seek American support in the face of China's perceived truculence backed by an ever-increasing Chinese military buildup.[67]

Rising frictions between China and Southeast Asian neighbors, especially over the South China Sea, came along with rising frictions in China's relations with the United States over a range of issues including American military presence in the South China Sea and other waters near China. The United States and Vietnam, the Philippines, and other Southeast Asian countries appeared to deepen military, political, and other cooperation in part in order to support their interests in their respective disputes with China. The cooperation came as the United States and many other countries in the Asia-Pacific region reacted negatively to what was widely seen as new and assertive Chinese approaches—in some cases backed by military or other government-supported maritime shows of force—to disputed territories and other issues around its periphery.[68] By solidifying cooperation with the United States in a period of enhanced disputes with China, many Southeast Asian governments appeared to join the United States and other regional governments in signaling to China that its assertive actions were fostering regional trends adverse to China's interests.

Against this background, American and regional leaders tended to see as a positive development a shift beginning in late 2010 toward greater moderation in Chinese policy in regard to disputes over regional waters near China, including the South China Sea. Chinese commentary muted differences with the United States over Southeast Asian and other issues in the lead-up to President Hu Jintao's summit in Washington, DC, in January 2011.[69] The moderate Chinese public profile toward Southeast Asian neighbors, the United States, and others was broadly welcomed by regional governments and the United States.

Unfortunately, Chinese truculence and assertiveness reemerged strongly in 2012. Chinese authorities took extraordinary measures and used impressive demonstrations of Chinese security, economic, administrative, and diplomatic power to have their way in the South China Sea:[70]

- China employed its large and growing force of maritime and fishing security ships, targeted economic sanctions, and repeated diplomatic warnings to intimidate and coerce Philippine officials, security forces, and fishermen to respect China's claims to disputed Scarborough Shoal.
- China showed stronger resolve to exploit more fully the contested fishing resources in the South China Sea with the announced deployment of one of the world's largest (thirty-two-thousand-ton) fish-processing ships to the area and the widely publicized dispatch of a fleet of thirty fishing boats supported by a supply ship to fish in disputed South China Sea areas.

- China created a new, multifaceted administrative structure backed by a new military garrison that covered wide swaths of disputed areas in the South China Sea. The coverage was reported to be in line with China's broad historical claims depicted in Chinese maps with a nine-dashed line encompassing most of the South China Sea. The large claims laid out in Chinese maps also were seen by foreign experts to provide the justification for a state-controlled Chinese oil company to offer nine new blocks of foreign oil companies' development in the South China Sea that were far from China but very close to Vietnam, with some of the areas already being developed by Vietnam. Against this background, little was heard in recent Chinese commentary of the more moderate explanation of Chinese South China Sea territorial claims made by the Chinese Foreign Ministry spokesperson on February 29, 2012, who said that China did not claim the "entire South China Sea" but only its islands and adjacent waters.
- China advanced cooperative relations with the 2012 ASEAN chair, Cambodia, thereby ensuring that with Cambodia's cooperation South China Sea disputes did not receive prominent treatment in ASEAN documents in the 2012 ASEAN Ministerial Meeting. A result was strong division in ASEAN on how to deal with China that resulted in a remarkable display of ASEAN disunity in the first failure of the annual ASEAN Ministerial Meeting to conclude with an agreed-upon communiqué in the forty-five-year history of the group.

Chinese officials and official Chinese media commentaries endeavored to bound and compartmentalize the South China Sea disputes. Their public emphasis remained heavily on China's continued pursuit of peaceful development and cooperation during meetings with Southeast Asian representatives and those of other concerned powers including the United States. Thus, what emerged was a Chinese approach having at least two general paths:

- One path showed South China Sea claimants in the Philippines, Vietnam, and others in Southeast Asia, as well as their supporters in the United States and elsewhere, how powerful China had become in disputed South China Sea areas, how China's security, economic, administrative, and diplomatic power was likely to grow in the near future, and how Chinese authorities could use those powerful means in intimidating and coercive ways short of overt use of military force in order to counter foreign "intrusions" or public disagreements regarding Chinese claims.
- Another path forecast ever-closer "win-win" cooperation between China and Southeast Asian countries, ASEAN, and others including the United States. It focused on burgeoning Chinese–Southeast Asian trade and economic interchange and was premised on treatment of the South China Sea dispute and others in ways that avoided public controversy and eschewed

actions challenging or otherwise complicating the extensive Chinese claims to the area. In this regard, China emphasized the importance of all concerned countries to adhere to efforts to implement the 2002 Declaration of the Conduct of the Parties in the South China Sea (DOC). It duly acknowledged recent efforts supported by ASEAN to reach the "eventual" formulation of a code of conduct (COC) in the South China Sea, implying that the process of achieving the latter may take some time.

In sum, China set forth an implicit choice for the Philippines, Vietnam, other Southeast Asian disputants of China's South China Sea claims, AS-EAN, and other governments and organizations with an interest in the South China Sea, notably the United States. On the one hand, based on recent practice, pursuit of policies and actions at odds with Chinese claims in the South China Sea would meet with more demonstrations of Chinese power along the lines of the first path above. On the other hand, recent Chinese leaders' statements and official commentary indicated that others' moderation and/or acquiescence regarding Chinese claims would result in the mutually beneficial development seen in the second path.

Subsequently, Xi Jinping's government married its tough policy on South China disputes with visionary publicity of China's proposed Silk Road Belt, Maritime Silk Road, and related economic initiatives. On May 2, 2014, China abruptly deployed in the disputed Paracel Islands of the South China Sea a forty-story oil rig along with a protecting armada of more than one hundred fishing, coast guard, and reportedly military vessels. The move shocked the region and particularly Vietnam, leading to paramilitary resistance at sea and violent Vietnamese demonstrations destroying Chinese-owned factories and killing and injuring some Chinese.[71]

In 2015 China's bold tactics involved massive dredging and rapid construction of disputed South China Sea islets, shows of force involving large military exercises, deployments of China's impressive coast guard fleet, and movement of massed fishing vessels and large oil rigs. In 2016 American-led challenges to Chinese expansion were military shows of force, expanded military presence, and freedom of navigation operations accompanied by strong rhetoric from American defense leaders warning of Chinese ambitions. China rebuked the American actions and pressed ahead with military deployments, construction of defense facilities, and island expansion.

When China reacted with harsh rhetoric and intimidating threats to the July 2016 decision of an international tribunal in The Hague ruling against China's South China Sea claims, the onslaught worked to China's advantage. The United States was in the lead among regional powers in calling for restraint and moderation, and no other regional country was willing to get out in front of Washington. In contrast to the high tempo of large-scale US and US-led naval exercises and other military maneuvers in the South China Sea prior to the decision, there were no US military actions signaling pressure on China in the weeks following the July 12 decision. Japan and Australia, important American allies in the Asia-Pacific and concerned with China's territorial expansion, joined the United States in restricting reactions mainly to official statements of approval of the tribunal's decision. The Philippines, a US ally and the initiator of the case, had come under a new government on June 30 and was much more interested in seeking common ground with China. In 2017 Chinese officials showed growing confidence and satisfaction that the cooling tensions in the South China Sea demonstrated increasing regional deference to Beijing's interests, while China's economic importance to Southeast Asia loomed larger in a period of anticipated international economic retrenchment.

RELATIONS WITH AUSTRALIA, NEW ZEALAND, AND THE PACIFIC ISLANDS

Growing disputes over the South China Sea, stronger involvement of Australia and New Zealand in Asian regional bodies, and an expanded US role in President Obama's rebalance policy reinforced growing Chinese interests in relations with Australia, New Zealand, and the Pacific Island countries. China's economic and political prominence has grown. China's relations with Australia have improved markedly, based notably on an upswing in Australian raw material exports to China and an increase in Chinese exports to Australia. Official Chinese attention to Australia, New Zealand, and the Pacific Islands has been extraordinary, with numerous high-level and other official visits. Nonetheless, officials and elites in regional governments often register wariness as they carefully calculate the pros and cons of closer China ties.[72]

Australia was among the group of leading Western nations establishing diplomatic relations with China in the early 1970s as China reached out for greater international contact and support in the face of growing power and pressure of the Soviet Union directed at China at that time. It became a major trading partner of China. China's rapid economic development required increasing imports of energy, iron ore, foods, and other resources, which Australia willingly provided; Chinese exports of manufactured goods to Australia also grew. A close ally of the United States, Australia generally adhered to a moderate policy and developed positive approaches in engagement with China, seeking to avoid the acrimonious disputes and controversies that sometimes marked the erratic course of US-Chinese relations in the recent period. However, Australia publicly sided with Washington during the Taiwan Strait crisis of 1996. In the face of China's steady military buildup and assertive policies along its rim in recent years, Australia adopted military buildups and coordinated closely with the United States in countering perceived Chinese coercive practices in nearby seas and in support of the American strategic reengagement with the Asia-Pacific, including deployments of US forces to Australia. Adding to Australian wariness of China was a major controversy in 2017 over the perceived negative influence Chinese investors, donors, and government officials had on Australian politicians, prompting stricter laws and government enforcement against such practices.[73]

China and New Zealand established diplomatic relations in 1972. In following years, relations developed along the lines of Chinese relations with Australia and other Western-oriented governments. New Zealand welcomed and sought economic opportunities in China as a result of post-Mao economic reforms and supported China's entry into the World Trade Organization. In 2004 it was the first developed country to recognize China's market economy status, which provided China more assurances regarding possible trade protection and restrictions by New Zealand. And in 2008 New Zealand was the first developed country to sign a free-trade agreement with China. China overtook Australia in 2013 to become New Zealand's largest trading partner. The two countries also maintained active political and defense interchanges. Among differences, New Zealand joined with Australia and India in participating in the East Asian Leadership Summit meetings beginning in 2005. China had not favored broadening the scope of these meetings to include these three countries. New Zealand also joined with Australia to sharply criticize the competition between the governments of the People's Republic of China (PRC) and the Republic of China (ROC) for diplomatic recognition among states in the Pacific Islands, arguing that the competition led to poor governance and instability in a region of high importance for New Zealand. Like Australia, New Zealand warmly welcomed the Obama government's rebalance policy, notably initiatives to improve US relations with New Zealand and the Pacific Island countries. As with its Australian neighbor, New Zealand also experienced controversy in 2017 over the perceived negative influence of Chinese investors, donors, and government officials in the country's politics.[74]

RELATIONS WITH SOUTHERN ASIA

The People's Republic of China's interaction with southern Asia began with China's long-standing concern to control Tibet. In October 1950, China started to consolidate its control of Tibet as tens of thousands of Chinese military forces entered eastern regions of Tibet and defeated Tibetan defenders. In May 1951, China and Tibet reached a seventeen-point agreement deepening China's control of Tibet.[75]

Neighboring India was under the leadership of Jawaharlal Nehru. As the first prime minister of newly independent India until his death in 1964, Nehru presided over, and in many cases directed, the tortuous turns of Sino-Indian relations during this formative period of relations. Nehru chartered a course for India independent of the United States and the Soviet Union. He pioneered a policy on nonalignment and became a leader of the international Non-Aligned Movement. He quickly established diplomatic relations with China, argued in favor of China's entry into the United Nations, and refused to condemn China as the aggressor in the Korean War.[76]

In the mid-1950s, Nehru built a relationship with Chinese premier Zhou Enlai, then emphasizing Chinese moderation consistent with the Five Principles of Peaceful Coexistence. He seemed surprised by revelations in 1958 of Chinese road building across Indian-claimed territory known as the Aksai Chin. Amid a Tibetan uprising and Chinese crackdown in 1959, the Dalai Lama and many thousands of Tibetans fled to India. Backing the Dalai Lama's cause, the US government clandestinely supported armed resistance to Chinese rule in Tibet during the 1960s. Some reports also highlighted the role of Taiwan and Indian authorities in these clandestine operations. Nehru allowed the Dalai Lama and the many thousands of his followers escaping a Chinese crackdown to reside in India. Chinese-Indian border tensions worsened, though Nehru again seemed surprised by the Chinese military action overrunning Indian defenses along the eastern boundary in 1962, the nadir of Sino-Indian relations in the modern period.[77]

The rising border tension with India added incentives for China to settle boundaries and build constructive relations with Burma in 1960, noted in the previous section on Southeast Asia, and other neighboring states. Nepal, a Himalayan mountain state bordering China, at first deepened economic and security ties with India in the aftermath of China's military occupation of Tibet in 1950. Nepal improved relations with China in the mid-1950s in tandem with improvement in India's relations with China. Nepal and China established diplomatic relations in 1955. Subsequently, relations continued to improve while Indian-Chinese relations declined. During the Sino-Indian War of 1962, Nepal maintained neutrality.[78]

As China's relations with India worsened, leading to the border war of 1962, Beijing moved to establish close ties with Pakistan, India's South Asian rival and main security concern. Since then, China and Pakistan have established an unbroken record of continued close relations, often bordering on an alliance, that has been unique in the history of twists and turns in the foreign relations of the People's Republic of China. A tentative border agreement was reached in 1962, contingent on the settlement of India and Pakistan's differences over Kashmir. China for years supported Pakistan's claims to this disputed territory along the India-Pakistan border, the catalyst of repeated military clashes and confrontations between the two South Asian powers.[79]

Chinese relations with India were poor during the lengthy tenure of Indian prime minister Indira Gandhi, 1966–77, 1980–84. During this time, India aligned more closely with China's main international adversary, the Soviet Union. India became directly involved in the breakup of China's main South Asian partner, Pakistan, supporting East Pakistan's independence as Bangladesh. In response to the perceived threat from nuclear-armed China, India developed a nuclear weapons program and carried out an underground nuclear test in 1974. China did little against India when India backed the breakaway of East Pakistan in 1971, leading to the creation of Bangladesh. But strong Chinese military, political, and economic support for Pakistan included the reported provision of nuclear weapons technology and missile delivery systems. China worked closely with Pakistan and the United States in supporting armed resistance to the Soviet Union's military presence in Afghanistan in the 1980s.[80]

Chinese-Indian relations began to improve with the visit to China in 1988 of Indira Gandhi's son, Prime Minister Rajiv Gandhi; this marked the first visit by an Indian prime minister in thirty-four years. Both sides appeared interested in avoiding conflict, expanding exchanges, and managing differences in less acrimonious ways than in the recent past.[81]

Post–Cold War Chinese policy toward southern Asia generally was in line with broader efforts by China at that time to reduce tensions around its periphery and stabilize the "peaceful international environment" needed for China's ambitious agenda of economic and other domestic changes and reforms. Beijing publicly emphasized the positive and endeavored to minimize the negative with all its southern Asian neighbors, including India. In this process, Chinese authorities avoided compromising important Chinese territorial, economic, political, and other interests while they sought to benefit through methodical and generally constructive interaction with the southern Asian countries.[82]

Nevertheless, India remained at odds with China over territorial issues and over China's long-standing support for Pakistan. India and China also vied for influence and leadership in Asian and world affairs. They also competed actively for international energy to fuel their respective burgeoning economies. Energy security added to factors influencing each power to view warily the other's military improvements and alignments, especially those affecting transportation routes from the oil-rich Middle East.[83]

The incremental efforts to ease tensions and improve relations moved forward in the 1980s and appeared to receive an added boost from the collapse of the Soviet Union. For many years, the latter had fostered a close strategic relationship with India based in part on Soviet-Indian mutual suspicion of China. Premier Li Peng visited India in 1990, and President Jiang

Zemin traveled there in 1996.[84] The regular visits by top-level Chinese and Indian leaders in following years were accompanied by many agreements, along with positive rhetoric asserting mutual determination to settle the border issue and other differences and to build on rapidly expanding economic cooperation and trade.[85]

As India and China improved relations, China continued to modify its long-standing support for Pakistan.[86] It was already evident in the 1970s that China was unwilling to take significant military action against India in the event of an Indo-Pakistani war. During the 1965 Indo-Pakistani war, Chinese forces did take assertive actions along the Indian border in order to divert Indian forces and weaken their assault against Pakistan. But when India defeated Pakistan in the late 1971 war, which brought about the dismemberment of Pakistan and the creation of an independent Bangladesh, China took no significant military action.

In the 1980s and 1990s, China further modified its public stance in support of Pakistani claims against India over territorial and other issues. Beijing notably adhered to an increasingly evenhanded approach over the sensitive Indo-Pakistani dispute over Kashmir. By 2008 it was reported that Chinese president Hu Jintao offered to mediate between India and Pakistan in order to help resolve the issues regarding Kashmir. Terrorist attacks in Mumbai's financial district in November 2008 were linked to a Pakistani-based organization reportedly involved in resisting Indian control in Kashmir. China changed its past unwillingness to have the UN Security Council condemn the group and sided with a UN Security Council vote declaring the group to be a terrorist organization.[87]

China continued its close military and economic support for Pakistan. Numerous reports showed that China played a major role for many years in assisting Pakistan's development of nuclear weapons and related ballistic missile delivery systems, though Chinese officials denied this. In an interview published on June 3, 1998, President Jiang Zemin was asked, "Has China helped Pakistan to make its nuclear bomb?" He replied, "No, China has not helped Pakistan."[88] Continuing to benefit from Chinese military, economic, and political support, Pakistan chose to emphasize the positive in Sino-Pakistani relations and deemed counterproductive any significant show of irritation with Beijing's shift toward a more evenhanded public posture in the subcontinent.

The US-led war in Afghanistan begun in 2001 quickly toppled the terrorist-harboring Taliban regime and had a major effect on China's relative influence in southern Asia.[89] The United States at the time became the most influential foreign power in Afghanistan, Pakistan, and India. Chinese leaders generally adjusted pragmatically and continued incremental improvements in regional relations. The withdrawal of US and NATO forces from Afghanistan came with the Obama government's strong focus on India as a western anchor in the US government's rebalance policy of enhanced engagement in Asia. US involvement in Afghanistan and Pakistan declined. The US moves raised China's profile in the now more unstable Afghanistan situation and in Pakistan; the moves also complicated Chinese influence in India.

The foreign policy initiatives of President Xi Jinping's signature "Silk Road" Belt and Road Initiative (BRI) highlighted multibillion-dollar infrastructure plans involving $46 billion of commitments in Pakistan. India was in the lead of Asian powers wary of Xi's development scheme, partly because Chinese-planned building in Pakistan would come in areas claimed by India. Xi Jinping's assertiveness in defending Chinese territorial claims saw an increase in publicized Sino-Indian border tensions.[90]

Even in periods when Sino-Indian relations improved, issues continued to be raised periodically and often strongly by officials on both sides, demonstrating slow overall progress in advancing ties.[91]

- *Border issues:* Large expanses of territory along India's northwestern and northeastern frontier remain in dispute. Many rounds of border talks for decades have kept tensions under control but they periodically flare up, most recently with a standoff of border forces in Bhutan in 2017.
- *Chinese ties with Pakistan, Myanmar, and other southern Asian states:* Long-standing close Chinese military ties with Pakistan and with Myanmar's military regime up to 2011 were viewed by some Indian officials as a Chinese "pincer movement" to contain India. Long-standing Chinese ties with Bangladesh, Sri Lanka, and Nepal added to the Indian suspicion that China sought to use such ties to hobble India's ambitions by causing New Delhi strategic concerns in southern Asia. China's military and political support assisted the Sri Lankan government in its final victory in the long-running war with the separatist Tamil Tigers in 2009, opening the way to closer strategic as well as economic and political cooperation. At times in the past, some in India also saw the United States playing a supporting role through its engagement policy toward China. Over the past two decades, however, India transformed this concern by nurturing a closer relationship, notably closer military relations, with the United States. Officials in the United States said that they were interested in developing these ties with India, along with nuclear, economic, and other ties, for a variety of important reasons, including as a strategic hedge in case of Chinese moves contrary to American interests.
- *Tibet:* Beijing gave high priority in the post–Cold War period to countering the efforts by the Dalai Lama and his supporters to seek a greater international profile for Tibet. Despite some greater Indian recognition of China's control of Tibet, China remained at odds with New Delhi over

India's continued hosting of the spiritual leader and his government in exile.

- *Trade, energy, and energy security:* Continued Indian efforts to open the economy and increase exports led to greater cooperation between the economies of China and India but also Indian economic competition with China for investment and markets and more direct competition for international energy resources. Concern over securing sea-lanes from the oil-rich Persian Gulf prompted India to increase its already powerful naval force in the Indian Ocean and China to develop closer ties with Pakistan, Myanmar, Sri Lanka, and others in developing port and communications assets that would help secure Chinese access to Persian Gulf oil. Chinese naval forces occasionally patrolled in the region.
- *Asian and world leadership:* India wanted a permanent seat on the UN Security Council. China on the one hand said that it supported India's bid and on the other hand made sure that UN reform was so slow that China would remain Asia's only permanent member on the council. India reportedly resented Chinese efforts to gain admission to the Indian-dominated South Asian Association for Regional Cooperation, while New Delhi was pleased that Japan and some Southeast Asian powers resisted Chinese efforts to exclude India and other interested outside powers from the new East Asian Summit of December 2005; New Delhi played a prominent role in the new organization. China appeared unenthusiastic in the face of India's efforts with Russian support to gain observer status and membership in the Shanghai Cooperation Organization (SCO). China, India, and others competed for influence in Southeast Asia through their respective free-trade initiatives and involvement with efforts to secure sea-lanes through the region. China also maneuvered unsuccessfully within the Nuclear Suppliers Group to thwart approval in 2008 of India's landmark nuclear cooperation agreement with the United States. It continued to block India's entry into the group.

As suggested above, further complicating smooth Sino-Indian relations has been the prominent role of the United States. India has benefited substantially from strong US support under the Clinton, Bush, Obama, and Trump administrations. The record of arms sales, military exchanges and exercises, trade, investment, and nuclear cooperation between Washington and New Delhi has underscored the repeated US declaration that it seeks to support India's rise as a major power. US relations with China involve many areas of competition and controversy as well as cooperation. US policy is not nearly as enthusiastic about China's rising power as it is about India's ascendance.

RELATIONS WITH RUSSIA AND CENTRAL ASIA

Relations with Russia

The role of the Soviet Union in China's relations with Asia is discussed at some length in chapters 2 and 3. China and Russia have had a long and often troubled history. Czarist Russia's expansion into the Far East came largely at the expense of the declining Chinese empire. Nineteenth-century treaties made vast stretches of territory formerly under China's rule part of the Russian empire. China's internal weakness and political dislocation during the first half of the twentieth century provided opportunities for Soviet leaders Vladimir Lenin and Joseph Stalin to seek allies and foster revolutionary movements favorable to the Soviet Union. Soviet involvement was often ham-handed and, on occasion, worked against the immediate interests of the Communist guerrilla movement in China led by Mao Zedong.[92]

Seeking economic support and strategic backing in the face of an indifferent or hostile West, Mao Zedong's newly formed People's Republic of China (PRC) sought an alliance with Stalin's Soviet Union in 1949. After many weeks of hard bargaining, the alliance was signed on February 14, 1950. The alliance relationship was essential to China's security and its military, economic, and social development in the 1950s. Soviet aid, advisors, and guidelines were key features fostering the changes under way in China. But steadily escalating differences arose over strategy toward the United States and international affairs, the proper ideological path to development, and the appropriate leadership roles of Mao Zedong and Soviet leader Nikita Khrushchev in the world communist movement. Soviet aid was cut off in 1960. Polemics over strategy and ideology led to more substantive disputes over competing claims to border territories. Armed border clashes reached a point in 1969 at which the Soviet Union threatened to attack Chinese nuclear installations, and Chinese leaders countered with a nationwide war preparation campaign against the "war maniacs" in the Kremlin. Party relations were broken, trade fell to minimal levels, and each side depicted the other in official media as a dangerous international predator.[93]

The start of Sino-Soviet talks on border issues in October 1969 eased the war crisis, but each side continued preparations for the long-term struggle against its neighboring adversary. As the weaker party in the dispute, China attempted to break out of its international isolation and gain diplomatic leverage against perceived Soviet efforts at intimidation and threat. Beijing's opening to the Nixon administration was an important element in this policy. The Soviet Union continued its previous efforts to build up military forces along the Sino-Soviet and Sino-Mongolian borders in order to offset any perceived threat from China. It also pursued this course to provide a counterweight against any Chinese effort to exert pressure on countries around China's periphery that were interested in developing closer relations with the Soviet Union (for example, India and Vietnam).[94]

The death of Mao Zedong in 1976 and the gradual emergence of a more pragmatic leadership in China reduced the importance of ideological and leadership issues in the Sino-Soviet dispute, but the competition in Asia again reached a crisis in 1979. China countered Soviet-backed Vietnam's invasion of Cambodia by launching a limited military incursion into Vietnam. The Soviet Union responded with warnings and large-scale military exercises along China's northern border. China also denounced the Soviet invasion of Afghanistan in 1979 and sided with the US-backed anticommunist guerrillas in Afghanistan.[95]

Chinese leaders spent much of the two decades from the late 1960s on building military defenses and conducting diplomatic and other international maneuvers to deal with the perceived dangers of the prime strategic threat to China posed by the Soviet Union. Particularly important were the buildup of Soviet military forces along the Sino-Soviet and Sino-Mongolian borders and Soviet military and political presence and influence in key areas along China's periphery, notably Vietnam, Laos, Cambodia, India, Afghanistan, North Korea, and the western Pacific and Indian Oceans.[96]

Over time, both countries attempted to moderate the tensions. Soviet leader Leonid Brezhnev made several public gestures calling for improved economic, government, and party relations with China before he died in 1982. This prompted the start of a series of political, economic, technical, and cultural contacts and exchanges.

By 1982, the Soviet leadership concluded that its post-1969 strategy toward China (including the massing of forces along the eastern sector of the border and media campaigns against China's domestic and international policies) had backfired. The post-1972 normalization of China's relations with the United States and Japan and the signing of the 1978 China-Japan friendship treaty showed a strategic convergence among the United States, China, and Japan, which added to the Soviet defense burden and worsened the security environment on its long, remote, and thinly populated eastern flank. To undo this problem, Brezhnev and later leaders held out an olive branch to the Chinese leadership. Political contacts and trade increased and polemics subsided, but real progress came only after Mikhail Gorbachev consolidated his power in the mid-1980s and made rapprochement with China a priority.[97]

Gorbachev was prepared to make major changes in what China referred to as the "three obstacles" to improved Sino-Soviet relations: Soviet troops in Afghanistan, the buildup of Soviet forces along the border (including the deployment in Mongolia), and the Soviet-backed Vietnamese military occupation of Cambodia.[98] Motivated by a desire to repair relations with China, to ease the defense burden on the Soviet economy, and to reciprocate China's reduction of its 4 million troops to 2.95 million from 1982 to 1986, the Soviet government announced in 1987 that a phased reduction of its troops (roughly 65,000 in total number) from Mongolia would be initiated with the aim of eliminating the deployment by 1992.[99] The Soviet formations in Mongolia had been kept at a higher level of readiness than others along the border, and the Chinese had long viewed them as a first-echelon strike force aimed at Beijing. In December 1988, Gorbachev announced at the United Nations that Soviet conventional forces would unilaterally be reduced by 500,000. Soviet spokesmen later clarified that, of the total, 120,000 would come from the troops arrayed against China and that remaining Far East units would progressively be configured in a defensive mode. In late 1989, following Gorbachev's visit to Beijing in May, Chinese and Soviet officials began negotiations on reducing forces along the border, and during Prime Minister Li Peng's visit to Moscow in April 1990, an agreement was reached on governing principles regarding force reductions. By the time the Soviet Union collapsed in 1991, five rounds of talks on force reductions had been conducted.

The reduction of the conventional threat to China was complemented by the 1987 US-Soviet intermediate nuclear forces (INF) treaty, under which Moscow dismantled all its medium- and intermediate-range nuclear missiles, including 180 advanced mobile SS-20 missiles that were based in the Asian regions of the Soviet Union with missions including targeting China. Meanwhile, the Soviet Union agreed under the April 1988 Geneva Accords to withdraw its combat forces from Afghanistan by May 1989 and Moscow encouraged Vietnam to evacuate its troops from Cambodia by the end of 1989.

High-level political contacts helped to alter the adversarial character of Sino-Soviet relations, the most important being the visits of Foreign Minister Eduard Shevardnadze and Gorbachev to Beijing in 1989 and of Li Peng and Chinese Communist Party General Secretary Jiang Zemin to Moscow in 1990 and 1991, respectively. Talks on resolving the border dispute, which had been derailed by the Soviet invasion of Afghanistan, resumed in 1987. A treaty delimiting the eastern sector of the border was signed in May 1991. These military and political transformations in Sino-Soviet relations were supplemented by a significant growth in trade—especially along the border—and agreements providing for thousands of Chinese workers to be employed in construction projects in Siberia and the Soviet Far East.[100]

With the demise of the Soviet Union following the end of the Cold War, Beijing's relationship with Moscow further improved amid massive changes in the relative power between the two former adversaries. China advanced dramatically in economic modernization and international prominence, becoming the world's fastest-rising power. Russia seemed to flounder for a decade, losing the military, economic, and other elements that had made the Soviet Union a major power in Asian as well as European and global affairs. The sparsely populated eastern Russia saw a steep decline in population, living standards, and military readiness as neighboring China boomed and its military modernized rapidly, partly with the help of Russian weapons and technical specialists.[101]

In recent years, international energy scarcities and the more disciplined administration of Vladimir Putin raised Russia's economic importance as an exporter of oil, gas, and other commodities to Asian as well as other consumers. Russia was positioned as a key player in international disputes such as the controversies over the US-led invasion of Iraq and Iran's nuclear development program. Russia also remained critically important for Chinese interests in central Asia and for supplies of modern weaponry. However, Chinese efforts in the 1990s to forge a united front with Russia against US "hegemonism" failed in part because Putin in early 2001 steered Russian policy in a direction that gave primacy to businesslike relations with the United States. China soon followed suit.

Chinese and Russian leaders subsequently issued occasional joint statements and engaged in some military and diplomatic activities in opposition to US interests and international leadership. Under Putin's leadership, Russia shifted for a time to a tougher stance against the United States and the West on a variety of issues, including perceived intrusions on Russia's power and influence along its periphery, notably NATO expansion and planned deployment of US-backed antiballistic missile systems (ABM) in the Czech Republic and Poland. China gave some political support to the Russian position, but when Russian military forces in August 2008 attacked Western-backed Georgia over territorial issues, Chinese leaders avoided taking sides. The weakness of any Russian-Chinese commitment against the United States and the West showed again when Russia shifted in 2010 to a more cooperative stance with the United States and NATO on arms control, security, and economic issues that stood in contrast with Chinese truculence toward the United States at this time over Taiwan arms sales, Tibet, US military surveillance near China, and economic issues.[102]

Closer Russia-China Collaboration

Putin's resumption as Russian president in 2012 was accompanied by hardening in Russian positions at odds with the United States and strengthening Russian ties with China. Putin found China's newly installed party leader and president, Xi Jinping, a like-minded partner in opposition to various aspects of the US-led international order. The partnership between Moscow and Beijing matured and broadened, with serious negative consequences for American and allied interests. The momentum was based on (1) common objectives; (2) perceived Russian and Chinese vulnerabilities in the face of US and Western pressures; and (3) perceived opportunities for the two powers to expand their influence at the expense of US and allied leaders seen as cautious, distracted, and in decline. The relationship went well beyond the previous common view that Russian-Chinese ties represented an "axis of convenience" with limited impact on US interests. [103]

Russia and China posed increasingly serious challenges to the US-supported order in their respective priority spheres of concern—Russia in Europe and the Middle East, and China in Asia along China's continental and maritime peripheries. Russia's challenges involved military maneuvers and interventions as well as cyber and political warfare undermining elections in the United States and Europe, European unity, and NATO solidarity. China's cyber attacks focused more on massive theft of information and intellectual property to accelerate China's economic competitiveness to dominate world markets in key advanced technology at the expense of leading US and other international companies. Russia and China worked separately and together to complicate and curb US power and influence in world politics, economy, and security. They supported one another in their respective challenges to the United States, allies and partners in Europe, the Middle East, and Asia. These joint efforts also involved diplomatic, security, and economic measures in multilateral forums and bilateral relations involving US adversaries in North Korea, Iran, and Syria. The two powers also supported one another in the face of US and allied complaints about Russian and Chinese coercive expansion and other steps challenging regional order and global norms and institutions backed by the United States. [104]

The US and allied ability to deal with these rising challenges was commonly seen as being in decline. The US position in the triangular relationship among the United States, Russia, and China deteriorated, to the satisfaction of leaders in Moscow and Beijing opportunistically seeking to advance their power and influence. Russia's tension with the West and ever-deepening dependence on China and active US constructive engagement with China gave Beijing the advantageous "hinge" position in the triangular relationship that the United States used to occupy. [105]

Recent Russian and Chinese policy calculations showed the importance of improved relations with the United States was low for President Vladimir Putin and the Russian leadership; their worldview focuses on dealing with the American threat with coercive means short of war including military deployments, cyber attacks, and security assistance to American adversaries. President Xi Jinping's government continued to balance strong opposition to US international leadership and perceived US encirclement in Asia with managing differences with the United States in order to avoid confrontation and conflict. China had a much greater stake in the US-led international order than did Russia. But Beijing struck the balance in ways that seriously undermined America. Notable in this regard were coercive advances to control disputed territory along its rim in ways that undermine the American position as regional security guarantor and an ever-expanding military budget that supports increasingly sophisticated weapons systems seeking to turn the military balance of power in Asia against the United States.[106]

Up to this point, it remained hard to find instances when Russia took substantial risks in support of China's serious challenges to the United States that did not involve overlapping Russian interests, and vice versa. At the same time, as the Russian-Chinese relationship became closer, American and other specialists carefully perused the behavior of both sides for signs of such closer collaboration with negative implications for the United States.

Relations with Central Asia

After the end of the Cold War and the fall of the Soviet Union, China expanded its ties across central Asia in order to stabilize its western frontier, gain access to the region's energy resources, and balance Western influence in an area Beijing traditionally viewed as Russia's reserve.[107] Beijing calculated that improved ties with central Asian states, which were also concerned about problems arising from the linkage of religion and politics, could shield Xinjiang Province and its ethnically Turkic Uighur population from outside Muslim and pan-Turkic influence. China worried that its neighbors might lack sufficient resolve to control and suppress the threat. In this context, US, Russian, and Chinese efforts to support antiterrorist initiatives in central Asia beginning in 2001 seemed to reflect some important common ground among the three powers.[108]

China's central Asian energy projects reflected PRC efforts to obtain secure supply lines and avoid overdependence on a few sources of energy. Beijing concluded agreements to develop Kazakhstan oil and gas fields and construct a pipeline to Xinjiang, and China developed gas pipeline links with Uzbekistan, Turkmenistan, and other countries. As in the case of pipeline and related energy deals involving Russia, the projects were expensive, logistically difficult, and complicated by inadequate energy-processing and transport systems. There were many signed agreements but slower progress toward completing the pipelines and filling them to capacity.[109]

On September 24, 1997, China and Kazakhstan signed agreements worth $9.5 billion that involved development of two major oil and gas fields and the construction of pipelines in Kazakhstan. One pipeline covered 3,000 kilometers from Kazakhstan into western China and began operation in 2006. China signed an agreement with Turkmenistan in 2006 to export natural gas through a new pipeline reaching China through Uzbekistan and Kazakhstan. This pipeline was completed expeditiously, and was supported by a separate natural gas pipeline linking Uzbekistan and Kazakhstan with China. The new efforts undercut what had been a situation of control of the exporting of central Asian natural gas by Russian pipeline administrators.[110]

Beijing adopted an evenhanded public stance on the most contentious political issue in central Asian politics since the 1990s: the continuing civil war in Afghanistan. China urged all warring parties to stop fighting and to discuss their problems among themselves without any outside interference. China typically supported a major role for the United Nations, where China had a permanent seat on the Security Council. With the increase of US-led combat operations against a resurgent Taliban threat during the administration of US president Barack Obama, China was careful to straddle the fence and avoid commitments not seen in its longer-term interests. China endorsed the May 2, 2011, killing of Osama Bin Laden by American special forces in Pakistan as "a positive development in the international struggle against terrorism."[111]

China continued to monitor carefully the growing Western commercial presence in central Asia and tended to view expanding NATO activities as indicative of US efforts to extend its influence to the region, squeeze out Russia, and contain China. China's expanding influence in central Asia generally prompted little overt opposition from Moscow. China usually pursued its interests in central Asia cautiously, presumably in part to avoid provoking its Russian strategic partner into discontinuing the supply of arms to China and possibly risking a strong nationalist backlash from Russia's leadership.[112]

China's interest in using multilateral organizations to pursue Chinese interests around its periphery in the post–Cold War period showed first in central Asia. Building on a growing "strategic partnership" with Russia, China hosted in Shanghai in April 1996 the first meeting of representative leaders of what became known as the Shanghai Five. The Shanghai Five consisted of China, Russia, and the three other former Soviet republics that border on China: Kazakhstan, Kyrgyzstan, and Tajikistan. The group focused at first on finalizing border settlements between China and the four former Soviet republics, demilitarizing their frontiers, and establishing confidence-building measures. Uzbekistan joined the group in July 2001, establishing the SCO, with six members: Russia, China, Kazakhstan, Kyrgyzstan, Tajikistan, and Uzbekistan. The declaration on the creation of the SCO showed strong attention to regional security issues involving terrorism, drug trade, and other transnational crimes affecting the countries. Work in subsequent annual summit meetings of the group included efforts to establish a charter and small budget for the organization, to start a small antiterrorism center in Kyrgyzstan, and to set up an SCO secretariat headquartered in Beijing and paid for by China to foster cooperation on terrorism and other transnational issues. Chinese leaders showed strong interest in broadening the scope of the SCO to include strong economic development efforts, notably in building transportation infrastructure that would benefit western China.[113] At the SCO prime ministers' meeting in Tajikistan in September 2006, Prime Minister

Wen Jiabao announced that China had set a goal of doubling the current level ($40 billion) of Chinese trade with SCO members in the next few years. [114]

Looking out, China's approach to the central Asian region seemed coherent, reasonably successful, and likely to continue along existing lines. While Chinese leaders have had several important interests and goals in pursuing relations with central Asia, they have managed them without significant conflict, reinforcing the likelihood of continuity and durability in China's approach to the region. Notably in contrast to Chinese approaches in eastern and southern Asia, there has been less tension between China's national development emphasis on promoting peace and development abroad and Chinese national security, territorial, and national unification objectives that emphasize China's use of force against foreign threats in ways that have alienated and alarmed some of China's neighbors and other concerned powers.

Chinese interests and goals in central Asia continued to focus on the following:

- Borders and security, curbing outside support to separatists in Xinjiang Province, and seeking common ground with regional governments in working against terrorist and criminal elements
- Access to central Asian oil and gas supplies and development of strong trade relations
- Fostering a stable and productive environment along this segment of China's periphery while enhancing China's regional and international prominence through effective bilateral and multilateral diplomacy

One of the reasons that China's government has been able to develop and sustain a coherent approach in post–Cold War central Asia despite potentially conflicting goals is that external forces that the Chinese government does not control and that strongly influence Chinese foreign policy in other areas do not play much of a role in its relations with central Asia. For example, Taiwan is insignificant in central Asia. Chinese threats to use force against Taiwan separatism have much less disruptive impact on China's central Asian neighbors than they do elsewhere around China's periphery. Japan's role in central Asia also is relatively small. China's sometimes strident reactions to disputes with Japan have a less disruptive impact on China's relations with central Asian neighbors than on Chinese relations with neighbors in other parts of China's periphery.

The upswing in US military presence and influence in central Asia after the terrorist attack on the United States in 2001 was an important change impacting China's strategic calculus in central Asia. However, its overall importance has been offset by the fact that the foundation of US power in central Asia is much weaker than in other parts of China's periphery. In addition, the record of relatively low levels of follow-on US aid and official involvement in the region and Russia's continued leading importance among the central Asian republics also have diminished Chinese concerns about the US military presence and influence in central Asia.[115]

Meanwhile, changes in Chinese foreign policy and behavior influenced by Chinese leaders' lack of confidence and uncertainty in their legitimacy at home and abroad are less in the case of central Asia than in other parts of China's periphery.[116] Notably, the need for Chinese leaders to adopt tough policies on territorial or other nationalistic issues with central Asian neighbors is less than in the case of Chinese relations with some neighbors to China's east and south. Part of the reason is that the Chinese government has been successful in keeping Chinese media and other public attention focused away from territorial and nationalistic issues with central Asian neighbors. In addition, Chinese territorial and nationalistic issues with central Asian neighbors seem less salient to important Chinese interests in development and national power than such Chinese issues with some other neighbors. And the generally authoritarian central Asian governments have endeavored to deal constructively, pragmatically, and generally quietly with China over territorial and other disputes, a contrast with the nationalistic posturing of some of China's eastern and southern neighbors.

Although the course of China's strategy toward central Asia seems more stable than in other areas of Chinese foreign relations, there remain significant uncertainties clouding the longer-term outlook. For one thing, specialists are divided on China's long-term goals in the region and how these goals could lead to a major change in China's approach to the region. Some emphasize strongly that the prevailing Chinese interest in regional stability and energy trade will remain the important determinants of Chinese policy and will reinforce continuity in the Chinese policy and behavior we see today.[117]

However, others argue that recent accommodating and moderate Chinese policies and behavior presage the creation of an emerging central Asian order dominated by China that will be reminiscent of the Sino–central Asian relationship during the strong dynasties in Chinese history.[118]

Meanwhile, China's influence in central Asia and developments in the region depend heavily on the power and policies of Russia. Russian weakness in the 1990s provided the opportunity for expanding Chinese influence in central Asia and the foundation of Russian inclination to cooperate closely with rising China on trade, including arms trade, and a variety of international issues. Under the leadership of Vladimir Putin, Russia has endeavored to rebuild elements of national strength and to use them to reassert Russian interests against those perceived as encroaching on Russian interests. Thus far, the Russian relationship with China generally has remained cordial and cooperative, though Russia-China competition for influence in central Asia and over other issues continues.[119] If China were to be seen to seek regional dominance in central Asia, Russia might adopt more competitive and perhaps confrontational policies that would have a major impact on China's existing approach to the region. At the same time, if Russia successfully pursues a more assertive leadership role in the region, China's leaders presumably would be forced to choose between accommodating rising Russian power and possibly losing Chinese equities and influence or resisting the Russian advances.

These dilemmas in China-Russia-Central Asian relations rose prominently with Xi Jinping's international activism focused on the Belt and Road Initiative. Russia and China have failed to coordinate well their economic strategies to the region. China has much more to offer and has gained political influence through its trade and investment activities. China plans to do much more in Central Asia with its various new "Silk Road" programs and related initiatives, which holds the prospect of orienting these economies more toward China than Russia. Russia's relative discomfort with this is an open question, but China is dedicated to continuing this effort, for both security and economic reasons. This situation has produced today a rough division of labor with China as the primary provider of economic goods and Russia as the security provider. A looming question, and potential source of tension, is whether China's growing economic role will inevitably lead to an increased security role—and how Russia responds.[120]

NOTES

1. Findings from an off-the-record seminar with US government and nongovernment China specialists, Washington, DC, area, November 10, 2011.
2. Christopher Buckley, "Xi Jinping Opens China's Party Congress," *New York Times*, October 17, 2017, https://www.nytimes.com/2017/10/17/world/asia/xi-jinping-communist-party-china.html.
3. Martin Indyk, Kenneth Lieberthal, and Michael O'Hanlon, *Bending History: Barack Obama's Foreign Policy* (Washington, DC: Brookings Institution Press, 2012), pp. 61–62.
4. Trade figures used in this section are from the UN COMTRADE database at comtrade, http://un.org/db.
5. Richard McGregor, *Asia's Reckoning* (New York: Viking 2017); Michael Yahuda, *Sino-Japanese Relations after the Cold War* (New York: Routledge, 2014); June Teufel Dreyer, *The Middle Kingdom and the Empire of the Rising Sun* (New York: Oxford University Press, 2016).
6. Chae-Jin Lee, *Japan Faces China* (Baltimore: Johns Hopkins University Press, 1978).
7. A. Doak Barnett, *China and the Major Powers in East Asia* (Washington, DC: Brookings Institution Press, 1977), pp. 105–8.
8. Barnett, *China and the Major Powers in East Asia*, pp. 108–22; Ezra Vogel, *Deng Xiaoping and the Transformation of China* (Cambridge, MA: Harvard University Press, 2011), pp. 294–310.
9. Allen Whiting, *China Faces Japan* (Berkeley: University of California Press, 1989); Robert Sutter, *China's Rise in Asia* (Lanham, MD: Rowman & Littlefield, 2005), pp. 131–32.
10. Donald Klein, "Japan and Europe in Chinese Foreign Relations," in *China and the World*, ed. Samuel Kim (Boulder, CO: Westview, 1998), pp. 137–46.
11. Robert Sutter, *Chinese Policy Priorities and Their Implications for the United States* (Lanham, MD: Rowman & Littlefield, 2000), p. 82.

12. McGregor, *Asia's Reckoning*; Yahuda, *Sino-Japanese Relations*; Dreyer, *The Middle Kingdom*; Minxin Pei and Michael Swaine, *Simmering Fire in Asia: Averting Sino-Japanese Strategic Conflict*, Policy Brief 44 (Washington, DC: Carnegie Endowment for International Peace, December 1, 2005); Susan Shirk, *China: Fragile Superpower* (New York: Oxford University Press, 2007), pp. 140–80; Richard Bush, *The Perils of Proximity: China-Japan Security Relations* (Washington, DC: Brookings Institution Press, 2010).

13. "TPP Negotiators Work to Revise Trade Deal after US Withdrawal," *Japan Times*, September 21, 2017, https://www.japantimes.co.jp/news/2017/09/21/business/tpp-negotiators-work-revise-trade-deal-u-s-withdrawal/#.WhA2FkqnGM8.

14. Yoshihisa Komori, "Rethinking Japan-China Relations: Beyond the History Issue," paper presented at scholarly conference at the Sigur Center for Asian Affairs, George Washington University, Washington, DC, December 5, 2001.

15. Shirk, *China*, 140–80; Denny Roy, *Stirring Samurai, Disapproving Dragon* (Honolulu: Asia Pacific Center for Security Studies, September 2003). See also "Noted Scholar Discusses 'New Thinking' in Sino-Japanese Relations," *Renmin Wang* (Beijing), January 1, 2004; Liu Xiaobiao, "Where Are Sino-Japanese Relations Heading?" *Renmin Wang* (Beijing), August 13, 2003; and Shi Yinhong, "On Crisis Formation, Control in Sino-Japanese Relations," *Wen Hui Po* (Hong Kong), June 1, 2005, cited in Robert Sutter, *China's Rise in Asia*, 151.

16. Wu Xinbo, "The End of the Silver Lining: A Chinese View of the U.S.-Japanese Alliance," *Washington Quarterly* 29, no. 1 (Winter 2005/2006): pp. 119–30.

17. Robert Sutter, "China-Japan: Trouble Ahead?" *Washington Quarterly* 25, no. 4 (2002): pp. 37–49; Mike Mochizuki, "Terms of Engagement: The U.S.-Japan Alliance and the Rise of China," in *Beyond Bilateralism: U.S.-Japan Relations in the New Asia-Pacific*, ed. Ellis Krauss and T. J. Pempel (Stanford, CA: Stanford University Press, 2004), pp. 96–100; Michael Yahuda, *The International Politics of the Asia-Pacific* (London: Routledge, 2011), pp. 324–28.

18. Ralph Clough, *Island China* (Cambridge, MA: Harvard University Press, 1978), pp. 148–72.

19. John Copper, *Taiwan: Nation State or Province?* (Boulder, CO: Westview, 2009), pp. 50–53.

20. Denny Roy, *Taiwan: A Political History* (Ithaca, NY: Cornell University Press, 2003), pp. 152–82.

21. Charles Freeman, "Preventing War in the Taiwan Strait," *Foreign Affairs* 77, no. 4 (July–August 1998): pp. 6–11; Steven Goldstein, *Taiwan Faces the Twenty-First Century* (New York: Foreign Policy Association, 1997).

22. John Garver, *Face-Off* (Seattle: University of Washington Press, 1997).

23. Richard Bush, *Untying the Knot* (Washington, DC: Brookings Institution Press, 2005), pp. 27–141.

24. Steven Goldstein and Julian Chang, eds., *Presidential Politics in Taiwan: The Administration of Chen Shui-bian* (Norwalk, CT: Eastbridge, 2008).

25. Nancy Bernkopf Tucker, *Strait Talk: United States-Taiwan Relations and the Crisis with China* (Cambridge, MA: Harvard University Press, 2009); Philip Yang, "Cross Strait Relations under the First Chen Administration," in Goldstein and Chang, eds., *Presidential Politics in Taiwan*, pp. 211–22.

26. Robert Sutter, *Chinese Foreign Relations* (Lanham, MD: Rowman & Littlefield, 2012), p. 158.

27. David G. Brown, "China-Taiwan Relations: Campaign Fallout," *Comparative Connections*, January 2005, http://www.csis.org/pacfor.

28. Brown, "China-Taiwan Relations"; interviews with Chinese government officials and specialists, Washington, DC, January–March 2004.

29. Sutter, *Chinese Foreign Relations* (2012), p. 159.

30. At this time, Taiwanese media reported that George H. W. Bush had used an epithet to refer to Chen Shui-bian (Brown, "China-Taiwan Relations").

31. David Brown, "Taiwan Voters Set a New Course," *Comparative Connections* 10, no. 1 (April 2008): p. 75.

32. Dennis Hickey, "Beijing's Evolving Policy toward Taipei: Engagement or Entrapment," *Issues and Studies* 45, no. 1 (March 2009): pp. 31–70; Alan Romberg, "Cross Strait Relations:

'Ascend the Heights and Take a Long-Term Perspective,'" *China Leadership Monitor* 27, Winter 2009, http://www.chinaleadershipmonitor.org; author's interviews and consultations with international affairs officials, including repeated meetings with senior officers up to minister level, Taipei, May, July, August, and December 2008, April 2009.

33. David Brown, "Economic Cooperation Framework Agreement Signed," *Comparative Connections* 12, no. 2 (July 2010): pp. 77–79.

34. David Brown, "Post-Election Continuity," *Comparative Connections* 14, no. 1 (May 2012): pp. 81–86.

35. David Brown, "Looking Ahead to 2012," *Comparative Connections* 12, no. 4 (January 2011), http://www.csis.org/pacfor.

36. Donald Zagoria, *Trip to Seoul, Taipei, Beijing, Shanghai, and Tokyo—May 8–25, 2010* (New York: National Committee on American Foreign Policy, 2010), pp. 2–6.

37. Author's interviews and consultations with international affairs officials, including repeated meetings with senior officers up to minister level, Taipei, May, July, August, and December 2008, April 2009.

38. Shirley Kan, *Taiwan: Major US Arms Sales since 1990*, Report RL 30957 (Washington, DC: Library of Congress, Congressional Research Service, October 8, 2008); Kathrin Hille and Demetri Sevastopulo, "US and China Set to Resume Military Talks," *Financial Times*, June 21, 2009, http://www.ft.com.

39. David Shear, "Cross-Strait Relations in a New Era of Negotiation," remarks at the Carnegie Endowment for International Peace, Washington, DC, July 7, 2010, http://www.state.gov.

40. Bonnie Glaser, "The Honeymoon Ends," *Comparative Connections* 12, no. 1 (April 2010): pp. 23–27; Bonnie Glaser, "US Pivot to Asia Leaves China Off Balance," *Comparative Connections* 13, no. 3 (January 2012): pp. 37–38.

41. David Brown, "Adjusting to New Realities," *Comparative Connections* 18, no. 3 (January 2017): pp. 51–57.

42. Alan Romberg, "Tsai Ing-wen Takes Office: A New Era in Cross-Strait Relations," *China Leadership Monitor* no. 50 (Summer 2016), http://www.hoover.org/research/tsai-ing-wen-takes-office-new-era-cross-strait-relations.

43. Bonnie Glaser and Alexandra Viers, "Trump and Xi Break the Ice at Mar-a-Lago," *Comparative Connections* 19, no. 1 (May 2017): pp. 21–32; Robert Sutter, "Trump and China," *EastAsia Forum Quarterly* 9, no. 2 (April–June 2017): pp. 21–24.

44. Samuel Kim, *The Two Koreas and the Great Powers* (New York: Cambridge University Press, 2006).

45. Robert Sutter, *China-Watch* (Baltimore: Johns Hopkins University Press, 1978), p. 65.

46. Sutter, *China-Watch*, pp. 85, 95–96; Ria Chae, "East German Documents on Kim Il Sung's April 1975 Visit to China," *North Korea International Documentation Project* (Washington, DC: Woodrow Wilson Center for Scholars, 2012), http://www.wilsoncenter.org/publication/east-german-documents-kim-il-sung%E2%80%99s-april-1975-trip-to-beijing (accessed July 7, 2012).

47. Ezra Vogel, *Deng Xiaoping and the Transformation of China* (Cambridge, MA: Harvard University Press, 2011), pp. 278–80.

48. Robert Sutter, *Chinese Foreign Policy: Developments after Mao* (New York: Praeger, 1986), pp. 185, 189–91.

49. Kim, *The Two Koreas and the Great Powers*, pp. 52–63, 118–21.

50. Robert Sutter, "China and North Korea after the Cold War: Wariness, Caution and Balance," *International Journal of Korean Studies* 14, no. 1 (2010): pp. 19–34.

51. Samuel Kim, "The Changing Role of China on the Korean Peninsula," *International Journal of Korean Studies* 8, no. 1 (2004): pp. 79–112.

52. Jae Ho Chung, "China's 'Soft' Clash with South Korea," *Asian Survey* 49, no. 3 (2009): pp. 468–83.

53. Scott Snyder, "Post Olympic Hangover: New Backdrop for Relations," *Comparative Connections* 10, no. 3 (October 2008): pp. 101–7.

54. Scott Snyder, "Lee Myung-bak and the Future of Sino-South Korean Relations," Jamestown Foundation, *China Brief* 8, no. 4 (February 14, 2008): pp. 5–8.

55. Bonnie Glaser, "China's Policy in the Wake of the Second DPRK Nuclear Test," *China Security* 5, no. 2 (2009): pp. 1–11.

56. Christopher Twomey, "Chinese Foreign Policy toward North Korea," *Journal of Contemporary China* 17, no. 56 (2008): p. 422.

57. Scott Snyder, "DPRK Provocations Test China's Regional Role," *Comparative Connections* 12, no. 4 (January 2011), http://www.csis.org/pacfor.

58. Scott Snyder, "Consolidating Ties with New DPRK Leadership," *Comparative Connections* 12, no. 3 (October 2010), http://www.csis.org/pacfor.

59. David Jackson, "Analysis: Trump's Trip to Asia Is Over: Now What," *USA Today*, November 14, 2017; Choe Sang Hun and Motoko Rich, "South Korean Leader Boxed In as Trump Threatens North Korea," *New York Times*, November 3, 2017, https://www.nytimes.com/2017/11/03/world/asia/south-korea-trump-nuclear.html.

60. Harold Hinton, *Communist China in World Politics* (Boston: Houghton Mifflin, 1966), pp. 394–441.

61. Nayan Chanda, *Brother Enemy* (New York: Harcourt, 1986); Hinton, *Communist China in World Politics*, pp. 408–22.

62. Robert Sutter, *Historical Dictionary of Chinese Foreign Policy* (Lanham, MD: Scarecrow, 2011), p. 125.

63. Sutter, *Historical Dictionary of Chinese Foreign Policy*, p. 55.

64. Chanda, *Brother Enemy*; Sophie Richardson, *China, Cambodia, and the Five Principles of Peaceful Coexistence* (New York: Columbia University Press, 2010).

65. Richardson, *China, Cambodia, and the Five Principles of Peaceful Coexistence*, pp. 110–98.

66. Robert Sutter, *China's Rise: Implications for US Leadership in Asia*, Policy Studies 21 (Washington, DC: East-West Center, 2006), pp. 9–16.

67. "US Profile Rises, China Image Falls, North Korea Changes?" *Comparative Connections* 12, no. 3 (October 2010): pp. 1–11.

68. "China Reassures Neighbors, Wary of US Intentions," *Comparative Connections* 12, no. 4 (January 2011), http://www.csis.org/pacfor.

69. "China–Southeast Asia Relations," *Comparative Connections* 13, no. 1 (May 2011): p. 65.

70. "China–Southeast Asia Relations," *Comparative Connections* 14, no. 2 (September 2012): pp. 61–62.

71. These and later developments are reviewed in Robert Sutter, *US-China Relations* (Lanham, MD: Rowman & Littlefield, 2017), pp. 223–30.

72. *The Rise of China in the Pacific*, Policy Briefing Note, no. 2 (Canberra: Australian National University, 2007); *China and Taiwan in the South Pacific: Diplomatic Chess versus Pacific Political Rugby* (Sydney: Lowy Institute, 2007); Tamara Shie, "Rising Chinese Influence in the South Pacific," *Asian Survey* 47, no. 2 (March–April 2007): pp. 307–26; Linda Jacobson, "Australia-China Ties: In Search of Political Trust," *Policy Brief*, Lowy Institute, June 2012.

73. Sutter, *Historical Dictionary of Chinese Foreign Policy*, p. 49; Jacobson, "Australia-China Ties"; "Australia–East Asia/US," *Comparative Connections* 18, no. 2 (September 2017), https://www.csis.org/analysis/comparative-connections-v18-n2-australia-east-asia-and-us.

74. Sutter, *Historical Dictionary of Chinese Foreign Policy*, pp. 179–80; Mark Manyin, coord., *Pivot to the Pacific? The Obama Administration's "Rebalancing" Toward Asia*, Report R42448 (Washington, DC: Library of Congress, Congressional Research Service, March 28, 2012), pp. 2–6; Joshua Kurlantzick, *Australia, New Zealand Face China's Influence* (Washington, DC: Council on Foreign Relations, December 13, 2017), https://www.cfr.org/expert-brief/australia-new-zealand-face-chinas-influence (accessed January 22, 2018).

75. Sutter, *Historical Dictionary of Chinese Foreign Policy*, pp. 241–42.

76. Sutter, *Historical Dictionary of Chinese Foreign Policy*, p. 178.

77. John Garver, *Protracted Contest* (Seattle: University of Washington Press, 2001), pp. 3–109; Alice Lyman Miller and Richard Wich, *Becoming Asia* (Stanford, CA: Stanford University Press, 2011), pp. 90–93.

78. Garver, *Protracted Contest*, pp. 138–66; Sutter, *Historical Dictionary of Chinese Foreign Policy*, pp. 178–79.

79. Garver, *Protracted Contest*, pp. 187–215; Miller and Wich, *Becoming Asia*, pp. 179–82.

80. Miller and Wich, *Becoming Asia*, pp. 182–93.

81. Sutter, *Historical Dictionary of Chinese Foreign Policy*, p. 105.

82. Abu Taher Salahuddin Ahmed, "India-China Relations in the 1990s," *Journal of Contemporary Asia* 26, no. 1 (1996): pp. 100–115; Robert Sutter, *China's Rise in Asia: Promises and Perils* (Lanham, MD: Rowman & Littlefield, 2005), pp. 231–48.

83. Gurpreet Khurana, "Securing the Maritime Silk Route: Is There a Sino-Indian Confluence?" *China and Eurasia Forum Quarterly* 4, no. 3 (August 2006): pp. 89–103.

84. Denny Roy, *China's Foreign Relations* (Lanham, MD: Rowman & Littlefield, 1998), pp. 170–74.

85. "Indian Prime Minister Ends China Visit," *China Daily*, January 15, 2008, p. 1; Fu Xiaoqiang, "Wen's Visit Benefits South Asia," *China Daily*, December 23, 2010, p. 8.

86. Garver, *Protracted Contest*, pp. 216–42.

87. Tarique Niazi, "Sino-Pakistani Relations Reach New Level after Zadari's Visit," *China Brief* 8, no. 24 (December 19, 2008): pp. 7–9; Christopher Griffin, "Hu Loves Whom? China Juggles Its Priorities on the Subcontinent," *China Brief* 6, no. 25 (December 19, 2006): pp. 1–3.

88. *Hong Kong AFP in English*, June 3, 1998, https://www.afp.com/ (accessed June 4, 1998), cited in Robert Sutter, *Chinese Policy Priorities and Their Implications for the United States* (Lanham, MD: Rowman & Littlefield, 2000), p. 135.

89. For developments in recent years in Chinese relations with South Asia see Robert Sutter, *The United States and Asia* (Lanham, MD: Rowman & Littlefield, 2015), pp. 233–68; Han Hua, "China, India Vital to Asia's Growth Story," *China Daily*, May 15, 2015, http://www.chinadaily.com.cn/opinion/2015-05/15/content_20722050.htm; Satu Limaye, "Acting East under Prime Minister Modi?" *Comparative Connections* 16, no. 3 (January 2015), pp. 141–60; Satu Limaye, "Back in the Same Orbit and Back on Earth," *Comparative Connections* 17, no. 1 (May 2015): pp. 133–48; Marina Golovnina, "China Offers to Mediate in Stalled Afghan Taliban Peace Talks," Reuters, February 12, 2015, http://www.reuters.com/article/2015/02/12/us-pakistan-china-idUSKBN0LG1UP20150212.

90. Satu Limaye, "India-East Asia Relations: Robust but Not Riveting," *Comparative Connections* 18, no. 3 (January 2017): pp. 117–25; Sutter, *Chinese Foreign Relations* (Lanham, MD: Rowman & Littlefield, 2016), pp. 231–32; Philippa Brant, "China Pledges $46 Billion for Pakistan, but Will Beijing Deliver?" Lowy Institute, *Interpreter*, April 21, 2015, http://www.lowyinterpreter.org/post/2015/04/21/China-pledges-$46-billion-for-Pakistan-but-will-Beijing-deliver.aspx?COLLCC=866310007&.

91. Mohan Malik, "Chinese-Indian Relations in the Post-Soviet Era," *China Quarterly* 142 (June 1995): pp. 317–55; Garver, *Protracted Contest*; Sutter, *China's Rise in Asia*, 233; Jonathan Holslag, *China and India: Prospects for Peace* (New York: Columbia University Press, 2010); C. Raja Mohan, "Sino-Indian Relations: Growing Yet Fragile," *RSIS Commentaries* 174, December 20, 2010; "India and China Eye Each Other Warily," *IISS Strategic Comments* 9, no. 27 (December 2010); Sutter, *The United States and Asia*, pp. 233–68; Limaye, "Acting East under Prime Minister Modi?"; "Back in the Same Orbit and Back on Earth"; "India-East Asia Relations: Robust but Not Riveting."

92. John Garver, *Foreign Relations of the People's Republic of China* (Englewood Cliffs, NJ: Prentice Hall, 1993), pp. 31–39, 304–13; Lowell Dittmer, *Sino-Soviet Normalization and Its International Implications, 1945–1990* (Seattle: University of Washington Press, 1992).

93. Miller and Wich, *Becoming Asia*, pp. 116–36.

94. Miller and Wich, *Becoming Asia*, pp. 161–93.

95. Sutter, *Chinese Foreign Relations* (2012), p. 270.

96. Robert Ross, ed., *China, the United States and the Soviet Union: Tripolarity and Policy Making in the Cold War* (Armonk, NY: M. E. Sharpe, 1993).

97. Miller and Wich, *Becoming Asia*, pp. 196–201.

98. Rajan Menon, "The Strategic Convergence between Russia and China," *Survival* 39, no. 2 (Summer 1997): pp. 101–25.

99. James Clay Moltz, "Regional Tension in the Russo-Chinese Rapprochement," *Asian Survey* 35, no. 6 (June 1995): pp. 511–27.

100. Stephen Uhalley, "Sino-Soviet Relations: Continued Improvement amidst Tumultuous Change," *Journal of East Asian Affairs* 6, no. 1 (Winter–Spring 1992): pp. 171–92.

101. Sutter, *Chinese Foreign Relations* (2012), pp. 272–78.

102. Sutter, *Chinese Foreign Relations* (2016), pp. 269–74.

103. Bobo Lo, *Axis of Convenience: Moscow, Beijing, and the New Geopolitics* (Washington, DC: Brookings Institution Press, 2008); *Russia-China Relations: Assessing Common Ground and Strategic Fault Lines* (Seattle: National Bureau of Asian Research, 2017), http://www.nbr.org/publications/issue.aspx?id=349 (accessed January 22, 2018).

104. *Russia-China Relations*, pp. v–vi.

105. Ibid., pp. 37–49.

106. Ibid., pp. 1–25.

107. Bates Gill and Matthew Oresman, *China's New Journey to the West* (Washington, DC: Center for Strategic and International Studies, August 2003).

108. Gill and Oresman, *China's New Journey to the West*, pp. viii–ix.

109. Zhou Yan, "A Lifeline from Central Asia," *China Daily*, February 17, 2011; Sebastien Peyrouse, "Sino-Kazakh Relations: A Nascent Strategic Partnership," *China Brief* 8, no. 21 (November 7, 2008): pp. 11–15.

110. Peyrouse, "Sino-Kazakh Relations," p. 12; Kevin Sheives, "China and Central Asia's New Energy Relationship: Keeping Things in Perspective," *China-Eurasia Forum Quarterly*, April 2005, p. 18; Stephen Blank, "The Strategic Implications of the Turkmenistan-China Pipeline Project," *China Brief* 10, no. 3 (February 4, 2010): pp. 10–12.

111. "China Says Bin Laden's Death a Milestone for Anti-Terrorism," *China Daily*, May 3, 2011, http://www.chinadaily.com.cn; Andrew Small, "China's Caution on Afghanistan-Pakistan," *Washington Quarterly* 33, no. 3 (July 2010): pp. 81–97.

112. Sutter, *Chinese Policy Priorities and Their Implications for the United States*, p. 143.

113. Wang Jianwei, "China's Multilateral Diplomacy in the New Millennium," in *China Rising: Power and Motivation in Chinese Foreign Policy*, ed. Yong Deng and Fei-Ling Wang (Lanham, MD: Rowman & Littlefield, 2005), pp. 177–87.

114. Qin Jize, "Wen: SCO Trade Is Set to Double," *China Daily*, September 16–17, 2006, p. 1.

115. Michael Mihalka, "Not Much of a Game: Security Dynamics in Central Asia," *China and Eurasia Quarterly* 5, no. 2 (2007): pp. 21–39; Dan Burghart, "The New Nomads? The American Military Presence in Central Asia," *China and Eurasia Quarterly* 5, no. 2 (2007): pp. 5–19.

116. Compare Shirk, *China*, pp. 140–254, with Matthew Oresman, "Repaving the Silk Road: China's Emergence in Central Asia," in *China and the Developing World*, ed. Joshua Eisenman, Eric Heginbotham, and Derek Mitchell (Armonk, NY: M. E. Sharpe, 2007), pp. 60–83.

117. Kevin Sheives, "China Turns West: Beijing's Contemporary Strategy toward Central Asia," *Pacific Affairs* 79, no. 2 (Summer 2006): pp. 205–24.

118. Niklas Swanstrom, "China and Central Asia: A New Great Game or Traditional Vassal?" *Journal of Contemporary China* 14, no. 45 (November 2005): pp. 569–84.

119. Celeste Wallander, "Russia: The Domestic Sources of a Less-Than-Grand Strategy," in *Strategic Asia 2007–2008*, ed. Ashley Tellis and Michael Wills (Seattle: National Bureau of Asian Research, 2007), pp. 138–75.

120. Nadege Rolland, *China's Eurasian Century* (Seattle: National Bureau of Asian Research, 2017), pp. 121–50.

Chapter Nine

Relations beyond Nearby Asia

The remarkable resource-intensive growth of China's export-oriented economy in the twenty-first century was accompanied by an upsurge in development of Chinese infrastructure and expanded urbanization and industrialization in China. As a result, there was a major increase in Chinese imports of oil, metals, timber, and other raw materials and agricultural products needed for Chinese economic development and industrial production. An authoritative Chinese commentator in 2010 said that China consumed over four times the amount of oil to advance its GDP than the United States did, and over eight times the amount of oil to advance its GDP than did Japan. The voracious need for energy and other resources China did not have in adequate supply in turn increased the importance of Chinese foreign relations with resource-rich countries throughout the world, notably in the Middle East, Africa, and Latin America.[1]

Those areas of the developing world received steady but generally low levels of Chinese government attention in the 1990s. The importance of the three regions to China grew in tandem with the growth of Chinese trade and other economic involvement focused on Chinese purchases of oil and other raw materials. Striving to balance Chinese imports and pursue economic opportunity, the Chinese government fostered programs that facilitated widespread use of Chinese companies in construction projects and rapid development of Chinese exports of manufactured goods to these regions. The impressive influx of Chinese merchants, construction laborers, and others saw close to 1 million Chinese working for 1,600 Chinese firms in Africa in 2010. China's large and growing share of foreign economic interactions in these regions received prominent attention in international media. In contrast to sometimes sensational media reports, however, China did not dominate the economic interaction, as the Western-oriented developed countries led by the

United States, countries of the European Union, Japan, and international financial institutions played a far more important role than China as investors, aid providers, and markets for regional exports. Notably, China's flattened global trade and the sharp decline of exports to China from Africa and Latin America beginning in 2015 caused China's economic importance to stall.[2]

Political activism and some military support backed improved Chinese relations with governments throughout the three regions. The imperatives of economic development underlined pragmatism in Chinese diplomacy. China sought to maintain good relations with all countries that eschewed formal contacts with Taiwan. It tried to avoid taking sides or alienating important actors in salient disputes such as the Middle East peace process and international efforts to curb Iran's suspected development of nuclear weapons. It adjusted in practical ways to changes affecting its energy and other interests, notably the breakaway of oil-rich southern Sudan as an independent country after a long armed struggle against the Chinese-backed regime in Khartoum. Some Chinese initiatives sought to reduce the power and influence of the United States.

The Xi Jinping government stressed less resource-intensive production and curbed investment in domestic infrastructure, which was seen to have reached the point of diminishing returns. It emphasized Chinese Silk Road plans that pledged tens of billions of dollars of Chinese investment in and financing of large transportation, electric power, and other infrastructure projects to be built by the massive excess capacity of Chinese construction firms no longer able to find work in China as a result of recent economic policy changes. Chinese policy in the Middle East, Africa, and Latin America continued to seek to build infrastructure that provided access to needed resources and gave much more attention to deals involving Chinese infrastructure projects like high-speed rail lines, roads, power plants, and airports that senior leaders promised would be supported with multibillion-dollar Chinese financing arrangements.

Coincident with China's intense publicity on its Silk Road initiatives, there was a growing awareness in China and abroad about the serious shortcomings of China's emphasis since the start of the previous decade on investment and financing in seeking oil and other resources abroad. On the positive side, trade to the Middle East, Africa, and Latin America grew rapidly for a decade and benefited a wide range of Chinese firms. Millions of Chinese went to the three regions to seek economic advantage. Multibillion-dollar Chinese and sometimes World Bank and other foreign financing supported numerous Chinese-built projects that provided good access to raw materials needed by China. Chinese debts for these efforts were often repaid in oil or other commodities.

On the negative side, the decline in oil and raw material prices in recent years caused countries where China had a heavy debt exposure such as Venezuela, Ecuador, and Angola to seek debt relief that China was reluctant to grant without some compensation or other assurance of repayment. Eventually, Chinese repayment was achieved through Chinese gaining direct ownership and control of important raw materials, infrastructure, or large tracts of land, causing critics to point to China's "debt trap" awaiting poorer countries taking on large debts from China. Another limitation was the failure of many of the widely touted Chinese deals to materialize. In countries like Pakistan and Indonesia, the vast majority of widely publicized past Chinese investment deals saw no effective follow-through. Meanwhile, China's worldwide foreign investment efforts reportedly were more often than not in unprofitable ventures. Mining ventures were particularly volatile, with over 80 percent failing to be realized Also, the Chinese practice to build infrastructure with Chinese firms and minimizing local involvement, and a variety of Chinese practices involving labor standards, environmental standards, and corrupt dealings with partner governments ran up against sometimes strong opposition by affected interest groups and people.[3]

The Xi government basically stuck with the playbook of the previous government, with less emphasis on seeking resources and more emphasis on infrastructure to be built by Chinese firms. The heavy publicity Xi's public actions received from Chinese propaganda organs meant that foreign policy in these regions often seemed to have a higher public profile than in the past. In fact, however, China's emphasis in foreign affairs was more on China's periphery. In the Middle East, Africa, and Latin America, China's trade position was strong but stalled; its position as an investor remained surprisingly small against the backdrop of Chinese leaders' repeated multibillion-dollar pledges. China probed for political advantage in competition with the United States, but it generally took care to avoid high-profile political or military actions that would seriously complicate relations with Washington.[4]

Overall Chinese policy remained in line with its "win-win" formula. What the win-win concept means for China is that China is prepared to work with foreign parties in areas of mutual interest but is not going to take actions or adopt changes in policy and behavior that are not within the limited scope of carefully defined Chinese national interests. Against this background, in regions of the world beyond the scope of Chinese nationalistic, security, and related interests in nearby Asia, China has followed practices that avoid involvement in contentious disputes and foster as stable an environment as possible that is beneficial for Chinese commercial and related interests.

The imperatives driving Chinese policy among the more-developed countries of Europe also had a limited scope. The European Union (EU) and its members were far away from China. They engaged in few military activities in areas of key importance to China. However, China's trade depended increasingly on access to European markets, and European investment in China was an important boost to China's modernization. As China began investing more in recent years, stable and prosperous European countries were an important destination. Educational and technical contacts between China and Europe grew along with economic relations. Chinese leaders also sought to encourage European opposition to US policies, notably making thus-far-unsuccessful efforts to get the European countries to override US opposition and end their embargo on transfers of military equipment to China. Burgeoning Sino-European economic and cultural ties along with strong common antipathy among leading European states and China regarding controversial Bush administration policies, notably the US-led invasion of Iraq, led to predictions of ever-closer Sino-European alignment against Washington. However, such predictions soon foundered on the realities of widely diverging interests and values between China and European countries. Notably, Chinese efforts to build infrastructure and closer relations with less-developed Eastern European countries in line with Beijing's broad-ranging Silk Road plans were viewed with suspicion by EU leading countries, as were adverse Chinese trade and investment practices.[5]

RELATIONS WITH THE MIDDLE EAST

During the Cold War, Chinese officials viewed the Middle East as an arena of the so-called East-West (i.e., U.S-Soviet) competition for world domination and of resistance by developing countries and liberation movements against outside powers and their local allies. Beijing lined up on the side of what it conceived of as progressive forces resisting the United States. It later encouraged opposition as well to the Soviet Union in the 1960s. China supported Gamal Abdel Nasser leading Egypt against Western powers in the 1950s. It supported Arab countries backing Palestinian resistance to Israel and the United States. China provided some military training, assistance, and other support to some resistance movements, notably the Palestine Liberation Organization under the leadership of Yasir Arafat. In general, however, Chinese leaders saw the Middle East as distant from primary Chinese foreign policy concerns. China avoided major commitments and was in a good position to change policies and practices in the region as Chinese foreign policy priorities shifted, sometimes dramatically.[6]

That China's policies in the Middle East for many years involved more rhetoric than substance was evident in relations with Egypt under Nasser. As noted in chapter 2, China showed strong interest in ties with Egypt following Nasser's coming to power in the 1950s. The Egyptian leader gave an anti-Western cast to the prevailing ideas in the Afro-Asian and Non-Aligned

Movements. He also was a proponent of pan-Arabism and sought to reduce Western influence in Egypt, notably by nationalizing the Suez Canal.

Egypt's confrontation with Great Britain and France led it to reach out to China and establish diplomatic relations in 1956, and China responded positively. Egypt became the first country in Africa or the Middle East to establish diplomatic relations with the People's Republic of China. Egypt's militant anticolonialist stance and its role as the largest and most influential Arab state reinforced Chinese interest in close relations. However, the two governments came to differ, notably over China's increasingly strident opposition to the Soviet Union, which caused a major split in the Afro-Asian People's Solidarity Organization and other Afro-Asian groups. China made the case that participants should receive assistance from only Afro-Asian countries, thereby excluding not only the West but also the Soviet Union, a major economic partner of and aid provider to Egypt. It opposed efforts by Cairo to include Soviet delegates in the proceedings of Afro-Asian groups in the 1960s. China's advice to Nasser and the Egyptians after the defeat at the hands of US-backed Israeli forces in the 1967 war was to engage in a protracted guerrilla war with Israel; this advice was deemed unhelpful and naïve among the Arab leaders.[7]

In the 1960s and 1970s, China actively supported the armed struggle of the PLO as a Palestinian political and paramilitary organization against the policies and practices of Israel. It recognized and had diplomatic relations with the PLO, supported its observer status in the United Nations, and maintained close relations with its longtime leader, Yasir Arafat.[8]

As China in the 1970s changed foreign policy priorities to emphasize an international front targeting Soviet expansion and to improve relations with the United States and Western-aligned countries, policy shifts in the Middle East resulted. In 1967 China began supporting Dhofar Province's struggle for independence from the central authority of the Sultanate of Oman. Chinese assistance diminished and ended in the middle 1970s in favor of Chinese diplomatic ties with the Shah of Iran, who was aligned with the United States and wary of the Soviet Union. Iran supported the Sultanate of Oman as a force for regional stability.[9]

China's strong interest in developing closer relations with the pro-Western Iranian leader brought expanding Chinese diplomatic, foreign trade, and other commercial ties with Iran. Chinese leader Hua Guofeng was one of the last major international leaders to visit the Shah prior to his overthrow in the Iranian revolution of 1979. China adjusted quickly and pragmatically to the change and was able to build ties with the new, more radical Iranian regime, which strenuously opposed the United States.[10]

China approved when Anwar Sadat of Egypt in 1972 expelled Soviet military personnel and abrogated the Egyptian Friendship Treaty with the Soviet Union. It offered immediate Chinese economic and military aid in response. By the end of the decade, China was reported to be selling to Egypt advanced weapons like submarines, jet fighters, and surface-to-air missiles worth hundreds of millions of dollars.[11]

China eschewed joining the harsh Arab criticism of Anwar Sadat for signing the Camp David Accords of 1978 and seeking peace with Israel. It came to view the accords negotiated by Sadat and the Israeli prime minister with mediation provided by US president Jimmy Carter as a positive step toward regional stability.

Other changes in Chinese policy at this time included a large cutback in Chinese military supplies, training, and other support for radical groups engaged in terrorist acts against Israel. By 1980, China clearly indicated opposition to terrorist acts and supported Israel's right to exist. During these years, Israel and China maintained a variety of intelligence operations and arms trade relationships, which helped to provide a foundation for China's decision to establish diplomatic relations with Israel in 1992.[12]

The twists and turns in Chinese Middle East policy at this time were also reflected in policy toward Iraq. China established relations with Iraq in 1958 after it withdrew from the US-backed Central Treaty Organization. China for years duly supported Iraq and other Arab governments opposed to Israel's policies and practices. As noted above, China's concern with the expansion of Soviet power and influence in the Middle East prompted its strong relations with Iraq's regional rival Iran in the 1970s. And China also diverged from Iraq in avoiding sharp criticism of Egypt in seeking peace with Israel in the Camp David Accords.[13]

China's maneuvering following the Iranian revolution of 1979 and subsequent war between Iran and Iraq (1980–88) was a remarkable display of pragmatism and fence straddling that benefited China's economic growth and military modernization. China was broadly successful in efforts to stay on good terms with both powers. While Chinese diplomats routinely denied reports of large Chinese arms sales to the combatants in the protracted conflict that killed a half-million people, China's actual supplying each with large amounts of weapons for the first time put China among the leading arms exporters in the international arms trade. China also developed close economic ties involving large purchases of oil and numerous Chinese construction and other projects in these two countries. The United States was critical of Chinese sales of missiles and other military equipment that Iran could use to threaten US forces and oil shipping in the Persian Gulf.[14]

Beijing was less successful in positioning China in reaction to Iraq's invasion of Kuwait in 1990. China opposed the invasion, but it also had reservations about moves led by the United States to organize efforts to drive out the Iraqi forces. China had developed important economic interests in Iraq, a supplier of oil to China. China's resistance slowed United Nations Security Council decisions condemning Iraq, and it abstained from endorsing the use of force against Iraq. When the US-led allied forces were successful in driving out Iraqi invaders and restoring stability in Kuwait with minimal allied casualties, China appeared temporarily isolated. China later criticized and resisted US-led efforts in the 1990s to continue military restrictions and other punishments against Iraq and to pressure Iraq to comply with international norms regulating the development of weapons of mass destruction.[15]

In the twenty-first century, Chinese policy and behavior toward the Middle East followed a pattern seen in Chinese policy and behavior toward the other regions of developing countries far from China—Africa and Latin America. On the one hand, there was an upswing of Chinese attention to the region, notably because of growing Chinese need for oil and other energy sources and resources that are required to support China's remarkable economic growth. On the other hand, there were complications in China's expanding engagement. In the Middle East, China's close relations with Iran complicated China's efforts to stay on good terms with the United States and developed countries important in Chinese foreign policy.[16] In much of the past two decades, Iran was seen as a major deviant from world norms regarding nuclear weapons proliferation, terrorism, human rights, and other sensitive issues that were supported by the United States, the EU, and other powers of importance to China.

The Chinese government was more reluctant than in the 1990s to take strong public positions against the United States and its allies in dealing with Iran, as well as Iraq and other issues of controversy.[17] The Chinese government generally did not allow its pervasive anti-US rhetoric to spoil its more important effort to stabilize US-China relations. For example, when the Chinese government came under pressure from the United States in the late 1990s to end nuclear cooperation with Iran, Chinese leaders did so. They suffered a serious downturn in relations with Tehran for the sake of ensuring smooth summit meetings with US leaders seriously concerned with Iran's nuclear weapons ambitions. Meanwhile, Chinese policy aimed at keeping on good terms with all sides, including notably Israel, in the often contentious politics of the region. In this way, China could serve its economic interests of ensuring diverse supplies of oil and access to regional markets for economic benefit and arms transfers.[18] In general, the Chinese leaders have tried to adopt positions on the many issues of controversy in the Middle East that are well balanced, have the broadest international appeal, and do the least damage to China's often conflicting interests in the Middle East.[19]

Heading the list of complications and conflicting imperatives in Chinese policy toward the Middle East is Chinese leaders' need to strengthen their relations with oil and gas exporters, including targets of US-backed international pressure (like Iran) and countries that periodically wish to show greater independence from the United States (like oil-rich Saudi Arabia). Building better Chinese relations with these two energy giants is further complicated by their deep mutual suspicion and conflicting interests. At the same time, Chinese leaders toned down their anti-US posturing seen in the 1990s for many reasons; notably, Chinese strategists see their access to the energy resources of the Persian Gulf heavily influenced by the strong US military presence in the gulf and the broader Middle East. Taken together, the previously mentioned imperatives and trends are often at odds. They appear contradictory, and they complicate China's approach toward the region.

Deepening the trend of the previous decade, Chinese policy aims as much as possible at keeping on good terms with all sides in the often contentious politics of the region.[20] The logic behind the Chinese approach to the Middle East seems clear, even though the Chinese goals seem in conflict and the resulting Chinese actions appear to be somewhat ambivalent and muddled. Chinese domestic economic growth and political stability depend on stable energy supplies. The main sources of Chinese energy demand involve industrial activities, infrastructure development, and transportation growth. The large increase in the number of cars in China strengthens the need for imported oil. Despite China's efforts to diversify the sources of oil imports, the Middle East accounts for over half of China's overall imports, with Saudi Arabia and Iran being the biggest suppliers in the region.[21] Graphic examples of China's stronger drive for international energy resources include a variety of high-level Chinese visits and energy-related agreements with Iran as well as even more interactions and agreements with the major energy power in the region, Saudi Arabia.

At the time of Chinese President Hu Jintao's visit to Saudi Arabia in February 2009, Sino–Saudi Arabian trade amounted to over $42 billion a year. This was almost half of China's overall trade with the Middle East. Bilateral trade declined along with international energy demand during the global economic downturn in 2009, but it rebounded to a value of $43 billion in 2010. China became the largest importer of Saudi oil.[22]

Meanwhile, even though China was well aware that Saudi Arabia and Iran had a number of serious differences and were often on opposite sides regarding Middle Eastern problems, China pursued its long-standing ties with Tehran with new vigor given its ever-growing energy needs. Chinese firms also were deeply involved in developing the Tehran subway, electrical grid, dams, and other industries and infrastructure. These steps reinforced Chinese reluctance to see sanctions or other pressure imposed on Tehran by the United States and Western powers concerned with Iran's nuclear development program, though China continued to show reluctance to stand alone against such international opposition.[23] Top-level Chinese leaders visited Iran less frequently than Saudi Arabia, but they met cordially with the controversial Iranian president in China and at international meetings elsewhere. Iranian officials said in 2011 that direct Chinese trade with Iran was valued at $29 billion, and indirect trade through countries neighboring Iran brought the total to $38 billion in 2010. Iran was China's third largest supplier of crude, providing China with roughly 12 percent of its total annual oil consumption. Trade reached a value of $50 billion in 2015.[24] Active collaboration between Iranian and Chinese energy firms indicated that China would continue to rely heavily on imports from the country, though the need to adhere to tightening US-backed international sanctions against Iran over its nuclear development programs were obstacles to oil trade between Iran and China.[25]

Regarding the controversy over Iran's nuclear program, the Chinese government acted as though it did not want to choose between its important energy and other ties with Iran and its concern to nurture the continued cooperation of the United States, the EU, and others who strongly pressed Iran over a variety of issues, notably its suspected efforts to develop nuclear weapons. Chinese officials at times endeavored to slow and delay actions in the United Nations that would result in condemnation of or sanctions against Iran, and at times they worked closely with Russia in fending off pressure from the United States and the EU powers for more decisive UN action. However, China was reluctant to stand alone against the Western pressure, and it bent to such pressure in allowing the issue to be brought before the UN Security Council despite earlier pledges to resist such a step. In June 2010 China voted for a UN Security Council resolution approving new sanctions against Iran on account of its suspected nuclear weapons development.[26]

Chinese relations with Israel have posed another set of contradictions and complications for Chinese foreign policy in the Middle East. China benefited greatly from economic and military transfers from Israel; the latter were especially valuable to China because of the continued Western arms embargo against China. China resented US pressure to curb Israeli military transfers to China.[27] Beijing accepted Israel's right to exist and eschewed past support for radical elements aiming at Israel's destruction—steps that significantly improved China's relations with the United States and other concerned Western powers. At the same time, China supported the Palestinian Authority (PA) in its opposition to various Israeli pressures and maneuvers seen as designed to weaken the PA and what were deemed legitimate Palestinian territorial claims. A serious set of complications was raised by the war in July–August 2006 between Israeli and Hezbollah forces based in southern Lebanon. Chinese commentary moved from a more-or-less evenhanded position to one that sided against Israel and to a degree against the United States. China did not want to seriously alienate any major party or make major commitments or take risks in the volatile situation; this finding was illustrated by the bland and noncommittal remarks of the Chinese media and the foreign ministry "special envoy" sent to tour the region. The United States, European powers, Israel, Iran, and Syria loomed much more important in the conflict and the efforts to resolve the conflict. As one veteran scholar of China–Middle East relations concluded, China's behavior during the crisis showed that Beijing continued to talk much and do little regarding serious regional issues.[28] China did respond to UN and European requests for peace-keeping forces and agreed to provide one thousand personnel for the UN peacekeeping operation in Lebanon. The Chinese personnel were used in support functions, according to Chinese diplomats.[29]

An additional set of contradictions is posed by China's ongoing efforts to suppress dissent and so-called splittist activities by Muslim adherents in Xinjiang. It is deemed essential that these elements be suppressed in order to preserve order and stability in China. At the same time, the tough Chinese measures negatively affect China's image among the Islamic governments in the Middle East. Also, Chinese antiterrorist efforts at home and abroad, notably in the Shanghai Cooperation Organization (SCO), are seen as vital to Chinese national security and regional stability and an important foundation for greater Chinese cooperation with the United States and other Western powers. At the same time, China's interests with Iran required Chinese lead-ers to allow the president of Iran to participate in the elaborate fifth anniver-sary summit of the SCO in Shanghai and later meetings of the group despite strong accusations from Israel, the United States, and Western powers that Tehran supports terrorist activities against Israel, in Iraq and elsewhere.[30]

President Xi Jinping wrestled with these contradictory imperatives. Though advancing a higher profile for China in other parts of the world, Xi and his colleagues found it difficult to get beyond China's traditional low profile in the Middle East. As discussed below, though Chinese economic interests in the region continued to grow along with the rapid rise of oil imports and Chinese exports of manufactured goods, the Chinese president and prime minister, widely traveled elsewhere, avoided visiting the region for over two years after coming to power in late 2012. The main reasons had to do with the pervasive violence throughout the region and resulting danger to Chinese leaders.

Caution and practicality determined China's reaction to the upsurge of mass demonstrations against authoritarian regimes throughout North Africa and nearby Asia in 2011. The Chinese government focused internally, tight-ening already extensive internal controls to guard against possible spillover effects that might challenge continued one-party rule in China. In the region, Chinese officials adjusted pragmatically to the new administrations taking form in Tunisia and Egypt. The armed conflict in Libya cost Chinese enter-prises invested there dearly; the Chinese government was effective in facili-tating the evacuation of over thirty thousand Chinese nationals from the country. China seemed to depart from its past practice in abstaining rather than blocking UN Security Council Resolution 1973 in March 2011, author-izing all measures, including military action, against the Libyan government of Muammar Gaddafi, then engaging in armed resistance to populist forces struggling for his ouster.[31]

Beijing came to regret this decision and began to oppose NATO military action against Gaddafi. It joined Russia in blocking UN action in opposition to the Bashar al-Assad government in the Syrian civil war. Still supporting the Assad government in Syria, China avoided full endorsement of US calls for strong action against the radical Islamic State in Iraq and Syria. Regional turmoil spread with the fall of the government of Yemen to militants in early 2015. Saudi Arabia intervened with bombing raids against the militants. Xi Jinping had been planning a visit to Saudi Arabia and Egypt, as well as Pakistan and Indonesia, in March 2015. In the wake of the Saudi bombings, he scrapped plans for both the Saudi Arabia and Egypt visits, and confined his trip to Pakistan and Indonesia. The Xi trip predictably underlined Chinese Silk Road economic initiatives that included the states in the Middle East, but security dangers combined with the various contradictions facing Chinese policy inclined Chinese leaders at least for now to avoid a potentially dangerous and counterproductive higher profile in the volatile Middle East. [32]

President Xi made his visits to Saudi Arabia and Egypt in early 2016; he added Iran to the trip following the international agreement on Iran's nuclear program and the ending of sanctions. [33] Subsequent Chinese activism included the establishment of China's first foreign military base (in Djibouti), the first Chinese "Arab Policy Paper," and the appointment of a special envoy regarding the Syria crisis. Despite the unremitting publicity on the vision of China's Belt and Road Initiative and its regional implications, the reality for now in the Middle East involved incremental steps focused on deepening economic engagement. [34]

RELATIONS WITH AFRICA

China's early involvement with Africa reflected efforts to throw off outside influence and foster rapid development and social progress. Chinese officials to this day continue a long-standing practice of comparing Africa's suffering under the European colonialists with China's so-called hundred years of humiliation. As in the Middle East and other areas of the developing world, Beijing aligned with what it saw as progressive forces resisting the United States and its Western allies and associates. It later encouraged opposition as well to the Soviet Union as China broke with the USSR in the 1960s. [35]

China was a disruptive force in African regional groups and liberation movements as it competed for influence against both the Western countries and the USSR and its allies. China's commitment to the efforts of liberation groups and states supporting armed struggles against colonial powers, white-ruled states, and African regimes closely aligned with the West or the USSR at times was substantial. China warned newly emerging African officials and leaders of militant liberation movements against Western and Soviet intentions, including foreign assistance from these governments, and it was for many years prepared to provide substantial assistance to favored governments and liberation movements despite its own pervasive poverty at home. Beijing was an important supplier of basic military equipment and training to a number of liberation groups and newly emerged governments. Premier Zhou Enlai in a wide-ranging visit to Africa in 1964 proclaimed that Africa was ripe for revolution, and China subsequently provided a variety of assistance to favored governments and resistance movements. The assistance ranged from providing help to dissident factions opposed to the UN-backed regime in Congo-Leopoldville to providing backing for the regime of President Mobutu in Zaire to help check Soviet-backed incursions from Angola in the 1970s. The Chinese were key backers of liberation fighters against the Portuguese in Angola and Mozambique, they supported Robert Mugabe in his struggle against white rule in Rhodesia, and they backed other radical groups in South Africa and elsewhere. [36]

Among African leaders who stayed close to China were Julius Nyerere of Tanzania and Kenneth Kaunda of neighboring Zambia. China nurtured ties with these long-serving presidents who enjoyed prominence among African leaders. In the 1960s and 1970s, China was a strong supporter of several of the armed resistance groups active in Nyerere's Tanzania and Kaunda's Zambia that were focused on opposition to white-ruled and colonial regimes in Africa. The groups included FRELIMO, Frente de Libertação de Moçambique, also known as the Liberation Front for Mozambique. This guerrilla movement founded in 1962 was focused on gaining freedom from Portugal's colonial rule; over the years it received important training and material support from China. Mozambique became an independent country under FRELIMO's rule in 1975 and soon established and sustained friendly ties with China. Also active in these countries was Robert Mugabe, who struggled for decades against the white-ruled government of Rhodesia. He led the Zimbabwe African National Movement (ZANU), which received support from China, in contrast to a competing resistance movement, the Zimbabwe African People's Union (ZAPU), which received support from the Soviet Union. China sustained support for Mugabe as he succeeded in his struggles against the white-ruled government and opposing forces, becoming head of government in Zimbabwe in the 1980s. [37]

As China developed close relations with Nyerere's Tanzania and Kaunda's Zambia, it provided favorable publicity to their international and domestic policies. A favorite subject highlighted for many years by Chinese media was Nyerere's socialist and rural-based development policies and practices that many foreign specialists and commentators now see as having been ineffective or counterproductive.

Tanzania under Nyerere's leadership and Zambia under Kaunda's leadership were among the few nations to remain on good terms with China during the radical policies and practices of the Cultural Revolution. Chinese assistance to Africa during this period and later involved building prominent demonstration projects. Most involved sports stadiums, government buildings, or roads, but a few were truly monumental. At the urging of Nyerere and Kaunda, Mao Zedong was willing to make the enormous Chinese sacrifices necessary to build the TanZam Railway that Zambia and Tanzania sought in order to allow Zambian copper to transit from landlocked Zambia through routes not controlled by white minority or colonial regimes. The TanZam Railway, designed to link Zambia's copper fields and the Tanzanian coast, was undertaken by Chinese engineers even though it was previously judged ill-advised by Western and other international experts. Despite great obstacles, Chinese government workers completed the project after many years of effort, the loss of many lives, and great expense. The railway was poorly maintained at various times during the ensuing years, making it less than reliable or efficient as a transportation route.[38]

As noted in chapter 3, China relied heavily on backing from African countries in its efforts to rally so-called third world support in order to gain entry for China and to remove Taiwan from the United Nations in 1971. Competition between China and Taiwan for diplomatic recognition in Africa and elsewhere continued.

The dramatic Chinese opening to improved relations with the United States and Western countries during an intensifying struggle against the expansion of the Soviet Union in the 1970s resulted in shifts in Chinese foreign relations in Africa. Chinese officials showed pragmatism as they developed relations with previously alienated African leaders who had strong ties with the United States. And unlike in the Maoist period, Chinese leaders became unwilling to make major economic or security commitments to these regimes. Focused on Chinese domestic needs and development, Deng Xiaoping and his colleagues proved much less generous in providing aid and other assistance.

Emblematic of the pragmatic and arguably expedient turns in Chinese policy at this time is the Chinese relationship with Sese Mobutu. China and this long-serving (1965–97) president of Zaire (also known at various times as the Democratic Republic of the Congo) were at first on opposite sides of the struggles afflicting the country. Mobutu seemed as suspicious of Chinese actions and motives as he was of the actions and motives of the Soviet Union. Mobutu opposed seating China at the United Nations.

However, by 1972, he began to see the Chinese in a different light, as a counterbalance to both the Soviet Union and his close ties with the United States, Israel, and South Africa. In November 1972, Mobutu extended diplomatic recognition to China, and the two governments established diplomatic relations. In 1973, he visited Beijing, where he met personally with Mao

Zedong and received promises of $100 million in technical foreign assistance.

In 1974, Mobutu made a surprise visit to both China and North Korea. At the time, China and Zaire shared a common goal in central Africa, namely opposing the expansion of Soviet power through Soviet-backed African resistance forces in Angola. Accordingly, both Zaire and China covertly funneled aid to Angolan resistance groups opposed to the Soviet-supported forces that seemed ascendant in Angola. The Soviet-backed forces also received the support of tens of thousands of combat troops from Cuba. China provided training, weapons, and money to the Angolan forces also backed by Zaire. Zaire itself launched an ill-fated preemptive invasion of Angola in a bid to install a pro-Zaire government, but the invasion was repulsed by Cuban troops. China sent military aid to Zaire during counterstrikes led by Cuban troops against Zaire.[39]

China subsequently pulled away from overt resistance to Soviet-backed movements in Angola and other parts of Africa. The shift involved ending support for the National Union for the Total Independence of Angola (União Nacional para a Independência Total de Angola—UNITA). This guerrilla movement founded in 1966 was one of the important African resistance movements that long received Chinese support. Largely peasant based, UNITA focused its armed struggle against the colonial rule by Portugal in Angola. Its leader was Jonas Savimbi, who had received paramilitary training in China and who adopted Maoist guerrilla tactics in his resistance against the Portuguese and competing resistance groups. After the end of Portuguese rule in Angola in 1975, a civil war among UNITA and competing resistance groups emerged that endured for more than two decades.[40]

China withdrew support from UNITA and generally eschewed involvement in the civil war. It remained on good terms with Mobutu, who visited China three times after his 1973 and 1974 visits. Chinese assistance projects were followed by a variety of commercial deals and China continued to provide some military assistance to Zaire. When Mobutu was overthrown in 1997, China continued normal relations with the now renamed Democratic Republic of the Congo without serious interruption.[41]

Post-Mao Chinese leaders were much less interested in spending money overseas, especially when their political standing at home rested heavily on their ability to improve economic conditions for the Chinese people. By the late 1970s, the overriding focus of domestic modernization led to a reduction in Chinese enthusiasm for funding expensive African assistance programs. Chinese officials also recognized that past efforts to roll back superpower influence in the region had not worked well. Aid levels dropped markedly in the late 1970s and remained around $100 million annually for the whole world. Chinese assistance increasingly took the form of training, export credits for Chinese goods, or joint financing plans. As the Chinese export-oriented economy grew, so did Chinese trade, from about $300 million with Africa in 1976 to $2.2 billion in 1988. Of course, this still was only a small fraction of overall Chinese trade.[42]

As post-Mao China was willing and anxious to receive foreign aid from the World Bank, the International Monetary Fund (IMF), and other international bodies and donor countries, this put China in direct competition with African states seeking aid from the same sources. The newly open Chinese economy also was seen by some to be taking foreign investment that might have gone to African ventures. African grumbling over these trends grew. Even some longtime African friends felt increasing ambiguity in their ties with China. With mixed results, Chinese officials used diplomacy, propaganda, and exchanges to preserve Beijing's self-described position as an intimate supporter of struggling African states. While acknowledging Chinese political support, African governments often recognized that they had to follow China's example in cultivating ties with developed economies, including the United States, Europe, and Japan, if they expected markedly to boost their modernization efforts. Meanwhile, long-standing Chinese efforts to offer university and other training for African students were clouded by several publicized incidents showing apparent Chinese social bias against Africans in the late 1980s.[43]

Chinese incentives to improve relations with African countries increased after the Tiananmen incident of 1989.[44] Officials anxiously sought African and other third world support to offset Beijing's isolation and to reduce international pressure against China. The period also saw Taiwan launch its pragmatic or flexible diplomacy policy. Taipei used offers of aid or other means to woo aid-dependent African countries and to have them establish official diplomatic relations with Taiwan even though they had diplomatic relations with Beijing. Whenever this occurred, Beijing broke ties with the African state concerned, providing a net diplomatic gain for Taipei. As discussed in chapter 8, China strongly intensified competition with Taiwan in Africa when Beijing gave higher priority to checking Taiwan's flexible diplomacy, especially following the visit by Taiwan's president, Lee Teng-hui, to the United States in 1995. Its efforts proved successful, diminishing Taiwan's official recognition in Africa to a few small states.

The deepening and broadening Chinese interaction with African countries in the twenty-first century featured an upsurge in Chinese trade, investment financing, and high-level official interaction with African countries that stood in contrast with the stagnant and contentious relations African countries often have had with developed countries and international financial institutions. A marked increase in Chinese purchases of oil and other raw materials from Africa and a concurrent effort to foster Chinese exports to African markets and an increase in Chinese construction projects throughout Africa were new and important drivers of Chinese interest in the continent.

Other patterns of the post–Cold War period have continued without major change. China continues to devote strong political attention to African countries in order to compete with Taiwan, enhance solidarity with members of the third world bloc in the United Nations and other world organizations, facilitate growing trade, and portray China internationally as a power of growing stature and importance. The Chinese government has had an active aid program in several African countries, but the cost of the program to China (that is, the amount of funds leaving China to aid African countries and not guaranteed to be paid back in commodities or other forms) remains small. With a few exceptions, Chinese arms transfers to Africa are small, and China has avoided taking positions that might be seen as interfering in the internal affairs of African countries or antagonistic to disputants in the continent's many conflicts. Though often sharply critical of the United States in Africa in the 1990s, China in the twenty-first century saw the wisdom of a less-contentious posture in African affairs, pursuing a path of "peaceful development" that tended to avoid criticizing US and other powers' policies incompatible with Chinese goals on the continent.[45]

In general, the advance of Chinese relations in Africa has faced fewer contradictions or complications than concurrent Chinese advances among developing countries in the Middle East or Latin America. In the latter two areas, the security, political, and economic roles of the United States, European countries, and other foreign powers generally have been significantly more important than China's newly rising prominence. Taken together, the roles of these other foreign powers have added to factors constraining the influence of China in those regions. In the case of Africa and especially sub-Saharan Africa, however, China's involvement has reached high prominence in a setting where other powers have appeared less vigorously involved. China, while not achieving the status of Africa's leading foreign power, clearly has played a leading role in regional affairs along with the United States and European countries and the international organizations they support. The latter powers sometimes have criticized aspects of Chinese involvement in Africa, but they also have moved to consult with and work more closely with China in dealing with regional issues. Meanwhile, though the Chinese government usually has sustained good relations with African government leaders, it has found that China's increasing impact on Africa has resulted in mixed reactions below the national government level, with some strong negative responses on the part of constituencies adversely affected by Chinese interaction with their countries.[46]

A landmark in China's efforts to formulate a comprehensive outreach to Africa came in October 2000 when China's leaders and the leaders of forty-five African countries met in Beijing to form the China-Africa Cooperation Forum (CACF). They agreed that CACF would meet every three years to further mutual economic development and cooperation. The Chinese government endeavored to enhance cooperation by using the first CACF meeting to pledge forgiveness of $1.2 billion in African debt covering thirty-two nations and to expand Chinese foreign aid to Africa. At the second ministerial CACF conference, held in Addis Ababa, Ethiopia, in December 2003, China promised to cooperate with Africa in priority sectors identified in the African governments' New Partnership for African Development. These African priorities included infrastructure development, prevention and treatment of diseases such as HIV/AIDS, human resources development, and agricultural development. China also agreed to begin negotiations on reducing tariffs to zero for some exports to China of the least-developed African countries.[47] Continued high-level attention to Africa included repeated top-level Chinese leaders' visits. In January 2006, the Chinese government's first official white paper on African policy was released. At the time, Chinese media reported that Chinese trade with Africa reached $40 billion in 2005, up rapidly from $10 billion in 2000.[48] China hosted the CACF summit in November 2006. It forecast that China's trade with Africa would reach $100 billion by 2010.[49]

Chinese government figures on Chinese investment in Africa tended to be significantly lower than figures used in Western and African media and other international reports. Thus, even with a widely reported and dramatic rise in Chinese involvement in gaining access to African oil and other natural resources needed for China's heavily resource-intensive economic growth trajectory, a Chinese government official said in April 2011 that Chinese investment in Africa was then "about $1 billion" a year, and was "dwarfed by the West" in contributions to overall annual foreign investment in Africa amounting to $80–90 billion.[50]

Chinese foreign assistance to African states also received prominent treatment in Chinese and international media and among concerned international relations specialists, even though the actual amounts of Chinese assistance to Africa (as opposed to large amounts of financing provided by China to be paid for with African commodities or other means) seemed modest and less than that provided by developed countries and international financial institutions.[51] For a variety of reasons, the actual amounts of Chinese foreign assistance have not been released in a comprehensive way by the Chinese government. China did issue an official document on Chinese foreign assistance in April 2011, but the information was very broad ranging. The second Chinese white paper on foreign assistance was issued in 2014; it offered better information focused on the three-year period 2010–12. China provided $14.4 billion in grants, interest-free loans, and concessional loans. Over half of that went to Africa, where fifty-one countries received Chinese aid.[52]

Salient indicators[53] underlining the importance of Africa in Chinese foreign relations at the start of the current decade included frequent Chinese leadership visits to Africa, involving regular participation in the China-Africa Cooperation Forum. Growing trade and investment saw China emerge as

Africa's largest trading partner in 2009 and trade amounting to $114 billion in 2010; China's cumulative investment at the end of 2010 was said to be worth $9.3 billion by official Chinese media. Chinese aid included forgiveness of debts to China of poorer African countries valued at almost $3 billion; several billions of dollars of financing provided by a special Sino-African development fund; and financing, including loans from official Chinese banks backed by commodities and other collateral, in support of large-scale infrastructure projects in Angola, Sudan, Congo, and other resource-rich countries. The over one million Chinese working in Africa included professionals in Chinese commercial and government institutions, Chinese laborers working on projects throughout the continent, and Chinese traders and small-business owners focused on selling Chinese commodities to African consumers. Pursuing active exchange programs with African countries involved African students in China, sending Chinese medical personnel to Africa, and Chinese-funded Confucius Institutes. Military exchanges saw Chinese arms sales generally remain at a modest level, though Chinese arms sales to controversial governments like Sudan and Zimbabwe received critical attention in international media. Chinese military and other security forces were active participants in UN-backed peacekeeping efforts in several African countries. Since 2009, China maintained warships along the Horn of Africa to work with international security efforts to counter pirate attacks against international shipping off the coast of Somalia.

Continuity and Change in Xi Jinping's Africa Policy

The highlights of Chinese interaction with Africa during the Xi Jinping government included President Xi Jinping's and Premier Li Keqiang's visits; growing trade reached $230 billion in 2014 and investment continued to grow from a low base. At first there were many widely touted plans for large-scale high-speed rail and other Chinese-financed and -built infrastructure highlighted during Li Keqiang's visit to Africa in 2014. In November 2014, China Railway Construction Corporation signed China's largest-ever overseas investment deal, agreeing to build a 1,400-kilometer railway along the coast of Nigeria. Another proposal involved a five-nation train line in East Africa.[54] China signed a deal with the African Union (AU) during the AU heads of state meeting in Ethiopia in 2015. It was publicized as "the most substantive project the AU has ever signed with a partner." It promised to connect African nations by road, rail, and air transportation.[55]

Reflecting the new priority on Chinese-financed and -built infrastructure, the leader of the Chinese Export-Import Bank told African representatives in November 2013 that China would invest the heretofore unimagined sum of $1 trillion in Africa over the next decade. He advised that the funds would be focused on the construction of transnational highways, railways, and airports.

He noted in particular that China was preparing to spend as much as $500 billion on a rail network that would span the continent, recalling to veteran African observers the dream of Cecil Rhodes of a Cape-to-Cairo rail link.[56]

Subsequently, despite the Xi government's various Silk Road initiatives and proposed investment, loans, and financing plans supporting Chinese interaction with other developing countries, in Africa hard realities undermined Chinese ambitions. The value of African exports to China collapsed in 2015, falling in value by 40 percent. Overall trade declined from $240 billion in 2014 to $149 billion in 2016.[57] Chinese investment in Africa also fell dramatically in 2015.[58] Against this background, a concrete indicator that China—as noted by the *Economist*—does not economically dominate Africa but is "one among many" foreign powers influencing Africa is the fact that while China is Africa's largest trader, there are many other important trading partners; China's share of 15 percent or less is hardly dominant. Foreign investment in Africa shows that China, even after all the pledges of multibillion-dollar "investment" deals, actually accounts for less than 5 percent of foreign investment in Africa.[59] Meanwhile, the net impact of the various widely touted Chinese-financed projects in Africa is less than first appearances if only for the fact that many and perhaps a majority of the proposed projects have not been implemented in the end.

A comprehensive study of failed Chinese implementation in Africa has not been done, but there are plenty of examples of very large promises followed by little implementation for a variety of reasons on the Chinese side and the side of the foreign partners. In Nigeria, for example, where official Chinese commentary focused on the massive 2014 deal to build Nigerian railways noted above, little is said of the fact that Chinese companies and proposed Chinese multibillion-dollar loans have been involved in failed deals to rebuild Nigeria's rail system since the 1990s.[60] Meanwhile, in July 2005, China and Nigeria signed an $800 million crude oil sale agreement involving the projected purchase by China of thirty thousand barrels of oil a day for five years. In April 2006, the Chinese state-owned company China National Offshore Oil Corporation (CNOOC) said that it had completed a deal to buy a share of a Nigerian oil license. The deal marked CNOOC's "biggest-ever overseas acquisition," costing over $2 billion. To win the bid, China agreed to build a hydropower station and to take over a privatized Nigerian oil refinery that was losing money. As it happened, several large Chinese deals with Nigeria fell through because of various reasons later in the decade. In 2010, the Chinese consul general in Lagos told the media that steadily growing China-Nigeria trade had reached an annual value in 2009 of over $6 billion. The composition and balance of the trade showed Chinese exports, mainly manufactured goods, were valued at $5.47 billion, while Nigerian exports to China were less than $1 billion. The Chinese official said this reflected the fact that "very limited crude oil is currently exported to China," an indication that earlier plans for Chinese purchase of Nigerian oil had failed to materialize.[61]

Though the majority of recent Chinese foreign policy initiatives in Africa remained commercial, the Xi Jinping government did take a few steps that increased China's foreign policy profile in noncommercial areas. China agreed for the first time to send combat troops to support UN peacekeeping missions; they were in Africa and involved deployments of 170 troops to Mali and 700 troops to South Sudan. China's special envoy for Africa took an active role in endeavoring to mediate the conflict in South Sudan. China's naval ships that participated in international antipiracy efforts off the Horn of Africa also were used to evacuate Chinese and other civilians from nearby crisis areas, most recently Yemen in 2015; they also were part of Chinese contingents participating in naval exercises with Russia in the eastern Mediterranean Sea and the Black Sea. Presumably to support the increased Chinese navy activities, China in 2015 engaged in discussions with Djibouti for what the Djibouti president said was "a military base." Against the background of this deployment, China established its first foreign military base, in Djibouti in the Horn of Africa, in 2017. China in the past strongly opposed Chinese foreign bases.[62]

RELATIONS WITH LATIN AMERICA AND THE CARIBBEAN

China historically has paid less attention to Latin America and the Caribbean (LAC) than to any other region in the developing world. Geographic distance and China's preoccupation with issues closer to home put Latin American issues low on China's list of priorities. In the East-West and Sino-Soviet competition for global influence during the Cold War, Beijing at first tried to make headway among radical Latin American groups. In general, however, there was little to show for this effort. The power and influence of the United States remained very strong among most established governments in Latin America, while leftists in Cuba, Chile, Nicaragua, and elsewhere tended to look to the Soviet bloc for tangible assistance rather than to seek the political advice and rhetorical support offered by Maoist China.[63]

Chinese leaders maneuvered to gain Fidel Castro's support in Cuba during the acrimonious Sino-Soviet split beginning in the 1960s. Pro-Chinese and pro-Cuban groups for several years pursued revolutionary tactics in ideological association. The break came in the mid-1960s, when the Cubans, presumably under Soviet pressure, became more cautious in exporting revolution. China went on giving financial aid and political encouragement to revolutionary groups in Latin America in the 1960s, but most of them adopted strongly pro-Soviet, pro-Cuban orientations.[64]

As China in the late 1960s and early 1970s opened to relations with the United States and a wide range of governments useful in China's search for greater recognition and international leverage against the growing coercion of the Soviet Union, China's past advocacy of violent revolution was replaced by championing the interests of third world governments. Forecasting themes seen in Deng Xiaoping's famous speech to the United Nations in 1974 announcing China's "Three Worlds" theory was the Chinese address at the UN Conference on Trade and Development meeting in Chile in 1972. China assumed the role as spokesperson for the developing world and chief opponent of both the Soviet Union and the United States in Latin America and elsewhere. Such rhetoric did not go very far in advancing Chinese regional influence, as China had few interests that coincided with those of the countries in Latin America and it had few resources to expend there.[65]

Later in the 1970s, Beijing for several years attempted to fit its Latin American policy into its dominant anti-Soviet orientation, but the results led to sometimes egregious excesses, notably China's support for the right-wing policies of General Augusto Pinochet in Chile. China's relations with Cuba worsened as Beijing strongly condemned Cuba's provision of thousands of combat forces in support of Soviet-backed regimes in Africa during the 1970s.[66]

China's more evenhanded criticism of the Soviet Union and the United States was evident at the turn of the decade and the emergence of China's "independent foreign policy" in the early 1980s. At an international summit in Cancún, Mexico, in October 1981, Chinese premier Zhao Ziyang stressed strong support for developing countries' demands for establishment of a new economic order, opposed by the United States and other developed countries. China sided with Argentina against US-backed Great Britain in the war over the disputed Falkland Islands in 1982. Regarding the conflicts in Nicaragua and El Salvador, China opposed the US use of force while supporting American and other efforts to use multilateral aid programs backed by political initiatives as the best means to achieve regional stability and keep out the USSR.[67]

Throughout much of the post–Cold War period, China followed a low-key and pragmatic effort to build better relations with Latin American countries. Beijing was well aware of China's limited standing in the region. The region has long been dominated by US power and influence and has also been developing improved economic and political relations with European powers, Japan, South Korea, and others. Radical movements in the region in the past looked to Moscow rather than Beijing for support and guidance. Throughout the 1990s and into the next decade, China maintained an active diplomatic presence; engaged in a wide variety of government-sponsored political, economic, and military contacts; and grew economic relations with the region to a point where China–Latin America trade, while only a small fraction of Chinese overall trade, surpassed Chinese trade with Africa.[68]

A rapid increase in Chinese purchases of Latin American commodities along with widely publicized Chinese leaders' visits to the region in 2004, 2005, and 2008 appeared to mark a significant change in China's approach to Latin America. President Hu Jintao's regional tour and participation at the November 2004 Asian-Pacific Economic Cooperation (APEC) summit in Chile saw an outpouring of media and specialist commentary that provided sometimes grossly exaggerated assessments of China's rising investments and other economic interests in Latin America. The commentary also exaggerated Chinese support for some regional leaders, such as Venezuela's president Hugo Chavez, who were determined to stand against US interests and influence in the region. Subsequent assessments provided a more sober view of China's increased interest in the region. China's interest appeared to focus heavily on obtaining access to resources needed for Chinese economic development; it showed little sign of a Chinese desire to undertake the costs and commitments involved in challenging the United States or adopting a significant leadership role in Latin America. The increased Chinese interest in acquiring Latin American resources generally was welcomed by regional leaders but also was accompanied by strong opposition and complaints over the impact of Chinese economic relations on regional economies.[69]

Throughout the post–Cold War period, Chinese motives in Latin America were similar to Chinese motives in the Middle East, Africa, and other developing countries without major strategic significance for China. Beijing sought to nurture common bonds with Latin American countries and strove to win their support for China's positions in the United Nations and other international organizations. Latin America, especially Central America and the Caribbean, represented the main battleground in Beijing's international competition with Taiwan. Chinese officials went to extraordinary lengths, even using China's veto power in the UN Security Council, in order to curb the still strong support for Taiwan on the part of many regional states.[70]

Chinese commentaries until 2001 also routinely criticized US policy in Latin America and highlighted European and Japanese resistance to the US efforts to have its way in the region. The rhetoric fit into the broader Chinese tendency at that time to see and encourage signs of emerging multipolarity in the world when the US superpower met resistance from other powers determined to protect their interests in an economically and politically competitive world environment. As a result of the improvement in US-Chinese relations in 1997–98, Chinese officials and commentary devoted less attention to these themes, suggesting that China was inclined, at least for the time being, to pursue its interests by not standing against the United States on a variety of world issues. This trend became more pronounced as in mid-2001 China muted most routine rhetoric against US hegemonism and later adopted an

emphasis on peaceful development that sought closer partnership and cooperation with the United States.[71]

By all accounts, economic relations between China and Latin American
countries took off in the previous decade. Growth in trade and investment
was large. Two-way trade flows increased over 500 percent, from $8 billion
in 1999 to $40 billion in 2004, and kept growing into the current decade.
Much of the activity centered on Chinese efforts to secure access to natural
resources. As a result, the large increases in Chinese imports focused on a
few Latin American countries that provide the raw materials that China has
been looking for, notably copper, nickel, iron ore, petroleum, grains, wood,
frozen fish, fish meal, sugar, leather, and chemical substances. Increased
trade also has seen a large upsurge in Chinese manufactured goods exported
throughout Latin American markets.[72]

The relative importance of China as a trading partner for Latin America
increased markedly. However, it was easy to exaggerate the extent of the
China–Latin America relationship. In 2011, reaching the height of the so-
called China boom in the region, China–Latin America trade flows were one-
fourth of the trade that occurred between Latin American countries and the
United States. Canada and the European Union remained major Latin
American trading partners. In the five years after that, the value of regional
exports to China declined markedly. Regional exports to China barely grew
up to 2017. Meanwhile, regional imports from China fell. The region continued to run a large trade deficit with China.[73]

Reports of large amounts of Chinese investment in Latin America, including a reported $100 billion in investment projected up to 2015, were featured
during President Hu Jintao's widely publicized visit to Latin America in late
2004.[74] For several years, Chinese investment levels remained low. Later
multibillion-dollar projects represented a significant shift in Chinese investment trends, which emerged as China's economy and its foreign exchange
holdings grew. The turn of the decade registered a big increase in Chinese
investment. Official Chinese media reported in April 2011 that cumulative
Chinese investment in Latin America had reached $41.2 billion at the end of
2009. The upswing continued in 2010, with Brazil being a major target of
investment. Various Chinese investment deals in Brazil in 2010 were valued
at $17 billion. Putting the advance in perspective, it was reported that a
Chinese investment of $100 billion in Latin America would make China's
portion of Latin America's cumulative stock a distinct minority share.[75]

China's investments have been directed toward projects that facilitated
the procurement of natural resources (for example, roads and port facilities)
and that were concentrated in a few countries where the resources base is
significant (Brazil, Argentina, Chile, Peru, Venezuela, and Ecuador). Meanwhile, as Chinese investment abroad grew, it became more widely known
that figures showing cumulative Chinese investment in Latin America could

be exaggerated, as a large proportion[76] of this "investment" went to such tax havens as the British Virgin Islands and the Cayman Islands,[77] and these tax havens also were the source of most of the Latin American investment going to China.[78]

The positive effects of growing economic ties on Chinese relations with Latin America were reduced to some degree by a variety of complications and negative features of the economic ties:

- Countries in Latin America that were not major exporters of resources tended to focus on the fact that they could not compete with incoming Chinese manufactured goods and that those goods also took their important markets in the United States and elsewhere. Countries that export products similar to those of China (notably Mexico but also many Central American and Caribbean countries) experienced intense competition with China.
- Chinese "tied loans," which carried low interest rates and led to the project being carried out by Chinese state-owned enterprises, tended not to increase local employment or related poverty reduction.[79]
- Much of the Chinese lending and investment was in extractive industries, and the profits made from the export of natural resources were reinvested into the extractive sector rather than in sustainable and social development. In other words, while Chinese lending and FDI might be an important source of foreign capital for Latin America—a region that experienced a decline in FDI since 2000—it was often less likely to be a driving force for major increases in local employment or marked poverty reduction.[80]
- Important constituents in the resource-exporting countries have reacted negatively to incoming Chinese manufactured imports and overall Chinese competition for world markets. Despite the rapid increase in Brazil-China trade and Chinese investment in Brazil, incoming Brazilian president Dilma Rousseff in 2011 steered policy in directions to defend Brazilian manufacturers suffering in the face of imported Chinese goods benefiting from the low value of China's currency; she also pressed China to open its market more to Brazilian aircraft and other manufactured goods.[81]
- Latin American countries had long been suppliers of raw materials to extraregional powers, and they often resented this role as well as the unfavorable terms of trade and environmental degradation that inevitably followed. As the pattern of Chinese trade and investment became more important and clear, past practice indicated that Latin American countries would see that the kind of relationship China was attempting to forge with the region was not all that different from the past imperialist and neoimperialist models that Latin Americans had come to resent. Some Chinese commentators expert in regional issues showed an awareness of negative

features in China's developing relationship with Latin America; they urged steps to foster a more balanced and complementary relationship in the broad interests of both sides.[82]

Meanwhile, several regional countries, notably Venezuela and Ecuador, had major difficulty managing massive Chinese debt. Venezuela by 2016 had accumulated $65 billion in loans since 2007 to fund gold mines, a high-speed railway, other logistics and trade facilities, and other unspecified items. In 2016, the Caracas government negotiated a postponement of payment of principal on its outstanding Chinese loans. Given the dire economic conditions in the country, the prospect for worsening default rose. The impact of a default is much larger for China as many big Chinese firms followed the lending splurge with their own financial involvement, with Chinese companies engaged in building power stations and phone networks along with oil refineries, pipelines, and railways. In some other such negative circumstances, Chinese lenders have sought control of equity, including land and ports. In the case of Venezuela, the main focus of China's interest has been to control oil.[83]

Diplomatically, the Taiwan factor continued to drive China's political relations in Latin America. Almost half of the governments that officially recognized Taiwan were in Latin America. Other than Paraguay, all were in Central America and the Caribbean. Notable breakthroughs were China wooing Costa Rica and Panama from Taiwan in 2007 and 2017, respectively.[84]

Latin America, including Central America and the Caribbean, also remained significant to China because of the number of votes the region represents in international bodies, especially the United Nations. China also was quietly seeking admittance to a number of regional organizations. It obtained observer status in the Organization of American States (OAS), the Association for Latin American Integration, and the Caribbean Development Bank; it sought to join and eventually did join the Inter-American Development Bank.

China's relations with Latin American countries also had a South-South dimension that supported Chinese efforts to work over the long term against US dominance and to create a multipolar world. China's support for Brazil's bid to become a permanent member of the UN Security Council, its cooperation agreements with regional governments in the areas of science and technology, and Chinese solidarity with developing countries in pushing for a favorable international trade regime were part of Beijing's South-South agenda that has long existed in Chinese foreign policy. Chinese leaders also participated actively and often cooperatively with Brazilian leaders in various international groups dealing with global development and governance. Notably, China collaborated closely with Brazil, India, and Russia in a new international grouping known as the BRIC, an acronym containing each member country's first letter. Another new grouping included South Africa along with China, India, and Brazil, and it was known as BASIC. As noted earlier, South Africa was asked and agreed to join the BRIC countries in 2011, with that organization becoming BRICS. [85]

Xi Jinping's Latin America Policy

The Xi Jinping government's policy toward Latin America advanced the same commercial features seen in Chinese policy toward other developing countries. There was heavy emphasis on Chinese investment in and loans for Chinese-supplied infrastructure, with the highlight being ambitious plans of Chinese support for transcontinental railways. Though the value of Chinese trade with Latin America stalled in recent years, President Xi in a visit to the region in 2013 said that trade would grow to $500 billion in ten years, and he pledged $250 billion in Chinese investment in that period. [86]

Xi's attendance at the annual APEC summit meeting in Chile in November 2016 saw him make his third visit to the region. The trip was accompanied by China's first policy paper on Latin America and other commentary that highlighted China's regional investment and trade and infrastructure development. Given the election of President Donald Trump and his sharp criticism of the Trans-Pacific Partnership and the North American Free Trade Agreement impacting Latin American countries, President Xi and Chinese commentary also highlighted China seeking to expand existing free-trade agreements with Peru, Chile, and Costa Rica to Colombia and Uruguay. Subsequent commentary in China and abroad focused on Argentina's agreement with China in June 2017 to facilitate its joining Brazil, Chile, Peru, Venezuela, and Bolivia as members of the China-backed Asian Infrastructure Investment Bank. And it contained analysis that China was eschewing engaging the region through the US-influenced Organization of American States (OAS) and was instead looking to increasingly interact with the region through the Community of Latin American and Caribbean States (CELAC). This multilateral organization is composed of thirty-three countries in the Americas but excludes the United States and Canada. In January 2015, the Xi Jinping government hosted an inaugural China-CELAC forum, and in 2017 China noted plans to bolster the forum by partnering with strong regional institutions like the Latin American Development Bank and the Economic Commission for Latin America and the Caribbean. [87]

RELATIONS WITH EUROPE

During the Cold War, Europe was viewed by China as an arena of competition between the United States and the Soviet Union that featured generally secondary concerns for China. East Germany and other countries aligned with the Soviet Union provided significant material and technical assistance to China during the 1950s. China took important positions in the discussions among Communist countries regarding the controversies involving the Soviet Union's relations with Poland and Hungary in 1956. China also was able to establish diplomatic and foreign trade relations with some non-Communist western European countries despite US pressure to impose a diplomatic and economic embargo against China. Amid the thaw in Chinese foreign relations after the Korean War and while China was joining the Soviet Union in highlighting the Five Principles of Peaceful Coexistence, Beijing reciprocated Great Britain's earlier appointment of a chargé d'affaires to its embassy, sent a trade delegation to London, signed a trade agreement with Finland, and began negotiations with the recently arrived Norwegian envoy on establishing formal diplomatic relations.[88]

Despite its alignment with the United States during the Cold War, Britain quickly recognized the People's Republic of China and worked to preserve its colonial administration in Hong Kong. As noted in chapter 2, a low point in relations came in 1967 at the height of China's Red Guard diplomacy during a particularly violent stage of the Cultural Revolution when a mob in Beijing protesting police arrests of pro-China demonstrators in Hong Kong burned the British mission and assaulted its officers.

French forces in Vietnam and Indochina were the target of the Viet Minh insurgents strongly backed by China in the early 1950s. Under the leadership of President Charles de Gaulle, France broke with its Western partners and in 1964 it established relations with the People's Republic of China (PRC) and ended ties with the Republic of China (ROC) based on Taiwan.[89]

The international communist movement was an important arena of early Sino-Soviet polemics over issues regarding Soviet leadership of world Communist parties and states, debates over how to assess Stalin's leadership, appropriate economic development strategies in Communist countries, and relations with the United States and other Western countries. Enver Hoxha was the leader of Albania's government, Communist Party, and military from the end of World War II until his death in the 1980s. As serious ideological and foreign policy issues emerged between the People's Republic of China (PRC) and the Soviet Union at the end of the 1950s, Albania under Hoxha's leadership sided with China and was publicly rebuked by Moscow beginning in the early 1960s. China provided strong material and political support for the hard-line leadership of the small European state for over a decade until relations declined as a result of disagreements over China's rapprochement with the United States and with Albania's more powerful regional neighbor, Yugoslavia.[90]

Regarding the latter, for many years, Chinese officials joined Albanians and a few others with similar views in attacking the "revisionist" policies of Josip Tito, the independent-minded Communist leader of Yugoslavia. China also encouraged Romania's Nicolae Ceauşescu to assert independence from policies in the Warsaw Pact favored by the Soviet Union. Signs of close relations included Chinese leaders using Ceauşescu to convey sensitive messages to and from leaders of the United States and the Soviet Union. The main Communist parties of Western Europe tended to side with Moscow against Beijing's challenges in the international communist movement. For many years, they were viewed critically by Chinese officials.[91]

The Chinese opening to the United States in the late 1960s and early 1970 was accompanied by many non-Communist governments in Europe establishing and upgrading official relations with China. China encouraged the trend and used the opportunity to urge European leaders to increase vigilance against the international expansion of the Soviet Union. China established official relations with West Germany in 1973, and it endeavored to balance these new relations with long-standing Chinese ties with East Germany. Beijing was wary of the implications of the moderate West German policy toward the Soviet Union and the Warsaw Pact under the leadership of Chancellor Willy Brandt (1969–74). At that time, China was under great pressure from the Soviet Union and was concerned that détente in Europe, the fulcrum of East-West confrontation, would allow Moscow to muster more forces to coerce China.[92]

Facing this strategic threat and pressure from the Soviet Union, Chinese officials moved pragmatically to improve relations with Yugoslavia, welcoming Tito on a landmark visit to China in 1977. They revived formal Communist Party relations and sent Party Chairman Hua Guofeng to Tito's funeral in 1980. The improvement of relations with Yugoslavia along with China's opening to the United States lay behind long-standing ally Albania's open break with China.

Beijing endeavored to keep on good terms with Ceauşescu's Romania, but while Chinese leaders were abandoning Maoist excesses and opening to the outside world in the late 1970s, Ceauşescu was moving toward erratic policies, a strong cult of personality, nationalism, and deterioration in relations with the West and the USSR. His eventual overthrow and execution by firing squad in 1989 as Communist regimes were collapsing throughout the world stood as a graphic reminder to leaders in China as to what can happen to authoritarian rulers who lose control of the levers of power.

China had mixed views of the implications of the labor strikes that undermined pro-Soviet rule in Poland in the early 1980s. On the one hand, China saw the workers' strikes and organization of Solidarity, a powerful independent labor organization, as weakening Moscow's international position in ways beneficial to China. On the other hand, the Polish example showed Communist rulers in China the kinds of challenges they would also face from an independent labor organization.[93]

China's pragmatic search for greater international influence, especially leverage to use against the USSR, brought changes in its approach to the main Communist parties in Western Europe. By 1976, official Chinese commentary no longer portrayed the Italian Communist Party, the largest in Western Europe, as subservient to the interests of the Soviet Union, but it continued to treat it as a revisionist party. Over time, China's commentary came to treat the party in an uncritical fashion, signaling an imminent reconciliation, which came during a summit meeting between the Chinese Communist Party and the Italian Communist Party leaders in 1980.[94]

Significant developments in Chinese relations with Europe in the 1980s included the Sino-British agreement on the future of Hong Kong, an important British colony. Interests in Hong Kong influenced Great Britain's decisions on policy toward China, notably its decision to recognize the People's Republic of China (PRC) in 1950. China generally was pragmatic in seeking economic and other advantage from interchange with Hong Kong, despite its colonial status. Hong Kong also served as a base for US and other foreign commercial and government activities dealing with China. Though Western trade with China was restricted during the first two decades of the Cold War, foreign trade and foreign investment in Hong Kong grew. As the Chinese government opened to foreign economic exchange in the 1970s, many foreign businesses used Hong Kong as a base of operations to take advantage of China's opening.[95]

Under the leadership of Prime Minister Margaret Thatcher, Britain was compelled to put aside colonial rights and negotiate the return of Hong Kong to Chinese sovereignty. Sino-British negotiations in 1982–84 to define Hong Kong's future status led to the Joint Declaration, an agreement in 1984 calling for the British colony to return to Chinese sovereignty in 1997. The Tiananmen crackdown and large-scale demonstrations in Hong Kong in 1989 prompted greater British interest in securing guarantees for democracy and stability in the territory. The United States shared this concern. US legislation conditioning the annual US renewal of most favored nation (MFN) tariff status for China routinely had provisions dealing with China's policy toward Hong Kong. The last British governor of Hong Kong, Christopher Patten, and prominent Hong Kong Democratic Party leader Martin Lee made annual visits to the United States seeking support while urging continued open US trade with China, an essential element in Hong Kong's economy. At congressional initiative, the United States passed the Hong Kong Policy Act in 1992 laying out US concerns about Hong Kong's future and calling for regular US reports monitoring China's treatment of the territory.[96]

In 1997, the territory of Hong Kong reverted to Chinese sovereignty as the Hong Kong Special Administrative Region (HKSAR) of the People's Republic of China (PRC). China followed through on commitments reached in the Joint Declaration while opposing efforts to advance democracy by advocates in Hong Kong and abroad. The Hong Kong administration integrated the region ever more closely to China's economy and sought to avoid controversy with Beijing over issues sensitive to the Chinese government. Hong Kong's status as a foreign gateway to China declined with the opening and development of the modern commercial hubs in Shanghai and other major Chinese cities. Foreign media and government attention to perceived Chinese efforts to curb those in Hong Kong seeking greater democracy for the people of Hong Kong also declined. In 2014, a series of street demonstrations against tightening Chinese control and in favor of greater democracy and autonomy in Hong Kong registered strong dissatisfaction with the Hong Kong authorities' subservience to Beijing's requirements. Foreign media highlighted this so-called umbrella movement and later demonstrations of dissatisfaction, but most foreign governments avoided serious controversy with China over Hong Kong.[97]

Although China strongly supported liberation movements engaged in armed struggle against Portuguese colonial rule in Angola, Mozambique, and other colonial possessions in Africa in the 1960s and the 1970s, China adopted a very different approach to the Portuguese colonial territory of Macao, which was near Hong Kong and was also claimed as part of China. The Portuguese government appeared willing to end colonial rule after changes in governments and colonial policies in the mid-1970s. Nevertheless, China waited until after reaching the Sino-British Joint Declaration, governing Hong Kong's transfer to China, before reaching agreement with Portugal on Macao's transfer to China. Macao was returned to Chinese rule in 1999, further advancing Portugal's relations with China under the rubric of a "strategic partnership."[98]

With its strong emphasis on economic modernization in recent decades, Beijing has remained anxious to gain economically from improved relations with Europe. The European powers joined the United States and Japan in imposing economic and other sanctions on China following the Tiananmen crackdown in 1989. Japan was the first in the group to break with the sanctions and resume trade, investment, and aid. It was followed by Great Britain and other European states.

Beijing also has shown interest from time to time in fostering greater European political and strategic independence from the United States. This is part of broader PRC efforts to develop a multipolar world more advantageous to China than the prevailing international order with the United States in the leading position. Throughout the 1990s and until 2001, Beijing publicly chafed under an international order where the Chinese saw the United States as the dominant power; this international order often pressed the PRC hard on a variety of sensitive international and domestic questions. Thus, for China, relations with Europe were viewed with an eye to other Chinese interests; Europe was said to represent a "card" China could play in the more important contest of US-Chinese relations. This line of thinking underscored the limits of Chinese interests in Europe and reflected the fact that in the order of PRC foreign policy priorities, primacy was given to the United States, followed by Japan and important countries in the Asian area. Europe and other areas more distant from China came in behind them.[99]

China notably opposed US-led NATO expansion and tried from time to time to play up intra-alliance rivalries and differences, especially between the US and French governments. But this effort was largely in vain given the strong and broad European alliance support for NATO and its expansion. Chinese opposition looked weak in the face of the US-led NATO war against Serbia in 1999. Chinese officials also had a long history of thinking of the EU and its members as oriented to protectionist tendencies that would try to impede the flow of Chinese exports to European markets.[100]

Because of organizational and institutional weaknesses, the European Union (EU) and its members had a hard time developing a comprehensive and coherent policy toward China. As Europe's interest in China was mainly economic, the EU and its members were seen as most effective when dealing with a country like China on the basis of economic issues, with other channels of interaction remaining weak.

As a diplomatic actor or as a force on security issues, the EU and its members were said to be less well suited to take action in relation to China, especially as EU members were reluctant to allow the EU very much leeway to deal with important defense and security issues. The EU was very slow to come out in support of the American show of force off the Taiwan Strait in the face of provocative PRC military exercises in 1996, though some member governments were prompt in supporting the move.[101]

Twenty-First-Century Developments

Though some observers saw Sino-European relations in the early twenty-first century as "a comprehensive and multidimensional relationship," a "strategic partnership," and "a new axis in world affairs,"[102] later development supported a less positive view. On balance, the record along with past practice suggested that the growing China-Europe ties will remain hampered by substantial and sometimes growing problems and competing interests.

Trade and economic ties are the foundation of the relationship. In January 2005, official Chinese media reported that according to Chinese trade data, the EU in 2004 surpassed Japan and the United States to become China's largest trade partner, and China became the second-largest trade partner of the EU, following the United States. The account acknowledged that the expansion of the EU to twenty-five members in 2004 obviously increased the size of the Chinese trade figures with the EU, though the main EU countries involved in China trade were those that were long-standing EU members—

Germany, the Netherlands, the United Kingdom, France, and Italy, which were said to account for 72 percent of EU trade with China at that time.[103] Trade grew impressively until the economic crisis of 2009. It rebounded and reached a value close to $500 billion in 2010 and $567.2 billion in 2011. Trade levels declined, and in 2016 trade was valued at $547 billion. It grew in value in 2017.[104]

Chinese sources reported EU countries were substantial foreign investors in China. They often were the largest exporter of technologies to China, which allowed for upgrades to Chinese manufacturing and related capabilities. Meanwhile, Chinese investment in Europe became significant. According to Xinhua, the EU invested $8.8 billion in China in 2016, a 35.1 percent increase from 2015, while China's nonfinancial direct investment in the EU stood at $7.29 billion, a 1 percent increase from 2015.[105]

That not all was positive in Chinese-European economic relations was seen in a growing trade deficit Europe ran with China. It tripled in size in five years, amounting to around $127 billion in 2005. It has been around $200 billion in recent years.[106]

Leading EU governments have become increasingly concerned in recent years about Chinese "Silk Road" schemes involving substantial infrastructure investments in Greece and east European countries that undermined EU standards of transparency and accountability and the unity of the union in dealing with China.[107] These governments have viewed the Chinese investments in advanced companies in more developed EU countries as predatory efforts to seek competitive advantages in international economic competition, and they cooperate with the United States and Japan in standing against Chinese deliberate efforts to promote excess capacity in steel production that disadvantage European and other foreign manufacturers and in standing against Chinese pressure to gain the advantages of international market status. Meanwhile, barriers to trade in China were estimated to cost EU businesses close to $30 billion in lost trade opportunities annually, and major losses came from counterfeiting and intellectual property rights violations in China.[108]

Regarding foreign assistance, in 2003, the EU Commission calculated that programs it was running in China amounted to annual expenditures of over $300 million. These programs did not take into account the sometimes large (as in the case of Germany) assistance programs in China offered by individual European countries.[109]

In the political realm, Chinese and European leaders held regular meetings. An annual China-EU summit has rotated between Brussels and Beijing.[110] China canceled the China-EU summit in 2008 over the French president's planned meeting with the Dalai Lama. Smooth relations took over a year to revive.[111]

Regarding continuing Chinese efforts to overturn the EU arms embargo against China, in 2004 China secured the support of the French government on this issue, and the French promised to persuade other EU members to lift the ban that had been in place since 1989. France managed to get the German government to change its view and to erode British opposition. However, US opposition was strong and firm, leading to a major crisis with the EU over whether to end the embargo. The United States was backed by many within Europe, including the new government in Germany in 2005, and had the strong support of Japan, which agreed with the United States that lifting the embargo would enhance the ability of Chinese forces to confront America and its allies in the event of a conflict over Taiwan. China's passage of a tough Anti-Secession Law directed at Taiwan in March 2005 halted the European movement to lift the embargo. At this time, European leaders also showed greater interest to coordinate policies with the United States on sensitive issues involving China, including the buildup of Chinese military forces and its implications for Taiwan and broader Asian security and stability.[112]

This string of setbacks for Chinese interests combined with rising trade frictions in EU-Chinese relations; a Chinese reassessment of European policy followed, according to specialists. While clearly determined to develop advantageous economic and other ties with European counterparts, Chinese officials were more realistic about developing any sort of a meaningful strategic partnership with Europe for the foreseeable future.

China viewed the EU and its members as collectively too weak, divided, and dependent on the United States to become an independent great power in international relations. Thus, the EU was not a particularly promising partner for China in its rise to power and influence in world affairs. Further, the EU was much more prone to side with the United States than with China on issues sensitive to China involving democracy and the rule of law in China, stability in eastern Asia, the implications of China's growing trade surpluses with both the United States and the EU members, antiterrorist efforts, and curbs on nuclear weapons proliferation in Iran.[113]

Developments underscored strong problems complicating Chinese-European relations. When French president Nicolas Sarkozy, then also serving as head of the European Union, indicated that he would meet the Dalai Lama and did so in late 2008, Beijing abruptly postponed the planned EU-China annual summit scheduled to be held in France. Also, China alienated many in Europe with its strident reaction and pressure on Norway and other European governments participating at the Nobel awards ceremonies in honor of a Chinese dissident receiving the 2010 Nobel peace prize.[114] In 2011 differences in Chinese-European relations saw Chinese complaints about NATO employing military force against the regime of Libya's Muammar Gadhafi.[115]

The Xi Jinping presidency has not seen such dramatic events in relations with Europe. China-European relations reflected the mix of positive developments and sustained differences evident since the outset of the twenty-first century. As noted above, trade and investment were accompanied by differences and disagreements. Neither side seemed prepared to give high priority to changing the status quo. An apparent breakthrough came with Xi Jinping's widely touted visit to England in 2016, launching the so-called golden era of China-British relations and the British government's seeking strong Chinese investment in sensitive power plants and other infrastructure. The afterglow faded with the British withdrawal from the European Union and the Theresa May government's much more wary view of Chinese involvement in sensitive British infrastructure.[116] Meanwhile, Europe had enormous economic preoccupations and a very difficult relationship with Russia. Xi Jinping developed a very close relationship with Russia. He showed little concern with EU sensitivities regarding Russian military shows of force designed to intimidate European neighbors as China took the unprecedented step of joining with Russia in conducting a military exercise in the Baltic Sea in 2017.

CANADA, THE ARCTIC, ANTARCTICA

A NATO member with strong ties to Europe and the United States, Canada was among the first of leading Western nations in establishing diplomatic relations with China, in 1970, as China reached out for greater international contact and support in the face of the growing power and pressure of the Soviet Union at that time. It became a major trading partner of China. China's rapid economic development required more imports of energy, foods, and other resources, which Canada willingly provided, while Chinese exports of manufactured goods to Canada grew enormously, leading to a large trade deficit for Canada.

Generally following a moderate course in dealing with China, Canada usually sought to avoid the acrimonious disputes and controversies that sometimes marked the erratic course of US-China relations in the recent period. An exception was the leadership of Prime Minister Stephen Harper (2006–15) whose government for several years in the first decade of the twenty-first century highlighted political disputes with China, notably over human rights and Tibet, before calming disputes in a more pragmatic pursuit of closer economic contacts. His successor Justin Trudeau (2015–) has actively engaged senior Chinese leaders in China and Canada, endeavoring to foster closer trade and economic relations while sustaining political values important to Canada and opposed by China.[117]

As post-Mao Chinese foreign relations developed, China began to play a more active role in Antarctica. Chinese scientists joined an Australian research expedition to the continent in 1979. China's growing interests showed in China's thirty-three Antarctic expeditions between 1984 and 2016 and the construction of four research stations (Great Wall, Zhongshan, Taishan, and Kun lun/Dome A). In a first for China, Beijing hosted the fortieth Antarctic Treaty Consultative Meeting in May 2017. During the meeting, it released the white paper "China's Antarctic Activities." Though Chinese longer-term interests reportedly involve developing the resources of the region, China promised to abide by existing arrangements restricting development while doing more research in Antarctica and reaffirming strong support of the Antarctic Treaty System (ATS).[118] China since 2008 has sought to become a permanent observer on the Arctic Council, an exclusive regional forum of eight member states (Canada, Denmark, Finland, Iceland, Norway, Russia, Sweden, and the United States) that was created in 1996 to promote collaboration and cooperation on Arctic issues. There are currently six non-Arctic observer states—France, Germany, the Netherlands, Poland, Spain, and the United Kingdom.

The five coastal states bordering the Arctic Ocean, Canada, Denmark, Norway, Russia, and the United States, signed a declaration in 2008 signaling that by virtue of their sovereignty, sovereignty rights, and jurisdiction in large areas of the Arctic Ocean, they are uniquely positioned to address the evolving contemporary issues of the Arctic. The declaration represented an explicit statement that there was no need for a comprehensive Arctic Treaty on the lines of what exists for Antarctica. Chinese commentary has taken the position that the Arctic region possesses a "shared heritage of humankind," suggesting China could oppose some of the Arctic states' sovereignty claims and assert claims of its own as the melting ice creates easier access to resources in the area and eases barriers to more efficient sea transportation between China and European and North American ports.[119]

NOTES

1. A Chinese government specialist wrote in an editorial in 2010 that China "consumed 0.82 ton of standard oil for every $1,000 increase in GDP value" while "in the U.S. and Japan, the figure was 0.20 ton and 0.10 ton respectively." Feng Zhaokui, "China Still a Developing Nation," *China Daily*, May 6, 2010, p. 12. Chinese perspectives on relations with the Middle East, Africa, and Latin America include the following: Li Shaoxian and Wei Liang, "New Complexities in the Middle East since 9.11," *Contemporary International Relations* (Beijing) 20, special issue (September 2010): pp. 22–32; Li Shaoxian and Tang Zhichao, "China and the Middle East," *Xiandai guoji guanxi* (Beijing) 17 (January 2007): pp. 22–31; Tang Jizan, "The Middle East Situation Is Full of Variables," *Foreign Affairs Journal* (Beijing) 79 (March 2006): pp. 63–72; "White Paper on China-Africa Economic Cooperation and Trade Cooperation," *China Daily*, December 24, 2010, p. 9; Zeng Qiang, "FOCAC: A Powerful Engine for the Continued Development of Friendship between China and Africa," *Contemporary International Relations* (Beijing) 20, no. 6 (November–December 2010): pp. 45–59; "Full Text of China's Africa Policy," *People's Daily*, January 12, 2006, accessed January 12, 2006, http://www.peoplesdaily.com.cn; He Wenping, "The Balancing Act of China's Africa Policy," *China*

Security 3, no. 3 (Summer 2007): pp. 23–41; Wu Hongying, "Latin America: Key Trends and Challenges," *Contemporary International Relations* (Beijing) 20, special issue (September 2010): pp. 33–42.

2. Thomas Lum, coord., *Comparing Global Influence: China's and U.S. Diplomacy, Foreign Aid, Trade, and Investment in the Developing World*, Congressional Research Service Report RL34620 (Washington, DC: Library of Congress, August 15, 2008); "China in Africa: One Among Many," *Economist*, January 17, 2015, http://www.economist.com/news/middle-east-and-africa/21639554-china-has-become-big-africa-now-backlash-one-among-many; *2013 China-Latin America Bulletin*, accessed June 5, 2015, http://www.bu.edu/pardee/files/2014/01/Economic-Bulletin-2013.pdf.

3. Robert Sutter, *Chinese Foreign Relations: Power and Policy since the Cold War* (Lanham, MD: Rowman & Littlefield, 2016), pp. 68–69, 209.

4. On recent Chinese relations with the Middle East, see Jon Alterman and John Garver, *The Vital Triangle: China, the United States, and the Middle East* (Washington, DC: CSIS, 2008); Lily Hindy, *A Rising China Eyes the Middle East* (New York: Century Foundation, April 6, 2017); Jon Alterman, *The Other Side of the World* (Washington, DC: CSIS, 2017); Joel Wuthnow, *Posing Problems without an Alliance: China-Iran Relations after the Nuclear Deal* (Washington, DC: INSS Strategic Forum, February 2016). On recent Chinese relations with Africa, see Howard French, *China's Second Continent* (New York: Vintage Books, 2014); David Shinn and Joshua Eisenman, *China and Africa* (Philadelphia: University of Pennsylvania Press, 2012); Deborah Brautigam, *The Dragon's Gift* (New York: Oxford University Press, 2010); Sarah Raine, *China's African Challenges* (London: Routledge Adelphi series, 2009); Christopher Alden, Daniel Large, and Ricardo de Oliveira, eds., *China Returns to Africa: A Superpower and a Continent Embrace* (London: Hurst, 2008). On recent Chinese relations with Latin America and the Caribbean, see R. Evan Ellis, *China in Latin America* (Boulder, CO: Lynne Rienner, 2009); Kevin Gallagher and Roberto Porzecanski, *The Dragon in the Room: China and the Future of Latin American Industrialization* (Stanford, CA: Stanford University Press, 2010); David Dollar, *China's Investment in Latin America* (Washington, DC: Brookings Institution Press, 2017).

5. Assessments and commentaries on these issues include Liu Mingli, "Reflection on EU-China Relations," *Contemporary International Relations* (Beijing) 20, no. 3 (May–June 2010): pp. 115–22; Xia Liping, "Sino-EU Security Relations," *Contemporary International Relations* (Beijing) 20, no. 1 (January–February 2010): pp. 102–8; David Shambaugh, "The New Strategic Triangle: U.S. and European Reactions to China's Rise," *Washington Quarterly* 29, no. 3 (Summer 2005): pp. 7–25; Lanxin Xiang, "China's Eurasian Experiment," *Survival* 46, no. 2 (Summer 2004): pp. 109–22; Bates Gill and Melissa Murphy, *China-Europe Relations: Implications and Policy Responses for the United States* (Washington, DC: Center for Strategic and International Studies, May 2008); David Shambaugh and Gudrun Wacker, eds., *American and European Relations with China* (Berlin: Stiftung Wissenschaft und Politik, 2008); Nicola Cassarini, *Remaking Global Order: The Evolution of Europe-China Relations and Its Implications for East Asia and the United States* (Oxford: Oxford University Press, 2009); David Shambaugh, Eberhard Sandschneider, and Zhou Hong, eds., *China-Europe Relations: Perceptions, Policies, and Prospects* (London: Routledge, 2007); Jing Men and Giuseppe Balducci, eds., *Prospects and Challenges for EU-China Relations in the Twenty-First Century* (Brussels: PIE–Peter Lang, 2010); European Commission, "Joint Statement: Deepening the EU-China Comprehensive Strategic Partnership for Mutual Benefit," press release, March 31, 2014; "Full Text of China's Policy Paper on the EU," Xinhua, April 2, 2014; Theresa Fallon, "China's Pivot to Europe," *America Foreign Policy Interests* 36 (2014): pp. 175–82; Frans-Paul van der Patten et al., *Europe and China's New Silk Roads* (Brussels: A Report by the European Think-Tank Network on China, December 2016); *China at the Gates: A New Power Audit of EU-China Relations* (Brussels: European Council on Foreign Affairs, April 2017).

6. Harold Hinton, *Communist China in World Politics* (Boston: Houghton Mifflin, 1966), pp. 178–87; Lillian Harris, *China Considers the Middle East* (London: I. B. Tauris, 1993); Guang Pan, "China's Success in the Middle East," *Middle East Quarterly*, December 1997, pp. 35–40; Lillian Harris, "Myth and Reality in China's Relations with the Middle East," in

Chinese Foreign Policy: Theory and Practice, ed. Thomas W. Robinson and David Shambaugh (New York: Oxford University Press, 1994), pp. 322–47.

7. Robert Sutter, *Historical Dictionary of Chinese Foreign Policy* (Lanham, MD: Scarecrow, 2011), pp. 41, 88–89.

8. Harris, "Myth and Reality in China's Relations with the Middle East," p. 336.

9. Sutter, *Historical Dictionary of Chinese Foreign Policy*, p. 85.

10. John Garver, *China and Iran* (Seattle: University of Washington Press, 2006), pp. 27–56.

11. Sutter, *Historical Dictionary of Chinese Foreign Policy*, p. 215.

12. Mao Yufeng, "China's Interests and Strategy in the Middle East," in *China and the Developing World: Beijing's Strategy for the Twenty-First Century*, ed. Joshua Eisenman, Eric Heginbotham, and Derek Mitchell (Armonk, NY: M. E. Sharpe, 2007), pp. 113–32; Yitzhak Shichor, "China's Middle East Strategy," in *China and the Developing World*, ed. Lowell Dittmer and George Yu (Boulder, CO: Lynne Rienner, 2010), pp. 157–76; Sutter, *Historical Dictionary of Chinese Foreign Policy*, p. 130.

13. Harris, "Myth and Reality in China's Relations with the Middle East," p. 332.

14. Garver, *China and Iran*, pp. 57–94.

15. Alexander Lennon, "Trading Guns, Not Butter," *China Business Review*, March–April 1994, pp. 47–49; Pan, "China's Success in the Middle East."

16. Garver, *China and Iran*, pp. 95–128.

17. Alterman and Garver, *The Vital Triangle*; John W. Garver, "Is China Playing a Dual Game in Iran?" *Washington Quarterly* 34, no. 1 (Winter 2011): pp. 75–88.

18. Harris, *China Considers the Middle East*; Pan, "China's Success in the Middle East."

19. Alterman and Garver, *The Vital Triangle*; Garver, "Is China Playing a Dual Game in Iran?"; Mao Yufeng, "China's Interests and Strategy in the Middle East," in *China and the Developing World: Beijing's Strategy for the Twenty-First Century*, ed. Joshua Eisenman, Eric Heginbotham, and Derek Mitchell (Armonk, NY: M. E. Sharpe, 2007), pp. 113–32; Shichor, "China's Middle East Strategy," pp. 157–76; Daniel Blumenthal, "Providing Arms," *Middle East Quarterly* (Spring 2005): pp. 11–19; Jing-dong Yuan, "China and the Iranian Nuclear Crisis," *China Brief* 6, no. 3 (February 1, 2006): pp. 6–8; Yitzhak Shichor, "China's Kurdish Policy," *China Brief* 6, no. 1 (January 3, 2006): pp. 3–6.

20. SUSRIS interview with Jon Alterman, October 13, 2008, http://www.saudi-us-relations.org/articles/2008/interviews/081013-alterman-interview.html (accessed October 14, 2008).

21. Flynt Leverett and Jeffrey Bader, "Managing China-U.S. Energy Competition in the Middle East," *Washington Quarterly* 29, no. 1 (Winter 2005/2006): pp. 187–201.

22. "China-Saudi Trade Reached Record High in 2010," Chinese embassy in Saudi Arabia, February 9, 2011, http://sa2.mofcom.gov.cn/.

23. Borzou Daragahi, "Iran Signs $3.2 Billion Natural Gas Deal with China," *Los Angeles Times*, March 14, 2009, http://www.latimes.com (accessed March 18, 2009); Garver, "Is China Playing a Dual Game in Iran?"

24. "Iran-China Trade Volume Reaches $38 billion," *PressTV*, February 13, 2011, http://www.presstv.ir/detail/165011.html (accessed May 18, 2011).

25. Mark Landler, "China Is Excluded from Waivers for Oil Trade with Iran," *New York Times*, June 11, 2012, http://www.nytimes.com.

26. Bonnie Glaser, "Pomp, Blunders and Substance: Hu's Visit to the U.S.," *Comparative Connections* 8, no. 2 (July 2006): pp. 35–36, 40; and Bonnie Glaser, "Cooperation Faces Challenges," *Comparative Connections* 12, no. 2 (July 2010): pp. 38–39.

27. Blumenthal, "Providing Arms," p. 6.

28. Yitzhak Shichor, "Silent Partner: China and the Lebanon Crisis," *China Brief* 6, no. 17 (August 16, 2006): pp. 2–4.

29. Consultations with Chinese diplomats, Washington, DC, December 18, 2006.

30. Yu Bin, "SCO Five Years On: Progress and Growing Pains," *Comparative Connections* 8, no. 2 (July 2006): p. 140.

31. "Smooth Evacuation," *People's Daily Online*, March 6, 2011, http://www.peoplesdaily.com.cn; Yun Sun, "China's Acquiescence on UNSCR 1973: No Big Deal," *PacNet* 20 (March 31, 2011), http://www.csis.org/pacfor.

32. Mu Chunshan, "Revealed: How the Yemen Crisis Wrecked Xi Jinping's Middle East Travel Plans," *Diplomat*, April 22, 2015, http://thediplomat.com/2015/04/revealed-how-the-yemen-crisis-wrecked-xi-jinpings-middle-east-travel-plans.

33. Jane Perlez, "President Xi Jinping of China Is All Business in Middle East Visit," *New York Times*, January 30, 2016, https://www.nytimes.com/2016/01/31/world/asia/xi-jinping-visits-saudi-iran.html.

34. Hindy, *A Rising China Eyes the Middle East.*

35. Hinton, *Communist China in World Politics*, pp. 188–96; Gerald Segal, "China and Africa," *Annals of the American Academy of Political and Social Science* 519 (January 1992): pp. 115–26; Philip Snow, "China and Africa: Consensus and Camouflage," in Robinson and Shambaugh, eds., *Chinese Foreign Policy*, pp. 283–321.

36. Philip Snow, *The Star Raft: China's Encounter with Africa* (Ithaca, NY: Cornell University Press, 1988); Alaba Ogunsanwo, *China's Policy in Africa, 1958–1971* (New York: Cambridge University Press, 1979); Peter Van Ness, *Revolution and Chinese Foreign Policy* (Berkeley: University of California Press, 1970).

37. Sutter, *Historical Dictionary of Chinese Foreign Policy*, pp. 140, 171–72, 185.

38. Brautigam, *The Dragon's Gift*, pp. 40–41, 83–85.

39. Sutter, *Historical Dictionary of Chinese Foreign Policy*, p. 169.

40. Snow, *The Star Raft*; Sutter, *Historical Dictionary of Chinese Foreign Policy*, p. 248.

41. Sutter, *Historical Dictionary of Chinese Foreign Policy*, p. 76.

42. Robert Sutter, *Chinese Policy Priorities and Their Implications for the United States* (Lanham, MD: Rowman & Littlefield, 2000), pp. 163–64.

43. Brautigam, *The Dragon's Gift*, pp. 22–70; Sutter, *Chinese Policy Priorities and Their Implications for the United States*, p. 164.

44. Snow, "China and Africa," pp. 318–21.

45. Brautigam, *The Dragon's Gift*; George Yu, "China's Africa Policy," in *China and the Developing World*, ed. Lowell Dittmer and George Yu (Boulder, CO: Lynne Rienner, 2010), pp. 129–56; Alden, Large, and de Oliveria, *China Returns to Africa*; Ian Taylor, *China's New Role in Africa* (Boulder, CO: Lynne Rienner, 2008); Robert I. Rotberg, ed., *China into Africa: Trade, Aid, and Influence* (Washington, DC: Brookings Institution Press, 2008); David Shinn and Joshua Eisenman, *Responding to China in Africa* (Washington, DC: American Foreign Policy Council, July 2008); Council on Foreign Relations, *More Than Humanitarianism: A Strategic U.S. Approach toward Africa*, Independent Task Force Report 56 (New York: Council on Foreign Relations, January 2006); *China and Sub-Saharan Africa*, Congressional Research Service Report RL 33055 (Washington, DC: Library of Congress, August 29, 2005).

46. *Africa and China: Issues and Insights—Conference Report* (Washington, DC: Georgetown University, School of Foreign Service, Asian Studies Department, November 7, 2008).

47. Chin-Hao Huang, *China's Rising Stakes in Africa*, Asian Studies Research Paper (Washington, DC: Georgetown University, April 2006), p. 7 (also reviewed in *China and Sub-Saharan Africa*).

48. *China's African Policy* (Beijing: State Council Information Office, January 2006), http://en.people.cn/200601/12/print20060112_234894.html; Yan Yang, "China-Africa Trade Prospects Look Promising: President Hu Jintao Promotes Nation on Tour of the Continent," *China Daily*, April 26, 2006, p. 9; "Support for Africa 'Not a Temporary Measure,'" *China Daily*, July 3, 2006, p. 3; Wenran Jiang, "China's Booming Energy Relations with Africa," *China Brief* 6, no. 13 (June 21, 2006): pp. 3–5.

49. Sun Shangwu, "Bright, Prosperous Relations," *China Daily*, November 6, 2006, p. 1.

50. Ding Qingfen, "Countries 'Seek More Investment for Development,'" *China Daily*, April 27, 2011, p. 1.

51. Phillip C. Saunders, *China's Global Activism: Strategy, Drivers, and Tools*, Occasional Paper 4 (Washington, DC: National Defense University Institute for National Strategic Studies, June 2006), p. 2; Lum, coord., *Comparing Global Influence*, pp. 62, 65.

52. Brautigam, *The Dragon's Gift*, p. 168; Sutter, *Chinese Foreign Relations* (2016), pp. 307–8.

53. Zeng Qiang, "FOCAC: A Powerful Engine for the Continued Development of Friendship between China and Africa," *Contemporary International Relations* (Beijing) 20, no. 6

(November/December 2010): pp. 45–59; "White Paper on China-Africa Economic Cooperation and Trade Cooperation," *China Daily*, December 23, 2010, http://www.chinadaily.com.cn; David Smith, "China Poised to Pour $10bn into Zimbabwe's Ailing Economy," *Guardian*, February 1, 2011, http://www.guardian.co.uk; He Wenping, "Equal Platform, Mutual Benefit," *China Daily*, July 17, 2010, p. 5; "China-Africa Trade Hits Record High," *China Daily*, December 24, 2010, p. 3.

54. "Li Pledges Larger Credit Line, High-Speed Rail Technology to Africa," *South China Morning Post*, May 7, 2014, http://www.scmp.com/news/china/article/1506229/li-pledges-larger-credit-line-high-speed-rail-technology-africa; Lauren Johnson, "China's Road to Growth in Africa," *East Asia Forum*, February 7, 2015, http://www.eastasiaforum.org/2015/02/07/chinas-road-to-growth-in-africa/.

55. Johnson, "China's Road to Growth in Africa."

56. Robert Rotberg, "China's $1 Trillion for Africa," *China-U.S. Focus*, November 26, 2013, http://www.chinausfocus.com/finance-economy/chinas-1-trillion-for-africa.

57. "China-Africa Trade Surges in Q1," Xinhua, May 11, 2017, http://english.gov.cn/state_council/ministries/2017/05/11/content_281475652349490.htm (accessed January 22, 2018); Valentina Romei, "China and Africa: Trade Relationship Evolves," *Financial Times*, December 3, 2015, https://www.ft.com/content/c53e7f68-9844-11e5-9228-87e603d47bdc (accessed November 1, 2017).

58. "China's Investment in Africa Down 40% on Year: Govt.," AFP, November 17, 2015, https://publiceyemaritzburg.co.za/afp/121414/chinas-investment-in-africa-down-40-on-year-govt (accessed January 22, 2018).

59. "China in Africa: One Among Many"; Johnson, "China's Road to Growth in Africa."

60. "Nigerian Railway Project: Derailed Too Many Times," *Notes by Nigeria Civil Rights Movement*, June 19, 2011, https://www.facebook.com/notes/nigerian-civil-right-movement/nigerias-railway-project-derailed-too-many-times-any-possible-logg-out-from-the-/136858396392560.

61. Lillian Wong, "The Impact of Asian National Oil Companies in Nigeria," *Nigerian Muse*, January 4, 2009, accessed April 9, 2009, http://www.nigerianmuse.com; Wang Ying, "CNOOC Buys Share in Nigerian Oil Mining License," *China Daily*, April 21, 2006, p. 9; Kate Linebaugh, "CNOOC Is Buying a 45% Stake in Nigerian Oil Field," *Wall Street Journal*, January 7, 2006, accessed January 9, 2006, http://www.wsj.com; Adam Wolfe, "The Increasing Importance of African Oil," *Power and Interest News Report*, March 2005, accessed April 2, 2006, http://www.pinr.com; "Nigeria Bilateral Trade with China: Increased by 76.3 Percent," *Vanguard*, June 23, 2010, accessed July 14, 2010, http://allafrica.com.

62. Yun Sun, *Xi Jinping's Africa Policy: The First Year* (Washington, DC: Brookings Institution Press, April 14, 2014), http://www.brookings.edu/blogs/africa-in-focus/posts/2014/04/10-jinping-africa-policy-sun; Kevin Wang, "Yemen Evacuation a Strategic Step Forward for China," *Diplomat*, April 10, 2015, http://thediplomat.com/2015/04/yemen-evacuation-a-strategic-step-forward-for-china/; Nicholas Bariyo, "China Deploys Troops in South Sudan to Defend Oil Field Workers," *Wall Street Journal*, September 9, 2014, http://www.wsj.com/articles/china-deploys-troops-in-south-sudan-to-defend-oil-fields-workers-1410275041; "China 'Negotiates Military Base' in Djibouti," *Aljazeera*, May 9, 2015, http://www.aljazeera.com/news/africa/2015/05/150509084913175.html; "China Formally Opens First Overseas Military Base in Djibouti," Reuters, August 1, 2017, https://www.reuters.com/article/us-china-djibouti/china-formally-opens-first-overseas-military-base-in-djibouti-idUSKBN1AH3E3 (accessed January 22, 2018).

63. Hinton, *Communist China in World Politics*, pp. 197–204; Cecil Johnson, *Communist China and Latin America* (New York: Columbia University Press, 1970); Robert Worden, "China's Balancing Act: Cancun, the Third World, Latin America," *Asian Survey* 23, no. 5 (May 1983): pp. 619–36.

64. Sutter, *Historical Dictionary of Chinese Foreign Policy*, p. 61.

65. Robert Sutter, *Chinese Foreign Policy: Developments after Mao* (New York: Praeger, 1986), p. 200.

66. Sutter, *Historical Dictionary of Chinese Foreign Policy*, pp. 65, 78.

67. Worden, "China's Balancing Act"; Sutter, *Chinese Foreign Policy*, pp. 200–202.

68. Samuel Kim, *The Third World in Chinese World Policy* (Princeton, NJ: Princeton University Press, 1989); Frank O. Mora, "Sino–Latin American Relations: Sources and Consequences," *Journal of Interamerican Studies and World Affairs* 41, no. 2 (Summer 1999): pp. 91–116; Chein-hsun Wang, "Peking's Latin American Policy in the 1980s," *Issues and Studies* 27, no. 5 (May 1991): pp. 103–18.

69. Jorge Dominguez, *China's Relations with Latin America: Shared Gains, Asymmetrical Hopes*, Working Paper (Washington, DC: Inter-American Dialogue, June 2006); R. Evan Ellis, *U.S. National Security Implications of Chinese Involvement in Latin America* (Carlisle, PA: U.S. Army War College Strategic Studies Institute, June 2005); Ellis, *China in Latin America*; Kerry Dumbaugh and Mark Sullivan, *China's Growing Interest in Latin America*, Report RS22119 (Washington, DC: Library of Congress, Congressional Research Service, April 20, 2005); Riordan Roett and Guadalupe Paz, eds., *China's Expansion into the Western Hemisphere* (Washington, DC: Brookings Institution Press, 2007); Robert Devlin, Antoni Estevadeordal, and Andrés Rodríguez-Clare, *The Emergence of China: Challenges and Opportunities for Latin America and the Caribbean* (Cambridge, MA: Harvard University Press, 2006); David Shambaugh, "China's New Foray into Latin America," YaleGlobal Online, November 17, 2008, http://www.yaleglobal.com (accessed November 18, 2008); Cynthia Watson, "Adios Taipei, Hola Beijing: Taiwan's Relations with Latin America," *China Brief* 4, no. 11 (May 27, 2004): pp. 8–10; "A Warming Friendship," *China Brief* 4, no. 12 (June 10, 2004): pp. 2–3.

70. Robert Sutter, *Chinese Foreign Relations: Power and Policy since the Cold War* (Lanham, MD: Rowman & Littlefield, 2012), pp. 326, 327, 333.

71. Sutter, *Chinese Foreign Relations* (2012), pp. 327–28.

72. *Asia and Latin America and the Caribbean: Economic Links, Cooperation and Development Strategies*, Discussion Paper for Annual Meeting of Governors (Washington, DC: Inter-American Development Bank, March 21, 2005); John Paul Rathbone, "China Is Now Region's Biggest Partner," *Financial Times*, April 26, 2011, http://www.ft.com; Rebecca Roy and Kevin Gallagher, *China–Latin America Economic Bulletin 2017 Edition*, Boston University Global Economic Governance Initiative Discussion Paper 2017-1, 2017, https://www.bu.edu/pardeeschool/files/2014/11/Economic-Bulletin.16-17-Bulletin.Draft_.pdf (accessed January 22, 2018).

73. Rathbone, "China Is Now Region's Biggest Partner"; Qin Jize and Wang Kenyan, "Argentina Visit to Boost Ties," *China Daily*, June 25, 2012, http://www.chinadaily.com.cn; Roy and Gallagher, *China–Latin America Economic Bulletin 2017 Edition*.

74. Dumbaugh and Sullivan, *China's Growing Interest in Latin America*.

75. Wang Xiaoping and Chen Ma, "RMB Fund Planned to Aid Latin America," *China Daily*, April 29, 2011, p. 13; Brian Winter and Brian Ellsworth, "Brazil and China: A Young Marriage on the Rocks," Reuters, February 3, 2011, http://www.reuters.com; "Brazil Leads Surge in Latam Foreign Investment," *UV10*, May 18, 2011, http://www.uv10.com/brazil-leads-surge-in-latam-foreign-investment_800548463.

76. Dumbaugh and Sullivan, *China's Growing Interest in Latin America*

77. Shambaugh, "China's New Foray into Latin America."

78. Thomas Lum, *China's Foreign Aid Activities in Africa, Latin America, and Southeast Asia*, Report R40361 (Washington, DC: Library of Congress, Congressional Research Service, February 25, 2009), p. 15; Erica Downs, *Inside China, Inc: China Development Bank's Cross-Border Energy Deals*, John Thornton China Center Monograph Series 3 (Washington, DC: Brookings Institution Press, March 2011), p. 1.

79. "Magic or Realism: China and Latin America," *Economist*, December 29, 2004, http://www.economist.com (accessed January 10, 2005); Stuart Grudgings, "Analysis: Surge in Chinese Investment Reshapes Brazil Ties," Reuters, August 10, 2010, http://www.reuters.com.

80. Roy and Gallagher, *China-Latin America Economic Bulletin 2017 Edition*.

81. Larry Rohter, "China Widens Economic Role in Latin America," *New York Times*, November 20, 2004, http://www.nytimes.com (accessed November 20, 2004); Winter and Ellsworth, "Brazil and China: A Young Marriage on the Rocks."

82. Sun Hongbo, "Tapping the Potential," *China Daily*, April 16, 2010, p. 9.

83. "China Rethinks Developing World Largesse as Deals Sour," *Financial Times*, October 13, 2016, https://www.ft.com/content/5bf4d6d8-9073-11e6-a72e-b428cb934b78 (accessed January 22, 2018).

84. "Ma Reaffirms 'Modus Vivendi' Diplomatic Approach," *China Post*, March 15, 2011, http://www.chinapost.com.tw; Chris Horton and Steven Lee Myers, "Panama Establishes Relations with China, Further Isolating Taiwan," *New York Times*, June 13, 2017, https://www.nytimes.com/2017/06/13/world/asia/taiwan-panama-china-diplomatic-recognition.html (accessed January 22, 2018).

85. Sutter, *Chinese Foreign Relations* (2012), p. 334.

86. "Backgrounder: China's Cooperation with Latin America," Xinhua, July 17, 2014, http://news.xinhuanet.com/english/china/2014-07/17/c_133491300.htm; "Recent High-Level Visits Showcase Strengthening Ties with Latin America," *China Daily*, May 27, 2015, http://www.chinadaily.com.cn/view.php?mid=138660&cid=80&isid=1887; "China's Financial Diplomacy: Rich but Rash," *Economist*, January 31, 2015, http://www.economist.com/news/finance-and-economics/21641259-challenge-world-bank-and-imf-china-will-have-imitate-them-rich.

87. "Latin America and China: A Golden Opportunity," *Economist*, November 17, 2016, https://www.economist.com/news/americas/21710307-chinas-president-ventures-donald-trumps-backyard-golden-opportunity (accessed January 22, 2018); Matt Ferchen, "What's New about Xi's 'New Era' in China–Latin America Relations," *Diplomat*, November 26, 2016, https://thediplomat.com/2016/11/whats-new-about-xis-new-era-of-china-latin-america-relations/ (accessed January 22, 2018); Ted Piconne, "The Geopolitics of China's Rise in Latin America," Brookings Institution Press, November 2016, https://www.brookings.edu/research/the-geopolitics-of-chinas-rise-in-latin-america/ (accessed January 22, 2018); R. Evan Ellis, *Indian and Chinese Engagement in Latin America and the Caribbean* (Carlisle, PA: US Army War College, 2017), https://ssi.armywarcollege.edu/pubs/display.cfm?pubID=1346 (accessed January 22, 2018).

88. Robert Sutter, *China-Watch* (Baltimore: Johns Hopkins University Press, 1978), p. 36.

89. Hinton, *Communist China in World Politics*, pp. 149–51.

90. Sutter, *Historical Dictionary of Chinese Foreign Policy*, p. 42.

91. Hinton, *Communist China in World Politics*, pp. 171–75; Sutter, *Historical Dictionary of Chinese Foreign Policy*, p. 94.

92. Sutter, *Historical Dictionary of Chinese Foreign Policy*, 107.

93. Sutter, *Chinese Foreign Policy*, pp. 57, 131, 145; Sutter, *Historical Dictionary of Chinese Foreign Policy*, pp. 61, 201, 242.

94. Sutter, *Historical Dictionary of Chinese Foreign Policy*, p. 131.

95. John Garver, *Foreign Relations of the People's Republic of China* (Englewood Cliffs, NJ: Prentice Hall, 1993), pp. 231–37.

96. Ezra F. Vogel, *Deng Xiaoping and the Transformation of China* (Cambridge, MA: Harvard University Press, 2011), pp. 495–511.

97. Richard Bush, *Hong Kong in the Shadow of China* (Washington, DC: Brookings Institution Press, 2016).

98. Sutter, *Historical Dictionary of Chinese Foreign Policy*, pp. 157, 202.

99. Michael Yahuda, "China and Europe: The Significance of a Secondary Relationship," in *Chinese Foreign Policy: Theory and Practice*, ed. Thomas Robinson and David Shambaugh (New York: Oxford University Press, 1994), pp. 266–82.

100. Sutter, *Chinese Policy Priorities and Their Implications for the United States*, pp. 149–56.

101. Sutter, *Chinese Policy Priorities and Their Implications for the United States*, p. 152; Wayne Morrison, *Chinese Economic Conditions*, Report RL 33534 (Washington, DC: Library of Congress, Congressional Research Service, June 26, 2012), p. 30.

102. David Shambaugh, "China and Europe: The Emerging Axis," *Current History* 103, no. 674 (September 2004): pp. 243–48.

103. "EU Becomes China's Largest Trade Partner," Xinhua, January 10, 2005, http://www.taiwansecurity.org (accessed January 19, 2005).

104. Stanley Crossick, Fraser Cameron, and Alex Berkofy, *EU-China Relations—Toward a Strategic Partnership*, Working Paper (Brussels: European Policy Centre, July 2005), p. 26;

"Senior Chinese Official Calls for Enhanced Trade, Economic Cooperation with EU," Xinhua, December 29, 2010, http://www.xinhua.com; "Facts and Figures: China-EU Trade," *New China*, Xinhua, June 1, 2017, http://www.xinhuanet.com/english/2017-06/01/c_136331819.htm (accessed January 22, 2018).

105. "Senior Chinese Official Calls"; Crossick et al., *EU-China Relations*, pp. 26–27; "Li's Visit Pushes China-EU Ties toward New Stage," *China Daily*, January 6, 2011, p. 8; "Facts and Figures: China-EU Trade."

106. Jean-Pierre Cabestan, "European Union–China Relations and the United States" (paper prepared for the 58th annual meeting of the Association for Asian Studies, April 6–9, 2006, San Francisco); "Senior Chinese Official Calls"; Crossick et al., *EU-China Relations*, pp. 26–27; "Press Release: EU-China Trade Deficit Massively Unbalanced," *Aegis Europe*, March 8, 2017, http://www.aegiseurope.eu/news/press-release-eu-china-trade-deficit-massively-unbalanced-175-billion-euros (accessed January 22, 2018).

107. Van der Patten, *Europe and China's New Silk Roads*.

108. European Commission, *Trade—China*, http://ec.europa.eu/trade/policy/countries-and-regions/countries/china/ (accessed June 24, 2015); "U.S., EU, Japan to Join Forces on Chinese Excess Capacity—Source," Reuters, December 12, 2017, https://uk.reuters.com/article/uk-trade-wto-china/u-s-eu-japan-to-join-forces-on-chinese-excess-capacity-source-idUKKBN1E6066 (accessed January 22, 2018); "EU Singles Out China as Distorted State-Run Economy," Reuters, December 21, 2017, http://www.jakartaglobe.beritasatu.com/news/eu-singles-china-distorted-state-run-economy (accessed January 22, 2018); "Europe Should Pursue a 'New Realism' in Its Dealings with China," press release, European Council on Foreign Relations, April 12, 2017, http://www.ecfr.eu/publications/summary/china_eu_power_audit7242 (accessed January 22, 2018).

109. Gillian Wong, "China Rises and Rises, Yet Still Gets Foreign Aid," Associated Press, September 27, 2010, http://www.ap.com.

110. "Full Text of Joint Statement Issued at 8th China-EU Summit," Xinhua, September 5, 2005, http://www.xinhuanet.com/english (accessed September 9, 2005).

111. Sutter, *Historical Dictionary of Chinese Foreign Policy*, p. 215.

112. Cabestan, "European Union–China Relations and the United States," pp. 6–8.

113. Neil King and Marc Champion, "EU, US Policy on China Converges on Key Issues: Trade, Defense Spats Foster Alignment, Worrying Beijing," *Wall Street Journal*, May 4, 2006, http://www.wsj.com (accessed May 4, 2006); Cabestan, "European Union–China Relations and the United States," p. 7.

114. Tania Branihan and Jonathan Watts, "Chinese PM Rebuts Criticism over Copenhagen Role," *Guardian*, March 14, 2010, http://www.guardian.uk.com; Geoff Dyer and Andrew Ward, "Europe Defies China's Nobel Threat," *Financial Times*, November 5, 2010, http://www.ft.com.

115. "China's Attitude on Libya: Give Peace a Chance," *People's Daily*, http://english.people.com.cn.

116. "Beijing Signals End of China-UK 'Golden Age,'" *Financial Times*, January 6, 2017, https://www.ft.com/content/4ab22b66-d42d-11e6-9341-7393bb2e1b51 (accessed January 22, 2018).

117. Sutter, *Historical Dictionary of Chinese Foreign Policy*, p. 60; "Li Meets Canadian Prime Minister Trudeau," *China Daily*, December 5, 2017, http://www.chinadaily.com.cn/china/2017-12/05/content_35208147.htm (accessed January 22, 2018).

118. Anne-Marie Brady, "China's Rise in Antarctica," *Asian Survey* 50, no. 4 (2010): pp. 759–85; Nengye Liu, "Demystifying China in Antarctica," *Diplomat*, June 9, 2017, https://thediplomat.com/2017/06/demystifying-china-in-antarctica/ (accessed January 22, 2018).

119. Francois Perrault, "Can China Become a Major Arctic Player?" *RSIS Commentaries* 073/2012 (April 24, 2012), https://www.rsis.edu.sg/rsis-publication/cms/1735-can-china-become-a-major-arcti (accessed July 8, 2012).

Chapter Ten

Outlook

The success of China's ascendance in Asia and the world, possibly leading to a regional and broader power shift from previous US leadership in the Asia-Pacific region, depends heavily on the policies and practices of China's strong-man ruler Xi Jinping amid varied circumstances in China and abroad. The Xi Jinping government has laid out, in uniformly laudatory commentary bordering on hagiography, various plans and ambitions in foreign affairs seen as very successful in their first five-year term (2012–17) as the outline of their intentions following the endorsement of party leader and President Xi during respectively the Nineteenth Communist Party Congress in October 2017 and the Thirteenth National People's Congress in March 2018. This chapter will examine the often visionary plans of the Xi Jinping government in foreign affairs and then assess the range of realities impacting China in Asia and the world to demonstrate that China faces serious obstacles and constraints regarding its regional and broader international ambitions. On this basis, the author judges that a power shift in the Asia-Pacific is not imminent; readers are encouraged to make their own judgments after considering the evidence and the argument.

CHINA'S FOREIGN POLICY VISION DURING XI JINPING'S SECOND TERM

Party leader and President Xi Jinping and supporting publicists have crafted a vision designed to consolidate and build upon gains in China's rising influence in Asian and world affairs in his first term. The vision is designed to meet with the approval of Chinese elite and popular opinion and to help legitimate Xi's rule at home and abroad.

The overall image of a powerful and benign China moving smoothly to lead Asia and world affairs proves to be weak when examined in the face of realities constraining China's international rise.

There are four major elements in Xi Jinping's foreign policy vision.

- The China Dream
- China building a "Community of Shared Future"
- China undertaking leading international obligations—no longer a "free rider"
- China's strengthened historical identity of benevolent rule over *Tianxia* (all under heaven)

The China Dream—The Central Mission in Xi's First Term

Xi Jinping's strong emphasis on achieving what he calls the China Dream of "national rejuvenation" after two centuries of struggle against national weakness and foreign exploitation seeks foreign policy–related goals that include a fully unified and ever more powerful China recognized as Asia's leader. As discussed in earlier chapters, to achieve these goals, Xi has broken with the more restrained policies of previous leader Hu Jintao (2002–12) and earlier Chinese leaders who followed the long-standing guidance of Deng Xiaoping that China should keep a low profile in foreign affairs and focus on domestic modernization. Xi has been much bolder and more assertive. Unlike Hu Jintao, he no longer emphasizes reassurance of the United States, Asian neighbors, and others that China's rise will be peaceful; those efforts now are seen as signs of weakness that were exploited by the United States and other states seen infringing on China's sovereignty and security.

As reviewed in earlier chapters, salient manifestations of China's new approach to foreign affairs have included:

- Using growing military, paramilitary, and other state power coercively, though generally short of military attack, to advance China's broad territorial claims at the expense of neighbors and key American interests.
- Using large foreign exchange reserves and massive excess industrial capacity to launch various self-serving international economic development programs (e.g., the so-called Belt and Road Initiative [BRI]) and institutions that undermine US leadership and/or exclude the United States.
- Advancing China's military buildup targeted mainly at the United States in the Asia-Pacific region.
- Cooperating ever more closely with Russia as both powers increasingly support one another as they pursue through coercive and other means disruptive of the prevailing order their revisionist ambitions in respective

spheres of influence, taking advantage of opportunities coming from weaknesses in Europe, the Middle East, and Asia.
- Continuing cyber theft of economic assets; widespread IPR violations; grossly unfair market access restrictions on US and other developed countries' companies; state-directed industrial policies leading to targeted acquisition of high-technology US and other developed countries' firms and massive overcapacity disadvantaging US and other foreign producers; and currency practices disadvantaging US and other foreign traders.
- Intensified internal repression and tightened political control—all with serious adverse consequences for US interests and those of other developed countries.

Breaking with his past reserved approach featuring only rare public criticism of China, President Barack Obama beginning in 2014 complained often about the above Chinese practices coming at US expense. President Xi tended to publicly ignore the complaints, which were dismissed by lower-level officials. Xi emphasized the positive in a purported "new great power relationship" with the United States. The Obama government did not endorse the concept. American critics saw Xi Jinping playing a double game, pretending to seek cooperation while relentlessly undermining America through pursuit of his China Dream.[1]

Xi continued to advance China's ambitions at US expense. Obama took some actions in response but generally remained restrained—seeking common ground with China on important global issues including climate change and nuclear nonproliferation. US opinion was negative about the Chinese government. The media and elites in both political parties shifted against Xi and his practices; calls for a tougher US approach toward China came from both leading candidates and most others in the 2016 US presidential election campaign.

Against this background, the key international factors facilitating Xi's foreign advances in pursuing the China Dream involved the following: an irresolute American government in the face of China's challenges; a decline in the ability and willingness of the United States, US allies, and partners in the West to take potentially risky and costly steps in the face of China's affronts, which paled in comparison to more immediate dangers posed by Syria and the Islamic State in the Middle East and Russian military–backed expansionism in Europe and new involvement in the Middle East. Also important were weaknesses in Asia, notably Southeast Asia, allowing Chinese expansion of control into the disputed South China Sea; and Russia, facing strong sanctions in the West, became more dependent on China. Longer-term Russian concerns about China's growing strategic influence in areas near Russia in Asia and Europe were suppressed in pursuing closer Russian collaboration with China against the United States and its allies and partners.[2]

Newly Prominent Elements in Xi's Foreign Policy Vision

Supporting the foreign policy implications of Xi Jinping's China Dream are other elements in China's foreign policy plan featured in the lead-up to the Chinese party and government congresses of 2017–18. The first is China building a "Community of Shared Future." Commentary on this aspect of current Chinese foreign policy argues that China recognizes its rising global status and seeks to do more to protect world peace, advance development, and promote international cooperation. Xi Jinping's speech at the international economic meeting in Davos, Switzerland, in January 2017, and an article by leading foreign policy publicist Ambassador Fu Ying in June 2017 both underlined the concept of a community of a shared future.[3] The concept prioritizes a UN-based international order and includes support for the World Trade Organization (WTO) and the World Bank; it opposes a US-led world order based on alliances and US-backed interventions beyond UN norms. China's publicists continue at times to call for a new world order, but the more recent emphasis on a community of a shared future implies preserving much of the existing US-led world order and changing it along lines favored by China.

In this regard, on security disputes, China is depicted as favoring consultations and as very reluctant to resort to force; it opposes US alliances and international interventions. On economics, China sees its so-called Silk Road or One Belt, One Road plans, now known as the Belt and Road Initiative (BRI), as an exemplary way to promote mutually beneficial (what China calls "win-win") economic development. On diplomacy, China argues for inclusiveness, allowing different government systems to develop without prejudice or interference. In this context, it opposes Western promotion of human rights, democracy, and good governance.

The second newly publicized element in the Xi Jinping government's foreign policy plans is an emphasis that China undertakes more international costs and leadership risks, contrary to its past reputation as a "free rider," leaving such costs and risks to the United States and other developed countries. Highlighted here are reports discussed earlier that China's UN dues and payments for UN peacekeeping now are in line with its economic advances, unlike in past decades when China worked hard to portray itself as a developing country warranting very small UN dues and payment responsibilities. Also, China has put aside its past status as a net recipient of foreign assistance, even though it still annually receives several billion dollars of international assistance. In particular, Chinese loans supporting infrastructure projects and other ventures are deemed as very important in promoting development among BRI participants and elsewhere in the developing world. Also, China's commitment to the Paris Agreement on climate change is portrayed as crucial to world support for the agreement. And China's support for economic globalization is welcomed amid signs of populist resistance in the United States and the West.

The third newly emphasized feature of the Xi Jinping government's foreign policy approach has to do with the Chinese government's long-standing practice of manipulating Chinese historical interpretation to serve the needs of the ruling authorities. In the current period, the interpretation being stressed is one that supports China's identity as historically peaceful—a benign leader of *Tianxia*—translated as "all under heaven" and historically referring to China and all the surrounding territories coming within the scope of the civilization of Chinese imperial dynasties in the previous two millennia.[4]

This emphasis is designed to influence opinion in China and abroad that Chinese governments and people have always been peace-loving. Xi Jinping is among the leading Chinese officials who use such a depiction of history to underline the assertion that peace and harmony are integral in the spirit and blood of Chinese people.[5] Responding to Xi's leadership, Chinese scholars and publicists reconstruct Chinese history to show a benevolent Chinese empire (*Tianxia*) based on royal ethics or the so-called *Wangdao*, which is translated as righteous rule shown by the Chinese leader. The governance model seen here is one of subjects and neighboring states being subservient to the Chinese ruler, whose governance secures lasting peace and order for the benefit of all. This image of past Chinese rule is contrasted favorably against Western practice in using coercive power to advance narrow state interests.

As noted in chapter 1, this Chinese identity of benevolence and righteousness fits well with government conditioning of opinion in China to view Chinese foreign policy as uniformly moral and correct. Thus, Chinese opinion is inclined to support the Chinese government positions in disputes with other countries. Many abroad also echo the Chinese claims of benevolence and righteousness. In contrast, foreign historians often find the interpretations historically wrong and professionally offensive, and foreigners subjected to past and recent Chinese expansion and intimidation often see them as propaganda and self-serving lies.

IMAGE MEETS REALITIES: CONSTRAINTS ON CHINA'S RISE

Though given little attention in prevailing laudatory Chinese government discourse on the success and righteousness of party leader and President Xi Jinping and his seemingly confident formulating and conducting China's policies in foreign affairs, circumstances impacting China's power and influence abroad seriously limit China's rise. In reality, there are major constraints hobbling China's international influence; adding to China's difficulties are major gaps and shortcomings in Chinese policies and how they are carried out.[6]

Five sets of factors limit China's rise. They are:

- Domestic preoccupations
- Strong interdependence, especially with the United States
- China's insecure position in Asia
- Gaps and shortcomings in China's international economic policies
- The US position in Asia and the world

Domestic Preoccupations

Constraints on Chinese influence in regional and world affairs start at home. The Chinese leaders face an ongoing and major challenge in trying to sustain one-party rule in the world's largest and very dynamic, and economically vibrant, society. To sustain one-party rule requires massive expenditures and widespread leadership attention regarding internal security and control and strong continued economic growth that advances the material benefits of Chinese people and ensures general public support and legitimacy for the Communist government. As shown below, these domestic concerns are multifaceted, expensive to deal with, and very hard to resolve; they represent the main focus of China's large government and Communist Party apparatus.[7]

Moreover, the prime importance of economic growth and continued one-party rule require stability at home and abroad, especially in nearby Asia where conflict and confrontation would have a serious negative impact on Chinese economic growth. Unfortunatety for uniform adherence to these policy priorities, the Chinese leaders have other seemingly contradictory priorities. They involve protecting Chinese security and advancing Chinese control of sovereign claims. These other top concerns are evident in the long and costly buildup of military forces to deal with a Taiwan contingency involving the United States and more recent use of various means of state power to advance territorial control in nearby disputed seas. Of course, these priorities seem to contradict the priority of stability in Asia for the sake of needed economic development. This makes for a muddled Chinese approach to its nearby neighbors and other concerned powers, notably the United States. China's protrayal as benevolent and focused on mutual benefit is mixed with strong determination to have its way at others' expense on sensitive sovereignty disputes and related security issues.

Meanwhile, looking beyond nearby Asia, there is less clarity among specialists in China and abroad as to where Chinese international ambitions for regional and global leadership fit in the current priorities of the Beijing leaders. However, there is little doubt that the domestic concerns get overall priority.

The wide range of domestic concerns preoccupying the Xi Jinping leadership involves:

- weak leadership legitimacy highly dependent on how the leaders' performance is seen at any given time;
- pervasive corruption that saps public support and undermines government efficiency;
- widening income gaps that are contrary to communist ideals and are sources of social division;
- widespread social turmoil (reportedly involving one hundred thousand to two hundred thousand mass incidents annually) that require domestic security budgets bigger than China's large national defense budget;[8]
- a highly resource-intensive economy and related enormous environmental damage; and
- over sixty major reforms proposed in 2013 for an economic model at the point of diminishing returns with no clear plan of how they can be implemented.

Among significant implications of these domestic preoccupations is the strong debate among foreign specialists regarding the stability of one-party rule in China.[9] A crisis and change in the Chinese political order would be unexpected largely because we know so little of the inner workings of the Chinese leadership; it probably would have a major impact on China's international role.

More immediately, domestic preoccupations mean China's continued reluctance to undertake the costs and risks of international leadership because it has so many important requirements at home. Thus, China may not like American leadership in Asian and world affairs, but it has important and enduring domestic reasons to avoid taking on the costly and risky leadership mantle on its own.

Strong Interdependence

China's record in foreign affairs shows a strong and ever-growing interdependence with the United States and with other aspects of the international order supported by the United States. This constrains China from asserting leadership in ways that confront the United States. The interdependence of the US and Chinese economies is particularly important, and any crisis would cause major harm to Chinese economic development—the linchpin of regime legitimacy in China. And China depends on the United States for secure passage of its growing imports of oil and gas from the Persian Gulf.

Moreover, neither side can deal effectively with North Korea without the other. Additional areas of interdependence involve climate change, antiterrorism, nuclear nonproliferation, and cyber security. Xi Jinping's foreign policy initiatives establish international financial organizations led by China and outside the scope of US-backed existing international financial institutions. Nevertheless, China still relies on the latter for important support and avows no interest in taking on the burden of replacing these organizations.

China's Insecure Position in Asia

As shown in chapter 8 and elsewhere in this volume, nearby Asia is a world area where China has always exerted greatest influence and where China devotes the lion's share of foreign policy attention. Nearby Asia contains security and sovereignty issues (e.g., Taiwan) of top importance. It is the main arena of interaction with the United States. The region's economic importance for China far surpasses the rest of the world.

Without a secure foundation in nearby Asia, China will have difficulty in undertaking major leadership roles in other world areas. China's actual influence in nearby Asia can be measured accurately, as can the influence in the region of the United States and other powers. As seen in chapter 8, an inventory of China's relationships with other leading regional powers, notably Japan and India, and important middle powers like South Korea and Australia, shows serious reversals over the past two decades. Similarly serious downturns have occurred in areas keenly sensitive to Chinese interests, Taiwan and North Korea. These setbacks offset widely touted gains China has made in the South China Sea, and among some Southeast Asian and other neighboring countries.

As discussed in chapter 8, China's mixed record in expanding influence in nearby Asia after the Cold War is explained in part by negative legacies of past violent and coercive policies and practices that prompt regional wariness of contemporary Chinese intentions. Chinese foreign policy in post–Cold War Asia shows the conflicting objectives noted above involving peaceful development of mutual interest on the one hand and steely determination to gain control of disputed territories at neighbors' expense on the other hand. The record shows repeated switches, at times stressing reassurance and peaceful development and at other times stressing determination and intimidation in pursuing sensitive issues of sovereignty and security.

Chinese strengths in nearby Asia involve large trade and large investment. The latter was one-way in the past—from Asia to China; now more Chinese investment flows to nearby Asia. Chinese strengths also are seen in the many newly built road, rail, waterway, and electric connections between China and neighbors. China's bilateral and multilateral "win-win" diplomacy is active, attentive, and prominent. Growing military capabilities along with the impressively increased capacity of China's coast guard, maritime militia, and other law enforcement agencies underline China's importance in the eyes of its neighbors. China has some cultural influence through Confucius Institutes,[10] student exchange programs, and affinity between the Beijing government and some of the ethnic Chinese citizens in Southeast Asian countries.

The record seen in chapter 8 and elsewhere shows the above Chinese strengths are constrained and offset by Chinese limitations and weaknesses. Heading the list is China's negative legacy, which the Chinese government refuses to recognize and Chinese opinion is unaware of. China's strong nationalism runs up against strong nationalism in neighboring countries, worsening relations over sensitive sovereignty and security matters in particular. The expansion of Chinese military and other security forces duly impresses neighbors but prompts many to engage in self-strengthening and seek ties with one another and the United States in order to avoid dominance by China. The secrecy of Chinese leadership decision making and the increasingly authoritarian restrictions it imposes on Chinese citizens reduce Chinese influence in some neighboring countries; Asian observers often judge that the way Beijing rulers treat their people reflects how the rulers would deal with them if China were dominant in Asia.[11]

As discussed in the next subsection, the perceived influence China has as a leading trader with its neighbors often is less than meets the eye. And the trade is heavily interdependent. Half of Chinese trade is done by foreign-invested enterprises in China. It depends on investment from abroad. It also depends on components and inputs from other countries in the production of many manufactured goods (an estimated 30 to 40 percent of the value of Chinese trade involves this so-called processing trade).[12] And it depends on foreign markets—headed by the United States and the European Union—to purchase these manufactured goods. Also discussed earlier and shown below are weaknesses in China's investments, large-scale loans, and much more limited foreign assistance in Asia and elsewhere.

Gaps and Shortcomings in China's International Economic Policies

The Belt and Road Initiative (BRI), also known as One Belt, One Road, and related Xi Jinping initiatives mimic the massive push for Chinese investment and financing abroad begun in the first decade of the twenty-first century, known as China's "going out" strategy. The Xi initiatives advance and modify the strong "going out" policies of Chinese investment and financing abroad seen in the previous decade.

The previous effort focused on attaining access to oil and other raw materials needed for China's resource-hungry economy. Recent Chinese economic reforms seek to reduce such intense resource use. As discussed in chapter 6, the new push for Chinese foreign investment and financing is to enable construction abroad of Chinese-supplied infrastructure provided by the enormous excess capacity of Chinese companies for such construction and supply now that major infrastructure development inside China is curtailed under recent economic reforms. Locating some of China's heavily resource-intensive and polluting industries abroad could ease China's serious pollution problems and enhance its ability to meet commitments to international climate-change agreements. Economically, the new push also helps to connect the poorer regions of western China to international markets and thereby advance their development; to provide investment opportunities promising better returns for the large part of China's $3 trillion foreign exchange reserves invested in low-yield US and other foreign securities; and to broaden the international use of China's currency. Strategically, it improves Chinese access to key land-and-sea international corridors and reduces China's vulnerability posed by actual or possible US military control of transit choke points for Chinese imported oil, gas, and other supplies, notably at the mouth of the Persian Gulf and the Malacca Strait; and it advances overall Chinese relations with important countries along its rim and globally.

THE IMAGE OF A CONFIDENT, GENEROUS, AND INFLUENTIAL CHINA VERSUS OFFSETTING REALITIES

China's Image

The image seen in Chinese and international commentary of an ever-stronger and influential China fostered by the BRI and other economic initiatives of Xi Jinping's government comes against the background of China's role as the world's second-largest economy, leading world manufacturer and world trader, and largest creditor nation. China's continued substantial economic growth contrasts with the notably more modest advances of all other leading international economies. Beijing's initiatives are said to show enormous Chinese largesse, unprecedented in size and scope, involving use of parts of China's $3 trillion in foreign exchange reserves in seeking mutually beneficial development throughout the world.

The results of the Xi Jinping government's initiatives include multibillion-dollar commitments to the BRI and other Chinese Silk Road funds and new development banks led by China and regional initiatives in Africa, Europe, Latin America, and the Middle East. Authoritative Chinese commentary eventually defined the scope of the BRI so broadly that it included the Western Hemisphere. Among notable developments cited earlier, China has pledged infrastructure in unstable Pakistan valued at $46 billion. A responsible Chinese official said Beijing's overall plan for investment in Africa will not lag given other priorities, and over the next decade will amount to $1 trillion. Latin America also will not be neglected as Xi personally pledged investment in Latin America of $250 billion over the next decade. Against this background, foreign commentary often echoed Chinese commentaries in seeing Beijing as the leader of international economic relations in Asia and much of the developing and developed world.

Offsetting Realities

Trade. The realities facing the Xi Jinping government's international economic initiatives forecast more modest Chinese impacts. The realities start with trade. For over two decades, and especially since China joined the WTO in 2001, Beijing relied on its burgeoning trade with Asian and international markets as a major source of Chinese international influence. For several years China's trade grew at double the rate of China's economic growth of around 10 percent. In contrast, while the Chinese economy continued to grow at a rate of around 7 percent in 2015 and 2016, the value of Chinese trade was flat in those two years. The value of trade began to rise again in 2017, but a return to the days of previous high annual growth seemed unlikely; accordingly, whatever influence rising trade would have for China in foreign affairs seemed likely to be less than in the first decade and a half of the twenty-first century.

Meanwhile, evidence that rising Chinese trade was often not as influential as Beijing and many foreign observers assessed came in reviewing Chinese relations with several important neighbors in recent years. Though very dependent on trade with China, Myanmar in 2011 shifted away from dependence on Beijing and opened relations with the United States and its allies and partners. Taiwan's dependence on trade with China grew during the ever-closer cross-strait relations during the rule of President Ma Ying-jeou (2008–16). Trade with China, including Hong Kong, came to be more than 40 percent of Taiwan's trade. Yet Taiwan's ever-closer economic relationship with China raised concerns in Taiwan about overdependence on China and was widely seen as a political liability for Ma and his Kuomintang party. One result was the landslide victory in January 2016 for President Tsai Ing-wen and her legislative colleagues on platforms opposing greater dependence on China.

Among other countries in the nearby Asia-Pacific region, there are very few that do more than 20 percent of their trade with China. South Korea and Australia are two notable exceptions. Yet such trade ties have not been able to halt growing suspicions of and antagonism toward China in both countries, worsening relations significantly from where they were over ten years ago.

Investment, loans. The "going out" policies begun at the start of the previous decade were accompanied by massive publicity for Chinese multi-billion-dollar agreements to invest in various developing countries and to promote infrastructure constructed by Chinese companies with loans from

Chinese banks. The recent BRI and related initiatives also are accompanied by massive publicity showing China's generosity and influence. In contrast, as noted in chapter 9, the *Economist* in 2015 assessed China's important economic footprint in Africa more soberly. China was viewed as far from dominant among many other foreign powers active in the region. It concluded that China was "one among many" foreign sources of economic influence and support.

Other data reviewed in chapter 9 showed that even after over a decade of publicity regarding multibillion-dollar Chinese investment pledges in developing countries, China investment in Africa and Latin America made up about 5 percent of the foreign investment received by these countries, and according to ASEAN data, Chinese investment made up about 10 percent of the foreign investment received by Southeast Asian countries.[13]

Meanwhile, despite the more recent and widely touted rise in Chinese investment abroad, and the often intense Chinese publicity on China's role in the BRI and related activities, as of the end of 2015 only 12 percent of Chinese investment had gone to the sixty-eight countries involved with the BRI, whereas those countries had received 17 percent of global investment. The situation worsened in 2016 when only 8.5 percent of Chinese investment went to the BRI countries.[14]

The reasons supporting a more sober view of the impact of Chinese investments and loans start with evidence showing that China often implements only a small fraction of its seemingly very expensive pledges. For example, Pakistan and Indonesia had numerous agreements involving investment and loans from China in the first decade and a half of the twenty-first century. Yet the record showed that less that 10 percent of these were implemented.[15] Myanmar in 2011 stopped a multibillion-dollar Chinese hydroelectric dam project; major railway projects in Nigeria and Mexico never made progress or were canceled; the big plans for Chinese investments and infrastructure development announced during meetings with Philippines president Rodrigo Duterte (2016–) recalled similarly large announced Chinese investment and loan commitments with Philippines president Gloria Arroyo in the previous decade that collapsed amid charges of corruption.

While Chinese commentary and Chinese representatives generally avoid detailed discussion of the negative aspects of Chinese investments and loans associated with China's outreach of investments and loans abroad, at various times Chinese representatives and official media provide important insights that support a more sober view on what influence and other gains China achieves through such efforts. Thus, for example, although Chinese mining deals are an important element in China's investment and infrastructure plans abroad, a prominent Chinese official with responsibility for mining disclosed in late 2012 that 80 percent of proposed Chinese mining deals fail to be implemented.[16] In 2015 a prominent Chinese expert on such matters disclosed that Chinese foreign enterprises resulting from Chinese investments abroad more often than not are losing money.[17] Indeed, Chinese investors and loan providers lost enormously in the conflicts in Iraq, Libya, and Syria.

The renewed push for investments and loans abroad raises the importance of recent scholarship based in part on interviews with officials in Beijing involved in deciding on China's state-supported loans and investments. One upshot of the analysis is that China employs a dual "win-win" approach when making these international deals. One part of the win-win story is well known. It is that China makes sure that these international deals serve China's national interests, usually centered on China's economic benefit, while China endeavors to make sure its international partner's national interests are served by the agreement. More important, the scholarship sheds light on the second part of the win-win story. It shows that such international deals must be of benefit for the win-set of different agencies in the Chinese government involved in such international ventures. Some of these agencies are strict in making sure that China will be repaid for its investments and loans. They support the widely seen pattern in Chinese lending and investment, which highlights China's assiduous demand for eventual repayment. If the foreign recipient cannot pay in money, China often arranges payment in goods—notably oil. If the foreign recipient does not have goods desired by China, China seeks repayment through control of factories, land, and other resources in the debtor country.[18]

Some of these repayment schemes have involved ninety-nine-year leases of territory in these countries, recalling for historians China's disadvantageous treatment by imperial powers seeking such control of Chinese territory in the nineteenth and twentieth centuries. Like Chinese in their sensitivity to past imperialist exploitation, Indian commentators have been in the lead in condemning China for creating "debt traps" in developing countries without the means to pay back large and often market-rate Chinese loans. Examples of such Chinese control of assets involve debt laggards Sri Lanka, Venezuela, and Ecuador. China also controls large swaths of coastal territory in Malaysia and Cambodia. Reported plans for Chinese loans and investment in Pakistan will involve large Chinese acquisitions of arable land there, and impoverished Laos's ability to pay back the costs for its planned $7 billion rail link with China presumably will involve greater Chinese control of assets in that neighboring country.[19]

Related, since the majority of states involved in the BRI initiative are poor credit risks without the means of easy repayment of Chinese loans or profit for Chinese investments, the fact that China has been disproportionately low among overall foreign investment in these states seems more understandable given scholarship showing the importance Chinese government agencies give to getting full return for their investments.

As noted earlier, other problems for China expanding its influence through investment and loans involve corrupt practices, nontransparent agreements with unaccountable foreign governments, unstable conditions in many developing countries, and China's recent diminishing need for some imported raw materials. Foreign labor unions and other politically active constituencies often resent China's tendency on the one hand to import Chinese labor crews in carrying out Chinese-supported projects and on the other hand to be less attentive to international labor standards when employing local workers. The environmental impact of Chinese development projects prompted local civil society groups in various countries to mobilize protests against Chinese practices.

The US Position in Asia

Until the advent of the Trump administration, a comparison of Chinese policies and practices in the Asia-Pacific region with those of the United States appeared to underline how far China had to go, despite more than two decades of post–Cold War efforts to strengthen its position in Asia, if it intended to be successful in seriously confronting and challenging the United States. And without a secure periphery, and facing formidable US presence and influence, China almost certainly calculated that challenging the United States under such circumstances would pose grave dangers for the PRC regime.

After several months of erratic behavior by the Trump government, there remains uncertainty as to whether the United States will persist in its past leadership role in competition with China in the Asia-Pacific region. Other possibilities range from retrenchment to conflict, with both at the extremes having potentially massive negative consequences for the existing Asian order. In particular, if retrenchment is pursued, then the existing constraints on China in Asia very likely will weaken substantially and China will have a freer hand in advancing toward regional dominance.

Nevertheless, it seems important to realize that any diminishment of US power and influence will take time. In a word, if rising China has some momentum, the United States benefits from massive inertia as the region's leading power.[20] America has a unique and remarkably strong foundation of nongovernment connections with Asian countries, topped off with many millions of Asians now settled in the United States and participating constructively in interchange connecting the United States and Asia. The deeply rooted US military and intelligence interchange with almost all Asia-Pacific governments has made the head of the US Pacific Command by far the most active senior US government representative in the region; these relationships remain of mutual benefit and do not depend on sentiment. And despite withdrawing from the TPP, the US market remains open and still absorbs a massive amount of manufactured goods from regional exporters and their component suppliers in the regional production chains.

Past US weaknesses in the Asia-Pacific included the often unilateral and arbitrary foreign policy decisions of the George W. Bush administration, which were very unpopular with regional elites and public opinion. As the Obama administration refocused US attention positively on the Asia-Pacific region, regional concerns shifted to worry that US budget difficulties and political gridlock in Washington would undermine the ability of the United States to sustain support for regional responsibilities. Overall, the Obama government's "rebalance" policy and recent US practice meshed well with the interests of the majority of Asia-Pacific governments that seek legitimacy through development and nation building in an interdependent world economic order and an uncertain security environment caused notably by Chinese assertiveness. However, major questions remained on whether the rebalance was sufficient to deal with China's recent challenges and whether it would be continued by the new US administration.

The basic determinants of US strength and influence in the Asia-Pacific region involve five factors, starting with security. In most of Asia, governments are viable and make the decisions that determine direction in foreign affairs. Popular, elite, media, and other opinion may influence government officials in policy toward the United States and other countries, but in the end the officials make decisions on the basis of their own calculus. In general, the officials see their governments' legitimacy and success resting on nation building and economic development, which require a stable and secure international environment. Unfortunately, Asia is not particularly stable, and most regional governments are privately wary of, and tend not to trust, each other. As a result, they look to the United States to provide the security that they need to pursue goals of development and nation building in an appropriate environment. They recognize that the US security role is very expensive and involves great risk, including large-scale casualties if necessary, for the sake of preserving Asian security. They also recognize that neither rising China, nor any other Asian power or coalition of powers, is able or willing to undertake even a small part of these risks, costs, and responsibilities.

Second, the nation-building priority of most Asian governments depends greatly on export-oriented growth. As noted above, much of Chinese and Asian trade depends heavily on exports to developed countries, notably the United States. America has run a massive trade deficit with China, and a total annual trade deficit with Asia valued at more than $400 billion. Asian government officials recognize that China, which consistently runs an overall trade surplus, and other trading partners in Asia are unwilling and unable to bear even a fraction of the cost of such large trade deficits, which, nonetheless, are very important for Asian governments.

Third, despite the negative popular view in Asia of the George W. Bush administration's policies in Iraq and the broader war on terror, it was generally effective in interaction with Asia's powers—notably China, Japan, and India. The Obama administration built on these strengths. The Obama government's broad rebalancing with regional governments and multilateral organizations had a scope ranging from India to the Pacific Island states to Korea and Japan. Its emphasis on consultation and inclusion of international stakeholders before coming to policy decisions on issues of importance to Asia and the Pacific also was broadly welcomed and stood in contrast with the previously perceived unilateralism of the Bush administration. Meanwhile, the US Pacific Command and other US military commands and security and intelligence organizations have been at the edge of wide-ranging and growing US efforts to build and strengthen webs of military and related intelligence and security relationships throughout the region.

Fourth, the United States for decades, reaching back to past centuries, has engaged the Asia-Pacific region through business, religious, educational, media, and other interchange. Such active nongovernment interaction puts the United States in a unique position and reinforces overall American influence. Meanwhile, more than fifty years of generally color-blind US immigration policy, since the ending of discriminatory American restrictions on Asian immigration in 1965, has resulted in the influx of millions of Asia-Pacific migrants who call America home and who interact with their countries of origin in ways that underpin and reflect well on the US position in the region.

Fifth, part of the reason for the success of US efforts to build webs of security-related and other relationships with Asia-Pacific countries has to do with active contingency planning by many Asia-Pacific governments. As power relations change in the region, notably on account of China's rise, regional governments generally seek to work positively and pragmatically with rising China on the one hand, but they seek the reassurance of close security, intelligence, and other ties with the United States, on the other hand, in case rising China shifts from its current avowed benign approach to one of greater assertiveness or dominance.

Against the background of recent Chinese demands, coercion, and intimidation, the Asia-Pacific governments' interest in closer ties with the United States meshed well with the Obama administration's engagement with regional governments and multilateral organizations. The US concern to maintain stability while fostering economic growth overlapped constructively with the priorities of the majority of regional governments as they pursued their respective nation-building agendas.

Under President Trump, the positive role of the Pacific Command, legal immigration, and nongovernment American engagement in Asia has continued. The president's campaign rhetoric raised questions about support for alliances, but they have subsided with high-level US reassurance. America's role as economic partner was in doubt with the scrapping of the TPP, but the US market has remained open to regional imports.

President Trump ended the rebalance and commitment to the TPP. Employing unpredictable unilateral actions, he cast doubt on past US commitment to positive regional relations. He also junked related policy transparency; carefully measured responses; and avoidance of dramatic action, linkage, or spillover among competing interests. Early in his presidency, his record in the region showed episodic engagement featuring intense pressure to prevent North Korea's nuclear weapons development and overall drift in dealing with most other issues. President Trump's strong defense posture and pragmatism on human rights issues were welcomed by many regional governments, but they failed to overshadow a muddled picture of a poorly staffed administration with conflicting impulses and many preoccupations leading to flawed engagement in the Asia-Pacific.

CONCLUSION

The discussion above shows continued Chinese advance in importance and influence. But the United States remains the region's leading power, and other important governments are wary of the implications of China's rise. Prevailing conditions, even including the mediocre record of the Trump administration in 2017, make it hard to foresee how China could emerge in a dominant position in Asia in the foreseeable future, notably during Xi Jinping's second term.

As a result, the reported dangers of US-China confrontation and conflict or dramatic US accommodation or appeasement of China, predicted in projections of power shift in Asia, are reduced. It appears more likely that Chinese policy makers will continue to rely on and to seek to exploit the US-led international order, avoiding taking on costs and obligations of replacing it while pushing for changes in line with Chinese interests.

Fairness requires noting variables that could upset the above forecast deemed most likely over the next five years and longer. Those variables include nationalistic elite and public opinion pushing for greater Chinese international assertiveness or domestic economic or political crises undermining China's government. US policy could withdraw from security commitments to the Asia-Pacific or close American markets to regional exporters. On the other hand, the United States could attempt strong and overt opposition to China. Meanwhile, abrupt and provocative actions by the always unpredictable North Korean government, by claimants in territorial disputes along China's rim, and by the bold leaders in power in Washington and Beijing could escalate tensions.

NOTES

1. Robert Sutter, "Obama's Cautious and Calibrated Approach to an Assertive China," YaleGlobal Online, April 19, 2016, http://yaleglobal.yale.edu/content/obamas-cautious-and-calibrated-approach-assertive-china.

2. *Russia-China Relations: Assessing Common Ground and Strategic Fault Lines* (Seattle: National Bureau of Asian Research, July 2017), http://nbr.org/publications/element.aspx?id= 950.

3. "Full Text of Xi Jinping Keynote at World Economic Forum," *CGTN*, January 17, 2017, https://america.cgtn.com/2017/01/17/full-text-of-xi-jinping-keynote-at-the-world-economic-forum (accessed January 23, 2018); Fu Ying, "China's Vision for the World: A Community of Shared Future," *Diplomat*, June 22, 2017, https://thediplomat.com/2017/06/chinas-vision-for-the-world-a-community-of-shared-future/ (accessed January 23, 2018).

4. Suisheng Zhao, "Reconstruction of Chinese History for a Peaceful Rise," YaleGlobal Online, June 13, 2017, https://yaleglobal.yale.edu/content/reconstruction-chinese-history-peaceful-rise (accessed January 23, 2018).

5. Frank Ching, "Does Chinese Blood Really Lack DNA for Aggression?" *South China Morning Post*, July 1, 2014, http://www.scmp.com/comment/article/1544186/does-chinese-blood-really-lack-dna-aggression (accessed January 23, 2018).

6. Over the past fifteen years, this writer has assessed the strengths and weaknesses of China's rise in Asian and world affairs in various publications. They include, notably, Robert Sutter, *China's Rise in Asia* (Lanham, MD: Rowman & Littlefield, 2005); an annual eight-thousand-word essay in a prominent yearbook, "China's Growing International Role," *Far East and Australasia* (London: Routledge, 2017); and three major studies that in sometimes multiple editions have addressed this topic. This section of this chapter builds on and updates the findings in those studies: Robert Sutter, *US-China Relations: Perilous Past, Uncertain Present*, 3rd ed. (Lanham, MD: Rowman & Littlefield, 2017), pp. 272–82; *Chinese Foreign Relations: Power and Policy since the Cold War*, 4th ed. (Lanham, MD: Rowman & Littlefield, 2016), pp. 327–33; and *The United States and Asia* (Lanham, MD: Rowman & Littlefield, 2015), pp. 112–32.

7. See, among others, David Shambaugh, *China's Future* (Cambridge: Polity Press, 2016); Bruce Dickson, *The Dictator's Dilemma: The Chinese Communist Party's Strategy for Survival* (New York: Oxford University Press, 2016); Arthur Kroeber, *China's Economy: What Everyone Needs to Know* (New York: Oxford University Press, 2016); Elizabeth Perry, "Growing Pains: Challenges for a Rising China," *Daedalus* 143, no. 2 (Spring 2014): pp. 5–13; Martin King Whyte, "China's Dormant and Active Volcanoes," *China Journal* (January 2016): pp. 9–37; Deborah Davis, "Demographic Challenges for a Rising China," *Daedalus* 143, no. 2 (Spring 2014): pp. 26–38; Cheng Li, "The End of the CCP's Resilient Authoritarianism? A Tripartite Assessment of Shifting Power in China," *China Quarterly* 211, September 2012, pp. 595–623; Minxin Pei, *China's Crony Capitalism: The Dynamics of Regime Decay* (Cambridge, MA: Harvard University Press, 2016); Daniel Lynch, *China's Futures: PRC Elites Debate Economics, Politics, and Foreign Policy* (Stanford, CA: Stanford University Press, 2015); William Callahan, *China: The Pessioptimist Nation* (Oxford: Oxford University Press, 2010).

8. Ben Blanchard and John Ruwitch, "China Hikes Defense Budget, to Spend More in Internal Security," Reuters, March 5, 2013, http://www.reuters.com/article/2013/03/05/us-china-parliament-defence-idUSBRE92403620130305.

9. Shambaugh, *China's Future*.

10. Confucius Institutes are part of a wide array of recent Chinese government efforts to influence opinion abroad about China. They have not been the source of major controversy among most developing countries, but significant controversy has accompanied their establishment in some developed countries, including the United States. Critics see them as one of a set of tools used by the Chinese government to influence officials and elite and popular opinion through legal and illegal means to support China's growing international ambitions for influence and control. Much more controversial than the Confucius Institutes are widespread reports of Chinese covert payments to government officials and to think tanks and opinion leaders seeking to influence their opinions and actions regarding China. "China Trying to Gain Politi-

cal Influence Abroad and the West Isn't Happy," CNBC, December 18, 2017, https://www.cnbc.com/2017/12/18/china-news-us-australia-criticize-beijing-political-influence-attempts.html (accessed January 26, 2018).

11. Joseph Nye, "Chinese Repression Undoes Its Charm Offensive," *Washington Post*, March 25, 2011, https://www.washingtonpost.com/opinions/chinas-repression-undoes-its-charm-offensive/2011/03/24/AFdlxRYB_story.html?utm_term=.4d21516623dc (accessed January 24, 2018); Evelyn Goh, *The Struggle for Order: Hegemony, Hierarchy and Transition in Post–Cold War East Asia* (Oxford: Oxford University Press, 2013).

12. Miaojie Yu and Wei Tian, "China's Processing Trade," *East Asia Forum*, October 27, 2012, http://www.eastasiaforum.org/2012/10/27/chinas-processing-trade/.

13. Top ten sources of foreign direct inflows in ASEAN (table 27), http://www.asean.org/images/2015/January/foreign_direct_investment_statistic/Table%2027.pdf (accessed June 6, 2015); "China in Africa: One Among Many," *Economist*, January 17, 2015, http://www.economist.com/news/middle-east-and-africa/21639554-china-has-become-big-africa-now-backlash-one-among-many; *2013 China–Latin America Bulletin*, p. 12, http://www.bu.edu/pardee/files/2014/01/Economic-Bulletin-2013.pdf (accessed June 5, 2015).

14. David Dollar, "Yes, China Is Investing Globally but Not So Much in Its Belt and Road Initiative," *Brookings Institution Order from Chaos*, May 8, 2017, https://www.brookings.edu/blog/order-from-chaos/2017/05/08/yes-china-is-investing-globally-but-not-so-much-in-its-belt-and-road-initiative/ (accessed January 24, 2018).

15. Linda Yulisman, "Indonesia: Indonesia to Push China to Realize Investment," *Jakarta Post*, April 4, 2015, http://www.thejakartapost.com/news/2015/04/04/indonesia-push-china-realize-investment.html; Dinna Wisnu, "Indonesia: Jokowi's Visits to Japan and China: What's in It for Us?" *Jakarta Post*, April 7, 2015, http://www.thejakartapost.com/news/2015/04/07/jokowi-s-visits-japan-and-china-what-s-it-us.html; Andrew Small, "Pakistan and the Belt and Road Initiative," *Asia Policy* 24 (July 2017): p. 80.

16. Toh Han Shih, "Chinese Investors Warned about African Mining Risks," *South China Morning Post*, December 16, 2013, http://www.scmp.com/business/commodities/article/1381796/chinese-investors-warned-about-african-mining-risks.

17. Huang Yiping, "Pragmatism Can Lead Silk Roads to Success," *China Daily*, February 25, 2015, http://repubhub.icopyright.net/freePost.act?tag=3.15484?icx_id=48971175.

18. Consultations with Professor James Reilly, University of Sydney. See James Reilly, *China's Economic Statecraft: Turning Wealth into Power*, Lowy Institute, November 2013, http://sydney.edu.au/arts/government_international_relations/downloads/documents/Reilly_China_Economic_Statecraft.pdf (accessed January 24, 2018).

19. In addition to citations in earlier chapters, see, among others, *The "New Great Game": China's Debt Trap Diplomacy*, European Foundation for South Asian Studies, October 2017, https://www.efsas.org/publications/study-papers/the-new-great-game-chinas-debt-trap-diplomacy (accessed January 24, 2018).

20. See the most recent review by this writer in *US-China Relations*, 3rd ed., pp. 278–81.

Chronology

1949[1]

October 1: The Communist-led People's Republic of China (PRC) was established on the Chinese mainland. **December:** The Chinese Nationalist government evacuated to Taiwan. Mao Zedong began a three-month visit to Moscow and the Soviet Union.

1950

February 14: China and the Soviet Union agreed to a Sino-Soviet alliance. **June:** North Korean forces attacked South Korea, starting the Korean War. **September:** A successful allied landing at Inchon marked the beginning of the end of the North Korean armed forces. **October:** Tens of thousands of Chinese military forces entered eastern regions of Tibet, defeating Tibetan defenders. **October–November:** Hundreds of thousands of Chinese military forces entered Korea and drove back advancing US and allied forces. A mass campaign in China, "resist America–aid Korea," saw the removal of US and other Western nongovernmental influence and personnel in China. **December:** The United States instituted a strict embargo on economic relations with China.

1951

May 23: China and Tibet reached a seventeen-point agreement deepening China's control of Tibet. **September 8:** The United States and Japan signed a defense treaty.

1953

March: Soviet authorities announced the death of Joseph Stalin. **July:** The armistice ending the Korean War was signed. The majority of Chinese troops held as prisoners by the United Nations forces chose not to return to China. **October 1:** The United States and South Korea signed a defense treaty.

1954

April 29: India and China signed an agreement dealing with Tibet that based Sino-Indian relations on the Five Principles of Peaceful Coexistence. **May:** French forces lost the battle of Dien Bien Phu to Chinese-supported Communist forces in Indochina. **June:** Premier Zhou Enlai visited India and Burma, issuing statements endorsing the Five Principles of Peaceful Coexistence. **July:** The Geneva Accords marking the end of the French war in Indochina were signed. China participated prominently in the talks leading to the accords. An upsurge in Chinese political and later military pressure led to a crisis in the Taiwan Strait. **September 8:** The Southeast Asian Treaty Organization was established. **December 2:** The United States and the Republic of China on Taiwan signed a defense treaty.

1955

February: Chinese raids on the Dachen Islands prompted evacuation of the islands by US-supported Chinese Nationalist forces. **April:** Chinese premier Zhou Enlai used a conference of Afro-Asian leaders in Bandung, Indonesia, to offer a more moderate Chinese approach to foreign relations. **July:** Zhou Enlai underlined Chinese interest in peaceful coexistence and forward movement in forthcoming talks with the United States. **August:** The US and Chinese governments began ambassadorial-level talks in Geneva. **September:** An agreement on repatriation of nationals reached at the US-China ambassadorial talks was released and quickly became an issue of debate and mutual recrimination.

1956

February: Soviet leader Nikita Khrushchev denounced Joseph Stalin in a speech to a closed session of the leaders of the Communist Party of the Soviet Union. Mao Zedong strongly disagreed with the speech. **July:** Egyptian leader Gamal Abdel Nasser announced a plan to nationalize the Suez Canal, precipitating the Suez crisis. China supported Nasser. **September:** China showed support for Polish Communist Party resistance to Soviet efforts to control the party's independent-minded leadership. **November:** Chinese leaders supported the intervention of Soviet troops into Hungary as they appeared to judge that the existing communist regime was unable to contain a burgeoning mass movement that was increasingly taking outright anticommunist forms.

1957

June: China began a crackdown against alleged "rightists" who criticized the government's policies and practices during the course of the previous year's campaign to encourage criticism and divergent thinking under the rubric of promoting a "Hundred Flowers." **September–October:** A plenary session of the Chinese Communist Party's Central Committee endorsed radical measures leading to China's intense national campaign for a Great Leap Forward. **November:** For the second time, Mao Zedong traveled to Moscow where he urged the Soviet Union and the international communist movement to adopt a more militant stance against US imperialism.

1958

August: Chinese forces began artillery bombardment of offshore islands held by US-supported Chinese Nationalist forces, prompting a new crisis in the Taiwan Strait. **October:** Chinese forces completed withdrawal from North Korea.

1959

March: Amid riots and Chinese troops firing on demonstrators, the Dalai Lama left Tibet, fleeing to India.

1960

January 28: Burma and China signed a Friendship and Mutual Non-Aggression Treaty. **July:** Amid deepening differences with China, the Soviet Union announced the withdrawal of its assistance and related personnel from China. Nepal and China established ambassadorial relations. **October 1:** A boundary treaty between China and Burma was signed in Beijing.

1961

July: China and North Korea signed a defense alliance. **October 5:** Nepal and China signed a boundary treaty.

1962

The United States repeatedly warned Chiang Kai-shek against attempting to attack mainland China at a time of the collapse of the Chinese Great Leap Forward. **July:** An international conference in Geneva ended with an agreement deferring a military crisis involving the United States and China over Laos. **October–November:** Culminating years of border maneuvers and tensions, Chinese military forces attacked and overwhelmed Indian defenses along the eastern boundary before withdrawing.

1963

March: Official Chinese media raised the issue of "unequal treaties" defining China's historical boundary with Russia, thereby broadening the Sino-Soviet split to include border issues. **December:** Zhou Enlai began a two-month trip to ten African countries, encouraging struggle in line with recent Chinese emphasis against the United States, the Soviet Union, and colonial and rightist regimes.

1964

March: The Fourth Afro-Asian People's Solidarity Conference held in Algeria saw Chinese delegates and their associates attack the policies and practices of the Soviet Union and nonaligned nations while urging support for more militant positions held by China. **August:** Several months of Sino-Soviet border talks ended without progress amid public Chinese complaints about the unequal treaties defining China's historic border with Russia. **October:** Nikita Khrushchev was removed as leader of the Soviet Union; he was replaced by Leonid Brezhnev. China successfully tested an atomic bomb.

1965

September: The outbreak of an India-Pakistan war over Kashmir saw China increase pressure along the China-India border and condemn what it depicted as Indian aggression supported by both the United States and the Soviet Union. **October:** In reaction to a coup attempt and growing influence of the Indonesian Communist Party (PKI) on the increasingly left-leaning President Sukarno, army officers under the leadership of General Suharto struck back. The resulting mass killings and arrests destroyed the PKI and killed many thousands of ethnic Chinese. Power now rested with Suharto and the army. China's influence collapsed in this important Southeast Asia country.

1966

January: The Soviet Union and Mongolia signed a defense treaty. Soviet motorized divisions and other forces began deploying along the Mongolian-Chinese border. **May:** A Chinese Communist Party circular attacked counterrevolutionary revisionists in the party, marking the start of the ten-year Cultural Revolution.

1967

January: Large numbers of Red Guard–led demonstrators began a sometimes violent siege of the Soviet embassy in Beijing. The Chinese military was instructed to intervene throughout China, stop factional fighting, and restore order. **June:** China successfully tested a hydrogen bomb. Confrontations caused by Chinese students and diplomats spreading Maoism in Rangoon, Burma, escalated into full-scale anti-Chinese riots. China called for the overthrow of the Burmese government and supported an armed struggle against it by insurgents of the Burmese Communist Party. **August:** Red Guard–led demonstrators seized the Chinese Ministry of Foreign Affairs building and burned the British mission in Beijing, beating British diplomats escaping the flames. **September:** With the support of Mao and Chinese leaders at the time, the Chinese military adopted sometimes tough measures to restore order and suppress disruptive Red Guard groups.

1968

January: Vietnamese Communist forces launched a major offensive during the Tet holiday in South Vietnam. **April:** The Vietnamese Communists agreed to enter peace talks proposed by the United States; China for a time opposed the talks. **August:** The Soviet Union invaded Czechoslovakia, toppled the government, and replaced it with a more pro-Soviet regime. This was justified by the so-called Brezhnev doctrine, asserting the right of Soviet leaders to intervene against other perceived deviant Communist regimes. **November:** In a moderately worded statement, the Chinese foreign ministry called for a resumption of moribund Sino-US diplomatic talks in Warsaw, Poland, with representatives of the administration of newly elected US president Richard Nixon.

1969

February: China abruptly canceled two days before the event scheduled talks with the United States at Warsaw. **March:** Publicized military clashes, with casualties on both sides, began along the Sino-Soviet border. **April:** The first Chinese Communist Party Congress in over a decade legitimated the restoration of order based heavily on military leadership with Defense Minister Lin Biao designated as Mao's successor. **July:** US president Nixon announced in Guam what later became known as the Nixon Doctrine calling for reduced US military involvement throughout Asia and the reassessment of the previous US policy of containment of China. **August:** A major clash along the western part of the Sino-Soviet border reportedly left "several dozen" Chinese soldiers killed. The clash was followed by reports in Western media that Soviet officials were telling various international sources that the USSR planned a military assault on China and that war, including the use of nuclear weapons, seemed likely. **September:** Soviet premier Alexei Kosygin stopped in Beijing's airport, where he held talks with Zhou Enlai. China launched urgent preparations to defend against nuclear war. **October:** China compromised its previous position and agreed to begin border talks with the Soviet Union. Zhou Enlai took the lead in signaling greater moderation and flexibility in Chinese foreign relations through initiatives directed at the Vietnamese Communists, North Korea, Cambodia, Algeria, Yugoslavia, and other countries. **November:** US naval forces ended previously regular patrols in the Taiwan Strait.

1970

January: US-Chinese ambassadorial talks resumed after a hiatus of many years. **March–May:** Cambodia's leader, Prince Norodom Sihanouk, was overthrown by a US-backed military coup. Sihanouk sought refuge and support in China, where he aligned with the Chinese-backed Cambodian resistance led by the Khmer Rouge. US and South Vietnamese forces made a large but temporary invasion of Cambodia. The US-China ambassadorial talks were suspended by China on account of the US-led invasion of Cambodia. Mao Zedong met with Sihanouk and issued a major statement denouncing the United States. **August:** A Central Committee plenary meeting revealed strong leadership differences, foreshadowing purges.

1971

Fourteen countries established official relations with China in 1971. **April:** US ping-pong players received a friendly welcome by senior Chinese officials in Beijing. **April–June:** The US government took steps to ease some travel and trade restrictions involving China. **July:** National Security Advisor Henry Kissinger made a secret visit to Beijing to talk with Chinese leaders, and President Richard Nixon subsequently announced that he would be visiting China. **September:** Defense Minister Lin Biao and his family died in a plane crash in Mongolia after an alleged coup attempt. Lin's allies in the military high command were arrested and purged from the leadership. **Octo-**

ber: The United Nations voted to admit the People's Republic of China; Taiwan walked out. **December:** India and Pakistan fought a brief war in the last stage of the breakaway of East Pakistan and creation of the independent country of Bangladesh; China sided with Pakistan and the Soviet Union sided with India.

1972

Eighteen countries established official relations with China in 1972. **February:** President Nixon visited China for talks with Chinese leaders. The so-called Shanghai Communiqué at the end of his visit set forth common US and Chinese positions on the Soviet threat and marked US willingness to pull back from Taiwan. **September 29:** Japan and China established diplomatic relations.

1973

January 27: The Paris Peace Accords were signed; China supported this international agreement intended to establish peace in Vietnam. Contrary to Chinese wishes, North Vietnam, with greater military support from the Soviet Union, prepared for and eventually launched military attacks against US-supported South Vietnamese forces in violation of the Paris Peace Accords that destroyed the resistance and reunified Vietnam in 1975. **February:** The United States and China agreed to establish official liaison offices in Beijing and Washington, even though the United States continued official ambassadorial relations with Taiwan.

1974

Eight governments established official relations with China in 1974. **January:** China defeated South Vietnamese forces and occupied islands they held in the Paracel Islands in the South China Sea. **April:** Deng Xiaoping delivered a major foreign policy speech at the United Nations, explaining China's so-called Three Worlds theory. **May 31:** Malaysia established diplomatic relations with China, the first noncommunist Southeast Asia country to do so following the United States ending armed operations in Vietnam under terms of the Paris Peace Accords of January 1973. **August:** President Nixon resigned under pressure as a result of his involvement in the Watergate scandal.

1975

January: Under terms of the so-called Jackson-Vanik amendment of the Trade Act of 1974, enacted in January 1975, conditions were established that

China and other Communist countries would have to meet in order to be eligible to receive most favored nation tariff status from the United States. **April:** Khmer Rouge forces were victorious over the US-backed government in Cambodia, and Vietnamese Communists defeated the US-backed government in South Vietnam. **April 5:** Chiang Kai-shek died in Taiwan. **June 9:** The Philippines established official relations with China. **July 1:** Thailand established official relations with China. **December:** President Gerald Ford visited China for talks with Chinese leaders. In addition to the Philippines and Thailand, seven other countries established official relations with China in 1975.

1976

January 8: Zhou Enlai died. **April:** Deng Xiaoping was purged from the Communist leadership. **September 9:** Mao Zedong died. **October:** Four radical Maoists in the Chinese leadership, known as the Gang of Four, were arrested.

1977

July: A Party Central Committee meeting restored Deng Xiaoping to his leadership positions. **August:** US Secretary of State Cyrus Vance visited China in an unsuccessful effort to move forward the normalization of US-China relations.

1978

May: US National Security Advisor Zbigniew Brzezinski visited China and told Chinese leaders of President Jimmy Carter's determination to move forward the normalization of US-China relations. **December:** The United States and China announced a joint communiqué establishing official US relations with China; the United States recognized the People's Republic of China as the government of China and acknowledged that Taiwan was part of China, ended official relations with Taiwan, and ended the US defense treaty with Taiwan. Vietnamese forces backed by the Soviet Union invaded Khmer Rouge–ruled Cambodia, driving out the Khmer Rouge and installing a pro-Vietnamese government.

1979

January 1: The United States officially established normal diplomatic relations with China. A letter by China's National People's Congress to "compatriots" in Taiwan laid out Chinese conditions for future relations with Taiwan. **January 29:** Chinese leader Deng Xiaoping began a seven-day visit to the United States. **February–March:** Chinese armed forces invaded Vietnamese border regions to punish Vietnam for its invasion of Cambodia. After withdrawing its forces in a few weeks, China exerted large-scale military pressure along Vietnam's border for over ten years, continued active support for Khmer Rouge guerrillas resisting the Vietnamese-backed Cambodian regime, and for a time publicly supported prominent Vietnamese officials working for the overthrow of the Vietnamese government. **March:** Chinese authorities closed down the so-called Democracy Wall in Beijing where prodemocracy advocates had been allowed since late 1978 to place posters supporting political reform. **April 10:** The United States approved the Taiwan Relations Act, a law to govern unofficial US relations with Taiwan. China strongly opposed the law. **July 7:** The United States and China signed a trade agreement, a step needed to allow Chinese exports to obtain most favored nation tariff status from the United States. **November:** Sino-Soviet talks to improve relations were carried out at the vice foreign minister level and made little progress. **December:** Soviet forces invaded Afghanistan; China soon began to cooperate clandestinely with the United States in support of Afghan insurgents resisting the Soviet military occupation.

1980

January: Defense Secretary Harold Brown visited China for talks with Chinese leaders focused on dealing with Soviet expansionism in Afghanistan and elsewhere. The United States and China reportedly reached agreement on using sites in China to assist the United States in monitoring Soviet missile tests. China suspended vice foreign minister talks with the Soviet Union. **April:** China formally joined the International Monetary Fund. **May:** China formally joined the World Bank. **September:** The Iran-Iraq war began. This eight-year conflict saw China deny selling arms when in fact it sold several billion dollars' worth of arms to the belligerents.

1981

September 30: China issued a nine-point proposal for economic and cultural exchanges across the Taiwan Strait and direct talks regarding reunification.

1982

January: The Reagan administration announced its decisions against the provision of more advanced jet fighters for Taiwan while continuing US coproduction of less advanced jet fighter aircraft for Taiwan. **August 17:** A communiqué between the United States and China saw the United States agree to gradually diminish its arms sales to Taiwan, and China agree to emphasize a peaceful approach to dealing with Taiwan. US officials provided to Taiwan leaders the "six assurances" regarding continued US support for Taiwan. **October:** Amid Chinese affirmations of a more independent foreign policy with stronger public criticism of the United States, China agreed to resume vice-ministerial talks with the Soviet Union.

1983

Under the leadership of recently appointed US Secretary of State George Shultz, US policy shifted from the previous emphasis of Secretary of State Alexander Haig on meeting Chinese demands on Taiwan and other issues, to a less solicitous and less accommodating US stance toward China while giving much higher priority to US relations with Japan. **June:** Deng Xiaoping announced the "one country, two systems" formula that provided the basis of China's approach to resolving Taiwan's and Hong Kong's reunification with China. **September:** China and the Soviet Union began a second channel of vice foreign minister talks. The new channel covered salient international issues; the old channel continued to cover bilateral relations.

1984

March: Japanese prime minister Yasuhiro Nakasone's visit to China reflected common economic interests and security concerns with checking Soviet power in Asia. **April 26–30:** President Ronald Reagan visited China. **September:** China and Great Britain announced the so-called joint declaration, an agreement governing the transfer of Hong Kong to Chinese sovereignty in 1997. **December:** A Soviet vice premier, the highest-level Soviet official to visit China since 1969, reached agreements in Beijing that modestly advanced Sino-Soviet economic relations but did little to ease major political and security differences.

1985

July: Chinese President Li Xiannian visited the United States, marking the first time a Chinese head of state had visited the United States.

1986

February: China entered the Asian Development Bank (ADB). Taiwan, a founding member of the bank, remained a member but with a name less offensive to Beijing. **July:** China applied for full membership into the General Agreement on Tariffs and Trade (GATT), the predecessor of the World Trade Organization (WTO). **December:** It was later disclosed that China and Saudi Arabia agreed in 1986 to the transfer of three dozen Chinese intermediate-range ballistic missiles to Saudi Arabia.

1987

January: Chinese Party General Secretary and leading reformer Hu Yao-bang was removed from top leadership positions. **September:** Martial law ended in Taiwan.

1988

January 13: President Chiang Ching-kuo died in Taiwan. **March:** The United States and China agreed to the dispatch of US Peace Corps volunteers to China. **May:** Soviet forces began withdrawing from Afghanistan. Vietnam said it was withdrawing troops from Cambodia.

1989

February: Soviet forces completed withdrawal from Afghanistan. **April:** Hu Yaobang, a popular Chinese leader whose reforms had angered Deng Xiaoping and other Communist leaders, died. His death prompted demonstrations of sympathy and in support of reform in Beijing's Tiananmen Square and other parts of China. **May:** Soviet leader Mikhail Gorbachev met senior Chinese leaders in Beijing, making substantial progress in normalizing Sino-Soviet relations. Mass demonstrations in Beijing's Tiananmen Square and other locations continued; Chinese leaders decided to use armed military force to wipe out the demonstrators and crack down on dissent. **June 4:** The military attack on Tiananmen Square shocked American and other international officials and public opinion. **June–July:** While imposing sanctions on China over the Tiananmen crackdown, President George H. W. Bush endeavored to keep open communications with senior Chinese leaders. President Bush sent National Security Advisor Brent Scowcroft and Deputy Secretary of State Lawrence Eagleburger on a secret mission to China. **November:** President Bush vetoed a Chinese student immigration bill, setting the stage for an acrimonious congressional effort to override the veto. **December:** President Bush sent National Security Advisor Scowcroft and Deputy Secretary of State Eagleburger on a second secret mission to China. The visit became known to the media, causing an uproar of US opposition. Chinese president Yang Shangkun, Premier Li Peng, and other senior leaders began using a series of visits to mainly developing countries in order to counter the isolation imposed on China by the United States and Western-aligned countries.

1990

Congressional efforts failed to override President Bush's veto of a Chinese student immigration bill, but bipartisan congressional opposition to the president's policies toward China remained strong. **April:** Premier Li Peng visited Moscow and reached agreement on how to demilitarize the Russian-Chinese border. **July:** Diverging from international sanctions against China after the Tiananmen crackdown, Japan announced resumed loans to China. **July 3:** China and Indonesia normalized diplomatic relations. **July 21:** China and Saudi Arabia established diplomatic relations. **October 3:** China and Singapore established diplomatic relations.

1991

August: Beijing said it would sign the nuclear Non-Proliferation Treaty (NPT). Using a compromise formula, China, Taiwan, and Hong Kong joined the regional economic grouping Asia-Pacific Economic Cooperation (APEC). **October 23:** A peace accord ending the conflict in Cambodia was agreed to by the United States, China, and other concerned powers.

1992

January 24: China and Israel established diplomatic relations. **April:** Great Britain appointed Christopher Patten as Hong Kong governor, beginning a period of much greater British activism to promote democracy in the territory prior to handover to China in 1997. The initiatives under Patten's leadership were strongly resisted by China. **August 24:** China and South Korea established diplomatic relations. **September:** President Bush approved the sale of 150 F-16 jet fighters to Taiwan, representing the most significant US arms sale following the break in official relations in 1979. **October 5:** The United States adopted the Hong Kong Policy Act demonstrating the US government's strong interest in promoting democracy and economic development in Hong Kong. **October 23:** Japan's emperor began a weeklong friendly visit to China, an unprecedented development in the history of the People's Republic of China. **November:** William Clinton won the November presidential election using sharp criticism of China and of President Bush's comparatively moderate policy toward China. **December:** US Special Trade Representative Carla Hills visited Taiwan, the first US cabinet official to do so since the break in official US relations with Taiwan in 1979. A joint communiqué marking Russian president Boris Yeltsin's visit to China called for reducing Russian and Chinese forces along the border to a minimum while enhancing defense ties between the two countries.

1993

May: The Clinton administration issued Executive Order 128590 that established human rights factors as conditions for extension of US most favored nation (MFN) tariff status for the PRC. **July:** The US Congress registered strong opposition to Beijing hosting the 2000 Olympic Games. **August:** The Clinton administration imposed sanctions on China over ballistic missile transfers to Pakistan. **September:** The International Olympic Committee turned down Beijing's bid to host the 2000 games. Chinese commentators blamed the United States for the decision.

1994

May: President Clinton reversed previous policy and announced that the United States would renew most favored nation tariff status for China, even though China had not met human rights requirements set the year before by the US government. **July:** The Association of Southeast Asian Nations (ASEAN) Regional Forum (ARF) was formed; China participated. **September:** The Clinton administration announced the results of a review of Taiwan policy that saw modest upgrades in US interchange with Taiwan.

1995

January: Chinese president and party leader Jiang Zemin issued an eight-point proposal to improve relations and foster reunification with Taiwan. **February:** Chinese military occupation of disputed territory known as Mischief Reef in the contested Spratly Island group in the South China Sea led to public disagreements with Southeast Asian countries, straining relations. **May:** President Clinton bowed to strong congressional and media pressure, reversed existing US policy, and allowed Taiwan president Lee Teng-hui to visit the United States. **June:** Taiwan president Lee visited the United States and gave a speech at his alma mater, Cornell University. China reacted strongly in following months, conducting ballistic missile tests and live-fire military exercises in the Taiwan Strait. **September:** Hillary Clinton gave a strong speech against international authoritarian practices at the UN Fourth Conference on Women in Beijing. **December:** China became a full dialogue partner of the Association for Southeast Asian Nations.

1996

March: The United States dispatched two aircraft carrier battle groups to the Taiwan area in reaction to China's provocative military exercises in the lead-up to the Taiwan presidential election. **April:** President William Clinton met the Japanese prime minister Hashimoto Ryutaro and issued a declaration strengthening the US-Japan alliance. The Shanghai Five, a group involving China, Russia, and three Central Asian states, was formed.

1997

October: Chinese president Jiang Zemin traveled to Washington for a summit meeting with President Clinton. China signed the International Covenant of Economic, Social and Cultural Rights. **November:** Prominent Chinese dissident Wei Jingsheng was allowed to leave China for the United States.

1998

January 1: China and South Africa established diplomatic relations. **March:** Prominent Chinese dissident Wang Dan was allowed to leave China for the United States. **June:** President Clinton traveled to China for a summit meeting with China's president Jiang Zemin. While in China, Clinton affirmed the so-called three nos, that is, the United States does not support Taiwan independence; two Chinas or one China, one Taiwan; and Taiwan's membership in international organizations where statehood is required. **October:** China signed the International Covenant on Civil and Political Rights. The US-led NATO air war against Yugoslavia over the Kosovo situation began, prompting strong protests from China.

1999

April: Chinese premier Zhu Rongji traveled to Washington in what turned out to be an aborted effort to reach agreement with the United States over conditions on China's entry into the World Trade Organization (WTO). Thousands of Falun Gong adherents demonstrated in front the Chinese Communist Party headquarters in Beijing, alarming Chinese leaders and leading to a major Chinese crackdown on the group. **May:** US bombs fell on the Chinese embassy in Belgrade, killing three, wounding twenty, and setting off demonstrations in China that saw the destruction of US diplomatic properties. A US congressional committee known as the Cox Committee issued a long report that was sharply critical of US security measures to protect nuclear weapons and other secrets in the face of Chinese spying efforts. **November:** US and Chinese negotiators agreed on conditions governing Chinese entry into the WTO.

2000

May 20: Democratic Progressive Party leader Chen Shui-bian was inaugurated as Taiwan president amid heightened Chinese worry over perceived Taiwan moves toward greater separation and independence from China. **September:** The US Congress passed legislation granting China permanent normal trade relations status, and ending the annual US government requirement to consider China's trade status.

2001

April 1: A US reconnaissance plane and a Chinese jet fighter collided in international airspace over the South China Sea, prompting a major incident. **April 25:** President George W. Bush said the United States would do "whatever it takes" to help Taiwan to protect itself from Chinese military attack. **June:** The Shanghai Cooperation Organization was formed. The members were China, Russia, Kazakhstan, Uzbekistan, Kyrgyzstan, and Tajikistan. **July:** Beijing was selected as the site for the 2008 Olympic Games. **September:** Chinese leaders reacted with messages of sympathy and support for the United States after the September 11 terrorist attack. **December:** The PRC formally joined the World Trade Organization.

2002

October 25: Chinese President Jiang Zemin met President Bush at his ranch in Crawford, Texas.

2003

August: Six-party talks on North Korean nuclear weapons and related issues began. They involved North Korea, South Korea, China, Japan, Russia, and the United States. **December:** Chinese premier Wen Jiabao's visit to Washington saw President Bush use a public meeting with the premier to register Bush's warning to Taiwan president Chen Shui-bian against further political or other actions by Taiwan that would disrupt stability in the Taiwan Strait.

2004

October: French president Jacques Chirac visited China, emphasizing his view that the European arms embargo against China should be lifted. China strongly supported the French move, which also had the support of Germany. The United States, Japan, and other concerned governments weighed in against the move and the embargo was not lifted.

2005

March: The annual meeting of China's National People's Congress saw consideration and passage of a law barring Taiwan's secession from China. **April:** Anti-Japanese demonstrations in Chinese cities destroyed property and expressed opposition to Japan's bid for a permanent seat on the UN Security Council. **July:** China and other Shanghai Cooperation Organization members called on the United States to set a deadline for withdrawal of US forces from Central Asia. China backed Uzbekistan's decision to close a US base in the country. **August:** Russia and China held a joint military exercise involving over ten thousand military forces that was seen as targeting Japan, Taiwan, and the United States. **September:** Participants in the six-party talks released a joint statement that committed North Korea to abandon its nuclear program and to rejoin the nuclear Non-Proliferation Treaty. **November:** Mongolia's president visited China, signing border and economic agreements. **December:** The first East Asian Leadership Summit meeting was held in Malaysia with all Association of Southeast Asian Nations members as well as China, Japan, South Korea, Australia, New Zealand, and India in attendance. This summit continued to meet annually and eventually saw Russia and the United States join the group. China had favored an East Asian Summit that would exclude Australia, New Zealand, and India and supported expanding the importance of the annual meeting of the ASEAN Plus Three (ASEAN members plus China, Japan, and South Korea) that continued to meet annually since the Asian economic crisis of the late 1990s.

2006

March: President Bush traveled to New Delhi to sign a civil nuclear cooperation agreement that solidified the burgeoning strategic and economic cooperation between the two countries. Russian president Vladimir Putin met with President Hu Jintao for the opening of the "year of Russia" celebrations in China. **April:** Chinese prime minister Wen Jaibao visited the Pacific Islands and pledged billions of dollars of aid in efforts to improve Chinese relations with the countries of the region. **August:** Japan's prime minister Junichiro Koizumi again visited the controversial Yasukuni Shrine. The visits were an annual occurrence during his term in office (2001–6). They prompted outrage from China and South Korea. **October:** China and Japan patched up relations during the visit to China of Prime Minister Shinzo Abe, who in September replaced Prime Minister Koizumi, whose policies had deepened divisions between China and Japan. North Korea conducted its first nuclear weapons test; China and other powers reacted negatively. North Korea later announced it would return to the six-party talks on North Korea's nuclear program. **December:** China and the rest of the United Nations Security Council voted to impose sanctions on Iran in order to curb its nuclear program.

2007

January: China destroyed one of its own satellites using a ground-based medium-range ballistic missile. The United States and other governments protested. **March:** China joined other UN Security Council permanent members in voting for additional sanctions against Iran. **June 7:** China announced establishing diplomatic relations with Costa Rica, breaking Taiwan's hold on official relations with Central American states.

2008

May: Foreign rescue teams arrived to help an area of China devastated by an earthquake; this reportedly marked the first time China had accepted such direct foreign assistance for a domestic disaster. Newly elected Taiwan Ppresident Ma Ying-jeou began sweeping changes designed to reassure China and improve relations across the Taiwan Strait. **July:** World Trade Organization talks on liberalizing trade collapsed when China, India, and the United States failed to resolve differences over protection for agricultural goods in developing countries. **August:** The Olympic Games were held successfully in China. China avoided taking sides in Russia's dispute and military conflict with Georgia. **November:** China announced an economic stimulus plan valued at $586 billion to be spent over two years in order to bolster its economy amid the global recession. China postponed a China-Europe summit on account of French president Nicolas Sarkozy's plan to meet the Dalai Lama. **December:** Chinese navy ships joined international efforts to curb piracy near Somalia.

2009

March: The United States protested publicly about Chinese harassment of US surveillance ships in the South China Sea. China countered the protest by claiming the surveillance violated Chinese rights. **April:** China and France agreed to restore high-level contacts that had been suspended because French president Nicolas Sarkozy met with the Dalai Lama in 2008. **May 25:** North Korea conducted a second nuclear weapon test. China strongly disapproved. **November:** President Barack Obama made his first visit to China. **December:** Chinese premier Wen Jiabao participated in the international climate talks in Copenhagen, Denmark; limited agreements were reached.

2010

January 1: China and the Association for Southeast Asian Nations officially initiated their free-trade agreement. **June:** After protracted negotiations, China joined other permanent members of the UN Security Council in voting for sanctions against Iran on account of its nuclear program. China and Taiwan signed a major trade agreement known as the Economic Cooperation Framework Agreement. **July:** At the United Nations, China refused to support efforts by South Korea and the United States to hold North Korea responsible for the torpedo attack on a South Korean warship in March that killed forty-six South Korean sailors. Also, the Chinese foreign ministry and media complained about plans by the United States and South Korea to hold military exercises in the Yellow Sea. Meanwhile, the Chinese foreign ministry and media reacted negatively to statements made by the United States and other countries at the Association of Southeast Asian Nations Regional Forum meeting in Hanoi on July 23 that were seen as critical of what were portrayed as China's assertive and unilateral policies and practices in the South China Sea. **August 26:** North Korean leader Kim Jong Il began a four-day visit to China, where he received a warm welcome by top-level Chinese leaders. **September 7:** The detention of a Chinese fishing boat by Japanese security forces near the disputed Diaoyutai Islands (known in Japan as the Senkaku Islands) led to the most serious dispute between the two countries in years. **November:** North Korea fired artillery rounds on Yeonpyeong Island, killing four and injuring dozens of South Koreans. China rebuffed US-backed efforts by South Korea in the UN Security Council to condemn North Korea.

2011

January: Chinese president Hu Jintao made an official visit to the United States. **November:** Senior US officials announced the Obama administration's "pivot" to the Asia-Pacific region; later they described it as an American "rebalance" policy, giving new emphasis to Asia-Pacific countries and regional groupings following the pullback of American forces and related economic and diplomatic attention from conflicts in Iraq and Afghanistan. China criticized the new approach.

2012

April: Although China strongly supported the ailing North Korean leader Kim Jong Il prior to his death in 2011 and backed his son, Kim Jong Un, as the new North Korean leader, China also joined other UN Security Council members in condemning Kim Jong Un's attempted satellite launch as a serious violation of previous UN Security Council resolutions. **August 3:** The US State Department released a statement criticizing what it said were China's recent application of coercive security power, economic sanctions, and diplomatic threats short of direct use of military force in order to take full control of Scarborough Shoal in the South China Sea. The statement accused China of blocking access to the shoal by Philippine claimants and taking similarly intimidating actions at odds with Vietnamese claims in the South China Sea. China strongly rejected the US statement. **September:** China and Russia blocked UN Security Council calls for stronger intervention in the conflict in Syria. Efforts by the Japanese government to head off the acquisition of the Senkaku (Diaoyutai) Islands by Japanese rightists by acquiring the islands set off a wave of mass demonstrations surpassing in size and scope previous large demonstrations against foreign targets in China. The demonstrations lasted several days and occurred in 120 cities; burning and looting of Japanese businesses were common; there were incidents of manhandling Japanese and Chinese thought to be sympathetic to Japan. There followed repeated patrols by Chinese coast guard vessels in the heretofore Japanese-controlled waters around the islands, and a few incidents involving military vessels and aircraft. The tense situation around the disputed islands continued into following years. **November:** China hailed the initiation of negotiations for the Regional Comprehensive Economic Partnership (RCEP) involving ASEAN leaders and their six regional free-trade partners (Australia, China, India, South Korea, Japan, and New Zealand). RCEP excluded the United States and was seen to be at odds with the US-backed Trans-Pacific Partnership free-trade agreement.

2013

February: China formally rejected a Philippine proposal to take their dispute regarding sovereignty issues in the South China Sea to the UN for arbitration; several US leaders were reported to support the Philippine proposal. **May:** The Obama administration escalated public charges against Chinese government entities using cyber espionage to steal US and international business secrets in order to advance Chinese economic enterprises. **June 7–8:** President Obama hosted President Xi at a two-day informal summit at an estate in Southern California. **September:** The Silk Road Economic Belt concept was introduced by Chinese president Xi Jinping during his visit to Kazakhstan. **October:** Visiting Indonesia, President Xi proposed building a close-knit China-ASEAN community and offered guidance on constructing a twenty-first-century Maritime Silk Road to promote maritime cooperation. Xi also proposed establishing the Asian Infrastructure Investment Bank (AIIB) to finance infrastructure construction and promote regional interconnectivity and economic integration. **November 23:** China announced establishment of its East China Sea Air Defense Identification Zone (ADIZ) that included areas claimed by Japan, South Korea, and Taiwan. Japan, South Korea, Taiwan, and the United States lodged protests. **December 26**: Japan's prime minister Shinzo Abe visited the Yasukuni Shrine. China and South Korea complained.

2014

March 30: Targeting China, the Philippine government filed a four-thousand-page memorandum on its claims on the South China Sea with an international Law of the Sea arbitration panel affiliated with the Permanent Court of Arbitration in The Hague. **May 2:** China deployed a deep-water drilling rig in disputed waters near the Paracel Islands in the South China Sea, prompting a violent face-off with opposing Vietnamese security forces. **July 1:** An estimated five hundred thousand protesters carrying banners saying "We want real democracy" and "We stand united against China" attended a rally in Hong Kong to mark the anniversary of the handover of the territory from the United Kingdom to China. **July 17:** China removed its offshore oil rig from contested waters near the Paracel Islands, a month before scheduled. **August 1:** China announced the development of the Dongfeng-41, a nuclear missile with multiple independently targetable reentry vehicles with a range of 7,500 miles.

2015

June 24: The US Congress renewed trade promotion authority for the president, which was needed to finalize negotiations on the Trans-Pacific Partnership (TPP). **September 3:** China marked the seventieth anniversary of the Chinese People's War of Resistance against Japanese Aggression and the World Anti-Fascist War over Japan with a large military parade in Tiananmen Square attended by Russian president Vladimir Putin and the president of South Korea but shunned by US and Western leaders. **November 7:** China's Xi Jinping and Taiwan's Ma Ying-jeou met in Singapore, marking the first such meeting since the 1940s.

2016

January: China's rapid and large-scale island building in the disputed South China Sea reached a point where Chinese aircraft landed on and took off from modern runways on the recently constructed outposts. The Asian Infrastructure Investment Bank (AIIB) began operations in Beijing. In a landslide victory, the Democratic Progressive Party (DPP) defeated the party of outgoing president Ma Ying-jeou and won the presidency and an outright legislative majority in Taiwan. **February:** Ministers from the twelve Trans-Pacific Partnership (TPP) member countries signed the final version of the trade agreement in Auckland, New Zealand. **March 2:** The UN Security Council unanimously adopted the toughest sanctions ever imposed on North Korea, in response to its fourth nuclear test and rocket launch. **July 12:** The UNCLOS Arbitral Tribunal at the Permanent Court of Arbitration issued a ruling in the Philippines v. China case over the maritime jurisdiction that went against China's claims in the South China Sea. Beijing responded strongly, seeking to mute international support for the ruling. **September:** China and Russia conducted a joint naval exercise in the South China Sea. The joint drill was described as a concrete action to promote the China-Russia comprehensive strategic partnership. **October:** Deepening a thaw in relations with

China, Philippine president Rodrigo Duterte led a delegation that included more than two hundred business leaders to China. **December 2:** Taiwan president Tsai Ing-wen and President-elect Donald Trump had a telephone conversation, marking the first time a Taiwan president had official contact with a US president or president-elect since the United States broke ties with Taiwan in 1979.

2017

January: Donald Trump became president; he withdrew from the Trans-Pacific Partnership (TPP) economic agreement. **February 9:** Presidents Donald Trump and Xi Jinping talked by phone. Both sides characterized the conversation as "extremely cordial" and Trump confirmed his administration would adhere to the "one-China policy." **February 10–13:** Prime Minister Abe visited President Trump in Washington and at the Trump resort Mar-a-Lago in Florida. They agreed that the friendship between the United States and Japan was "very, very deep" and their alliance was "a cornerstone of peace in the East Asian region." **April 6–7:** President Trump hosted Chinese president Xi Jinping at Mar-a-Lago, Florida. **May 2:** China called for the immediate dismantlement of the THAAD missile defense system in South Korea. May 14–15: China hosted delegates from 138 countries for its Belt and Road Forum in Beijing. **June:** Indian Army troops intercepted and stalled road-laying efforts by Chinese in the Doka La area of the Doklam Plateau, leading to a standoff between the Indian and Chinese forces, which ended in late August. **August 6:** Foreign ministers from ASEAN endorsed a framework with China for the South China Sea code of conduct. **September 3:** North Korea conducted its sixth nuclear weapons test, which it claimed was a successful test of a hydrogen bomb. **November:** Xi Jinping hosted Donald Trump in Beijing during the US president's first visit to Asia.

Note

1. The citations covering 1949–2010 are adapted from Robert Sutter, *Historical Dictionary of Chinese Foreign Policy* (Lanham, MD: Scarecrow Press, 2011), pp. xix–xxxv.

Glossary of Key Terms

AGREED FRAMEWORK. This US–North Korean accord in 1994 was intended to halt North Korea's nuclear weapons program and was welcomed by China.

AKSAI CHIN. To secure its control in Tibet, China in the latter 1950s turned an old caravan trail across the Aksai Chin plateau into a motor road that provided a unique and strategically important western access to Tibet. China announced the road construction activities in 1958 and India protested.

AMBASSADORIAL TALKS. Facing congressional and Allied pressures to meet with PRC officials, Secretary of State John Foster Dulles agreed to low-level ambassadorial talks that began in Geneva in 1955. At the talks, the two sides reached some agreement on repatriating detained personnel, but the agreement was subsequently disputed. The talks were suspended for a time before resuming in Warsaw in 1958 where the two sides met periodically without much result. They were used effectively in 1970 when two sessions were held in Warsaw before being suspended on account of the US military invasion of Cambodia in 1970.

ANTISECESSION LAW. China passed this formal legislation in March 2005 concerning its strong opposition to moves by Taiwan toward greater separation from China.

ASIA-PACIFIC ECONOMIC COOPERATION (APEC). APEC was set up in 1989 as a loose arrangement among twelve countries. The United States helped to engineer a compromise in 1991 allowing China, Taiwan, and Hong Kong to join this regional body that initially focused on economic issues but later broadened its scope to include political, security, and other issues. The membership grew to over twenty countries.

ASIAN ECONOMIC CRISIS. Beginning in 1997, this crisis lasted more than a year and severely damaged the economies of South Korea, Thailand, Indonesia, Malaysia, and several other Asian countries.

BANDUNG CONFERENCE. This conference of Afro-Asian leaders was hosted by Indonesia in April 1955. China was a prominent participant.

BREZHNEV DOCTRINE. Named after Soviet leader Leonid Brezhnev following his orders for Soviet troops to invade Czechoslovakia to topple what was seen as a deviant Communist government in August 1968, this doctrine asserted the Soviet Union had the right to intervene against other such regimes.

BRICS. China collaborated closely with Brazil, India, Russia, and South Africa in this international grouping that developed at the end of the first decade of the twenty-first century.

CHINA LOBBY. These organized American supporters of Chiang Kai-shek and his Republic of China (ROC) government strongly backed Chiang and the ROC and opposed the Chinese Communist Party leaders and policies during the Cold War. Subsequently, journalists discerned the emergence of a new China Lobby, focused on American businesses concerned with developing interests in China.

"CHINA'S PEACEFUL DEVELOPMENT ROAD." A document with this title was issued by the Chinese government in 2005 to underline a strategy that emphasized peaceful development and China's need to foster a cooperative and peaceful international environment.

CODE OF CONDUCT. China and the members of the Association of Southeast Asian Nations (ASEAN) have held off-and-on talks over the past decade involving preparations for formal negotiations to reach a code of conduct to deal with disputes in the South China Sea.

DEMOCRATIC PROGRESSIVE PARTY (DPP). Formed illegally in Taiwan in 1986 by groups of opponents of Nationalist Party rule in Taiwan, the DPP was soon accepted by the liberalizing Nationalist rulers and became the main opposition party. It grew in strength, emphasizing issues including advocacy of greater Taiwan independence from China, anathema to Beijing. Rejecting Beijing's warnings, Taiwan voters elected DPP candidate Chen Shui-bian president in 2000 and reelected Chen in 2004. Amid poor governance, corruption scandals, and seeming voter fatigue with repeated crises with China, the party was overwhelmingly defeated in legislative and presidential elections in 2008. Those elections returned the Nationalist Party to power with a mandate to ease tensions and improve relations with China. However, the voters turned against the Nationalist Party's accommodation of

China and overwhelmingly chose DPP candidates for the president and the legislature in 2016.

DEMOCRACY WALL MOVEMENT. During the reforms that started after Mao's death, Wei Jingsheng and other Chinese dissidents and reformers were allowed to post pro-reform tracts on a wall in Beijing beginning in December 1978. When by March 1979 the posters began to challenge Chinese Communist Party rule, the posters were torn down by the authorities. Wei Jingsheng and other activists were arrested and given long prison sentences.

DIEN BIEN PHU. In this culminating battle of the French war against Communist forces in Indochina, Chinese-supported Vietnamese Communists defeated French forces backed by the United States at this fortress in Indochina on May 7, 1954.

ECONOMIC COOPERATION FRAMEWORK AGREEMENT (ECFA). During the administration of President Ma Ying-jeou of the Republic of China based on Taiwan, representatives from Taiwan and China reached after long negotiations an agreement in 2010 that promised to greatly advance economic and related relations across the Taiwan Strait.

ENGAGEMENT. This term was used by officials in the George H. W. Bush and later US administrations to describe interaction by the United States with China. The term also was used more generally by other developed countries in their interaction with China in the post–Mao Zedong period and by the United States and others in their constructive interaction with other countries, like North Korea.

EP-3 INCIDENT. On April 1, 2001, a Chinese jet fighter crashed with a US reconnaissance plane, an EP-3, in international waters off the China coast. The jet was destroyed and the pilot killed, resulting in a major dispute in US-China relations.

FALUN GONG. The Chinese government's harsh crackdown against this religious movement in China began in 1999 and added to the array of negative features of Chinese government human rights practices as seen by US and other government officials and opinion leaders.

FIVE PRINCIPLES OF PEACEFUL COEXISTENCE. The Five Principles of Peaceful Coexistence were used by China in relations with India, Burma, and some other countries in the 1950s and were later featured when China sought to emphasize moderation and accommodation in Chinese foreign relations. The principles are respect for territorial integrity and sovereignty; nonaggression; noninterference in each other's internal affairs; equality and mutual benefit; and peaceful coexistence.

GANG OF FOUR. These four radical Chinese Communist Party leaders rose to prominent positions as members of the party's Politburo during the Cultural Revolution (1966–76). They were arrested and purged after Mao's death in 1976.

GENEVA ACCORDS. These agreements dealing with issues in Indochina reached at the Geneva Conference in 1954 represented a compromise brokered in part by China that did not satisfy the Vietnamese Communists who sought full control of Vietnam. After the conference, US policy makers worked to support a non-Communist regime in South Vietnam that resisted steps toward reunification set forth in the Geneva Accords.

GLOBAL ECONOMIC CRISIS, 2008–9. The economic chaos and decline in Western and other markets in this crisis impacted world consumption of Chinese consumer and manufactured goods, causing slowdown in China's foreign trade. China enacted a large stimulus package that pumped resources into infrastructure and capacity building as well as supporting greater consumption by Chinese people. China emerged from the crisis more quickly than other large international economies and continued its rapid economic growth without major interruption.

GOGURYEO. In the twenty-first century, China and South Korea developed sharply competing views as to whether this northeast Asian historical kingdom was Chinese or Korean.

GREAT LEAP FORWARD. This utopian mass campaign promoted rapid economic modernization in China in the late 1950s. Its catastrophic results included mass starvation and premature deaths of thirty million people.

GROUP OF SEVEN (G-7). China disapproved of the policies and practices of this organization representing the United States, Japan, Canada, and leading powers of Europe, especially when it isolated China after the Tiananmen crackdown of 1989.

GROUP OF TWENTY (G-20). This forum active since 1999 seeking cooperation and consultation on matters pertaining to the international financial system on the part of nineteen nations and the European Union saw China play an active role after the global economic crisis of 2008–9.

HEGEMONISM. Chinese officials often used this term and the term "hegemony" in the 1970s to refer to the expansionism and encirclement of China by the Soviet Union. After the Tiananmen crackdown, Chinese officials tended to refer to the United States and its policy toward China and others as hegemonism.

INDEPENDENT FOREIGN POLICY. Beginning in 1981 and emerging in 1982, China moved away from its previous emphasis on creating and strengthening a united front with the United States and other powers in opposition to perceived expansionism by the Soviet Union. It adopted a publicly balanced policy of seeking peaceful coexistence with both super-powers. It also gave more attention to Chinese relations with developing countries and with governments and parties in the international communist movement.

JACKSON-VANIK AMENDMENT. This amendment of the US Trade Act of 1974 said that each year the president had to inform Congress of the intention to extend most favored nation (MFN) tariff status to China in re-gard to China's foreign trade with the United States. Congress had ninety days to reject the move by majority vote in both houses of Congress. The president could veto the congressional action and Congress had the option to override the veto by a two-thirds vote in both houses. This annual exercise became a focal point of US debate on China policy after the Tiananmen crackdown until China was granted permanent normal trade relations (PNTR) status in 2000.

JOINT DECLARATION, 1984. Negotiations in 1982–84 between China and Great Britain over the future of Hong Kong led to this agreement calling for the British colony to return to Chinese sovereignty in 1997.

KASHMIR. Dispute over control of Kashmir was the catalyst of repeated military clashes and confrontations between India and Pakistan; China for many years supported Pakistan. As China endeavored to improve relations with India in the post–Cold War period, it adopted a more even-handed position on the dispute.

KHMER ROUGE. China strongly supported the victory of this radical and ruthless insurgency in Cambodia in 1975. After Vietnam, backed by the Soviet Union, toppled the regime in 1978, the Chinese supported the Khmer Rouge insurgents and worked together with the United States and Southeast Asian governments and others to resist and roll back the Vietnamese military occupation.

KOSOVO. China, along with Russia, supported the authoritarian Yugoslavia regime and viewed Kosovo, officially part of Yugoslavia, as an internal affair of the Belgrade government. In October 1998, when Serbian repression of ethnic Albanians, the majority of Kosovo's population, prompted North At-lantic Treaty Organization (NATO) forces, including forces of the United States, to begin an air war against the Belgrade regime, Chinese leaders protested strongly.

KUOMINTANG (KMT). *See* NATIONALIST PARTY.

KYOTO PROTOCOL. At the December 1997 Third Conference of the Parties to the United Nations Framework Convention on Climate Change in Kyoto, Japan, at which the Kyoto Protocol was drafted, China pressed to exempt developing countries from greenhouse gas reduction targets. It favored putting the burden for such reductions on the United States and other developed countries.

LEADING GROUP ON FOREIGN AFFAIRS. This CCP body oversaw foreign policy making and implementation and deliberated choices on major issues for top decision makers in the Chinese leadership. It was established in the 1950s and became moribund during the disruptive Cultural Revolution. It became more important during the post–Cold War period, especially following the retirement of senior leader Deng Xiaoping, who tended to personally dominate foreign policy decision making, as had Mao Zedong.

LIAISON OFFICES. Prior to the establishment of official diplomatic relations between the United States and the People's Republic of China in 1979, the two governments established official liaison offices, headed by senior diplomats, in their respective capitals in 1973.

LONG MARCH. In the mid-1930s, Chinese Communist Party forces retreated from locations in southern China pressured by Nationalist Party forces and moved to more secure locations in northern and western China. Many of the surviving veterans of this retreat rose to prominent positions in China after 1949.

MARKET ECONOMY STATUS. China sought to achieve market economy status under World Trade Organization (WTO) rules. Achieving that goal had several benefits; notably it would help the country avoid punitive anti-dumping measures caused by foreign trade disputes.

MISSILE TECHNOLOGY CONTROL REGIME (MTCR). Under pressure from the United States, China agreed in 1992 and 1994 to abide by the guidelines of this international arms control group that endeavored to restrict the transfer of nuclear-capable missiles and related technology. But Chinese adherence to the regime was disputed by the US government.

MOST FAVORED NATION (MFN) TARIFF STATUS. In the last half of the twentieth century, the United States applied the low tariff rates mandated under this status to most countries. Under US law, certain conditions had to be met for a country like China to receive MFN tariff treatment. Notably, the Jackson-Vanik amendment of the Trade Act of 1974 said that each year the president had to inform Congress of his intention to extend MFN tariff status to China; then Congress had ninety days to reject the move by majority vote in both houses of Congress. The president could veto the congressional action and Congress had the option to override the veto by a two-thirds vote in both houses. The annual MFN extension became very contentious after the Tiananmen crackdown in 1989. The extension process became an annual focal point of congressional-executive wrangling over China policy, with various interest groups, lobbyists, specialists, and others engaging in some-times bitter debates as they anticipated the president's waiver and the con-gressional reaction. US legislation later changed the name of MFN to normal trade relations. After the United States agreed in late 1999 to China joining the World Trade Organization (WTO), US legislation passed granting China permanent normal trade relations (PNTR) in 2000. This ended the occasion for the annual congressional debate over China policy.

MULTIPOLAR WORLD. After the Cold War, China worked with larger countries like Russia, France, and others to seek the creation of a "multipolar world" of several large powers that from China's perspective would provide protection from the dominance and pressure of the United States.

NATIONALIST PARTY. The party traced its origins to Sun Yat-sen. Chiang Kai-shek emerged as party leader after a power struggle following Sun's death in 1925. He remained the dominant leader of the party as it fostered one-party authoritarian rule in China, and in Taiwan after Chiang and his followers retreated there in 1949. With political liberalization in Taiwan beginning in the 1980s, the party competed with a major opposition party, the Democratic Progressive Party (DPP), losing control of the presidency to the DPP in 2000, regaining the presidency in 2008, and losing again in 2016.

NEW SECURITY CONCEPT. Chinese official pronouncements in the late 1990s highlighted this concept, which reworked the Five Principles of Peace-ful Coexistence to develop a more accommodating and reassuring Chinese posture in Asian and world affairs.

NIXON DOCTRINE. President Richard Nixon announced his so-called Nix-on Doctrine while speaking in Guam on July 25, 1969. It called for major reductions in American military involvement in all of Asia.

NON-ALIGNED MOVEMENT (NAM). The ostensible common feature of countries in this movement was that they aligned neither with the US or the USSR. China's relations in the Non-Aligned Movement waxed and waned during the decades of Maoist rule. Chinese officials at times showed modera-tion and flexibility, and at other times they pushed a hard line against the United States, Soviet Union, and other targets that alienated these govern-ments. During the latter decades of the Cold War, China saw its interests as better served in staying on the sidelines and avoiding involvement and pos-sible entanglement in the many issues that divided the states in the move-ment. China upgraded modestly its interaction with the movement in the 1990s when China became an observer state in the Non-Aligned Movement.

NORMAL TRADE RELATIONS (NTR). On a subject important to China, US law in the late 1990s changed the name of most favored nation (MFN) tariff status to normal trade relations.

ONE CHINA. This term was used in discourse by and between officials from the People's Republic of China and officials from the Republic of China on Taiwan, particularly as Taiwan officials beginning in the 1990s repeatedly emphasized Taiwan as an entity distinct and separate from China. In reaction, Chinese officials insisted on the recognition by Taiwan, the United States, and other countries that Taiwan is part of one China. They called this the one-China principle.

ONE CHINA, ONE TAIWAN POLICY. Chinese officials often criticized the United States and other governments for following this policy that they said was designed to treat Taiwan as a country separate from China. The charges often came together with charges that the United States or other governments were following a two-Chinas policy; that is, a policy that treated Beijing and Taipei as representing two separate and distinct Chinese governments.

ONE-CHINA POLICY. Chinese leaders repeatedly called on US officials to affirm support for a one-China policy set forth in the three joint communiqués governing US policy toward China. Among other things, the US policy recognized the People's Republic of China as the legitimate government of China, acknowledged that Taiwan was part of China, and determined that US relations with Taiwan would be unofficial. Despite Chinese objections, US officials often included US adherence to the terms of the Taiwan Relations Act, which Chinese leaders opposed, as part of America's vaguely defined one-China policy.

ONE-CHINA PRINCIPLE. *See* ONE CHINA.

ONE COUNTRY, TWO SYSTEMS. This proposal for reunifying the Republic of China (ROC) government on Taiwan and the People's Republic of China (PRC) was made by Chinese leaders beginning in the 1980s. The proposal said that reunification would not affect Taiwan's political, economic, or social systems. The one country, two systems proposal also was used to govern China's approach to Hong Kong's return to Chinese sovereignty in 1997 and Macao's return to Chinese sovereignty in 1999.

PEACEFUL REUNIFICATION. Post-Mao Chinese leaders highlighted this concept as their goal for Taiwan, as well as Hong Kong and Macao. The new emphasis was a change from past emphasis on the use of Chinese military force to "liberate" Taiwan.

PERMANENT NORMAL TRADE RELATIONS (PNTR). US legislation granted China permanent normal trade relations in 2000. This ended the need for annual presidential requests and congressional reviews regarding China keeping normal trade relations tariff status, previously known as most favored nation (MFN) tariff status.

RED GUARD DIPLOMACY. This term was used in the West and elsewhere in the world to describe the radical behavior of Chinese foreign affairs officials and representatives during the first years of the Cultural Revolution. Chinese diplomats and sympathizers abroad took to the streets to demonstrate loyalty to the strident ideological line coming from Maoist radicals in China. The results damaged Chinese relations with many countries.

REGIONAL COMPREHENSIVE ECONOMIC PARTNERSHIP (RCEP). This proposed regional free-trade agreement involved ASEAN members and their six regional free-trade partners (Australia, China, India, South Korea, Japan, and New Zealand). RCEP excluded the United States and was seen to be at odds with the US-backed Trans-Pacific Partnership (TPP) free-trade agreement.

SIX ASSURANCES. In tandem with US signing of the communiqué of August 17, 1982, with China agreeing to reduce US arms sales to Taiwan, the Ronald Reagan administration assured the government on Taiwan of the following points: The United States would not set a specific date to end arms sales to Taiwan; would not hold talks with China regarding US arms sales to Taiwan; would not play a mediating role between China and Taiwan; would not revise the Taiwan Relations Act; would not change the US position on the sovereignty of Taiwan; and would not pressure Taiwan to negotiate with China.

SIX-PARTY TALKS. A major impasse in late 2002 and early 2003 between the United States and North Korea over North Korea's nuclear weapons program raised the prospect of war. China was instrumental in persuading North Korea to participate first in three-party (China, North Korea, and the United States) talks that soon changed into six-party talks (adding Japan, Russia, and South Korea). The talks reached a series of agreements, but they fell into disuse and became moribund in 2009 as a result of the repeated North Korean nuclear weapons and ballistic missile tests and other provocative international behavior.

TAIWAN INDEPENDENCE MOVEMENT. Opponents of the Nationalist Party government, the Republic of China (ROC) in Taiwan, that was dominated by officials who came from mainland China with Chiang Kai-shek in 1949 often advocated independence for Taiwan. They were harshly suppressed or fled abroad. With greater political liberalization in Taiwan beginning in the 1980s, many oppositionists returned to the island and joined with indigenous oppositionists in the Democratic Progressive Party and more extreme political parties in pushing for greater self-determination and independence for Taiwan. The People's Republic of China (PRC) threatened to use military force to stop them. The influence of those pushing for greater self-determination and independence for Taiwan seemed to wane during the administration of ROC President Ma Ying-jeou, beginning in 2008, that followed a policy of encouraging closer Taiwan ties with the PRC. But it revived somewhat with the election of a Democratic Progressive Party president and legislature in 2016.

TAIWAN RELATIONS ACT (TRA) This legislation was passed by the US Congress in March 1979 and signed by President Jimmy Carter on April 10, 1979. The legislation was proposed by the Carter administration to govern US relations with Taiwan once official US ties were ended in 1979. Congress rewrote the legislation, notably adding or strengthening provisions on US arms sales, opposition to threats and use of force, foreign trade, foreign investment and other economic relations, human rights, and congressional oversight.

THREE CONDITIONS. To normalize official relations with China in 1978, the United States acceded to "three conditions" that China demanded. They were withdrawal of all US military forces from Taiwan, severance of official relations between the United States and Taiwan, and termination of the US-Taiwan security treaty.

THREE NOS. In June 1998, President William Clinton affirmed that the United States does not support Taiwan independence; or two Chinas, or one Taiwan, one China; and that the United States does not believe Taiwan should be a member of an organization where statehood is required. The Clinton administration claimed the statement was a reaffirmation of longstanding US policy, but it was roundly criticized in the Congress and American media as undermining Taiwan.

THREE WORLDS THEORY. China announced the so-called Three Worlds theory during a speech by Deng Xiaoping at the United Nations in 1974. The theory divided the world into three categories of governments: the first were the two superpowers, the United States and the Soviet Union, whose domineering policies and practices were seen as the main cause of international problems; the second were the other developed countries of Europe, North America, and the Asia-Pacific; the third were the vast majority of world countries that made up the developing or third world. China saw the third world as the main source of resistance to the "hegemonism" of the superpowers and sought to align with them and, where possible, countries of the second world in order to resist the superpowers and create a more equitable and just international order.

TRANS-PACIFIC PARTNERSHIP (TPP). This proposed Asia-Pacific free-trade accord was strongly supported by the Barack Obama government. It involved twelve countries seeking to liberalize trade in goods and services in ways that would support the interests of developed countries disadvantaged by perceived unfair practices by state-directed economies, notably China. The Donald Trump administration withdrew from the TPP.

TWO-CHINAS POLICY. The PRC insisted that it represented the only legitimate government of China. The Chinese Nationalists on Taiwan for many years stuck to a similar rigid stance, though they became more flexible in the 1990s under ROC president Lee Teng-hui and were willing to accept the legitimacy of two Chinese governments, one based in Beijing and one based in Taipei. In that context, Beijing worked against what it saw as some countries endeavoring to have official relations with both Beijing and Taipei. It accused them as following a two-Chinas policy.

UNEQUAL TREATIES. Chinese patriots called unequal treaties those treaties imposed on China by the foreign powers in the nineteenth and twentieth centuries. At various times during the Cold War, China accused Western powers and later the Soviet Union of attempting to impose conditions on China reminiscent of the unequal treaties.

WEDGE STRATEGY. Leaders of the United States, notably Secretary of State John Foster Dulles, sought ways to drive a wedge between the Soviet Union and China and thereby weaken the Sino-Soviet alliance. Dulles favored using hard tactics against China, forcing it to make demands that Moscow could not meet and thereby splintering the Sino-Soviet alliance.

WIN-WIN DIPLOMACY. In the twenty-first century, Chinese leaders used the concept of win-win in Chinese foreign interaction. In making a deal with a foreign government or other entity, China averred that it sought a "win" for the foreign government or entity as China worked to assure a "win" for China's win-set focused on strengthening China's wealth and power. The Chinese depicted their approach as reassuring other countries, international groups, or other world actors that were impacted by China's rise. China endeavored to reassure them that Chinese behavior and interaction with them would benefit them as well as China.

YASUKUNI SHRINE. China strongly objected to Japanese leaders visiting this controversial memorial in Tokyo that commemorates Japan's war dead including war criminals convicted of atrocities in China.

Selected Bibliography

Alden, Christopher, Daniel Large, and Ricardo de Oliveria. *China Returns to Africa: A Super-power and a Continent Embrace*. New York: Columbia University Press, 2008.

Alterman, Jon, and John Garver. *The Vital Triangle: China, the United States, and the Middle East*. Washington, DC: Center for Strategic and International Studies, 2008.

Austin, Greg. *Cybersecurity in China*. New York: Springer Publishers, 2018.

Austin, Greg, and Stuart Harris. *Japan and Greater China*. Honolulu: University of Hawaii Press, 2001.

Ba Zhongtan et al. *Zhongguo Guojia Anquan Zhanlue Wenti Yanjiu*. Beijing: Zhongguo Junshi Kexue Chubanshe, 2003.

Bachrack, Stanley D. *The Committee of One Million: "China Lobby" Politics, 1953–1971*. New York: Columbia University Press, 1976.

Bader, Jeffrey. *Obama and China's Rise*. Washington, DC: Brookings Institution Press, 2012.

Barnett, A. Doak. *China and the Major Powers in East Asia*. Washington, DC: Brookings Institution Press, 1977.

———. *Communist China and Asia: Challenge to American Policy*. New York: Harper and Brothers, 1960.

Barnouin, Barbara, and Yu Changgen. *Chinese Foreign Policy during the Cultural Revolution*. New York: Columbia University Press, 1997.

Bergsten, C. Fred, et al. *China's Rise: Challenges and Opportunities*. Washington, DC: Peterson Institute for International Economics and Center for Strategic and International Studies, 2008.

Bhattasali, Deepak, Shantong Li, and Will Martin. *China and the WTO*. Washington, DC: World Bank, 2004.

Blackwill, Robert, and Ashley Tellis. *Council Special Report: Revising U.S. Grand Strategy toward China*. Washington, DC: Council on Foreign Relations, April 2015.

Blasko, Dennis. *The Chinese Army Today*. London: Routledge, 2012.

Brautigam, Deborah. *The Dragon's Gift*. New York: Oxford University Press, 2009.

Bush, Richard. *Hong Kong in the Shadow of China*. Washington, DC: Brookings Institution Press, 2016.

———. *The Perils of Proximity: China-Japan Security Relations*. Washington, DC: Brookings Institution Press, 2010.

———. *Uncharted Strait: The Future of China-Taiwan Relations*. Washington, DC: Brookings Institution Press, 2012.

———. *Untying the Knot: Making Peace in the Taiwan Strait*. Washington, DC: Brookings Institution Press, 2005.

351

Bush, Richard, and Michael O'Hanlon. *A War Like No Other: The Truth about China's Challenge to America*. Hoboken, NJ: John Wiley & Sons, 2007.

Cai, Peter. *Understanding the Belt and Road Initiative*. Sydney: Lowy Institute, March 2017.

Campbell, Kurt. *The Pivot*. New York: Twelve Hachette Book Group, 2016.

Carlson, Allen. *Unifying China, Integrating with the World: Securing Chinese Sovereignty in the Reform Era*. Stanford, CA: Stanford University Press, 2005.

Carlson, Allen, and Ren Xiao. *New Frontiers in China's Foreign Relations*. Lanham, MD: Lexington, 2011.

Chanda, Nayan. *Brother Enemy: The War after the War*. New York: Harcourt Brace Jovanovich, 1986.

Chang, Gordon. *Fateful Ties: A History of America's Preoccupation with China*. Cambridge, MA: Harvard University Press, 2015.

———. *Friends and Enemies: The United States, China, and the Soviet Union, 1948–1972*. Stanford, CA: Stanford University Press, 1990.

Chase, Michael, et al. *Russia-China Relations: Assessing Common Ground and Strategic Fault Lines*. Seattle: National Bureau of Asian Research, 2017.

Chen Jian. *China's Road to the Korean War*. New York: Columbia University Press, 1994.

———. *Mao's China and the Cold War*. Chapel Hill: University of North Carolina Press, 2001.

Chi, Su. *Taiwan's Relations with Mainland China: A Tail Wagging Two Dogs*. New York: Routledge, 2008.

Christensen, Thomas. *The China Challenge: Shaping the Choices of a Rising Power*. New York: W. W. Norton, 2015.

———. *Useful Adversaries: Grand Strategy, Domestic Mobilization, and Sino-American Conflicts, 1949–1958*. Princeton, NJ: Princeton University Press, 1996.

Chu Shulong. "Quanmian jianshe xiaokang shehui shiqi de zhongguo waijiao zhan-lue." *Shijie Jingji yu Zhengzhi* 8 (August 2003).

Chung, Jae Ho. *Between Ally and Partner*. New York: Columbia University Press, 2007.

Clough, Ralph. *Cooperation or Conflict in the Taiwan Strait?* Lanham, MD: Rowman & Littlefield, 1999.

———. *Island China*. Cambridge, MA: Harvard University Press, 1978.

Cohen, Jerome, and Hungdah Chiu. *People's China and International Law*. Princeton, NJ: Princeton University Press, 1974.

Cohen, Warren I. *America's Response to China: A History of Sino-American Relations*. New York: Columbia University Press, 2010.

Cole, Bernard. *Great Wall at Sea*. Annapolis, MD: Naval Institute, 2010.

Council on Foreign Relations. *More Than Humanitarianism: A Strategic U.S. Approach toward Africa*. Independent Task Force Report 56. New York: Council on Foreign Relations, January 2006.

———. *U.S.-China Relations: An Affirmative Agenda, a Responsible Course*. New York: Council on Foreign Relations, 2007.

Cui Liru. "A Multipolar World in the Globalization Era." *Contemporary International Relations* (Beijing) 20, Special Issue (September 2010): 1–11.

Cumings, Bruce. *The Origins of the Korean War*. Princeton, NJ: Princeton University Press, 1990.

Dahlman, Carl. *The World under Pressure: How China and India Are Influencing the Global Economy and Environment*. Stanford, CA: Stanford University Press, 2011.

Dai Bingguo. "Stick to the Path of Peaceful Development." *Beijing Review* 51 (December 23, 2010). http://www.beijingreview.com.cn.

Deng Hao. "China's Relations with Central Asian Countries: Retrospect and Prospect." *Guoji Wenti Yanjiu* (Beijing), May 13, 2002, 8–12.

Deng Xiaoping. *Selected Works of Deng Xiaoping, 1982–1992*. Beijing: Foreign Languages Press, 1994.

Deng, Yong. *China's Struggle for Status: The Realignment of International Relations*. New York: Cambridge University Press, 2008.

Deng, Yong, and Thomas Moore. "China Views Globalization: Toward a New Great-Power Politics." *Washington Quarterly* 27, no. 3 (Summer 2004): 117–36.

Deng, Yong, and Fei-Ling Wang, eds. *China Rising: Power and Motivation in Chinese Foreign Policy*. Lanham, MD: Rowman & Littlefield, 2005.

Dittmer, Lowell. *China's Asia: Triangular Dynamics since the Cold War*. Lanham, MD: Rowman & Littlefield, 2018.

———. *Sino-Soviet Normalization and Its International Implications, 1945–1990*. Seattle: University of Washington Press, 1992.

Dittmer, Lowell, and George T. Yu, eds. *China, the Developing World and the New Global Dynamic*. Boulder, CO: Lynne Rienner, 2010.

Dollar, David. *China's Investment in Latin America*. Washington, DC: Brookings Institution Press, 2017.

Downs, Erica. *Brookings Foreign Policy Studies Energy Security Series: China*. Washington, DC: Brookings Institution Press, 2006.

———. *Inside China, Inc: China Development Bank's Cross-Border Energy Deals*. John Thornton China Center Monograph Series 3. Washington, DC: Brookings Institution Press, March 2011.

Dreyer, June Teufel. *Middle Kingdom and Empire of the Rising Sun*. New York: Oxford University Press, 2016.

Dulles, Foster Rhea. *American Policy toward Communist China, 1949–1969*. New York: Thomas Y. Crowell, 1972.

Economy, Elizabeth. *The River Runs Black*. Ithaca, NY: Cornell University Press, 2004.

Economy, Elizabeth, and Michael Levi. *By All Means Necessary*. New York: Oxford University Press, 2013.

Economy, Elizabeth, and Michel Oksenberg. *China Joins the World*. New York: Council on Foreign Relations, 1999.

Eisenman, Joshua, and Eric Heginbotham. *China Steps Out*. New York: Routledge, 2018.

Eisenman, Joshua, Eric Heginbotham, and Derek Mitchell, eds. *China and the Developing World*. Armonk, NY: M. E. Sharpe, 2007.

Ellis, R. Evan. *China in Latin America*. Boulder, CO: Lynne Rienner, 2009.

Fang Ning, Wang Xiaodong, and Qiao Liang. *Quanqihua Yinying xia de Zhongguo Zhilu*. Beijing: Chinese Academy of Social Sciences, 1999.

Fairbank, John. *The United States and China*. Cambridge, MA: Harvard University Press, 1983.

Fairbank, John, and Merle Goldman. *China: A History*. Cambridge, MA: Harvard University Press, 1999.

Fang Ning, Wang Xiaodong, and Qiao Liang. *Quanqihua Yinying xia de Zhongguo Zhilu*. Beijing: Chinese Academy of Social Sciences, 1999.

Fewsmith, Joseph. *China since Tiananmen*. New York: Cambridge University Press, 2012.

Finkelstein, David. *China Reconsiders Its National Security: The Great Peace and Development Debate of 1999*. Alexandria, VA: CNA, December 2000.

Foot, Rosemary. "Chinese Strategies in a U.S.-Hegemonic Global Order: Accommodating and Hedging." *International Affairs* 82, no. 1 (2006): 77–94.

———. *The Practice of Power: U.S. Relations with China since 1949*. New York: Oxford University Press, 1997.

Foot, Rosemary, and Andrew Walter. *China, the United States and the Global Order*. New York: Cambridge University Press, 2011.

Fravel, M. Taylor. *Strong Borders, Secure Nation: Cooperation and Conflict in China's Territorial Disputes*. Princeton, NJ: Princeton University Press, 2008.

Fravel, M. Taylor, and Evan Medeiros. "China's Search for Assured Retaliation." *International Security* 35, no. 2 (Fall 2010): 48–87.

French, Howard. *China's Second Continent*. New York: Vintage, 2014.

Friedberg, Aaron. *A Contest for Supremacy: China, America, and the Struggle for Mastery in Asia*. New York: W. W. Norton, 2011.

———. *Beyond Air-Sea Battle: The Debate over US Military Strategy in Asia*. Adelphi Paper 444. London: International Institute for Strategic Studies, 2014.

Frost, Ellen. *Rival Regionalisms and the Regional Order*. Seattle: National Bureau of Asian Research, December 2014.

Fu Mengzi. "China and Peace Building on the Korean Peninsula." *Xiandai guoji guanxi* (Beijing) 17 (July 2007): 27–40.

———. "Sino-US Relations." *Xiandai guoji guanxi* (Beijing) 17 (January 2007): 32–46.

Gallagher, Kevin, and Roberto Porzecanski. *The Dragon in the Room: China and the Future of Latin American Industrialization*. Stanford, CA: Stanford University Press, 2010.

Gao Lianfu. "East Asia Regional Cooperation Entered the Stage of Institutionalization." *Taipingyang Xuebao* 2 (2001).

Gao Zugui. "An Analysis of Sino-U.S. Strategic Relations on the 'Western Front.'" *Xiandai Guoji Guanxi* 12 (December 20, 2004).

Garnett, Sherman, ed. *Rapprochement or Rivalry? Russia-China Relations in a Changing Asia*. Washington, DC: Carnegie Endowment for International Peace, 2000.

Garrison, Jean. *Making China Policy: From Nixon to G. W. Bush*. Boulder, CO: Lynne Rienner, 2005.

Garver, John. *China and Iran: Ancient Partners in a Post-Imperial World*. Seattle: University of Washington Press, 2006.

———. *China's Quest*. New York: Oxford University Press, 2016.

———. *Face-Off*. Seattle: University of Washington Press, 1997.

———. *Foreign Relations of the People's Republic of China*. Englewood Cliffs, NJ: Prentice Hall, 1993.

———. "Is China Playing a Dual Game in Iran?" *Washington Quarterly* 34, no. 1 (Winter 2011): 75–88.

———. *Protracted Contest: Sino-Indian Rivalry in the 20th Century*. Seattle: University of Washington Press, 2001.

Gill, Bates. *Rising Star: China's New Security Diplomacy*. Washington, DC: Brookings Institution Press, 2007.

Gill, Bates, and Melissa Murphy. "China's Evolving Approach to Counterterrorism." *Harvard Asia Quarterly*, Winter/Spring 2005, 21–32.

Gill, Bates, and Matthew Oresman. *China's New Journey to the West*. Washington, DC: Center for Strategic and International Studies, August 2003.

Glaser, Bonnie, and Evan Medeiros. "The Changing Ecology of Foreign Policy Making in China: The Ascension and Demise of the Theory of 'Peaceful Rise.'" *China Quarterly* 190 (2007): 291–310.

Goh, Evelyn. *Constructing the US Rapprochement with China, 1961–1974: From "Red Menace" to "Tacit Ally."* Cambridge: Cambridge University Press, 2005.

———. *Meeting the China Challenge: The United States in Southeast Asian Regional Security Strategies*. Policy Studies 21. Washington, DC: East-West Center, 2006.

———. *The Struggle for Order: Hegemony, Hierarchy and Transition in Post–Cold War East Asia*. Oxford: Oxford University Press, 2013.

Goh, Evelyn, ed. *Rising China's Influence in Developing Asia*. New York: Oxford University Press, 2016.

Goldstein, Avery. *Rising to the Challenge: China's Grand Strategy and International Security*. Stanford, CA: Stanford University Press, 2005.

Goldstein, Lyle. *Meeting China Halfway*. Washington, DC: Georgetown University Press, 2015.

Goldstein, Steven. *China and Taiwan*. Cambridge: Polity Press, 2015.

———. *Taiwan Faces the Twenty-First Century*. New York: Foreign Policy Association, 1997.

Goldstein, Steven, and Julian Chang, eds. *Presidential Politics in Taiwan: The Administration of Chen Shui-bian*. Norwalk, CT: Eastbridge, 2008.

Gong Li. "Deng Xiaoping Dui Mei Zhengce Sixing yu Zhong-Mei Guanxi." *Guoji Wenti Yanjiu* 6 (2004): 13–17.

———. *Kuayue: 1969–1979 nian Zhong Mei guanxi de yanbian* [Across the chasm: The evolution of China-US relations, 1969–1979]. Henan: Henan People's Press, 1992.

————. "The Official Perspective: What Chinese Government Officials Think of America." In *Chinese Images of the United States*, edited by Carola McGiffert, 25–32. Washington, DC: CSIS, 2006.

Gottlieb, Thomas. *Chinese Foreign Policy Factionalism and the Origins of the Strategic Triangle.* Santa Monica, CA: RAND Corporation, 1977.

Green, Michael. *By More Than Providence.* New York: Columbia University Press, 2017.

————. *Japan's Reluctant Realism.* New York: Palgrave, 2003.

Gries, Peter. *China's New Nationalism.* Berkeley: University of California Press, 2004.

Guoji Zhanlue yu Anquan Xingshi Pinggu 2001–2002. Beijing: Shishi Chubanshe, 2002.

Guoji Zhanlue yu Anquan Xingshi Pinggu 2003–2004. Beijing: Shishi Chubanshe, 2004.

Guoji Zhanlue yu Anquan Xingshi Pinggu 2004–2005. Beijing: Shishi Chubanshe, 2005.

Gurtov, Melvin, and Byong-Moo Hwang. *China under Threat.* Baltimore: Johns Hopkins University Press, 1981.

Halper, Stefan. *The Beijing Consensus.* New York: Basic Books, 2010.

Hao, Yufan, and Lin Su, eds. *Chinese Foreign Policy Making: Societal Force and Chinese American Policy.* Burlington, VT: Ashgate, 2005.

Harding, Harry. *China's Foreign Relations in the 1980s.* New Haven, CT: Yale University Press, 1984.

————. *China's Second Revolution.* Washington, DC: Brookings Institution Press, 1987.

————. *A Fragile Relationship: The U.S. and China since 1972.* Washington, DC: Brookings Institution Press, 1992.

————. "Has U.S. China Policy Failed?" *Washington Quarterly* 38, no. 3 (2015): pp. 95–122.

Harris, Lillian Craig, and Robert Worden, eds. *China and the Third World.* Dover, MA: Auburn House, 1986.

Heginbotham, Eric, and George Gilboy. *Chinese and Indian Strategic Behavior.* New York: Cambridge University Press, 2012.

Heginbotham, Eric, et al. *China's Evolving Nuclear Deterrent.* Santa Monica, CA: RAND Corporation, 2017.

Herberg, Mikkal, and Kenneth Lieberthal. "China's Search for Energy Security: Implications for U.S. Policy." *NBR Analysis* 17, no. 1 (April 2006): 1–54.

Hinton, Harold. *China's Turbulent Quest.* New York: Macmillan, 1972.

————. *Communist China in World Politics.* Boston: Houghton Mifflin, 1966.

Holslag, Jonathan. *China and India: Prospects for Peace.* New York: Columbia University Press, 2010.

Horsburgh, Nicola. *China and Global Nuclear Order.* New York: Oxford University Press, 2015.

Hou Yousheng. "Oumeny yu Meiguo dai Hua zhanlue bijiao." *Xiandai guoji guanxi* (Beijing) 8 (August 2006): 1–6.

Hou Zhengdo. "Guanyu Zhong Ou zhanlue guanxi jige xiangfa." *Guoji Wenti Yanjiu* (Beijing) 2 (April 2005).

Hu Angang. *Daguo Zhanlue Liyi yu Shiming.* Liaoning: Liaoning Renmin Chubanshe, 2000.

Hu Angang and Meng Honghua. "Zhongmeiriieying youxing zhanlue ziyuan bijiao." *Zhanlue yu Guanli* 2 (2002): 26–41.

————, eds. *Jiedu Meiguo Dazhanlue.* Hangzhou: Zhejiang Renmin Chubanshe, 2003.

Hu Guocheng. "Chinese Images of the United States: A Historical Review." In *Chinese Images of the United States*, edited by Carola McGiffert, 3–8. Washington, DC: CSIS, 2006.

Hu, Sheng. *Imperialism and Chinese Politics.* Beijing: Foreign Language Press, 1985.

Huang Renwei. *Zhongguo Jueji de Shijian he Kongjian.* Shanghai: Shanghai Academy of Social Sciences, 2002.

Huchet, Jean-Francois. "Emergence of a Pragmatic India-China Relationship: Between Geostrategic Rivalry and Economic Competition." *China Perspectives* 3 (2008): 50–67.

Hughes, Christopher. *Chinese Nationalism in a Global Era.* London: Routledge, 2006.

Hunt, Michael H. *The Genesis of Chinese Communist Foreign Policy.* New York: Columbia University Press, 1996.

Institute for International and Strategic Studies. *China's Grand Strategy: A Kinder, Gentler Turn.* London: Institute for International and Strategic Studies, November 2004.

Institute of Strategic Studies, CCP Central Party School. *Zhongguo Heping Jueji Xindaolu.* Beijing: Zhonggong Zhongyang Dangxiao Chubanshe, 2004.

International Crisis Group. *China and North Korea: Comrades Forever?* Asia Report 112. Brussels: International Crisis Group, February 1, 2006.

———. *China's Growing Role in UN Peacekeeping.* Asia Report 166. Brussels: International Crisis Group, April 17, 2009.

———. *China's Myanmar Strategy.* Asia Briefing No.112. Brussels: International Crisis Group, September 21, 2010.

———. *China's Thirst for Oil.* Asia Report No. 153-9. Brussels: International Crisis Group, June 2008.

———. *China-Taiwan: Uneasy Détente.* Asia Briefing 42. Brussels: International Crisis Group, September 21, 2005.

———. *North Korea's Nuclear Test: The Fallout.* Asia Briefing 56. Brussels: International Crisis Group, November 13, 2006.

Jacobson, Linda, and Dean Knox. *New Foreign Policy Actors in China.* SIPRI Policy Paper 26. Stockholm: Stockholm International Peace Research Institute, September 2010.

Ji Zhiye. "Strategic Prospects for Russia." *Contemporary International Relations* (Beijing) 20, no. 5 (September/October 2010): 1–16.

Jia Qingguo. "Peaceful Development: China's Policy of Reassurance." *Australian Journal of International Affairs* 59, no. 4 (December 2005): 493–507.

Jiang Changbin and Robert S. Ross, eds. *1955–1971 Nian de Zhong Mei Guanxi—Huanhe Zhigian: Lengzhan Chongtu yu Keshi de Cai Tantao* [U.S.-China relations 1955–1971—before détente: An examination of Cold War conflict and restraint]. Beijing: Shijie Zhishi Chubanshe, 1998.

———. *Cong Duizhi zouxiang Huanhe: Lengzhan Shiqi Zhong Mei Guanxi zai Tantao* [From confrontation toward détente: A reexamination of U.S.-China relations during the Cold War]. Beijing: Shijie Zhishi Chubanshe, 2000.

Johnson, Christopher. *Decoding China's Emerging "Great Power" Strategy in Asia.* Washington, DC: Center for Strategic and International Studies, June 2014.

Johnston, Alastair Iain. "How New and Assertive Is China's New Assertiveness?" *International Security* 37, no. 4 (Spring 2013): pp. 7–48.

———. *Social States: China in International Institutions, 1980–2000.* Princeton, NJ: Princeton University Press, 2008.

Johnston, Alastair Iain, and Robert S. Ross, eds. *New Directions in the Study of China's Foreign Policy.* Stanford, CA: Stanford University Press, 2006.

Kan, Shirley. *China and Proliferation of Weapons of Mass Destruction and Missiles: Policy Issues.* Report RL31555. Washington, DC: Library of Congress, Congressional Research Service, January 31, 2006.

Kang, David. *American Grand Strategy and East Asian Security.* New York: Cambridge University Press, 2017.

———. *China Rising: Peace, Power, and Order in East Asia.* New York: Columbia University Press, 2007.

———. "Getting Asia Wrong: The Need for New Analytical Frameworks." *International Security* 27, no. 4 (2003): 57–85.

Keefe, John. *Anatomy of the EP-3 Incident.* Alexandria, VA: Center for Naval Analysis, January 2002.

Keller, William, and Thomas Rawski, eds. *China's Rise and the Balance of Influence in Asia.* Pittsburgh: University of Pittsburgh Press, 2007.

Kent, Ann. *Beyond Compliance: China, International Organizations, and Global Security.* Stanford, CA: Stanford University Press, 2007.

Kim, Samuel. *China, the United Nations and World Order.* Princeton, NJ: Princeton University Press, 1979.

———. *The Third World in Chinese World Policy.* Princeton, NJ: Center of International Studies, Woodrow Wilson School of Public and International Affairs, Princeton University, 1989.

———. *The Two Koreas and the Great Powers.* New York: Cambridge University Press, 2006.

———, ed. *China and the World: New Directions in Chinese Foreign Relations.* Boulder, CO: Westview, 1989.

Kissinger, Henry. *On China.* New York: Penguin, 2011.

———. *White House Years.* Boston: Little, Brown, 1979.

———. *Years of Upheaval.* Boston: Little, Brown, 1983.

Kleine-Ahlbrandt, Stephanie, and Andrew Small. "China's New Dictatorship Diplomacy." *Foreign Affairs* 87, no. 1 (January–February 2008): 38–56.

Koen, Ross Y. *The China Lobby in American Politics.* New York: Harper and Row, 1974.

Kroeber, Arthur. *China's Economy: What Everyone Needs to Know.* New York: Oxford University Press, 2016.

Kurlantzick, Joshua. *Charm Offensive: How China's Soft Power Is Transforming the World.* New Haven, CT: Yale University Press, 2007.

Lall, Arthur. *How Communist China Negotiates.* New York: Columbia University Press, 1968.

Lampton, David M. *Following the Leader: Ruling China from Deng Xiaoping to Xi Jinping.* Berkeley: University of California Press, 2014.

———. *Same Bed, Different Dreams.* Berkeley: University of California Press, 2001.

———. *The Three Faces of Chinese Power: Might, Money, and Minds.* Berkeley: University of California Press, 2008.

———. ed. *The Making of Chinese Foreign and Security Policy in the Era of Reform, 1978–2000.* Stanford, CA: Stanford University Press, 2001.

Lancaster, Carol. *The Chinese Aid System.* Washington, DC: Center for Global Development, June 2007.

Lardy, Nicholas. *Integrating China in the Global Economy.* Washington, DC: Brookings Institution Press, 2002.

Larkin, Bruce. *China and Africa, 1949–1970.* Berkeley: University of California Press, 1971.

Lee, David Tawei. *The Making of the Taiwan Relations Act.* New York: Oxford University Press, 2000.

Lee Teng-hui. *Creating the Future: Towards a New Era for the Chinese People* (a compilation of speeches and remarks by President Lee Teng-hui). Taipei: Government Information Office, 1992.

Leverett, Flynt, and Jeffrey Bader. "Managing China-U.S. Energy Competition in the Middle East." *Washington Quarterly* 29, no. 1 (Winter 2005/2006): 187–201.

Li, Cheng, ed. *China's Changing Political Landscape: Prospects for Democracy.* Washington, DC: Brookings Institution Press, 2008.

———. *China's Leaders: The New Generation.* Lanham, MD: Rowman & Littlefield, 2001.

Li Li. "India's Engagement with East Asia and the China Factor." *Contemporary International Relations* (Beijing) 20, no. 5 (September/October 2010): 97–109.

Li Shaoxian. "China-Russia Bond." *Xiandai guoji guanxi* (Beijing) 17 (January 2007): 5–21.

Li Shaoxian and Tang Zhichao. "China and the Middle East." *Xiandai guoji guanxi* (Beijing) 17 (January 2007): 22–31.

Li Shaoxian and Wei Liang. "New Complexities in the Middle East since 9.11." *Contemporary International Relations* (Beijing) 20, Special Issue (September 2010): 22–32.

Li Shengming and Wang Yizhou, eds. *Nian quanqiu Zhengzhi yu Anquan Baogao.* Beijing: Shehui Kexue Wenxian, 2003.

Lieberthal, Kenneth, and Mikkal Herberg. "China's Search for Energy Security: Implications for U.S. Policy." *NBR Analysis* 17, no. 1 (April 2006): 1–54.

Lieberthal, Kenneth, and David Sandalow. *Overcoming Obstacles to US-China Cooperation on Climate Change.* John L. Thornton China Center Monograph Series, no. 1. Washington, DC: Brookings Institution Press, January 2009.

Lieberthal, Kenneth, and Wang Jisi. *Addressing U.S.-China Strategic Distrust.* Brookings Institution Press, March 2012.

Liu Baolai. "Broad Prospects for China-Arab Relations." *Foreign Affairs Journal* (Beijing) 79 (March 2006): 38–44.

Liu Jianfei. *Meiguo yu Fangong Zhuyi: Lun Meiguo Dui Shehui Zhuyi Guojia de Yishixingtai Wijiao*. Beijing: Chinese Social Science Press, 2001.

Liu Ming. "China and the North Korean Crisis." *Pacific Affairs* 76, no. 3 (Fall 2003): 347–73.

Liu Tainchun. *Riben Dui Hua Zhengce yu Zhongri Guanxi*. Beijing: Renmin Chubanshe, 2004.

Lo, Bobo. *A Wary Embrace*. Sydney: Lowy Institute, 2017.

———. *Axis of Convenience: Moscow, Beijing, and the New Geopolitics*. Washington, DC: Brookings Institution Press, 2008.

Lou Yaoliang. *Diyuan Zhengzhi yu Zhongguo Guofang Zhanlue*. Tianjin: Tianjin Press, 2002.

Lu Fanghua. "An Analysis of U.S. Involvement in the South China Sea." *Contemporary International Relations* (Beijing) 20, no. 6 (November/December 2010): 132–41.

Lu Gang and Guo Xuetang. *Zhongguo Weixie Shui: Jiedu "Zhong Weixie Lun."* Shanghai: Xueling Chubanshe, 2004.

Lu Ning. *The Dynamics of Foreign Policy Decision Making in China*. Boulder, CO: Westview, 1997.

Lum, Thomas, coord. *Comparing Global Influence: China's and U.S. Diplomacy, Foreign Aid, Trade, and Investment in the Developing World*. Report RL34620. Washington, DC: Library of Congress, Congressional Research Service, August 15, 2008.

Luthi, Lorenz M. *The Sino-Soviet Split: Cold War in the Communist World*. Princeton, NJ: Princeton University Press, 2008.

Ma Jiali. "Emerging Sino-Indian Relations." *Xiandai guoji guanxi* (Beijing) 17 (May 2007): 71–80.

Ma Licheng. "Duiri Guanxi Xinsiwei." *Zhanlue yu Guanli* 6 (2002): 41–47.

MacFarquhar, Roderick, and John K. Fairbank, eds. *The Cambridge History of China*, Vol. 14: *The People's Republic, Part 1: The Emergence of Revolutionary China, 1949–1965*. Cambridge: Cambridge University Press, 1987.

———. *The Cambridge History of China*, Vol. 15: *The People's Republic, Part 2: Revolutions within the Chinese Revolution, 1966–1982*. Cambridge: Cambridge University Press, 1991.

MacFarquhar, Roderick, and Michael Schoenhals. *Mao's Last Revolution*. Cambridge, MA: Harvard University Press, 2006.

Mann, Jim. *About Face: A History of America's Curious Relationship with China, from Nixon to Clinton*. New York: Knopf, 1999.

McGiffert, Carola, ed. *Chinese Images of the United States*. Washington, DC: CSIS, 2006.

McGregor, Richard. *Asia's Reckoning*. New York: Penguin Random House, 2017.

Medeiros, Evan. "Is Beijing Ready for Global Leadership?" *Current History* 108, no. 719 (September 2009): 250–56.

———, ed. *Pacific Currents: The Responses of U.S. Allies and Security Partners in East Asia to China's Rise*. Santa Monica, CA: RAND Corporation, 2008.

———. *Reluctant Restraint: The Evolution of China's Nonproliferation Policies and Practices, 1980–2004*. Stanford, CA: Stanford University Press, 2007.

———. "Strategic Hedging and the Future of Asia-Pacific Stability." *Washington Quarterly* 29, no. 1 (2005–2006): 145–67.

Medeiros, Evan, and R. Taylor Fravel. "China's New Diplomacy." *Foreign Affairs* 82, no. 6 (November–December 2003): 22–35.

Mei Zhaorong. "Sino-European Relations in Retrospect and Prospect." *Foreign Affairs Journal* (Beijing) 79 (March 2006): 17–27.

Men Honghua. *China's Grand Strategy: A Framework Analysis*. Beijing: Beijing Daxue Chubanshe, 2005.

Menon, Rajan. "The Strategic Convergence between Russia and China." *Survival* 39, no. 2 (Summer 1997): 101–25.

Miller, Alice Lyman, and Richard Wich. *Becoming Asia*. Stanford, CA: Stanford University Press, 2011.

Mitter, Rana. *A Bitter Revolution: China's Struggle with the Modern World*. New York: Oxford University Press, 2004.

Mochizuki, Mike, and Deepa Ollapally. *Energy Security in Asia and Eurasia*. New York: Routledge, 2017.

Morck, Randall, Bernard Yeung, and Minyuan Zhao. *Perspectives on China's Outward Foreign Direct Investment.* Working Paper. Washington, DC: International Monetary Fund, August 2007.

Morrison, Wayne. *China's Economic Conditions.* Report RL33534. Washington, DC: Library of Congress, Congressional Research Service, 2012.

———. *China's Economic Rise.* Report RL33534. Washington, DC: Library of Congress, Congressional Research Service, 2017.

———. *China-U.S. Trade Issues.* Report 33536. Washington, DC: Library of Congress, Congressional Research Service, 2017.

Murray, William S. "Revisiting Taiwan's Defense Strategy." *Naval War College Review*, Summer 2008, 13–38.

Nathan, Andrew, and Robert Ross. *The Great Wall and Empty Fortress.* New York: W. W. Norton, 1997.

Nathan, Andrew, and Andrew Scobell. *China's Search for Security.* New York: Columbia University Press, 2012.

Naughton, Barry. *The Chinese Economy.* Cambridge, MA: MIT Press, 2007.

Niu Haibin. "China's International Responsibility Examined." *Xiandai guoji guanxi* (Beijing) 17 (July 2007): 81–93.

Niu Jun. *From Yan'an to the World: The Origin and Development of Chinese Communist Foreign Policy.* Steven I. Levine, ed. and trans. Norwalk, CT: Eastbridge, 2005.

Norris, William J. *Chinese Economic Statecraft: Commercial Actors, Grand Strategy and State Control.* Ithaca, NY: Cornell University Press, 2016.

O'Rourke, Ronald. *China's Naval Modernization.* Report RL33153. Washington, DC: Library of Congress, Congressional Research Service, 2017.

———. *Maritime Territorial and Exclusive Economic Zone (EEZ) Disputes Involving China.* Report R42784. Washington, DC: Library of Congress, Congressional Research Service, 2017.

Pang Guang. "An Analysis of the Prospects of 'Shanghai Five'." In *Thinking of the New Century*, ed. Ling Rong. Beijing: Central Party School Press, 2002.

———. "China's Asian Strategy: Flexible Multilateralism." *World Economy and Politics* (Beijing) 10 (2001).

———, ed. *Quanqiuhua, Fanquanqiuhua yu Zhongguo: Lijie Quanqiuhua de Fuzhanxin yu Duoyangxin.* Shanghai: Renmin, 2002.

———. "SCO under New Circumstances: Challenge, Opportunity and Prospect for Development." *Journal of International Studies* (Beijing) 5 (2002): 40–52.

Paulson, Henry. "The Right Way to Engage China: Strengthening U.S.-Chinese Ties." *Foreign Affairs*, September–October 2008. http://www.foreignaffairs.org.

Pei Jianzhang. *Yanjiu Zhou Enlai: Waijiao sixiang yu shijian* [Researching Zhou Enlai: Diplomatic thought and practice]. Beijing: Shijie Zhishi Chubanshe, 1989.

———. *Zhonghua renmin gongheguo waijiao shi, 1949–1956* [A diplomatic history of the People's Republic of China, 1949–1956]. Beijing: Shijie Zhishi, 1994.

Pei, Minxin. *China's Crony Capitalism: The Dynamics of Regime Decay.* Cambridge, MA: Harvard University Press, 2016.

———. *China's Trapped Transition: The Limits of Development Autocracy.* Cambridge, MA: Harvard University Press, 2006.

Pei, Minxin, and Michael Swaine. *Simmering Fire in Asia: Averting Sino-Japanese Strategic Conflict.* Policy Brief 44. Washington, DC: Carnegie Endowment for International Peace, December 1, 2005.

People's Republic of China Ministry of Foreign Affairs. "China's Africa Policy." *People's Daily.* http://www.peoplesdaily.com.cn, January 12, 2006.

———. *China's EU Policy Paper.* Beijing: Ministry of Foreign Affairs, October 13, 2003.

———. Department of Policy Planning. *China's Foreign Relations 2010.* Beijing: World Affairs Press, 2010.

People's Republic of China State Council Information Office. *China's Foreign Aid.* Beijing: People's Republic of China State Council Information Office, April 21, 2011.

———. *China's Foreign Aid (2014)*. Beijing: People's Republic of China State Council Information Office, August 23, 2014.

———.*China's National Defense in 2002*. Beijing: People's Republic of China State Council Information Office, December 9, 2002.

———. *China's National Defense in 2004*. Beijing: People's Republic of China State Council Information Office, December 27, 2004.

———. *China's National Defense in 2006*. Beijing: People's Republic of China State Council Information Office, December 29, 2006.

———. *China's National Defense in 2008*. Beijing: People's Republic of China State Council Information Office, January 2009.

———. *China's National Defense in 2010*. Beijing: People's Republic of China State Council Information Office, March 2011.

———. *China's Peaceful Development Road*. http://www.peoplesdaily.com.cn, December 22, 2005.

———. *The One-China Principle and the Taiwan Issue*. http://www.gwytb.gov.cn, February 21, 2000.

———. *The Taiwan Question and the Reunification of China*. http://www.gwytb.gov.cn, September 1, 1993.

Percival, Bronson. *The Dragon Looks South: China and Southeast Asia in the New Century*. Westport, CT: Praeger, 2007.

Pillsbury, Michael. *The Hundred Year Marathon*. New York: Holt, 2015.

Plesner, Jonas Parello, and Mathieu Duchatel. *China's Strong Arm: Protecting Citizens and Assets Abroad*. London: International Institute for Strategic Studies, 2015.

Pollack, Jonathan. *No Exit: North Korea, Nuclear Weapons, and International Security*. New York: Routledge, 2011.

Qian Qichen. "Adjustment of the United States National Security Strategy and International Relations in the Early New Century." *Foreign Affairs Journal* (Beijing) 71 (March 2004): 1–7.

———. "Xinshiji de Guoji Guanxi." *Xuexi Shibao*, October 18, 2004.

Rachman, Gideon. *Easternization: Asia's Rise and America's Decline*. New York: Penguin Random House, 2017.

Raine, Sarah. *China's African Challenges*. London: Routledge, 2009.

Reilly, James. *China's Economic Statecraft: Turning Wealth into Power*. Sydney: Lowy Institute, November 2012.

Richardson, Sophie. *China, Cambodia, and the Five Principles of Peaceful Coexistence*. New York: Columbia University Press, 2010.

Rigger, Shelley. *Taiwan's Rising Rationalism: Generations, Politics, and "Taiwanese Nationalism."* Washington, DC: East-West Center, 2006.

———. *Why Taiwan Matters*. Lanham, MD: Rowman & Littlefield, 2014.

Rinehart, Ian. *The Chinese Military: Overview and Issues for Congress*. CRS Report 44196. Washington, DC: Congressional Research Service, Library of Congress, March 24, 2016.

Robinson, Thomas W., and David Shambaugh, eds. *Chinese Foreign Policy: Theory and Practice*. New York: Clarendon, 1997.

Rolland, Nadege. *China's Eurasian Century?* Seattle: National Bureau of Asian Research, 2017.

Rose, Caroline. *Sino-Japanese Relations: Facing the Past, Looking to the Future*. New York: RoutledgeCurzon, 2005.

Rosen, Daniel, and Thilo Hanemann. *An American Open Door: Maximizing the Benefits of Chinese Foreign Direct Investment*. New York: Asia Society, 2011.

Ross, Robert S., ed. *After the Cold War*. Armonk, NY: M. E. Sharpe, 1998.

———. *The Indochina Tangle*. New York: Columbia University Press, 1988.

———. *Negotiating Cooperation: The United States and China, 1969–1989*. Stanford, CA: Stanford University Press, 1995.

———. "Taiwan's Fading Independence Movement." *Foreign Affairs* 85, no. 2 (March–April 2006): 141–48.

Ross, Robert, and Jiang Changbin, eds. *Re-examining the Cold War: U.S.-China Diplomacy 1954–1973*. Cambridge, MA: Harvard University Press, 2001.

Ross, Robert, and Oystein Tunsjo, eds. *Strategic Adjustment and the Rise of China.* Ithaca, NY: Cornell University Press, 2018.

Ross, Robert, and Zhu Feng, eds. *China's Ascent: Power, Security and the Implications for International Politics*. Ithaca, NY: Cornell University Press, 2009.

Roy, Denny. *China's Foreign Relations*. Lanham, MD: Rowman & Littlefield, 1998.

———. *Return of the Dragon: Rising China and Regional Security.* New York: Columbia University Press, 2013.

———. *Taiwan: A Political History*. Ithaca, NY: Cornell University Press, 2003.

Rozman, Gilbert. *Chinese Strategic Thought toward Asia*. New York: Palgrave Macmillan, 2010.

Sa Benwang. "Some Observations on Building a Harmonious World." *Foreign Affairs Journal* (Beijing) 80 (June 2006): 37–42.

Saich, Tony. *Governance and Politics of China*. New York: Palgrave, 2010.

Samuels, Richard. *Securing Japan: Tokyo's Grand Strategy and the Future of East Asia*. Ithaca, NY: Cornell University Press, 2007.

Saunders, Phillip. "China's America Watchers: Changing Attitudes toward the United States." *China Quarterly*, March 2000, 41–65.

———. *China's Global Activism: Strategy, Drivers, and Tools*. Occasional Paper 4. Washington, DC: National Defense University Institute for National Strategic Studies, June 2006.

Saunders, Phillip, and Andrew Scobell, eds. *PLA Influence on China's National Security Policymaking.* Stanford, CA: Stanford University Press, 2015.

Schaller, Michael. *The United States and China: Into the Twenty-First Century* (New York: Oxford University Press, 2015).

Schell, Orville, and Susan Shirk. *US Policy toward China: Recommendations for a New Administration.* New York: Asia Society, 2017.

Self, Benjamin. "China and Japan: A Façade of Friendship." *Washington Quarterly* 26, no. 1 (Winter 2002–2003): 77–88.

Shambaugh, David. *Beautiful Imperialist*. Princeton, NJ: Princeton University Press, 1991.

———. *China Goes Global: Partial Power*. New York: Oxford University Press, 2013.

———. *China's Communist Party: Atrophy and Adaptation*. Washington, DC: Woodrow Wilson Center, 2008.

———. *China's Future*. Cambridge: Polity Press, 2016.

———. *Modernizing China's Military*. Berkeley: University of California Press, 2002.

———, ed. *Power Shift: China and Asia's New Dynamics*. Berkeley: University of California Press, 2005.

———, ed. *Tangled Titans*. Lanham, MD: Rowman & Littlefield, 2012.

Sheives, Kevin. "China Turns West: Beijing's Contemporary Strategy toward Central Asia." *Pacific Affairs* 79, no. 2 (Summer 2006): 205–24.

Sheng Lijun. *China's Influence in Southeast Asia*. Trends in Southeast Asia Series 4. Singapore: Institute of Southeast Asian Studies, 2006.

Shi Yinhong. "Zhongri Jiejin yu 'Waijiao Geming.'" *Zhanlue yu Guanli* (Beijing) 2 (2003): 71–75.

Shie, Tamara. "Rising Chinese Influence in the South Pacific." *Asian Survey* 47, no. 2 (March–April 2007): 307–26.

Shinn, David, and Joshua Eisenman. *China and Africa*. Philadelphia: University of Pennsylvania Press, 2012.

Shirk, Susan. *China: Fragile Superpower*. New York: Oxford University Press, 2007.

Small, Andrew. *The China-Pakistan Axis*. New York: Oxford University Press, 2015.

Snyder, Scott. *China's Rise and the Two Koreas: Politics, Economics, Security*. Boulder, CO: Lynne Rienner, 2009.

———. *South Korea at the Crossroads*. New York: Columbia University Press, 2018.

Stahle, Stefan. "China's Shifting Attitude towards United Nations Peacekeeping Operations." *China Quarterly* 195 (September 2008): 631–55.

Storey, Ian James. "Living with the Colossus: How Southeast Asian Countries Cope with China." *Parameters*, Winter 1999–2000, 111–25.

———. *Southeast Asia and the Rise of China*. London: Routledge, 2011.

———. *The United States and ASEAN-China Relations: All Quiet on the Southeastern Asian Front*. Carlisle, PA: Strategic Studies Institute, U.S. Army War College, 2007.

Stueck, William W. *The Road to Confrontation: American Policy toward China and Korea, 1947–1950*. Chapel Hill: University of North Carolina Press, 1981.

Su Ge. *Meiguo: Dui hua Zhengce yu Taiwan wenti* [America: China policy and the Taiwan issue]. Beijing: Shijie Zhishi Chubanshe, 1998.

Suettinger, Robert. *Beyond Tiananmen*. Washington, DC: Brookings Institution Press, 2003.

Sun, Yun. *Chinese National Security Decision-making: Process and Challenges*. Washington, DC: Brookings Institution Press, May 2013.

Sutter, Robert. *China's Rise: Implications for U.S. Leadership in Asia*. Washington, DC: East-West Center, 2006.

———. *China's Rise in Asia: Promises and Perils*. Lanham, MD: Rowman & Littlefield, 2005.

———. *Chinese Foreign Relations: Power and Policy since the Cold War*. Lanham, MD: Rowman & Littlefield, 2016.

———. *The United States and Asia*. Lanham, MD: Rowman & Littlefield, 2015.

———. *U.S.-China Relations: Perilous Past, Uncertain Present*. Lanham, MD: Rowman & Littlefield, 2018.

Swaine, Michael. *America's Challenge: Engaging a Rising China in the Twenty-First Century*. Washington, DC: Carnegie Endowment for International Peace, 2011.

———. *Chinese Views of Global Governance since 2008–2009: Not Much New*. Washington, DC: Carnegie Endowment for International Peace, February 8, 2016.

———. *Creating a Stable Asia*. Washington, DC: Carnegie Endowment for International Peace, 2016.

Swaine, Michael, and Ashley Tellis. *Interpreting China's Grand Strategy, Past, Present and Future*. Santa Monica, CA: RAND Corporation, September 2001.

Swaine, Michael, Tousheng Zhang, and Danielle F. S. Cohen. *Managing Sino-American Crises: Case Studies and Analysis*. Washington, DC: Carnegie Endowment, 2006.

Swanstrom, Niklas. "China and Central Asia: A New Great Game or Traditional Vassal." *Journal of Contemporary China* 14, no. 45 (November 2005): 569–84.

Tang Shiping and Zhang Yunling. "Zhongguo de Diqu Zhanlue." *Shijie Jingli yu Zhengzhi* 6 (2004): 8–13.

Taylor, Ian. *China's New Role in Africa*. Boulder, CO: Lynne Rienner, 2008.

Taylor, Jay. *The Generalissimo*. Cambridge, MA: Harvard University Press, 2009.

———. *The Generalissimo's Son: Chiang Ching-kuo and the Revolutions in China and Taiwan*. Cambridge, MA: Harvard University Press, 2000.

Tellis, Ashley J., and Travis Tanner, eds. *Strategic Asia 2012–13: China's Military Challenge*. Seattle: National Bureau of Asian Research, 2012.

Tian Peiliang. "China and Africa in New Period." *Foreign Affairs Journal* (Beijing) 70 (December 2003): 36–42.

———. "Nationalism: China and Japan." *Foreign Affairs Journal* (Beijing) 63 (March 2002): 63–83.

Tian Zengpei, ed. *Gaige kaifang yilai de Zhongguo waijiao* [Chinese diplomacy since reform and opening]. Beijing: Shijie Zhishi Chubanshe, 1993.

Tiang Zhongqing. *East Asia Cooperation and China's Strategic Interest*. Dangdai Yatai 5. Beijing: Chinese Academy of Social Sciences, 2003.

Tsou, Tang. *America's Failure in China, 1941–1950*. Chicago: University of Chicago Press, 1963.

Tucker, Nancy Bernkopf. "China-Taiwan: U.S. Debates and Policy Choices." *Survival* 40, no. 4 (Winter 1998–1999): 150–67.

———, ed. *Dangerous Strait: The U.S.-Taiwan-China Crisis*. New York: Columbia University Press, 2005.

———. *Strait Talk: United States-Taiwan Relations and the Crisis with China*. Cambridge, MA: Harvard University Press, 2009.

———. *Taiwan, Hong Kong, and the United States, 1945–1992: Uncertain Friendships*. New York: Twayne, 1994.

US Congress, House Committee on Foreign Affairs. *Executive-Legislative Consultations over China Policy, 1978–1979*. Washington, DC: US Government Printing Office, 1980.

US Congress, House Committee on International Relations. *United States–Soviet Union-China: The Great Power Triangle*. Washington, DC: US Government Printing Office, 1976.

US Department of Defense. *Military and Security Developments Involving the People's Republic of China, 2017*. https://www.defense.gov/Portals/1/Documents/pubs/2017_China_Military_Power_Report.PDF.

US National Intelligence Council. *China and Weapons of Mass Destruction: Implications for the United States*. Conference Report. Washington, DC: US National Intelligence Council, November 5, 1999.

———. *China's Future: Implications for U.S. Interests*. Conference Report CR99-02. Washington, DC: US National Intelligence Council, September 1999.

US Senate, Committee on Foreign Relations. *China's Foreign Policy and "Soft Power" in South America, Asia, and Africa*. Washington, DC: US Government Printing Office, 2008.

Van Ness, Peter. *Revolution and Chinese Foreign Policy*. Berkeley: University of California Press, 1970.

Vogel, Ezra. *Deng Xioaping and the Transformation of China*. Cambridge, MA: Harvard University Press, 2011.

Wachman, Alan. *Why Taiwan: Geostrategic Rationales for China's Territorial Integrity*. Stanford, CA: Stanford University Press, 2007.

Wan, Ming. *Sino-Japanese Relations: Interaction, Logic, and Transformation*. Stanford, CA: Stanford University Press, 2006.

Wang, Bingnan. *Zhongmei huitan jiunian huigu* [Nine years of Sino-American ambassadorial talks]. Beijing: Shijie Zhishi, 1985.

Wang, Fei-Ling. *The China Order*. Albany: State University of New York Press, 2017.

Wang Gungwu. *China and Southeast Asia: Myths, Threat, and Culture*. EAI Occasional Paper 13. Singapore: National University of Singapore, 1999.

———. "The Fourth Rise of China: Cultural Implications." *China: An International Journal* 2, no. 2 (September 2004): 311–22.

Wang Jianwei. "China's Multilateral Diplomacy in the New Millennium." In *China Rising: Power and Motivation in Chinese Foreign Policy*, edited by Yong Deng and Fei-Ling Wang, 177–87. Lanham, MD: Rowman & Littlefield, 2005.

Wang Jisi. "China's Search for a Grand Strategy." *Foreign Affairs* 90, no. 2 (March/April 2011): 68–79.

———. "China's Search for Stability with America." *Foreign Affairs* 84, no. 5 (September–October 2005): 39–48.

———. "'Marching Westwards': The Rebalancing of China's Geostrategy." International and Strategic Studies Report 73 (Beijing: Peking University), October 7, 2012.

Wang Shida. "The Way to a Secure and Stable Afghanistan." *Contemporary International Relations* (Beijing) 20, no. 6 (November/December 2010): 123–31.

Wang Shuzhong, ed. *Mei-Su zhengba zhanlue wenti* [The question of contention for hegemony between the United States and the Soviet Union]. Beijing: Guofang Daxue Chubanshe, 1988.

Wang, Taiping, et al. *Zhonghua renmin gongheguo waijiao shi, 1957–1969* [A diplomatic history of the People's Republic of China, 1957–1969]. Beijing: Shijie Zhishi, 1998.

Wang, T. Y. "Taiwan's Foreign Relations under Lee Teng-hui's Rule, 1988–2000." In *Sayonara to the Lee Teng-Hui Era*, edited by Wei-chin Lee and T. Y. Wang, 250–60. Lanham, MD: University Press of America, 2003.

Wang Xiaolong. "The Asia-Pacific Economic Cooperation and the Regional Political and Security Issues." *Dangdai Yatai* (Beijing) 4 (2003).

Wang Yizhou. *Quanqiu zhengzhi he zhongguo waijiao*. Beijing: Shijie Zhishi Chubanshe, 2004.

Weatherbee, Donald. *International Relations in Southeast Asia: The Struggle for Autonomy.* 3rd ed. Lanham, MD: Rowman & Littlefield, 2014.

Weiss, Jessica. *Nationalist Protests in China's Foreign Relations.* New York: Oxford University Press, 2014.

Westad, Odd Arne. *Brothers in Arms: The Rise and Fall of the Sino-Soviet Alliance, 1945–1963.* Stanford, CA: Stanford University Press, 1998.

White, Hugh. *The China Choice.* Collingwood, Australia: Black, 2012.

Whiting, Allen S. *China Crosses the Yalu.* New York: Macmillan, 1960.

———. *The Chinese Calculus of Deterrence: India and Indochina.* Ann Arbor: University of Michigan Press, 1975.

Wilson, Jeanne. *Strategic Partners: Russian-Chinese Relations in the Post-Soviet Era.* Armonk, NY: M. E. Sharpe, 2004.

Wishnick, Elizabeth. "Russia and China: Brothers Again?" *Asian Survey* 41, no. 5 (September–October 2001): 797–821.

Womack, Brantly. *China and Vietnam: The Politics of Asymmetry.* New York: Cambridge University Press, 2006.

Wong, John, and Sarah Chan. "China-ASEAN Free Trade Agreement." *Asian Survey* 43, no. 3 (May–June 2003): 507–26.

Wu Hongying. "Latin America: Key Trends and Challenges." *Contemporary International Relations* (Beijing) 20, Special Issue (September 2010): 33–42.

———. "A New Era of Sino-Latin American Relations." *Xiandai guoji guanxi* (Beijing) 17 (January 2007): 64–71.

Wu Xinbo. "Chinese Perspectives on Building an East Asian Community in the Twenty-First Century." In *Asia's New Multilateralism*, edited by Michael Green and Bates Gill, 55–77. New York: Columbia University Press, 2009.

———. "The End of the Silver Lining: A Chinese View of the U.S.-Japanese Alliance." *Washington Quarterly* 29, no. 1 (2005): 119–30.

———. "Four Contradictions Constraining China's Foreign Policy Behavior." *Journal of Contemporary China* 10, no. 27 (May 2001): 293–302.

Wuthnow, Joel, and Phillip Saunders. *Chinese Military Reforms in the Age of Xi Jinping.* Washington DC: National Defense University, March 2017.

Xie Yixian. *Zhongguo Waijiao Shi: 1949–1979* [China's diplomatic history: 1949–1979]. Henan: Henan Renmin Chubanshe, 1988.

Xing Guangcheng. "Work for Mutual Trust and Mutual Benefit in Deepening Sino-Russian Relations." *Foreign Affairs Journal* (Beijing) 80 (June 2006): 8–13.

Xiong Guangkai. "Dongqian Quanqiu Fankongxing shi Jiqi Qiying Zhanwang." *Guoji Zhanlue Yanjiu* (Beijing) 2 (2003).

Xu Weizhong. "Beijing Summit Promotes Sino-African Relations." *Xiandai guoji guanxi* (Beijing) 17 (January 2007): 72–79.

Yahuda, Michael. *China's Role in World Affairs.* New York: St. Martin's, 1978.

———. *The International Politics of the Asia-Pacific, 1945–1995.* New York: Routledge, 1996.

———. *Sino-Japanese Relations after the Cold War.* London: Routledge, 2013.

Yan Xuetong. "The Instability of China-US Relations." *Chinese Journal of International Politics* 3, no. 3 (2010): 1–30.

———. "The Rise of China and Its Power Status." *Chinese Journal of International Politics* 1 (2006): 5–33.

Yan Xuetong et al. *Ancient Chinese Thought, Modern Chinese Power.* Princeton, NJ: Princeton University Press, 2011.

———. *Zhongguo Jueji—Guoji Huanjin Pinggu.* Tianjin: People's Press, 1998.

Yang Jianmian. *Da Mo He.* Tianjin: Renmin Chubanshe, 2007.

Yang Wenchang. "Sino-U.S. Relations in Retrospect and Prospect." *Foreign Affairs Journal* (Beijing) 80 (June 2006): 1–7.

Ye Zicheng, *Inside China's Grand Strategy: The Perspective from the People's Republic.* Lanham, MD: Lexington Press, 2011.

————. *Xin Zhongguo Waijiao Sixiang: Cong Maozedong dao Dengxiaoping*. Beijing: Beijing Daxue Chubanshe, 2001.

Yee, Herbert, and Ian Storey. *The China Threat: Perceptions, Myths, and Reality*. London: Routledge, 2002.

Yu Bin. "China and Russia: Normalizing Their Strategic Partnership." In *Power Shift: China and Asia's New Dynamics*, edited by David Shambaugh, 228–46. Berkeley: University of California Press, 2005.

Yuan, Jing-dong. "China's Role in Establishing and Building the Shanghai Cooperation Organization (SCO)." *Journal of Contemporary China* 19, no. 67 (November 2010): 855–70.

————. "The Dragon and the Elephant: Chinese-Indian Relations in the 21st Century." *Washington Quarterly* 30, no. 3 (Summer 2007): 131–44.

Yuan Peng. "9.11 Shijian yu Zhongmei Guanxi." *Xiandai Guoji Guanxi*, November 11, 2001, 19–23, 63.

————. "A Harmonious World and China's New Diplomacy." *Xiandai Guoji Guanxi* (Beijing) 17 (May 2007): 1–26.

Zagoria, Donald. *The Sino-Soviet Conflict, 1956–1961*. New York: Atheneum, 1964.

Zeng Qiang. "FOCAC: A Powerful Engine for the Continued Development of Friendship between China and Africa." *Contemporary International Relations* (Beijing) 20, no. 6 (November/December 2010): 45–59.

Zhang Biwu. "Chinese Perceptions of American Power, 1991–2004." *Asian Survey* 45, no. 5 (September–October 2005): 667–86.

Zhang Wenmu. "Quanqiuhua Jincheng Zhong de Zhongguo Guojia Liye." *Zhanlue yu Guanli* 1 (2002): 52–64.

Zhang Yunling. "East Asian Cooperation and the Construction of China-ASEAN Free Trade Area." *Dangdai Yatai* (Beijing) 1 (2002): 20–32.

————, ed. *Huoban Haishi Duishou: Tiao Zheng Zhong de Mei Ri E Guanxi*. Beijing: Social Science Departments Press, 2000.

————, ed. *Making New Partnership: A Rising China and Its Neighbors*. Beijing: Social Sciences Academic Press, 2008.

————. "New Thinking Needed to Promote East Asian Cooperation." *Foreign Affairs Journal* (Beijing) 96 (September 2010): 17–23.

————, ed. *Weilai 10-15 Nian Zhongguo Zai Yatai Diqu Mianlin de Guoji Huanjing*. Beijing: Zhongguo Shehui Kexue Chubanshe, 2003.

Zhang Yunling and Tang Shiping. "China's Regional Strategy." In *Power Shift: China and Asia's New Dynamics*, ed. David Shambaugh, 48–70. Berkeley: University of California Press, 2005.

Zhao, Huasheng. "China's View of and Expectations from the Shanghai Cooperation Organization," *Asian Survey* 53, no. 3 (2013): 436–60.

Zhao, Suisheng. "Chinese Nationalism and Its International Orientations." *Political Science Quarterly* 115, no. 1 (Spring 2000): 1–33.

————. *A Nation-State by Construction: Dynamics of Modern Chinese Nationalism*. Stanford, CA: Stanford University Press, 2004.

————, ed. *China in Africa*. New York: Routledge, 2015.

Zheng Bijian. "China's 'Peaceful Rise' to Great-Power Status." *Foreign Affairs* 84, no. 5 (2005): 18–24.

Zheng Ruixiang. "New Development of Relations between China and South Asian Countries." *Foreign Affairs Journal* (Beijing) 76 (June 2005): 40–46.

Zhou Yuhao. *Liyi Youguan*. Beijing: Zhongguo Chuanmei Daxue Chubanshe, 2007.

Zhu Feng. "Zai Lishi Gui yi Zhong Bawo Zhong Mei Guanxi." *Huanqiu Shibao Guoji Luntan*, February 28, 2002.

Zhu Liqun, *China's Foreign Policy Debates*. Brussels: Chaillot Papers, September 2010.

Zhu Tingchang et al., eds. *Zhongguo Zhoubian Anquan Huanjin yu Anquan Zhanlue*. Beijing: Shishi Chubanshe, 2002.

Zi Zhongyun. *Meiguo duihua zhengce de yuanqi he fazhan, 1945–1950* [The origins and development of American policy toward China, 1945–1950]. Chongqing: Chongqing, 1987.

———. *No Exit? The Origin and Evolution of U.S. Policy toward China, 1945–1950.* Norwalk, CT: Eastbridge, 2004.
Zou Jingwen. *Li Denghui Zhizheng Gaobai Shilu.* Taipei: INK, 2001.

Index